Gramsci and Education

CULTURE AND POLITICS SERIES
GENERAL EDITOR: HENRY A. GIROUX, PENNSYLVANIA STATE UNIVERSITY

FORTHCOMING

Gramsci and Education

EDITED BY
CARMEL BORG
JOSEPH BUTTIGIEG
PETER MAYO

ROWMAN & LITTLEFIELD PUBLISHERS, INC.
Lanham • Boulder • New York • Oxford

ROWMAN & LITTLEFIELD PUBLISHERS, INC.

Published in the United States of America
by Rowman & Littlefield Publishers, Inc.
A Member of the Rowman & Littlefield Publishing Group
4720 Boston Way, Lanham, Maryland 20706
www.rowmanlittlefield.com

PO Box 317
Oxford
OX2 9RU, UK

British Library Cataloguing in Publication Information Available

Library of Congress Cataloging-in-Publication Data Available

ISBN: 0-7425-0032-2 (cloth: alk. paper)
ISBN: 0-7425-0033-0 (pbk. : alk. paper)

Printed in the United States of America

♾™ The paper used in this publication meets the minimum requirements of American National Standard for Information Sciences—Permanence of Paper for Printed Library Materials, ANSI/NISO Z39.48-1992.

Contents

Introduction

Gramsci and Education:
A Holistic Approach

Carmel Borg, Joseph A. Buttigieg, and Peter Mayo

There is no term more closely associated with the figure of Antonio Gramsci than "hegemony." Indeed, more has been written on Gramsci's concept of hegemony, its nuances, its continuing relevance, its applicability to critical analyses of contemporary politics and culture, and so on, than on any other feature of his voluminous and wide-ranging work. Yet, if one were asked to identify a specific passage or section in Gramsci's massive *opus* wherein he succinctly and systematically expounds his concept of hegemony—and, we are sure most Gramsci scholars have, at some point or another, received such a request from a student or a colleague in search of a quick way to grasp the significance of the term—one would find it impossible to oblige. To be sure, the enormous bibliography of secondary literature on Gramsci abounds in books and scholarly articles that purport to offer methodical and orderly expositions of the concept of hegemony stitched together from various passages scattered throughout the *Prison Notebooks*. Gramsci himself, however, never thought of gathering the numerous notes that touch directly and explicitly on the question of hegemony into a "special" thematic notebook as he did with his notes on Machiavelli, the Risorgimento, Americanism and Fordism, culture, literary criticism, the intellectuals, the history of subaltern social groups, and other topics that figure prominently in his prison writings. Nor does one find, in the notebooks, clusters of notes under the rubric "hegemony" similar, say, to the numerous notes entitled "Past and Present.

There has been a tendency to assume that the absence of a clearcut, self-contained formulation of the concept or theory of hegemony in the notebooks is attributable to the fragmentary and unfinished character of the project that Gramsci undertook to carry out under the impossibly difficult conditions of prison life. This is a faulty assumption which not only overlooks the complexity of Gramsci's methods of study, research, and critique (by conveniently ascribing the unique characteristics of his text to extraneous factors), but also obscures the fact that hegemony is not simply one more (albeit overwhelmingly important) topic, or theme, out of many that Gramsci dwelt on in his notebooks. It is not an accident that "hegemony" does not appear among the "main topics" that Gramsci jotted down on the opening page of his first notebook when he outlined a program of study that would protect his intellect from the corrosive effects of prison life; nor is it mere coincidence that "hegemony" is not among the themes listed in the opening pages of Notebook 8, where Gramsci, in an effort to provide some order to his multidirectional inquiries, tries to sketch a system for grouping, more or less systematically, the clusters of notes on various topics he had already composed.

Gramsci's idea or concept of hegemony emerges somewhat tentatively in two early notes of the first notebook: one is devoted to a discussion of the leadership role played by the Moderate Party of Cavour in the initial formation of the Italian State (QC, pp. 40-54), and the other, a few pages later, deals with Charles Maurras's reactionary political movement in France (QC, pp. 58-64). At this early stage in the composition of the notebooks, it is quite clear that Gramsci has not yet formulated a theory of hegemony. Hegemony, in other words, does not make its appearance in the prison notebooks as a readymade theory or concept with which to explain historical or political phenomena. Instead, it is the analyses of specific phenomena that induce Gramsci to consider employing the term "hegemony" in a sense that is markedly different from—or, at least, much more nuanced than—the meaning attached to it by Lenin. Gradually, in the course of his research and writing, Gramsci elaborates his concept of hegemony, but it is important to note that this elaboration never takes the form of an abstract, systematic, and comprehensive theoretical exposition of the concept of hegemony as such. The development of the concept of hegemony by Gramsci always occurs in conjunction with his treatment of the increasingly diverse issues and phenomena that he undertakes to examine in his everexpanding field of inquiry. Gramsci's concept of hegemony is, thus, enriched, expanded, and reinforced by his critical examination of a wide variety of topics and problems, even as it helps to illuminate his understanding of those same topics and problems, enabling him to achieve his original insights into them.

The prison notebooks, then, do not so much contain a fragmented theory of hegemony that is waiting for scholars to assemble it into a coherent form, as constitute a record of the unfolding of the concept of hegemony *pari passu* with Gramsci's analyses of the various political, social, historical, philosophical, cultural, economic, religious, and literary questions to which he devoted his intellectual energy during his years of imprisonment. Virtually every aspect of Gramsci's program of study in prison is, in some manner, linked to, sheds light on, and is in turn illuminated by several others; and running through every major element of Gramsci's multifaceted inquiries—whether it be the notes on the medieval communes and Machiavelli's political theory, the extensive investigation of the state of journalism in late nineteenth and early twentieth-century Italy, the study of the philosophy of Benedetto Croce, or even the outline for a monograph on grammar and linguistics—one encounters the leitmotif of hegemony. Hence, in order to arrive at a thorough understanding of Gramsci's concept of hegemony, one needs to embark upon nothing less than a diligent reading of all the notebooks along the chrono-logical lines of their composition.

Gramsci's views on education, if their true significance and far reaching implications are to be fully appreciated, call for as thorough a study of the entire *corpus* of the notebooks as does the concept of hegemony (see Aronowitz and Monasta in this book). Indeed, one has to go even further, for unlike the concept of hegemony, multiple aspects of the spheres of activity and the diverse institutions encompassed by the term "education" occupied Gramsci's attention long before his arrest. An exhaustive study of Gramsci's views on and attitudes toward education in its many aspects would have to take into account his journalistic writings and many of his activities as a militant politician and party leader, in addition to his prison writings—including the letters where he frequently discusses questions of education in relation to the development and schooling of his two sons, Delio and Giuliano, and his niece, Edmea. Scattered throughout the letters from prison one also finds a number of poignant autobio-

graphical vignettes in which Gramsci recounts some of his early experiences as a schoolboy in Sardinia. Here is an example from a letter
that he wrote to his sister-in-law, Tatiana Schucht, on 9 April 1928:

> When I was a boy I had a pronounced preference for the exact sciences and
> mathematics. I lost it during my high school studies, because I didn't have
> any teachers worth a straw. And so, after my first year in *liceo*, I stopped
> studying math and chose Greek instead (there was an option at the time);
> but during my third year in *liceo* I suddenly gave proof that I had a remark-
> able "ability." In those days in the third year of *liceo*, in order to study
> physics one had to know the elements of mathematics that the pupils who
> had opted for Greek were not obliged to know. The physics professor, who
> was a most distinguished gentleman, got great amusement out of embarrass-
> ing us. During the last interrogation of the third trimester, he presented me
> with questions in physics linked to mathematics, saying that my answers
> would determine my average for the year and thus whether I would or would
> not have to take exams for my diploma: he was very amused at seeing me
> stand in front of the blackboard where he let me stand as long as I pleased.
> Well, I stood in front of the blackboard for half an hour, I covered myself
> with chalk from head to toe. I tried, tried again, wrote, erased, but finally I
> "invented" a demonstration that was considered excellent by the professor,
> even though it did not exist in any treatise. This professor knew my older
> brother in Cagliari and he tormented me with his cackling all through the
> school year; he called me the Hellenistic physicist. (LP, Vol. 1, pp. 195-96)

The schools he attended were poor, most of the teachers inept,
and their pedagogical methods atrocious. As he put it succinctly in a
letter to Giuliano (25 January 1936): "the scholastic method by which
I was taught was very backward" (LP, Vol. 2, p. 356). Only through
sheer willpower and determined resilience was the physically impaired
young Gramsci able to gain the skills and knowledge necessary to win
the scholarship that would permit him to escape the antiintellectual
and retrograde provincial milieu of his upbringing, and gain admission
to the University of Turin. The frustrations he encountered and the
enormous hurdles he had to overcome in order to satisfy his thirst for
learning instilled in Gramsci a spirit of rebellion against the rich. They
also convinced him, at an early age, that the liberation of the subaltern classes required a massive educational effort—an effort that
would somehow overcome the formidable obstacles posed by a state
educational system that was designed to serve the rich and perpetuate
their leading role in society.

Gramsci's journalistic and political activity in Turin was animated
first and foremost by a profound conviction that the most pressing
task of the socialist movement was cultural and educational in nature.
The subordinate classes needed to free themselves from their depend-
ence on bourgeois intellectuals so that they could develop and dis-

seminate their own culture or, as Gramsci often preferred to say, to elaborate their own conception of the world and of life. This entailed, among other things, breaking away from antiquated approaches to learning and dissociating themselves from the dominant philosophical currents of the time. Gramsci's lifelong battle against positivism (which pervaded socialist thought as much, if not more, than it did the general culture) stemmed from his firm belief that it encouraged a fatalistic worldview, a passive attitude that inhibited the subordinate classes from embracing the notion that they could be the agents of historical transformation. Education, culture, philosophy, socialism: all were intertwined in the mind of the young Gramsci; and, of course, by the time Gramsci finished his life's work, he would have demonstrated with greater clarity and thoroughness the complexities of this web of connections.

Socialism, in Gramsci's view, required nothing less than a complete intellectual reform. Fellow socialists were for the most part skeptical, if not openly hostile, to his cultural/intellectual emphasis. The mainstream socialist view was typified by an article that appeared in the syndicalist journal, *Guerra di classe*, in which Enrico Leone expressed disdain towards culture and education: "The modern worker learns much more from his class institutions than from any book of official knowledge [. . .]. There is no salvation except within labourism, within the classes of calloused hands and a brain uncontaminated by culture and by scholastic infection." Gramsci used Leone's article as a point of departure in one of his finest early essays, "Socialism and Culture," published in *Il Grido del Popolo* of 29 January 1916. It is an essay in which Gramsci articulates both a positive and a negative definition of culture (i.e., the definition of culture which socialists must jettison). In his negative definition of culture, Gramsci's targets are simultaneously positivism and degenerate forms of education:

We must rid ourselves of the habit of conceiving of culture as encyclopedic knowledge; a concept in which man is regarded as a mere receptacle to be stuffed with empirical data and disjointed brute facts which he must then file away in his brain as in the columns of a dictionary so that he can, on any given occasion, respond to the different stimuli of the world around him. This form of culture is really harmful, especially to the proletariat. It can only serve to create misfits [. . .]. The smug little student who knows some Latin and history, the vain little lawyer who has taken advantage of his teachers' laziness and apathy to eke out for himself a cheap degree—these people regard themselves as superior to the most skilled of skilled workers [. . .]. But this is not culture, it is pedantry; it is not intelligence, but intellectualism; and any attack on it is more than justified. (SPW, pp. 10-11)

On the positive side of the equation, Gramsci stresses the acquisition of self-knowledge (hence the need for reflection) and self-discipline, the study of history and of "others," and the cultivation of the spirit of critique. Echoing Vico, he explains how, historically, people gained independence from the laws and social hierarchies imposed upon them by ruling minorities only after they attained a greater level of awareness, a higher consciousness, "by means of which one succeeds in understanding one's own historical value, one's own function in life, one's own rights and duties" (SPW, p. 11). Also, arguing along the same Vichian lines (while also invoking Novalis's axioms), Gramsci drives home the point that culture and history are human constructs:

> To know oneself means to be oneself, to be master of oneself, to distinguish oneself, to get out of chaos, to be an element of order and of one's own discipline in pursuit of an ideal. And one cannot achieve this without knowing others, their history, the succession of efforts they made to be what they are, to create the civilisation they have created and which we want to replace with our own. (SPW, p. 13)

The last sentence, composed by Gramsci in 1916, adumbrates the research project he embarked upon thirteen years later in his prison cell at Turi di Bari. For the notebooks are, to a very large extent, the record of an extensive study aimed at "knowing others"—primarily, the bourgeoisie—through an examination of their history from the period of the medieval communes to the fascist era, and a close scrutiny of the institutions and activities by means of which they constructed and sustained their hegemonic civilization.

In 1916, Gramsci had not yet arrived at a concept of hegemony, but as is evident in "Socialism and Culture" (and in numerous other articles he wrote, and in the kind of initiatives he promoted as a political activist), he already believed that what enabled the ruling class to secure and maintain power was not brute force alone but also, and perhaps more importantly, the attainment of cultural dominance—i.e., its ability to permeate an entire society with its philosophies, values, tastes, and so on. In other words, the bourgeois revolution, as Gramsci explains in "Socialism and Culture," was not a spontaneous affair; rather, it was, the culmination of "a long process of intense critical activity, of new cultural insight and the spread of ideas" (SPW, p. 12). The phrases "critical activity," "cultural insight," and "spread of ideas" are all aspects of and variations on Gramsci's idea of "education." Gramsci held what one might call an active or activist concept of education; that is to say, he associated education not with the passive reception of information and the solitary refinement of an individual's sensibility, but with the transformative power of ideas, the capacity to bring about radical social change and construct a new order through the elaboration and dissemination of a new philosophy, an alternative world view. In this regard, his account of the connection between the Enlightenment and the French Revolution is especially revealing:

> the Enlightenment, a period which has been so slandered by facile critics of theoretical reason, was in fact not—or at least not entirely—a featherweight gathering of superficial, dilettante intellectuals, discoursing about anything and everything with complacent indifference [. . .]. It was not, that is to say, simply a phenomenon of pedantic, arid intellectualism, like the one we see before our eyes now, exhibited in its full glory in the low-grade popular universities. The Enlightenment was a magnificent revolution in itself [. . .] it created a kind of pan-European unified consciousness, a bourgeois International of the spirit, with each part sensitive to the tribulations and misfortunes of the whole, which was the best preparation for the bloody revolution which would subsequently take place in France.
>
> In Italy, in France, in Germany, the same things were being discussed, the same institutions, the same principles [. . .]. The bayonets of Napoleon's armies found their way already cleared by an invisible army of books and tracts, which had been swarming out of Paris since the first half of the eighteenth century, preparing men and institutions for their badly needed renovation. (SPW, p. 12)

Gramsci then goes on to declare that socialism was preparing the ground for a new revolution "through a critique of capitalist civilization;" that is, through the kind of intellectual, cultural, and educational work that was giving rise to "a unified proletarian consciousness" (SPW, p. 13). The youthful Gramsci, as he would discover later, was being inordinately optimistic. There were moments in the immediate postwar period when Italy seemed to be on the brink of a socialist revolution; but in the end, the forces of reaction prevailed. In the wake of the devastating political defeats that drove the Italian Communist Party underground and sent its leaders into exile or to prison, Gramsci was compelled to radically reassess his views. What was it that rendered bourgeois "civilization" so resilient? It is important to note that even though Fascism protected the interests of the conservative ruling strata of society by force and suppressed the radical opposition by violent means, Gramsci did not accept the easy explanation that his party's failure to bring about the radical transformation of Italian society was attributable solely, or even primarily, to the overwhelming coercive power of the State. Instead, he arrived at the conclusion that the modern State derives its strength from and is protected by something far more formidable than firepower, namely its powers and mechanisms of persuasion. This is not to say that Gramsci believed that Fascism truly exercised hegemony (as opposed to domination) over the Italian nation. If it did, it would not have had to resort to brutal coercive measures. Fascism, however, did not represent for Gramsci an example, much less a paradigm, of the modern State. Indeed, Gramsci considered Fascism in Italy to be the outcome of the impoverished, retrograde condition of the nation's culture and education for which he held the leading intellectuals (and, specifically, their detachment from the people) responsible.

Modern bourgeois civilization, in Gramsci's view, perpetuates itself through the operations of hegemony—i.e., through the activities and initiatives of a vast network of cultural organizations, political movements, and educational institutions that instill its conception of the world and its values in every capillary of society. Yet, one must hasten to add, Gramsci does not conceive of hegemonic operations as unidirectional; they do not consist solely in the transmission and dissemination of ideas and views from the leading groups of society down to the subordinate strata. Cultural activity, in the broadest sense of the term, also stimulates new thinking among the privileged echelons of society, enables them to address new problems, permits them to remain attuned to the demands and aspirations of all segments of society; in short, it reinforces the ability of the leading groups to look beyond their narrow corporative self-interest and, hence, to extend their reach and influence over the rest of society. Hegemony, as Gramsci conceives it, is an educational rapport.

For Gramsci, education means much more than schooling (see Monasta in this book); education, in Gramsci's conception, amounts to nothing less than the fundamental operations of hegemony. In a note entitled "Introduction to the Study of Philosophy," he writes:

> This problem [i.e., the question of collectively attaining a single cultural "climate"] can and must be related to the modern way of considering educational doctrine and practice, according to which the relationship between teacher and pupil is active and reciprocal so that every teacher is always a pupil and every pupil a teacher. But the educational relationship should not be restricted to the field of strictly "scholastic" relationships [...]. This form of relationship exists throughout society as a whole and for every individual relative to other individuals. It exists between intellectual and non-intellectual sections of the population, between the rulers and the ruled, *élites* and their followers, leaders and led, the vanguard and the body of the army. Every relationship of "hegemony" is necessarily an educational relationship and occurs not only within a nation, between the various forces of which the nation is composed, but in the international and world-wide field, between complexes of national and continental civilization. (SPN, pp. 349-50; QC, p. 1331)

In this particular passage Gramsci is thinking of the kind of hegemonic relationships that characterize the modern bourgeois liberal state and of the sort of relations that he envisaged a Communist Party fostering and cultivating if it aspired to have a leadership role in society. At the same time, though, this passage makes starkly explicit what can already be detected in the very earliest pages of the prison notebooks; namely, that educational relationships constitute the very core of hegemony, that any analysis of hegemony necessarily entails a careful study of educational activities and institutions, and that neither the complexities of hegemony nor the significance of education can be understood as long as one thinks of education exclusively in terms of "'scholastic' relationships."

Unfortunately, a number of critics and commentators who have written on Gramsci's views on education focused their attention primarily on a few pages that deal directly with questions of schooling, and particularly on a couple of long notes that Gramsci first composed in Notebook 4—"The Common School" (QC, pp. 485-88) and "The Educational Principle in Elementary and Secondary Schools" (QC, pp. 498-503)—and that he later incorporated (with some minor modifications) in a "special" thematic notebook devoted to "notes and jottings for a group of essays on the history of the intellectuals" (QC, pp. 1512-51). The reading of these two notes in isolation from the rest of Gramsci's corpus has given rise to many misunderstandings, misuses, and instrumentalizations of Gramsci's ideas. E. D. Hirsch, for example, has invoked Gramsci to buttress his view that "mainstream culture is not a class culture" (1987, p. 104). (See the chapters by Giroux and Buttigieg in this book for a critique of this use.) What such critics overlook, first of all, is that these particular notes have a specific historical context; i.e., the controversy surrounding the educational reforms put in place by the Fascist ideologue and minister of education, Giovanni Gentile. In the second place, they ignore the fact that the school system, the educational bureaucracy, the cultural milieu, and the social structures that prevailed in Italy during the first third of the twentieth century bear little, if any, resemblance to the problems and conditions of our time. Third, they obscure and confuse the most fundamental, and much broader issues that preoccupied Gramsci and that are still very much our problems today—namely, the disparities between the education received by the privileged classes and the disadvantaged sectors of the population, the consequences of increasing specialization in education; and the gulf that separates intellectuals from the people and "science" from "life." Worst of all, they deflect attention from Gramsci's revealing analysis of the relations between education (in the broader sense of the term) and power; that is to say, the ensemble of relations that constitute hegemony.

Gramsci's views on education, like his concept of hegemony, can only be usefully understood and appreciated if examined in the full context of and in relation to the diverse aspects of his entire life's work. The essays in this volume start with precisely this premise. They also relate to many different concerns in contemporary educational debates and focus on multiple sites of educational and social practice. Gramsci's impact on theory and research pertaining to schooling and adult education (including both formal and nonformal learning) has been substantial in recent years, and this consideration serves as justification for the publication of this anthology. Always bearing in mind the caveat that a knowledge of Gramsci's whole corpus is central to an understanding of his ideas on education, it would not be amiss to devote special attention to his notes that are directly concerned with schooling and that figure prominently in the educational literature (e.g., Manacorda, 1970; Lombardi, 1971; Broccoli, 1972; Entwistle, 1979; De Robbio Anziano, 1987; Senese, 1991).

Schooling Working-Class Intellectuals

As indicated above, Gramsci conceived of education as central to any process of intellectual and moral reform. In fact, he equated the reform's success with the party's ability to have a substantial nucleus of intellectuals, "'specialised' in conceptual and philosophical elaboration of ideas" (SPN, p. 334), who "arise directly out of the masses but remain in contact with them to become, as it were, the whalebone in the corset" (SPN, p. 340).

Mussolini's educational reform of 1923 (i.e., the *riforma Gentile*), the first major reform in Italian education since the *Casati Act* of 1859, dramatically increased the number of vocational schools. This particular aspect of the Gentile reform militated against Gramsci's conception of how education can contribute to political emancipation. He interpreted the division into classical and vocational schools as an accentuation of "juridically fixed and crystallized estates rather than moving towards the transcendence of class divisions. The multiplication of vocational schools which specialise increasingly from the very beginning of the child's educational career is one of the most notable manifestations of this tendency" (SPN, p. 41). As an alternative to what Gramsci perceived as a bourgeois and clerical model of educational reform, the Sardinian intellectual suggested a common basic education that imparted a general, humanistic, and formative culture. In Gramsci's view, such a curriculum provided a comprehensive background for eventual specialization. In fact, from this type of common schooling, via repeated experiments in vocational orientation, pupils proceeded to one of the specialized schools or to productive work: "The common school or school of humanistic formation (taking the term 'humanism' in a broad sense rather than simply in the traditional one) or general culture, should aim to insert young men and women into social activity after bringing them to a certain level of maturity, or capacity for intellectual and practical creativity, and of autonomy of orientation and initiative" (SPN, p. 29).

Within Gramsci's educational formula, working-class youth would not only have received the same formative preparation as youth from other classes, but would also have acquired the "fundamental power to think" and problematize traditional conceptions of the world. In Gramsci's words, "the scientific ideas the children learnt conflicted with the magical conception of the world and nature which they absorbed from an environment steeped in folklore; while the idea of civic rights and duties conflicted with tendencies towards individualistic and localistic barbarism—another dimension of folklore" (SPN, p. 34).

While dismissing the popular conception that the "gentlemen" are engaged in some kind of "trick" when completing with apparent speed and ease "work which costs their sons tears and blood" (SPN, p. 43), Gramsci challenged the ideology of meritocracy by explaining how

> the child of a traditionally intellectual family acquired this psycho-physical adaptation more easily. Before he ever enters the classroom he has numerous advantages over his comrades, and is already in possession of attitudes learnt from his family environment; he concentrates more easily, since he is used to "sitting still," etc. (SPN, p. 42)

Therefore, what came relatively easy for middle- and upper-class children—sitting still, concentrating more easily—had to be acquired, often painfully, through diligent and precise labor over texts.

In view of the discrepancy between the reality obtained in schools and the expectations and skills acquired by working-class children within their natural environment, Gramsci argued that if working-class and peasant children were to develop into "organic intellectuals," they had, in learning how to study, to acquire "physical self-discipline and self-control." In Gramsci's words, "if our aim is to produce a new stratum of intellectuals, including those capable of the highest degree of specialisation, from a social group which has not traditionally developed the appropriate attitude, then we have unprecedented difficulties to overcome" (SPN, p. 43).

Gramsci's obsession with discipline and rigor, and his insistence on working-class children's exposure to disinterested knowledge "as was intended by the ancients and more recently by the men of the Renaissance" (SG, p. 57), has been interpreted by some scholars as a conservative agenda (Saviani, in da Silva & McLaren, 1993; Entwistle, 1979; Senese, 1991) with radical ends. Harold Entwistle (1979) challenged Hoare and Smith's interpretation that "the apparently 'conservative' eulogy of the old curriculum in fact often represents a device which allowed Gramsci to circumvent the prison censor, by disguising the future (ideal system) as the past in order to criticize the present" (p. 24). Echoing Manacorda (1976), Entwistle argues that Gramsci embodied the educational principles of the old school, as expressed in the *Casati Act* of 1859, to the extent that his organization of a school for prisoners—*scuola dei confinati*—on the island of Ustica was modeled on the pattern of the traditional elementary school. Entwistle dedicated a lengthy chapter to Gramsci and the schooling of children to illustrate how the Italian intellectual's educational vision for school-aged children contained all the characteristics traditionally associated with conservative agendas in education; that is: (a) a deficit model of education, with working-class and peasant cultures perceived as inadequate cultural resources, flawed with superstition, incoherence, and fragmentation; (b) an inordinate emphasis on the accumulation of "truths already discovered;" (c) a traditional view of academic standards and of the function of examinations; and (d) the glorification of didactic pedagogy.

Angelo Broccoli (1972) argued that Gramsci's plan for the organization of schools stems from the democratic need for the promotion of a wide educational base, as opposed to the accentuation of an elitist tripartite system of education characterized by classical schools for the dominant classes, technical schools for the new urban intellectuals, and professional schools for the instrumental (read: subaltern) classes. Within Gramsci's basic educational framework, formative and disinterested knowledge for all meant a homogenization of opportunities and outcomes in basic education, and eventual full participation in a cultural milieu of the highest order. Broccoli contends that, while Gramsci seemed to have favored a classical type of education, he was equally keen on democratizing its access (for a critique of this, see the chapters by Giroux and by Borg and Mayo). Broccoli states that, for Gramsci, it was limited or no access to the cultural capital associated with power, rather than the content itself, which was elitist. The accumulation of this type of capital, through a disciplined, rigorous and, antispontaneous educational regime, provided the basis for the creative phase of cultural production. It is at the latter stage, "through the conquest by the popular, proletarian-led movement of the commanding heights of the adversary's culture" (Boothman, 1995, p. xxx), that the radical and transformative possibilities of education become apparent. The point concerning education's transformative possibilities is underscored by Italia De Robbio Anziano (1987) in one of the Italian works on Gramsci and education that devotes ample space to schooling (for other recently published Italian works, on Gramsci and education, see Monasta, 1993 and Capitani & Villa, 1999).

Adult Education

Arguably, it is in the field of adult education, and, more generally, adult learning, that Gramsci's influence is most pronounced. This section will focus on the importance being attached to Antonio Gramsci in a segment of the published English literature on adult education—primarily, that segment of the literature that deals with radical adult education. Writers who adopt this particular approach to adult education see potential in Gramsci's writings and actions primarily because the Italian theorist himself regarded forms of adult education as having an important role to play in a "war of position" intended to confront, surround, and eventually supersede the bourgeois state. Moreover, adult education incorporates a very large section (though not the entire section) of the vast domain that is civil society. This domain was of great interest to Gramsci since he regarded it as the terrain wherein much of the struggle for hegemony takes place. It is in this terrain, across its entire complex of ideological institutions, that the "war of position" occurs.

Many of those who adopt a radical approach to adult education derive inspiration from Gramsci's own writings concerning the Factory Council Movement, conceived of as a politically educative movement (see Livingstone in this book), and those other writings which emphasize the need to generate institutions and associations of proletarian culture. Furthermore, they also stress his role as a committed adult educator, and here one should mention his involvement in workers' education circles, including the *Club di Vita Morale*, and in the establishment of an Institute of Proletarian Culture, the PCI's correspondence school, and the *scuola dei confinati* (school for prisoners) at Ustica. Gramsci must have regarded radical adult education agencies as capable of playing an important part in that process of wide-ranging social organization and cultural influence that is carried out across the entire complex of "civil society" and is intended to challenge, rupture, and provide an alternative to capitalist social relations of production. Gramsci has shown how these relations are sustained and their contradictions mystified by dominant ideas and practices in most spheres of social life, even the most intimate ones.

Because of its flexibility and its potential to be carried out apart from state agencies and dominant institutions (often in clandestine settings), possibly within the context of a larger movement striving for social change, adult education (conceived of in its broader context) constitutes an excellent vehicle both for the development of views and practices that challenge hegemonic ones and for the unveiling of the underlying contradictions within the dominant ideology. It must also have seemed (to Gramsci and his followers) to constitute an important terrain wherein a social group aspiring to power can generate some of the ideas leading to the creation of an *historical bloc*. Finally, adult education constitutes an important terrain wherein much of the "intense labour of criticism," which, according to Gramsci must precede a revolution, may occur.

Gramsci's work is an important source of reference in English language books that contribute to the radical debate on adult education. In a study on nonformal education in Latin America, Carlos Alberto Torres (1990), a contributor to this book, devotes an entire section to Gramsci's theory of the State (see also Mayo on this, forthcoming) as part of the framework for analysis in this book. Gramsci and Gramscianism are referred to in another work by Torres (1995) and an edited compendium on education and social change in Latin America, especially in the chapter by Raymond A. Morrow (1995). In another book dealing with the same topic, Thomas J. La Belle (1986) states emphatically that Gramsci is the most cited Marxist theorist in the area of Latin American popular education. He then goes on to demonstrate the relevance of Gramsci's ideas, concerning the organization of workers through the Factory Councils, to the task of organizing the masses through popular education (p. 185). Gramsci's impact on left wing Latin American political thought and action has, of course, been great (see Aricó, 1988; Coutinho, 1995; Melis, 1995; and Fernández Diaz, 1995).

In exploring ingredients for a socialist approach to adult education, Frank Youngman (1986) stresses the importance of research into Gramsci's educational activities in Turin. He argues that research into these activities would be useful for the development of such an approach (pp. 233-34).

The potential in Gramsci's writings is explored in connection with various struggles worldwide. In a much cited work, Jane L. Thompson (1983) refers to Gramsci in the course of her review of continuing education provision and the effect of such provision on women. She argues:

> There is one small light amidst the general gloom, however, which, if we are to accept Gramsci's optimism, can be a focus for development. Gramsci was convinced that despite the all pervasive power of ruling groups, which he called hegemony, education has an important part to play in challenging its ubiquity—especially adult education, which he regarded as political education. Gramsci's analysis was formulated in the context of factory councils and working class industrial struggles, but the same conviction that education has the potential to affect political consciousness holds good. For women the opportunity of education can be enormously significant. (p. 97)

These are a few examples of works, within the radical debate on adult education, in which Gramsci and his ideas are taken up. However, it would be most useful at this stage to turn to works that deal at length with Gramsci's ideas that are relevant to adult education. One of the earliest articles in this respect is probably that by Tom Lovett (1978) who writes on community education among the working class in Northern Ireland and argues that progressive adult education should be developed in the context of social movements of workers (Jackson, 1981, p. 81). Harold Entwistle (1979) makes one of the first major contributions in the English language. His contribution is a chapter in the book discussed earlier in this introduction for its particular representation of Gramsci's conception of schooling. Entwistle's book deserves further comment in view of the fact that this work contains a vast section on adult education. The imparting of knowledge and the creation of educational experiences intimately tied to political and class struggle was, according to Entwistle's interpretation of Gramsci's work, to be the domain of politically committed adult education. "Adult Education" therefore constitutes a chapter on its own, one which deals with Gramsci's writings on political education, the formation of intellectuals (on this issue and its relevance to adult education, see Hommen, 1986), cultural production and dissemination, the factory councils, and technical and vocational education.

While Entwistle's chapter is the first lengthy study on the subject in English, Timothy Ireland's monograph (1987), in the well-known University of Manchester monograph series, is the first full-scale study published in English that focuses exclusively on Gramsci and adult education. It deals specifically with the influence of Antonio Gramsci on popular education in Brazil (for a related discussion, see

Morrow and Torres' chapter in this book and the chapter on the "two Gramscis" in Morrow & Torres, 1995). Ireland carried out his study at a delicate moment in Brazilian history as the former Portuguese colony embarked on a period of transition from authoritarian (military) to civilian rule—the *abertura*. One of his many observations is that the popular education movement is fragmented, lacking a "Modern Prince," a unifying organization. In this respect, Ireland asks the following questions:

> Can we assume that a multiplicity of unconnected efforts will eventually, through a kind of "snowball" effect, contribute to strong and representative working class organizations capable of uniting in a new historic bloc those forces struggling for a transformation of society? Or is the kind of strong revolutionary working class party which Gramsci envisaged central to this process of canalizing the struggle and destroying narrow sectarian interests? Is there any one party capable of such a task—the Workers' Party, the Brazilian Communist Party, the Communist Party of Brazil, etc.—or is the multiplicity of sectarian parties of the Left evidence that such a party remains to be created? (pp. 66-67)

Ireland returns to these questions in the concluding part of the monograph. His thorough investigation of the Gramscian influence on Brazilian popular education, an influence which extends to popular education throughout Latin America, would be very useful reading for anyone embarking on a project comparing or synthesizing the work of Gramsci and Freire, the latter another important theorizer of adult education (Ransome, 1992, pp. 183-85; Leonard, 1993; Morrow & Torres, 1995; Coben, 1998; M. Mayo, 1997; Mayo, 1999; Allman, 2000; Hill, 1999, 2000). Freire himself draws on Gramsci in his works and one finds a sustained discussion on the Italian theorist and his influence on Latin American intellectuals in his "talking book" with the Chilean exile, Antonio Faundez (1989). The Gramscian influence in this book is evident in Freire's discussion of the role of intellectuals as mediators between party and masses, the need to convert "common sense" to "good sense" (in the context of popular culture), and the concept of "national popular."

The one writer who refutes the uniting of Gramsci and Freire in the radical adult education debate is Diana Coben, a contributor to this book. She rejects the view that the ideas of the two thinkers are complementary: "Gramsci's and Freire's ideas are not sufficiently compatible to be usefully conjoined in the construction of a political theory of radical adult education" (1998, p. 201). She argues that Gramsci's ideas are more useful to adult educators than those of Freire, and, therefore, attacks the latter's work. This position is in stark contrast to those advocated by Mayo (1999) and Allman (2000) in their books and several articles. Mayo explores the possibilities for a synthesis, on the basis of a complementarity thesis, between Gramsci's and Freire's ideas with respect to adult education. Allman, a contributor to this book who has authored and coauthored numerous pieces on Gramsci (see Allman, 1988; Allman & Wallis, 1995; Allman & Mayo, 1997), discovers important "parallels in their thinking, because both base their ideas on an understanding of Marx's theory of consciousness" (Allman, 2000, p. 7). In an earlier piece (one of the first published pieces in English to bring Gramsci and Freire together), Allman (1988) draws on the ideas of Gramsci, Freire, and Illich, as she discusses the importance of ideology and dialectical (as opposed to linear) thinking in the process of the production and development of consciousness. One other writer, Debbie Hill (1999), from Waikato University, New Zealand, echoes Allman in arguing that an exploration of the dialectical method employed by Gramsci and Freire indicates that there is "overlap" between them. She goes on to argue that "both wrestle—albeit in their own unique (but not incommensurable) way—with the most decisive dichotomy of a 'democratic' way of life: between the goal of autonomous human existence and a hegemonic form of life in which all of us find ourselves unwittingly immersed" (p. 24).

In another article, published in the *International Journal of Lifelong Education* and dealing specifically with the relevance of Gramsci's writing and action to radical workers' education, W. John Morgan (1987) provides a comprehensive account of Gramsci's life and central themes, including hegemony and the State, the intellectuals, and the role of the party. Morgan (see his chapter on Gramsci and Raymond Williams in this book) underlines the relevance of intellectuals to counterhegemonic adult education practice. Morgan highlights aspects of Gramsci's own involvement in adult education, with particular emphasis on the Factory Council Movement and the Ustica prison school. In his discussion on intellectuals, Morgan, citing Entwistle, underlines Gramsci's belief that the proletariat is very slow at producing its stratum of organic intellectuals, the reasons for which lie in the "lack of resources and opportunity available to the working class" (p. 303). Gramsci argues that the proletariat has few institutions of its own and that education, religion, leisure, and the like are "segments" of the dominant class's hegemonic control.

In Morgan's view, "adult education presents an opportunity to break through this mesh and explains why Gramsci insisted on the conscious, active, educational intervention of the workers' party" (p. 303). A year later, another article on Gramsci appeared in the same journal. This article, by Paul F. Armstrong (1988), dwells on some of the most popular concepts in Gramscian and Marxian thought, namely the relationship between the dominant ideas and the ruling class, the nondeterministic relationship between base and superstructure, hegemony, the production of consciousness, and praxis. The last section deals specifically with Gramsci and the education of adults. The main point is that Gramsci conceived of adult education "as a significant vehicle" in the process of challenging the "dominant hegemony" (p. 158) and as the means of enabling intellectuals to remain organic to the working class. Since he had little faith in traditional adult education institutions, such as the popular universities, Gramsci primarily conceived of adult education, in this context, as "informal political education, which happened in the community and in the work place, especially in factory councils" (p. 158). In this regard, one would do well to read the chapters, "Political Education and Common Sense," in Adamson (1980), and "Political Consciousness: Education and the Intellectuals," in Ransome (1992). Equally pertinent are Federico Mancini's (1973) chapter on the Factory Councils, and the section on Gramsci and popular education in Andy Green's excellent comparative work concerning education and State formation (1990).

The issue of "Adult Political Education" is also taken up by Diana Coben (1994). It constitutes the penultimate section of a chapter in which Coben outlines some of Gramsci's major concepts, notably those of an "educative politics," hegemony, and the intellectuals. She provides a condensed account of Gramsci's own involvement as an adult educator. In this section, she highlights Gramsci's well-known critique of the kind of education for the working class provided by the popular universities. She also highlights Gramsci's view that, in adult political education carried out within the context of a revolutionary movement, the task is to facilitate the process whereby learners move from "common sense" to "good sense." She returns to this theme in a later article (Coben, 1995) and in her contribution to this book.

One other article on Gramsci to appear in an adult education journal is that by Ursula Apitzsch (1993), a well-known German contributor to the international debate on Gramsci's work, who has written other pieces on Gramsci's ideas concerning work, education, and culture (see Apitzsch, 1995). The focus in the 1993 article is on Gramsci's writings on migration, an area in which Apitzsch has a keen interest, and the issue of the South. She regards these writings as very relevant to the current debate on multiculturalism, and she revisits her article in this book to provide us with a more elaborate version of the argument, underlining its implications for contemporary adult education practice.

As is clear from this overview, Gramsci remains a key point of reference in the literature on education, especially literature that deals with radical and transformative approaches to education. And it seems most likely that more literature concerning Gramsci (or rather Gramsci's theoretical legacy) and education will emerge. A special issue of the journal *Education & Society* is being dedicated to the topic of "Rethinking Hegemony" (this confirms the point made in the opening section of this introduction, namely that more has been written on the concept of hegemony than on any other feature of Gramsci's work) and will contain empirical research. The issue will eventually be republished as a book (Clayton, forthcoming) containing some new papers in addition to the original collection.

The *Gramsci and Education* anthology, which we have put together mainly through electronic networking, attempts to bring some of the dispersed literature together in a single volume. It includes contributions by quite a number of writers cited in this introductory chapter, some providing fresh material, others revisiting their earlier pieces to update them with insights derived from more contemporary experiences and in the light of subsequent published literature. The book deals with Gramsci's ideas as they impinge on different aspects of learning and intellectual practice. They are written by scholars from Argentina, Canada, England, Germany, Italy, Malta, the United States, and Wales, many of whom have, over the years, contributed to the growing international literature on Gramsci's work. An attempt has been made, in the development of this compendium of essays, to incorporate different aspects of Gramsci's large *oeuvre* and to deal with a broad range of areas, including schooling, intellectual practice, hegemony as educational practice, popular education, workers' education, radical adult education in general, multiculturalism, and the cultural productions of dominant and subaltern groups.

We fervently hope that this compendium will serve as a companion book to the primary sources that inspired it; namely, Gramsci's writings that are now available in various editions and in many languages. We also hope that this book will continue to keep alive Gramsci's intellectual legacy in contemporary educational debates.

References

Adamson, W. (1980). *Hegemony and Revolution: Antonio Gramsci's Political and Cultural Theory.* Berkeley: University of California Press.

Alden, H. (1981). Gramsci's Theoretical Legacy. *Convergence,* 14 (3), 91-94.

Allman, P. (1988). Gramsci, Freire and Illich: Their contributions to education for socialism. In T. Lovett (Ed.), *Radical Approaches to Adult Education. A Reader* (pp. 85-113). London: Routledge.

Allman, P. (1999). *Revolutionary Social Transformation. Democratic Hopes, Political Possibilities and Critical Education.* Westport, CT: Bergin & Garvey.

Allman, P., & Wallis, J. (1995). Gramsci's Challenge to the Politics of the Left in "Our Times." *International Journal of Lifelong Education,* 14 (2), 120-43.

Allman, P., & Mayo, P. (1997). Freire, Gramsci and Globalisation: Some Implications for Social and Political Commitment in Adult Education. In P. Armstrong, N. Miller & M. Zukas (Eds.), *Crossing Borders. Breaking Boundaries: Research in the Education of Adults* (pp. 6-10). Proceedings of the 27th Annual SCUTREA Conference. Egham: Birkbeck College, University of London.

Apitzsch, U. (1993). Gramsci and the Current Debate on Multicultural Education. *Studies in the Education of Adults,* 25 (2), 136-45.

Apitzsch, U. (1995). Lavoro, cultura ed educazione tra fordismo e fascismo. In G. Baratta & A. Catone, (Eds.), *Antonio Gramsci e il 'Progresso Intellettuale di Massa'* (pp. 115-31). Milan: Edizioni Unicopli.

Aricó, J. (1988). *La Cola del Diablo. Itinerario de Gramsci en América Latina.* Caracas: Editorial Nueva Sociedad.

Armstrong, P. (1988). L'Ordine Nuovo: The Legacy of Antonio Gramsci and the Education of Adults. *International Journal of Lifelong Education,* 7 (4), 249-59.

Boothman, D. (Ed.). (1995). *Further Selections for the Prison Notebooks.* Minneapolis: University of Minnesota Press.

Broccoli, A. (1972). *Antonio Gramsci e l'educazione come egemonia.* Florence: La Nuova Italia.

Capitani, L., & Villa, R. (Eds.). (1999). *Scuola, intellettuali e identità nazionale nel pensiero di Antonio Gramsci.* Rome: Gamberetti Editrice.

Clayton, T. (forthcoming). *Rethinking Hegemony.* Melbourne: James Nicholas.

Coben, D. (1994). Antonio Gramsci and the Education of Adults. In *Adult Education and Social Change* (pp. 1-9). A collection of papers presented at the European Research Seminar of the European Society for Research on the Education of Adults (ESREA), Lahti, Finland, 7-11 August, 1993.

Coben, D. (1997). Revisiting Gramsci. *Studies in the Education of Adults*, 27 (1), pp. 36-51.

Coben, D. (1998). *Radical Heroes. Gramsci, Freire and the Politics of Adult Education*. New York: Garland.

da Silva, T., & McLaren, P. (1993). Knowledge Under Siege. The Brazilian Debate. In P. McLaren & P. Leonard (Eds.), *Paulo Freire: A Critical Encounter* (pp. 36-46). New York: Routledge.

De Robbio Anziano, I. (1987). *Antonio Gramsci e la Pedagogia del Impegno*. Naples: Ferrero.

Entwistle, H. (1979). *Antonio Gramsci: Conservative Schooling for Radical Politics*. London: Routledge & Kegan Paul.

Fernández Diaz, O. (1995). In America Latina. In E. J. Hobsbawm (Ed.) & A. Santucci (Trans.), *Gramsci in Europa e in America* (pp. 141-57). Rome: Sagittari Laterza.

Freire, P., & Faundez, A. (1989). *Learning to Question. A Pedagogy of Liberation*. Geneva: World Council of Churches.

Green, A. (1990). *Education and State Formation. The Rise of Educational Systems in England, France and the USA*. London: Macmillan.

Hill, D. (1999). [Review of the book *Radical Heroes. Gramsci, Freire and the Politics of Adult Education* by D. Coben]. *International Gramsci Society Newsletter*, 9, 19-26.

Hill, D. (2000). [Review of the book *Gramsci, Freire and Adult Education. Possibilities for Transformative Action* by P. Mayo]. *International Gramsci Society Newsletter*, 10, 17-22.

Hirsch, E. D. (1987). *Cultural Literacy* Boston: Houghton Mifflin.

Hommen, L. (1986). *On the "Organic Intellectualism" of Antonio Gramsci: A Study of the Concept as a Contribution to the Politics of Adult Education*. Unpublished master's thesis, University of Saskatchewan, Saskatoon.

Ireland, T. (1987). *Antonio Gramsci and Adult Education: Reflections on the Brazilian Experience*. Manchester: Manchester University Press.

Jackson, T. (1981). The Influence of Gramsci on Adult Education. *Convergence*, 14 (3), 81-86.

La Belle, T. J. (1986). *Non Formal Education in Latin America and the Caribbean—Stability, Reform or Revolution?* New York: Praeger.

22   Carmel Borg, Joseph A. Buttigieg, and Peter Mayo

Leonard, P. (1993). Critical Pedagogy and State Welfare—Intellectual Encounters with Freire and Gramsci, 1974-86. In P. McLaren & P. Leonard (Eds.), *Paulo Freire: A Critical Encounter* (pp. 155-76). New York: Routledge.

Lombardi, F. (1971). *La Pédagogie Marxiste d'Antonio Gramsci* (J. Gritti, Trans.). Toulouse: Edouard Privat.

Lovett, T. (1978). The Challenge of Community Education in Social and Political Change. *Convergence,* 11 (1), 42-51.

Manacorda, M. A. (1976). *Il Principio Educativo in Gramsci: Americanismo e Conformismo.* Rome: Armando Editore.

Mancini, F. (1973). *Worker Democracy and Political Party in Gramsci's Thinking.* Occasional Paper. Bologna: School of Advanced International Studies, The Johns Hopkins University Press.

Mayo, M. (1997). *Imagining Tomorrow. Adult education for Transformation.* Leicester: NIACE.

Mayo, P. (1999). *Gramsci, Freire and Adult Education. Possibilities for Transformative Action.* London: Zed.

Mayo, P. (forthcoming). Gramsci, War of Position, and Adult Education. In T. Clayton (Ed.), *Rethinking Hegemony.* Melbourne: James Nicholas.

Melis, A. (1995). Gramsci e l'America Latina. In G. Baratta & A. Catone (Eds.), *Antonio Gramsci e il 'progresso intellettuale di massa'* (pp. 227-34). Milan: Edizioni Unicopli.

Monasta, A. (1993). *L'educazione tradita: Criteri per una diversa valutazione complessiva dei Quaderni del Carcere di Antonio Gramsci.* Florence: McColl.

Morgan, W. J. (1987). The Pedagogical Politics of Antonio Gramsci—"Pessimism of the Intellect, Optimism of the Will." *International Journal of Lifelong Education,* 6 (4), 295-308.

Morrow, R. A. (1995). Post-Marxism, Post-Modernism, and Popular Education in Latin America. In C. A. Torres (Ed.), *Education and Social Change in Latin America* (pp. 111-26). Melbourne: James Nicholas.

Morrow, R. A., & Torres, C. A. (1995). *Social Theory and Education. A Critique of Theories of Social and Cultural Reproduction.* Albany: State University of New York Press.

Ransome, P. (1992). *Antonio Gramsci. A New Introduction.* London: Harvester/Wheatsheaf.

Senese, G. B. (1991). Warnings on Resistance and the Language of Possibility: Gramsci and a Pedagogy from the Surreal. *Educational Theory,* 41 (1), 13-22.

Thompson, J. L. (1983). *Learning Liberation: Women's Response to Men's Education.* London: Croom Helm.

Torres, C. A. (1990). *The Politics of Nonformal Education in Latin America*. New York: Praeger.
Torres, C. A. (Ed.) (1995). *Education and Social Change in Latin America*. Melbourne: James Nicholas.
Youngman, F. (1986). *Adult Education and Socialist Pedagogy*. Kent: Croom Helm.

Abbreviated Titles

LP: *Letters from Prison* (F. Rosengarten, Ed. and R. Rosenthal, Trans.). 2 vol. New York: Columbia University Press (1994).
QC: *Quaderni del carcere* (V. Gerratana, Ed.). Edizione critica dell' Istituto Gramsci. 4 vol. Torino: Einaudi (1975).
SG: *Scritti Giovanili 1914-1918*. Torino: Einaudi (1975).
SPN: *Selections from the Prison Notebooks of Antonio Gramsci* (Q. Hoare & G. Nowell Smith, Eds. and Trans.). London: Lawrence & Wishart (1971).
SPW: *Selections from Political Writings (1910-1920)* (Q. Hoare, Ed. and J. Mathews, Trans.). London: Lawrence & Wishart (1977).

1

Hegemony and Rhetoric: Political Education in Gramsci*

Benedetto Fontana

Antonio Gramsci's social and political theory is centered on his concept of hegemony, the analysis and interpretation of which has
spawned a plethora of works in various fields.[1] My purpose here is to
explore what appear to me as significant points of convergence between Gramsci's hegemony, his idea of education, and ancient rhetoric. Such a relationship, at first sight, might appear surprising, perhaps
even anomalous, yet, given Gramsci's references to the importance of
classical thought and culture, and to the role they played throughout
the politics and history of Italy, it is crucial to the understanding of
his notion of education. At the same time, much has been written and
debated on the revolutionary or reformist, conservative or radical,
nature of his concept of education.[2] Rather than rehearse the interpretations of the secondary sources, this chapter intends to return to
where Gramsci himself began—the attempt to construct "a humanistic school, as conceived by the ancients, and more recently by the
men of the Renaissance" (Gramsci, 1977a, p. 26)—and explore what
Gramsci means when he says he wants to go back to the "ancients."

For Gramsci, in his theoretical and practical concern with educational reformers, the ultimate purpose and goal was to uncover conditions that would lead to the transformation of State and society through the formation of a particular type of consciousness, that is, the generation within the proletariat and other subordinate groups of a culture and a politics which are both autonomous and hegemonic. Throughout his writings, during both the preprison years of active political and cultural struggle, and the prison years when he was compelled to confront the failure of the revolution in the West, Gramsci often addressed the kind of cultural and educational institutions he thought the subordinate classes required. In these articles and notes classical and humanist thought is crucial.

It is significant, therefore, that in his project to establish a culture and a practice independent of the dominant conception of the world, Gramsci believed it necessary to return to a type of school and education "as conceived by the ancients." In effect, Gramsci's concept of education can fruitfully be brought back to ancient thinkers such as Plato and Aristotle; in the same way, his concept of hegemony cannot be understood without recognizing its rhetorical (that is, speech and language) elements.

In the *Prison Notebooks*, in a note entitled "Passage from Knowing to Understanding and to Feeling and vice versa from Feeling to Understanding and to Knowing," Gramsci makes a distinction between intellectuals who "know" and the "people-nation" that merely "feels." The former may know but do not always understand or feel, while the latter may feel but does not always know. The intellectual, in order to know something politically and socially, and not merely abstractly or philosophically, must understand it with feeling and passion. Gramsci writes:

> The intellectual's error consists in believing that one can know without understanding and even more without feeling and being impassioned (not only for knowledge in itself but also for the object of knowledge); in other words that the intellectual can be an intellectual (and not a pure pedant) if distinct and separate from the people-nation, that is, without feeling the elementary passions of the people, understanding them and therefore explaining and justifying them in the particular historical situation and connecting them dialectically to the laws of history and to a superior conception of the world, scientifically and coherently elaborated—i.e. knowledge. One cannot make politics-history without this passion, without this sentimental connection between intellectuals and people-nation. (SPN, p. 418)

The abstract knowledge of the intellectual may be turned into life and politics as it becomes linked to the experience and passion felt by the people. At the same time, the feelings and passion of the people—by means of the intellectuals acting as filters or mediators—are infused with conscious direction and coherence.

Of course, such a description of the relation between thinking and feeling, thought and passion (action) recalls Marx's comments in the *Theses on Feuerbach* (1978, pp. 143-45). The reciprocal relation between intellectual and people-nation, and between knowledge and feeling-passion, is at the heart of the dichotomy between common sense and good sense. Common sense is opinion which is incoherent and ambiguous (SPN, p. 423) but which may nevertheless contain elements of truth to the extent that they are proliferated throughout a people. Good sense is the common sense of the people as their passion and experience are imbued with knowledge and reason—that is, as the people begin to "think" coherently by producing their own intellectuals, the organic intellectual, or the democratic philosopher (SPN, pp. 328-36, 348-50). As Gramsci says,

> critical self-consciousness means, historically and politically, the creation of an *élite* of intellectuals. A human mass does not "distinguish" itself, does not become independent in its own right without, in the widest sense, organising itself; and there is no organisation without intellectuals, that is without organisers and leaders [. . .]. (SPN, pp. 334-35)

Hence a link is made between thinking—"critical consciousness" of self—and cultural individuation and social differentiation, and intellectuals and political and social autonomy. The movement from incoherence to coherence in both the political and epistemological senses is one mediated by the social/cultural category of intellectuals. The formation of intellectuals, in particular of intellectuals closely tied to the people, and immersed in their life and activity is therefore fundamental. Such are the organic or the national-popular intellectuals, leaders, and organizers of the class or social groups from which they emerge. They are central to a movement that seeks to "replace common sense and the old concept of the world in general." As such their function is

> to raise the intellectual level of ever growing strata of the populace, in other words, to give a personality to the amorphous mass element. This means working to produce *élites* of intellectuals of a new type, which arise directly out of the masses, but remain in contact with them to become, as it were, the whale bone in the corset. (SPN, p. 340)

To produce organic intellectuals is to "give a personality" to the masses; and to give personality is to mold or shape a characteristic individuality, to differentiate and to concretize what was originally amorphous potential.

How to bring a people to think critically and coherently is the

fundamental problem posed by Gramsci, and it is a problem that combines political, epistemological, and educational spheres of activity.
As such, it is a theme that permeates the history of Western political
thought, one that was originally formulated by ancient and classical
thought.[3] It is a problem posed by Plato and taken up by Aristotle.
The relation between knowledge and politics, philosophy and rhetoric, ruler and people, and reason and desire/appetite[4] is addressed by
Plato in such dialogues as the *Gorgias*, the *Republic*, the *Statesman*,
and the *Laws*. The same theme is taken up by Aristotle in his *Politics*
and *Rhetoric*, where he revises Plato's original position.

The relation between knowledge and politics points to two fundamental questions: what is the nature of political rule? (that is, what
does it mean to exercise political power?) and, concomitantly, what is
the relation between ruler and ruled? Another way of putting the question is to inquire whether the "masses" or the "people" are competent and rational, that is, whether they are capable of ruling.

Gramsci's distinctions among the various type of intellectuals-
traditional/organic,   cosmopolitan/national-popular—summarize   and
underline the relation between mass and reason or thought. The first
term of these dyads describes a social category of intellectuals di-
vorced from the masses, and who therefore assert the primacy of
autonomous reason (the *logos* as the expression of what Gramsci
would call *alta cultura*). And the second term of the dyad depicts a
type of intellectual closely and intimately allied with the people, and
who therefore understands reason and thought as emerging from
within the life activity of the people (the *logos* as the expression of
cultura popolare). The former is reminiscent of Plato, while the latter evokes Aristotle. In either case, both are grounded within concrete
social and political structures. Gramsci, like Plato and Aristotle, understands that the *logos*, or its elaboration in a philosophy, is merely
sterile and ineffectual without grounding within a particular sociopolitical formation. That is to say, it is not enough to know the "truth"
tout court—rather, philosophy and knowledge are "realized" (to use a
Hegelian term) by means of their dissemination and proliferation
throughout a social group or society, which points to the necessary
role speech, language, and rhetoric play as the vehicles by which the
people or the masses are shaped and formed—that is, by which they
are persuaded and educated.

All of which brings us to hegemony. Gramsci develops hegemony
as a complex and densely articulated set of ideas constituted by multiple and interlocking layers. On one level, hegemony may be viewed as
the movement away from the economic-corporative to the political[5]—from the particular to the universal, exemplified by Gramsci in

his contrast between the narrowly based interests of the medieval Italian communes and the collective will he sees embodied in Machiavelli's new prince.[6] At the same time, hegemony also constitutes the generation of alliances by an increasingly preeminent social group. Thus, a group or class becomes hegemonic as it exercises intellectual and moral leadership over other groups in society in such a manner that the latter become "allies" and "associates" of the former. On the other hand, opposed to leadership is domination, which is the exercise of coercion or "armed force" over other groups. In Gramsci's words,

> the supremacy of a social group is manifested in two ways: as "domination" and as "intellectual and moral leadership." A social group is dominant over those antagonistic groups it wants to "liquidate" or to subdue even with armed force, and it is leading with respect to those groups that are associated and allied with it. (QC, p. 2010)

In addition, Gramsci sees modern Western societies—liberal and democratic political regimes—as systems of hegemonic equilibrium characterized by a "combination of force and consent which are balanced in varying proportions, without force prevailing too greatly over consent" (QC, p. 1638). Coercion and persuasion, force and consent, and domination and leadership together describe and constitute the defining and essential character of the political, such that the State in Gramsci is characterized by two analytically separate, but historically and mutually penetrating, spheres: "dictatorship + hegemony," and "political society + civil society," where the symbiotic unity of the two spheres represents to Gramsci what he calls the "integral State" (QC, pp. 763-64).

Moreover, Gramsci's distinction between the war of movement (possible in the East) and the war of position (necessary in the West) highlights his dichotomy between political society (the sphere of force and domination) and civil society (the sphere of hegemony). "In the East," Gramsci writes, "the State was everything, civil society was primordial and gelatinous; in the West there was a proper relation between the State and civil society, and when the State trembled a sturdy structure of civil society was at once revealed. The State was only an outer ditch, behind which there stood a powerful system of fortresses and earthworks" (SPN, p. 238). Civil society is the sphere of liberty and of contract (that is, of what Isaiah Berlin has called "negative liberty"), where consent and persuasion are generated (see Berlin, 1967). It is the sphere of cultural, ideological, and religious conflict, where this conflict is defined by the contest of voluntary and secondary associations such as trade unions, political parties, sects and churches, schools and universities, civic organizations, and interest groups of various kinds. In addition, Gramsci asserts that

> [t]he massive structures of modern democracies, both as State organizations, and as complexes of associations in civil society, constitute for the art of politics as it were the "trenches" and the permanent fortifications of the front in the war of position: they render merely "partial" the element of movement which before used to be "the whole" of war [. . .]. (SPN, p. 243)

In the West, a direct assault (the war of movement) on the State is not possible because sedimented layers of complex associations of civil society have rendered the "integral State" both politically powerful and ideologically resilient. Thus, a war of position, that is, ideological, cultural, and intellectual struggle, becomes necessary to overcome the established order. Radical social and political change in the West involves sociocultural and socioeconomic "trench warfare," whose purpose is to undermine the "ethico-political" and ideological structures of society. The necessity of waging a war of position in the West points to the moral and intellectual—that is, the persuasive, consensual (and thus educative)—nature of the State in the modern world. Gramsci underlines such a nature when he points to the radical and innovating activity of the bourgeoisie and to the emergence of a form of political rule not seen since the fall of the ancient Roman republic. He writes:

> The previous ruling classes were essentially conservative in the sense that they did not tend to construct an organic passage from the other classes into their own, i.e., to enlarge their class sphere "technically" and "ideologically": their conception was that of a closed caste. The bourgeois class poses itself as an organism in continuous movement, capable of absorbing the entire society, assimilating it to its own cultural and economic level. The entire function of the state has been transformed; the state has become an "educator," etc. (SPN, p. 260)[7]

The State as educator means that now it exerts moral, intellectual, and cultural force: it exercises power by presenting itself as "ethico-political,"[8] as the representative of universal values, independent of narrow economic, social, or class interests. In doing so, the dominant groups infuse the "entire society"—that is, the subordinate groups—with their specific and determinate "personality." The notion of the State as "educator" and the formation of a socio-cultural "personality" brings us back full swing to the notion of hegemony specifically construed as the movement from feeling to knowledge, from desire/appetite to reason, and from the economic to the political. In other words, hegemony is precisely described by the movement from a particular (or prepolitical) to a universal (or political) consciousness (Gramsci, SPN, pp. 326-36; QC II: 11, pp. 1378-87).

Parallel to the formation of a critical or political (that is, hegemonic) consciousness is the development of a common language and a common grammar or structure of discourse within the subordinate group class. Indeed, to Gramsci this effort is crucial to the germination and generation of a hegemonic conception of the world.[9] Such a conception must arise in opposition to that of the dominant groups, for the genesis and consequent proliferation of a *Weltanschauung* are rooted in, and elaborated through, sociopolitical conflicts and sociocultural contests. However, its primary locus is centered within the life and practical activity of the subordinate groups, giving the latter an autonomous and comprehensive interpretation of the material and social world. The formation of a hegemonic conception of the world is equivalent to the formation of the subordinate group into a determinate and political subject, and to the acquisition by such a group of moral, intellectual, and cultural autonomy. Hegemony presupposes and requires—indeed, is intimately and inherently defined and characterized by—the development of such a common language and common grammar. What is hegemony—the development and elaboration of a conception of the world and of a moral-intellectual structure—if not the discourse structure and speech so necessary to the elaboration of an autonomous personality? Gramsci explicitly identifies the necessary relation between the political and forms of speech and language. Such a relation constitutes the basis of the political and civic space envisioned as the sphere of public action (SPN, pp. 38-43, 323-25, 348-51).

The reciprocal relation between speech/language and politics (the *polis*) can be traced back to Plato, Aristotle, and eventually Isocrates, all of whom attempt to investigate the relation between knowledge and politics. In particular, it was Isocrates who asserted *logos hegemon panton*, that is, "speech and language are the leader and guide of all things," and it was Aristotle who made the *logos* both the basis for, and the product of, the political association.[10] In other words, *logos* and *polis* imply and presuppose each other. What this means is that the relation between speech/language (*logos*) and hegemony describes a power relationship based on the generation and dissemination of forms of knowledge and systems of value. Such a relationship presupposes a particular form of knowledge and practice—the art (*ars*) or *techne* of rhetoric,[11] which requires a particular relation between the speaker (intellectual) and the audience (masses) he is addressing, which, in turn, assumes a particular socio-political structure or order in existence which makes both necessary and useful the relation between the intellectual (speaker/writer) and the people. Aristotle writes that "speech based on knowledge is teaching, but teaching is impossible [with some audiences]; rather, it is necessary for *pisteis* [means of persuasion] and speeches [as a whole] to be formed on the basis of common [beliefs], as we said in the *Topics* about communication with the crowd [the people]" (trans. 1991, 1355 a-1355 b).

An understanding of the feelings, passion, and practices of the people is fundamental—that is, what in Gramsci comes under the general rubric of *cultura popolare*, such as folklore, dialectical speech, popular religion, and embryonic or immature expressions of thought and beliefs, cannot be discounted in the effort to develop a new and superior form of culture and knowledge. In this regard, as Aristotle writes, "the greatest and most important of all things in an ability to persuade and give good advice is to grasp an understanding of all forms of constitution [*politeia*] and to distinguish the customs and legal usages and advantages of each" (trans. 1991, 1365 b-1366 a). Moreover, it is only in a political community such as the *polis* that the *logos* as *hegemon* would be capable of generating consent by means of the persuasive and rhetorical devices of speech, language, and discourse. And it is only in a social and political order such as is found in the liberal and democratic regimes of the West—the "massive structures of modern democracies" (SPN, p. 243)—that a war of position, that is, the generation of a conception of the world in opposition to the established one, becomes possible. Thus, we have arrived where we began: Gramsci's concept of the organic intellectual, or the democratic philosopher—and thus too, Gramsci's hegemony, viewed as the proliferation of a conception of the world throughout a society by means of the generation of "permanent consent" (SPN, pp. 10, 80).

It is in this context that the famous formulation—"every relationship of 'hegemony' is necessarily an educational relationship"—should be understood. As Gramsci says, "the relationship between teacher and pupil is active and reciprocal so that every teacher is always a pupil and every pupil a teacher [. . .]. [Such a relationship] exists between intellectual and nonintellectual sections of the population, between the rulers and the ruled, *élites* and their followers, leaders and led, the vanguard and the body of the army" (SPN, p. 350). An educational relationship, since it is always hegemonic, is necessarily a political relationship: that is, the generation of permanent persuasion by means of speech and language. What this means is that Gramsci sees a reciprocal relation between politics and education: the political is educative, in the same way as education is political. In this sense, as Gramsci points out, education is not restricted to the merely "scholastic" (SPN, p. 350) or technical activity that occurs within schools and other pedagogic institutions. Still less is Gramsci's concept of education limited to the techniques and processes devised to produce various categories of workers and functionaries required and demanded by a modern economy. Rather, it is aimed at the sociocultural, moral, and intellectual mechanisms by which an integrated "personality" is formed. The ensemble of these mechanisms, taken together, would constitute for Gramsci an on-going moral and intellectual reform leading to the construction of a political and historical subject that is self-conscious and self-disciplined, and thus autonomous and self-ruling. In Gramsci's words,

> the labourer can become a skilled worker [. . .] the peasant a surveyor or petty agronomist. But democracy [. . .] cannot mean merely that an unskilled worker can become skilled. It must mean that every "citizen" can "govern" and that society places him, even if only abstractly, in a general condition to achieve this. Political democracy tends towards a coincidence of the rulers and the ruled (in the sense of government with the consent of the governed), ensuring for each non-ruler a free training in the skills and general technical preparation necessary to that end. (SPN, pp. 40-41)

On one level, as has been pointed out, Gramsci is launching a critique of contemporary systems of education. The ruling groups devise an educational structure geared toward technical and "vocational" training, which, while producing "petty agronomists" and technicians, would deny the lower classes the kind of "general" and "universal" education necessary to attain positions of power and political leadership.[12] As Gramsci notes, "from technique-as-work one proceeds to technique-as-science and to the humanistic conception of history, without which one remains 'specialised' and does not become 'leading' [*dirigente*] (specialised and political)" (SPN, p. 10). For the problem regarding the identification of the "skills and general technical preparation" necessary to achieve "a coincidence of the rulers and the ruled" is precisely the problem regarding the transformation of subordinate groups into ruling classes, which is also the problem regarding the formation of a political subject capable of rule (see Fontana, 1993 and Nardone, 1977).

In this sense, therefore, Gramsci's emphasis on revolutionary praxis, on the formation of an active historical subject capable of transforming society, requires a public educational system that transforms the children of the subordinate groups into young men and women who are both critical, conscious, and disciplined. As he notes, the reform of the schools is not a question of creating different kinds of vocational schools (still less of developing a "multicultural" curriculum in contemporary society), but rather "to create a single type of formative school (primary-secondary) which would take the child up to the threshold of his choice of job, forming him during this time as a person capable of thinking, studying and ruling—or controlling those who rule" (SPN, p. 40).

At the same time, Gramsci's understanding of "political democracy" as a "coincidence" of rulers and ruled, and thereby as a training ground for the skills and education necessary to the active participation of the people in such a system, demonstrates a close affinity to Aristotle's conception of rule in the *polis* and the education necessary to such a form of rule. In the *Politics*, Aristotle develops his idea of political rule in opposition to Plato's aristocratic conception of rule by the philosophers. Since, to Plato, ruling is a science and a form of knowledge, those who are able to reason ought to rule. The *Republic* is an attempt to establish a system of education, understood in the broadest sociocultural terms, by which the philosopher/ruler is to be discovered and shaped. In Books VIII and IX, the section dealing with the decline and degeneration of the ideal polity governed by Reason embodied in the class of philosopher/rulers, Plato underlines the intimate connection between social and cultural structures and the generation of a specific personality (or "character") (see Plato, trans. 1969, 543 A-576 B). Each type of personality—from the just to the timocratic to the oligarchic to the democratic to the despotic—informs, and is informed by the social, political, and cultural order within which it is embedded and from which it derives its form and content. In this sense, Plato understands the formation of the ruling class as a process that occurs at simultaneous and multiple levels: it is at once epistemological, educational, socioeconomic, and political. Aristotle accepts the close relation between the moral and the intellectual, and between the political and the cognitive, established by Plato. He rejects, however, the exclusive reduction of rule to the self-enclosed rational activity of the philosopher. Ruling to Aristotle is a reciprocal relation between the ruler and the ruled, in which both elements are active and engaged. The relation is no longer between reason (the ruler/philosopher) that rules, and appetite (the workers/ruled) that obeys. The relation is no longer vertical, but horizontal. Political rule is understood in terms of "ruling and being ruled in turn,"[13] where the operative term is "in turn." Without this reciprocity, ruling is no longer political (that is, free and consensual), but is rather despotic—in the original sense of rule of the master over his household of slaves.

Man is a *zoon politikon* because, to Aristotle, he realizes his full human potential only within the political association, the highest expression of cultural and social life. At the same time, the *polis*—and this is typically and classically central to ancient political practice and political speculation—is an association, or a way of life, that embodies, and is embodied by, speech and language (the *logos*).[14]

In this regard, it is interesting to note that the Marxian conception of the proletariat may be viewed as the elaboration and modernization of the Aristotelian notion of the *polis* as an association of equals, an association of citizens defined by ruling and being ruled in turn. In Marx the proletariat was the class which, through its concrete praxis and political activity, would realize philosophy in history; in Aristotle the *polis* is seen as the concrete realization of the *logos*, for it is only in and through the *polis* that man's nature as a rational and moral subject can be fulfilled. Thus, if in Aristotle the *logos* implies and presupposes the *polis*, in Marx the proletariat implies and presupposes philosophy, such that the proletariat in its self-becoming is none other than the incarnation in history of the *logos*. All of which is to say that the proletariat as a class may be conceptualized as the Aristotelian association of equals, whose realm of freedom is a truly universal space, since its existence does not presuppose and require the domination of others.

Of course, Marx, by standing Hegel on his feet, has substituted a socioeconomic category (the working class) for Hegel's State. Hegel, by making the State the concrete realization in history of Reason, historicizes Aristotle's and Plato's *logos*, and traces its various (sociopolitical, cultural, and ethical) manifestations as it moves through history. Gramsci, in developing his notion of hegemony, returns to the Hegelian notion of Spirit (culture) moving in history. For hegemony is precisely the synthesis of culture/knowledge and power as it moves in history and as it becomes realized concretely as a way of life and as an active practice—that is, as it becomes embodied in the "integral State" (SPN, p. 267). Hegemony is the proliferation throughout the people of a particular conception of the world, and of a particular way of life, which is, at the same time, the process by which a "great State" (SPN, p. 249) is founded. For the founding of the State is the realization in history (praxis) of a hegemonic conception of the world.

In effect, *polis* and *logos* presuppose one another, such that each can only be understood in terms of the other. Aristotle identifies three distinct kinds of rule: in the family, in the household (*despoteia*), and in the *polis* (see Aristotle, trans. 1958, 1252 a-1253 b). The first two delineate rule over unequals (such as women, barbarians, and slaves), and the last describes rule over equals. Women, slaves, and metics, which together formed the majority of the population of the *polis* (certainly of Athens), could not speak in the political space that defined the *polis*. Possessing no public persona, they could only speak and act within the household (ruled, we should note, by the citizen/master). The ability to speak openly and publicly within the political community or polity is thus the preeminent criterion for the development of equal citizenship (see Aristotle, trans. 1958, 1260 a-1260 b). Since, therefore, ruling and being ruled in turn implies the reciprocal and mutual relation of persuading and being persuaded, political education in Aristotle is directed to the formation of citizens capable of acting as autonomous and conscious political subjects.

Unlike Plato, who establishes rule on the strict and irreconcilable antithesis between those who know and those who do not know, Aristotle does not believe that "those who rule [should] be different from [. . .] those who are ruled" (see Aristotle, trans. 1997, 1332 b 12). Like Gramsci,[15] he believes that the "nonrulers" should have a "free training" to achieve "that end," namely, equal citizenship and participation in the life of the polity. Accordingly, education must be directed toward the formation of rulers and nonrulers who know how both to command and to obey "in turn." But, as Aristotle notes, "in one way the rulers and the ruled are the same but that in another they are different. Accordingly, it is necessary for their education also to be in one way the same and in another way different. For, they say, one who is going to rule well must first be ruled" (trans. 1997, 1332 b 41-1333 a). Or, to put it somewhat differently, one who wishes to rule over others must first learn how to rule himself.

Ruling and being ruled in turn encompass both self-mastery and self-discipline (that is, commanding and obeying oneself), and mastery and leadership as a relationship within the political community. Self-mastery (obeying self-imposed commands) is what Gramsci means when he talks about the generation of a critical self-consciousness as the basis for the development of an integrated "personality." All cultural activity is directed to the formation of this personality; and to Gramsci, culture presupposes moral and intellectual discipline achieved by means of labor and work.[16] As Gramsci puts it in one of his pre-prison essays,

> consciousness of self which is opposed to others, which is differentiated and, once having set itself a goal, can judge facts and events other than in themselves but also in so far as they tend to drive history forward or backward. To know oneself means to be oneself, to be master of oneself, to distinguish oneself, to free oneself from a state of chaos, to exist as an element of order—but of one's own order and one's own discipline in striving for an ideal. (Gramsci, 1977b, p. 13)

To move from a "state of chaos" to an order of one's own making is to move from undifferentiated desire to the self-positing of goals; it is to move from matter to idea, from economics to politics, from worker to citizen—in sum, from necessity to liberty.

Such a personality is autonomous precisely because it has learned how to be ruled, and thus in the process learns how to rule. In turn, such an education presupposes a particular and special kind of intellectual, the democratic philosopher whose activity is not to maintain the masses at the level of "feeling" and "animal appetite" (SPN, p. 298), but rather to lead (that is, in the sense of both *educere* and *educare*) them to the realization of their potential for critical thought and coherent knowledge. Thus the force of Gramsci's assertion that "every citizen can govern." Thus, too, we now see the relation between Gramsci's understanding of hegemony seen as moral and intellectual leadership, as the drawing out (*educere*) of consent from the people, and education conceived as the instilling of critical self-consciousness (*educare*). All of which brings us back to Gramsci's formulation, an educational relationship is a hegemonic relationship, where to educate means precisely to exercise moral and intellectual leadership. In the same way, to exercise hegemony means precisely to educate the masses toward a superior and more coherent conception of the world (moral and intellectual reform).

Notes

*For Doris, *quae laetificat vitam meam*.
1. The number of works on Gramsci's hegemony is enormous. Informative and interesting are Adamson (1980), Nardone (1971), Buzzi (1973), and Finocchiaro (1988).
2. For discussion and analysis of Gramsci's concept of education as well as its relation to other aspects of his thought, see Broccoli (1972), Manacorda (1976), Entwistle (1979), Morgan (1987), and Mayo (1995).
3. For a discussion of the relation between Gramsci's concept of hegemony and ancient political thought, see Fontana (2000).
4. See Gramsci's comments (SPN, p. 350). See also his Notebook 10 (II), §44 (QC, pp. 1331-32) and Notebook 1, §114 (QC, p. 114). In addition, Gramsci's comments in his preprison writings are noteworthy: see, especially, Gramsci (1977b); in Italian, "Socialismo e cultura," first published in *Il Grido del popolo*, 29 January 1916, and reprinted in Gramsci (1977c).
5. See Notebook 13, §17 (QC, pp. 1579-89).
6. See Notebook 6, §10, §79, and §97 (QC, pp. 690, 750, 772); and Notebook 10 (II), §22 and §41xiv (QC, pp. 1261, 1325).
7. "In reality," Gramsci notes, "the State must be conceived of as an 'educator,' in as much as it tends precisely to create a new type or

level of civilisation" (SPN, p. 247).

8. For Gramsci's discussion of the concept of the ethicopolitical, and his critique of Croce's use of it, see Gramsci (SPN, pp. 257-63; QC II: 8, pp. 1049-50, II: 10, pp. 1214-37).

9. See the section entitled "State and Civil Society" in *Selections from the Prison Notebooks of Antonio Gramsci.*

10. On this, see Sinclair (1968, pp. 115-42, and, especially, 130-39), and Aristotle (trans. 1958, 1252a-1253a, 1261a, 1278b, 1280). I use two translations of *Politics.* For citations up to but not including 1323a, I use Ernest Barker's edition. For citations beginning with 1323a, I use *Politics: Books VII and VIII,* translated and with commentary by Richard Kraut. For an excellent analysis of Isocrates and *logos politikos,* see Yun Lee Too (1995).

11. See Aristotle (trans. 1991, 1354a-1354b, and 1355a-1357a).

12. See Gramsci's 1916 essay "Men or Machines?" in *Avanti!,* where he writes that

> [t]he children of proletarians too should have all possibilities open to them; they should be able to develop their own individuality in the optimal way[. . .]. Technical schools should not be allowed to become incubators of little monsters aridly trained for a job, with no general ideas, no general culture, no intellectual stimulation[. . .]. Of course, meanly bourgeois industrialists might prefer to have workers who were more machines than men. (1977a, p. 27)

13. See Euripides' *The Suppliant Women* (400-40), where Theseus says, "there is no tyrant here. The city is not ruled by one man only, but is free. The people is the sovereign, and rulers succeed one another year by year in turn. No extra privilege is given to the rich man, and the poor is his equal" (trans. 1998, 403-08).

14. Aristotle writes: "man is a being meant for political association. [. . .] and man alone of the animals is furnished with the faculty of language" (trans. 1958, 1253a).

15. Gramsci states that

> [t]he philosophy of praxis does not tend to leave the "simple" in their primitive philosophy of common sense, but rather to lead them to a higher conception of life. If it affirms the need for contact between intellectuals and simple it is not in order to restrict scientific activity and preserve unity at the low level of the masses, but precisely in order to construct an intellectual-moral bloc which can make politically possible the intellectual progress of the mass and not only of small intellectual groups. (SPN, pp. 332-33)

16. See Gramsci's letter of 28 July 1930 to his mother (1975, pp. 358-59), and Notebook 3, §48 (QC, p. 330). See also Manacorda (1976, p. 17). On Gramsci's understanding of work and labor as the overcoming of nature and "instinct," see Fontana (1996).

References

Adamson, W. L. (1980). *Hegemony and Revolution: A Study of Antonio Gramsci's Political and Cultural Theory.* Berkeley: University of California Press.

Aristotle. (1997). *Politics: Books VII and VIII* (R. Kraut, Trans. and Commentary). Oxford: Clarendon Aristotle Series, Clarendon Press.

Aristotle. (1991). *Aristotle on Rhetoric: A Theory of Civic Discourse* (G. A. Kennedy, Trans. and Introduction). New York: Oxford University Press.

Aristotle. (1958). *Politics* (E. Barker, Ed. and Trans). Oxford: Oxford University Press.

Berlin, I. (1967). *Four Essays on Liberty.* Cambridge: Cambridge University Press.

Broccoli, A. (1972). *Antonio Gramsci e l'educazione come egemonia.* Florence: Editrice La Nuova Italia.

Buzzi, A. R. (1973). *La teoria politica di Gramsci* (S. Genovali, Trans.). Florence: La Nuova Italia Editrice.

Entwistle, H. (1979). *Antonio Gramsci: Conservative Schooling for Radical Politics.* London: Routledge & Kegan Paul.

Euripides. *Suppliant Women; Electra; Heracles* (D. Kovacs, Ed. and Trans.) Cambridge, MA: Harvard University Press, Loeb Classical Library

Finocchiaro, M. A. (1988). *Gramsci and the History of Dialectical Thought.* Cambridge: Cambridge University Press.

Fontana, B. (2000). Logos and Kratos: Gramsci and the Ancients on Hegemony. *Journal of the History of Ideas*, 61 (2), 305-26.

Fontana, B. (1996). The Concept of Nature in Gramsci. *The Philosophical Forum*, 27 (3), 220-43.

Fontana, B. (1993). *Hegemony and Power: On the Relation between Gramsci and Machiavelli.* Minneapolis: University of Minnesota Press.

Gramsci, A. (1977a). Men or Machines? In Q. Hoare (Ed.) and J. Matthews (Trans.), *Selections from Political Writings* (pp. 25-27). New York: International.

Gramsci, A. (1977b). Socialism and Culture. In Q. Hoare (Ed.) and J. Matthews (Trans.), *Selections from Political Writings* (pp. 10-13). New York: International.

Gramsci, A. (1977c). Socialismo e cultura. *Scritti giovanili 1914-1918* (pp. 22-26). Turin: Einaudi, 1977.

Gramsci, A. (1975). *Lettere dal carcere* (S. Caprioglio & E. Fubini, Eds.). Turin: Einaudi.

Manacorda, M. A. (1976). *Il principio educativo in Gramsci*. Rome: Armando Editore.

Marx, K. Theses on Feuerbach. In R. C. Tucker (Ed.), *The Marx-Engels Reader* (pp. 143-45). New York: W. W. Norton & Company.

Mayo, P. The "Turn to Gramsci" in Adult Education: A Review. *International Gramsci Society Newsletter*, 4, 2-9.

Morgan, W. J. (1987). The Pedagogical Politics of Antonio Gramsci: "Pessimism of the Intellect, Optimism of the Will." *International Journal of Lifelong Education*, 6 (4) 295-308.

Nardone, G. (1977). *L'Umano in Gramsci: evento politico e comprensione dell'evento politico*. Bari: Dedalo Libri.

Nardone, G. (1971). *Il pensiero di Gramsci*. Bari: De Donato.

Plato. (1969). *Republic*. Cambridge, MA: Loeb Classical Library, Harvard University Press.

Sinclair, T. A. (1968). *A History of Greek Political Thought* (2nd ed.). Cleveland: Meridian Books.

Too, Y. L. (1995). *The Rhetoric of Identity in Isocrates: Text, Power, Pedagogy*. Cambridge: Cambridge University Press.

Abbreviated Titles

QC: *Quaderni del carcere* (V. Gerratana, Ed.). Edizione critica dell' Istituto Gramsci. 4 vol. Torino: Einaudi (1975).

SPN: *Selections from the Prison Notebooks of Antonio Gramsci* (Q. Hoare & G. Nowell Smith, Eds. and Trans.). London: Lawrence & Wishart (1971).

2

Rethinking Cultural Politics and Radical Pedagogy in the Work of Antonio Gramsci*

Henry A. Giroux

Introduction

Sixty years after his death, Italian Marxist Antonio Gramsci still looms large as one of the great political theorists of the twentieth century. Refusing to separate culture from systemic relations of power, or politics from the production of knowledge and identities, Gramsci redefined how politics bore down on everyday life through the force of its pedagogical practices, relations, and discourses. This position is in stark contrast to a growing and insistent number of progressive theorists who abstract politics from culture and political struggle from pedagogical practices. In opposition to Gramsci, such theorists privilege a materialist politics that ignores the ways in which cultural formations have become one of the chief means through which individuals engage and comprehend the material circumstances and forces that shape their lives. In a strange twist of politics, many progressives and Left intellectuals now view culture as ornamental, a burden on class-based politics, or identical with a much maligned identity politics (for example, see Gitlin, 1995; and Rorty, 1998).

Gramsci's work both challenges this position and provides a theoretical framework for understanding how class is always lived through the modalities of race and gender.[1] Moreover, it provides an important political corrective to those social theories that fail to acknowledge how pedagogical politics work in shaping and articulating the divide between diverse institutional and cultural formations. For Gramsci, social theory at its best expands the meaning of the political by being self-conscious about the way pedagogy works through its own cultural practices in order to legitimate its own motivating questions, secure particular modes of authority, and privilege particular "institutional frameworks and disciplinary rules by which its research imperatives are formed" (Frow & Morris, in Grossberg, 1977, p. 268). Gramsci's work presents a much-needed challenge to this position. For Gramsci, culture needed to be addressed as part of a new political configuration and set of historical conditions that had emerged in the beginning of the twentieth century in the advanced industrial societies of the West. Critical intellectuals could not address the material machineries of power, the institutional arrangements of capitalism, and the changing politics of class formation without being attentive to how common sense and consent were being constructed within new public spheres marked by an expanding application of the dynamics and politics of specific, yet shifting, pedagogical practices. Such an understanding required not only a new attentiveness to "culture in its political role and consequences" (Cochran, 1994, p. 157), but foregrounded the issue of how alternative cultural spheres might be transformed into sites of struggle and resistance animated by a new group of subaltern intellectuals.

While the context for taking up Gramsci's work is radically different from the historical context in which his politics and theories developed, Gramsci's views on the relationship between culture, pedagogy, and power provide an important theoretical resource for addressing the challenge currently facing public and higher education in the United States. I want to analyze the importance of Gramsci's work, especially his work on education, by first outlining the nature of the current right-wing attempt to subordinate public and higher education to the needs of capital—substituting the purpose and meaning of education from a public to a private good—and the central role that cultural politics plays in spearheading such an assault. In addition, I want to analyze the attempt on the part of right-wing theorists such as E. D. Hirsch to appropriate Gramsci's views on education for a conservative educational project. Finally, I will conclude by analyzing the implications Gramsci's work might have for defending education as a public good and cultural pedagogy as central to any discourse of radical politics.

Democracy and Education under Siege

As the United States moves into the new millennium, questions of culture have become central to understanding how politics and power reorganize practices that have a profound effect on the social and economic forces that regulate everyday life. The politics of culture can be seen not only in the ways that symbolic resources and knowledge have replaced traditional skills as the main productive force, but also in the role that culture now plays as the main pedagogical force to secure the authority and interests of dominant groups. Media technologies have redefined the power of particular groups to construct a representational politics that plays a crucial role shaping self and group identities, as well as determining and marking off different conceptions of community and belonging. The notion that culture has become "a crucial site and weapon of power" (Grossberg, 1996, p. 142) has not been lost on conservatives and the growing forces of the new right.

Beginning with Reagan and Bush in the 1980s and culminating with the Gingrich-Republican revolution in the 1990s, conservatives have taken control over an evergrowing electronic media industry and new global communication systems—acknowledging that politics has taken on an important pedagogical function in the information age (see Schiller, 1989; and Barnouw, 1997). Recognizing the political value of defining culture as both a site of struggle and a sphere of education becomes central to social and political change, and conservatives have easily outmaneuvered progressives in the ongoing battle over control of the conditions for the production of knowledge, values, identities, desires, and those social practices central to winning the consent of diverse segments of the American public. Utilizing the power of the established press, electronic media, and talk radio as a site of cultural politics, conservatives have used their massive financial resources and foundations to gain control of various segments of the culture industry (Giroux, 1995). Conservative foundations and groups have also played a pivotal role in educating a new generation of public intellectuals in order to wage a relentless battle against all facets of democratic life; bearing the brunt of this vicious attack are groups disadvantaged by virtue of their race, age, gender, class, and lack of citizenship. With profound irony, conservative forces have appropriated Antonio Gramsci's insight that "every relationship of 'hegemony' is necessarily an educational relationship" (Gramsci, 1971, p. 350). In doing so, they have reasserted the role of culture as educational force for social and economic reproduction and have waged an intense ideological battle both within various cultural sites such as the media and over important cultural sites such as public schools, the arts, and higher education.

The effects of the current assault on democracy by the right can be seen in the dismantling of state supports for immigrants, people of color, and working people. More specifically, it is evident in the passage of retrograde social policies that promote deindustrialization, downsizing, and free market reforms, which in the case of recent welfare reform legislation will prohibit over 3.5 million children from receiving any type of government assistance, adding more children to the ranks of over 14.7 million children already living in poverty in the United States.[2] As conservative policies move away from a politics of social investment to one of social containment, state services are hollowed out and reduced to their more repressive functions—discipline, control, and surveillance.[3] This is evident not only in states such as California and Florida, which spend more to incarcerate people than to educate their college-age populations, but also in the disproportionate number of African-American males throughout the country who are being incarcerated or placed under the control of the criminal justice system (on this issue, see Tonry, 1995; Miller, 1996; and Butterfield, 1997). The aftermath of this battle against democracy and social and economic justice can also be seen in a resurgent racism, marked by antiimmigrant legislation such as Proposition 209 in California, the dismantling of affirmative action, and the re-emergence of racist ideologies attempting to prove that differences in intelligence are both racially distinctive and genetically determined.[4] In this instance, racially coded attacks on criminals, the underclass, and welfare mothers are legitimated, in part, through a politically invigorated rhetoric of Social Darwinism that both scapegoats people of color while simultaneously blaming them for the social problems that result in their exploitation, suffering, and oppression (see, for example, Hadjor, 1995; Hacker, 1995; and Marable, 1995).

As part of this broader assault on democracy, public education has become one of the most contested public spheres in political life at the turn of the century. More than any other institution, public schools serve as a dangerous reminder of both the promise and shortcomings of the social, political, and economic forces that shape society. Embodying the contradictions of the larger society, public schools provide a critical referent for measuring the degree to which American society fulfills its obligation to provide all students with the knowledge and skills necessary for critical citizenship and the possibilities of democratic public life. As sites that reflect the nation's alleged commitment to the legacy of democracy, schools offer both a challenge and threat to attempts by conservatives and liberals alike to remove the language of choice from the discourse of democracy and to diminish citizenship to a largely privatized affair in which civic responsibilities are reduced to the act of consuming. A euphemism for privatization, "choice" relieves schools of the pretense of serving the public good. No longer institutions designed to benefit all members of the community, they are refashioned in market terms designed to serve the narrow interests of individual consumers and national economic policies.

Dismissing the role that schools might play as democratic public spheres, conservatives have redefined the meaning and purpose of schooling in accordance with the interest of global capitalism. As financial support for public schools dries up, conservatives increasingly attempt to harness all educational institutions to corporate control through calls for privatization, vouchers, and so-called choice programs. Rewriting the tradition of schooling as a public good, conservatives abstract questions of equity from excellence and subsume the political mission of schooling within the ideology and logic of the market. Similarly, conservatives have waged a relentless attack on teacher unions, called for the return of authoritarian teaching approaches, and endorsed learning by drill and rote memorization. In this scenario, public education is replaced by the call for privately funded educational institutions that can safely ignore civil rights, exclude students who are class and racially disenfranchised, and conveniently blur the lines between religion and the state.

Given the prevailing attack on education, we are witnessing both the elimination of public school as a potential site for expanding the public good and the realignment of the mission of higher education within the discourse and ideology of the corporate world.[5] Within this perspective, higher education is aggressively shorn of its utopian impulses. Undermined as a repository of critical thinking, writing, teaching, and learning, universities are refashioned to meet the interests of commerce and regulation. Within the current onslaught against non-commodified public spheres, the mission of the university becomes instrumental; it is redesigned largely to serve corporate interests whose aim is to restructure higher education along the lines of global capitalism. In specific terms, this means privileging instrumental over substantive knowledge, shifting power away from faculty to administrations, and corporatizing the culture of the university. As the college curriculum is stripped of those subjects (typically in the humanities) that do not translate immediately into market considerations, programs are downsized and reduced to service programs for business. In this case, not only does instrumental knowledge replace substantive knowledge as the basis for research, writing, and teaching, but the university intellectual is reduced to low level technocrat whose role is to manage and legitimate the downsizing, knowledge production, and labor practices that characterize the institutional power and culture of the corporatized and vocationalized university.

The defining principle of the current right-wing attack against higher education and public schooling is the dismantling of all public spheres that refuse to be defined strictly by the instrumental logic of the market. As such, the battle waged over education must be understood as part of a much broader struggle for democratic public life, the political function of culture, the role of intellectuals, and the importance of pedagogy as a hegemonic technology in various aspects of daily life. At stake here is the issue of how we "think" politics in Gramscian terms, that is, how do we create a new culture through a reformulation of the meaning of cultural politics, intellectual engagement, and pedagogical change.[6] In short, how do we reassert the primacy of a nondogmatic, progressive politics by analyzing how culture as a force for resistance is related to power, education, and agency? This project suggests the need to understand how culture shapes the everyday lives of people: how culture constitutes a defining principle for understanding how struggles over meaning, identity, social practices, and institutional machineries of power can be waged while inserting the pedagogical back into the political, and expanding the pedagogical by recognizing the "educational force of our whole social and cultural experience [as one] that actively and profoundly teaches" (Williams, 1967, p. 15).

Gramsci's legacy is important for progressives because he provides a wide-ranging and insightful analysis of how education functions as part of a wider political set of discourses and social relations aimed at promoting ideological and structural change. But in spite of Gramsci's politics and intentions, his work has also been used by conservatives to legitimate a profoundly reactionary view of education and the processes of learning and persuasion. In opposition to such an appropriation, I want to analyze in detail how Gramsci's work has been used by Harold Entwistle, in *Antonio Gramsci: Conservative Schooling for Radical*

Politics (1979), and, more recently, by E. D. Hirsch, in *The Schools We Need* (1996), to push a deeply conservative educational agenda. While recognizing that Gramsci's writings on education represent a problematic legacy for progressives, I want to argue in opposition to Entwistle and Hirsch that Gramsci's work, when read within the appropriate historical context and in relation to Gramsci's revolutionary project, provides an invaluable theoretical service for helping radical educators rethink the political nature of educational work and the role it might play in the struggle for expanding and developing the relationship between learning and democratic social change, and committed intellectual practice and political struggle.[7]

Appropriating Gramsci

Although the works of Harold Entwistle and E. D. Hirsch are separated by a decade, the writers share similar views about the value of a conservative approach to schooling. Not only do both authors legitimate schools as agents of social and economic reproduction, they advocate classroom practices based on learning a common culture, rigid disciplinary rules, an authoritarian pedagogy, and a standardized curriculum. At the same time, it is important to note that Entwistle provides a far more serious engagement with Gramsci's work and makes some valuable contributions, both in his critiques of some progressive forms of political education and in his suggestions for rethinking the politics of adult education. While Hirsch's work on Gramsci was inspired by Entwistle, he attempts to reappropriate Entwistle in the service of a right-wing conservatism that blames educational progressives in the United States for the decline of teaching and learning in the public schools. Hirsch's "discovery" that Gramsci is in actuality a poster boy for conservative thought combines the bad faith of misrepresentation with the reductionism of an ideological fervor that seems to make a mockery of political sense and historical accuracy.[8] While the nature of the political appropriation of Gramsci's work by a diverse body of radical educators may be open to interpretation, it certainly stretches the bounds of plausibility when Hirsch aligns Gramsci with contemporary, right-wing educational theorists such as Dianne Ravitch and Charles Sykes. Not only does such an appropriation represent a form of theoretical disingenuousness and political opportunism, but it is also an affront to everything that Gramsci stood for as a Marxist revolutionary.

Entwistle and Hirsch share a view of schooling that stands in sharp contrast to the radical educational theories of their time; yet, they appropriate from Gramsci's work a rationale for conservative pedagogical practices as part of their attempt to redefine the relationship between schooling and society, and intellectuals and their social responsibilities. Although Entwistle's book, *Antonio Gramsci: Conservative Schooling for Radical Politics*, provides a more extensive reading of Gramsci, E. D. Hirsch applies the implications of such a conservative interpretation directly to matters affecting teaching and learning in the United States. Moreover, Hirsch draws upon Gramsci's work, in addition to that of his conservative contemporaries, in a spurious effort to produce what he calls a "pragmatic" and bipartisan, rather than "ideological" and conservative agenda for educational reform. In what follows, I will critically engage how Entwistle and Hirsch appropriate Gramsci, and analyze the implications of their work for a theory of schooling and pedagogy.

Harold Entwistle's book represents one of the first comprehensive analyses of the relevance of Gramsci's writings for educational theory and practice. Providing his own detailed interpretation of Gramsci's writings on schooling, Entwistle rejects as misguided the way Gramsci's work has been previously interpreted, and excoriates "new sociologists of education" as well as other radical educational theorists who rose to prominence in the 1970s and 1980s in England. After resurrecting the "real" Gramsci, Entwistle proceeds to dismiss those "radical" critics who have allegedly misinterpreted Gramsci's work. The remainder of Entwistle's book focuses on the relevance of Gramsci's writings for adult education, ending with the "remarkable" conclusion that the lesson to be learned from Gramsci's work is that schools do not provide the setting for "a radical, counterhegemonic education" (1989, p. 177).

Entwistle's reading of Gramsci's work portrays him as a "stern" taskmaster whose views on discipline, knowledge, and hegemony render him more compatible with Karl Popper and Jacques Barzun (both of whom are referred to positively), than the likes of Karl Marx, Paulo Freire, or, for that matter, even John Dewey. If we are to take Entwistle's version of Gramsci seriously as a model for socialist education, then we will have to accept the claim that Gramsci supported unproblematically a deference to authority, the rote memorizing of facts, and a subservience to imposed standards as core pedagogical principles for a theory and practice of schooling. Needless to say, such a claim is hardly consistent with Gramsci's call for an educational practice and project aimed at generating "more and more organic intellectuals from the children of the peasantry and the proletariat" (Holly, 1980, p. 319).

The conservative literary theorist, E. D. Hirsch, echoes a similar argument. Hirsch describes Gramsci's work as a critical response to Giovanni Gentile's educational reforms (enacted under Il Duce in the 1920s)—reforms which emphasized "'emotion,' 'feeling,' and the 'most immediate needs of the child'" (Hirsch, 1996, p. 7). The failure of these reforms, according to Hirsch, served as proof of the inadequacy of what he incorrectly terms the central tenets of critical educational theory. In opposition to the alleged failure of this form of "progressive" pedagogy, Hirsch argues that Gramsci offers a rationale for conservative methods, such as "phonics and memorization of the multiplication table," claiming that they are necessary for "the oppressed classes to learn how to read, write, and communicate—and to gain enough traditional knowledge to understand the worlds of nature and culture surrounding them."

What Hirsch and Entwistle fail to acknowledge in their selective readings of Gramsci is that his concern with "facts" and intellectual rigor makes sense only as a rightly argued critique of inane methodologies that separate facts from values, learning from understanding, and emotion from the intellect. As David Forgacs points out, in the introduction to *An Antonio Gramsci Reader*, Gramsci

> begins not from the point of view of the teacher but from that of the learner, and he emphasizes that the learning process is a movement toward self-knowledge, self-mastery and thus liberation. Education is not a matter of handing out "encyclopedic knowledge" but of developing and disciplining the awareness which the learner already possesses. (1988, p. 54)

Gramsci's emphasis on intellectual rigor and discipline can only be understood as part of a broader concern that students develop a critical understanding of how the past informs the present in order that they liberate themselves from the ideologies and common sense assumptions of the dominant order. Gramsci was quite clear on the distinction between learning facts that enlarged one's perception of the larger social order and simply gathering information. Even in his earlier writings, Gramsci understood the relationship between pedagogy of rote memorization and the conservative nature of the culture it served to legitimate. For instance, Gramsci wrote in 1916:

> We must break the habit of thinking that culture is encyclopedic knowledge whereby man [sic] is viewed as a mere container in which to pour and conserve empirical data or brute disconnected facts which he will have to subsequently pigeonhole in his brain as in the columns of a dictionary so as to be able to eventually respond to the varied stimuli of the external world. This form of culture is truly harmful, especially to the proletariat. It only serves to create misfits, people who believe themselves superior to the rest of humanity because they

have accumulated in their memory a certain quantity of facts and dates which
they cough up at every opportunity to almost raise a barrier between themselves
and others. (1975, pp. 20-21)

Hirsch ignores Gramsci's critique of encyclopedic knowledge and, in
doing so, argues that

> Romantic anti-intellectualism and developmentalism [critical thinking and criti-
> cal social theory], as Gramsci understood, are luxuries of the merchant class that
> the poor cannot afford [. . .]. Today, the Enlightenment view of the value of
> knowledge is the only view we can afford. When the eighteenth-century Ency-
> clopedists attempted to systematize human knowledge in a set of books, they
> were placing their hope for progress in the ever-growing experience of human
> kind. (1997, p. 113)

For Hirsch, the production of knowledge by the middle class is only
paved with good intentions. It seems unimaginable for Hirsch to engage
critically the relationship between knowledge and power, or ideology and
politics. To address how culture and power combined to produce
knowledge that often legitimates not the general interests but particular
racial, class, and gendered interests would work against his general
educational program: to teach children a core knowledge base of "facts."
For Hirsch, the most distinguishing mark of encyclopedic knowledge is
its use for inculcating mental discipline; moreover, the primary purpose
of education is not only to transmit such knowledge but to prevent it
from being undermined by forms of "anti-intellectualism" in the
American educational community—whose legacy, Hirsch argues,
extends from "'home economics' and 'shop' in the 1920s to all forms of
'critical thinking and problem solving skills' in the 1990s" (1997, p.
113).

For Gramsci, the production of knowledge and its reception and
transformation was historical, dialectical, and critical. Gramsci rejected
mere factuality and demanded that schooling be "formative, while being
'instructive.'" The pedagogical task entailed, in part, "mitigating and
rendering more fertile the dogmatic approach which must inevitably
characterize these first few years" (Gramsci, 1971, p. 30). Such a task
was not easy and demanded, the production of "limits on libertarian
ideologies," while, the recognition that "the elements of struggle against
the mechanical and Jesuitical school have become unhealthily exaggerated" (pp. 32-33). Underlying Gramsci's pedagogy is an educational
principle in which a comfortable humanism is replaced by a hardheaded
radicalism—not a radicalism that falsely separates necessity and
spontaneity, discipline and the acquisition of basic skills from imagina-

tion, but, instead, one that integrates them.

In contrast, Entwistle and Hirsch interpret Gramsci's view of schooling as one that surrenders pedagogy to dull routine, and, in doing so, implies that such a pedagogy can, and should, be maintained at the expense of the spirit. The interconnections between discipline and critical thinking in Gramsci's view of schooling only lend support to a conservative notion of pedagogy if the concept of physical discipline and self-control is abstracted from his emphasis on the importance of developing a counterhegemonic project, one "which demands the formation of a militant, self-conscious proletariat that will fight unyieldingly for its right to govern itself [. . .]" (Karabel, 1976, p. 172). In other words, Gramsci's claim that "it will always be an effort to learn physical self-discipline and self-control, the pupil, has, in effect, to undergo psycho-physical training" (Gramsci, 1971, p. 42) gets seriously distorted unless understood within the context of Gramsci's other remarks on learning and intellectual development. Gramsci stressed this view not only in his early writing in 1916, but just as forcefully, in the *Notebooks*. In the latter, he writes: "Many people have to be persuaded that studying too is a job, and a very tiring one with its own particular apprenticeship involving muscles and nerves as well as *intellect*" (1971, p. 42; my emphasis).

For Gramsci, there was a dynamic tension between self-discipline and critical understanding. Consequently, what in fact often appears like a paradox in Gramsci's work on education is in reality a nuanced and dialectical endorsement of a critical and disciplined educational practice informed by a notion of radical pedagogical authority. Distinguishing between classroom authority that works in the service of critical agency and authority that is used to promote conformity and allegiance to the state, Gramsci provides a political referent for criticizing schools that he claims are merely a bourgeois affair. According to Gramsci, any pedagogical practice has to be examined and implemented within a broader understanding of what the purpose of schooling might become and how such a view of political education articulates a wider democratic project. Schools, in this instance, are seen as central and formative sites for the production of political identities, the struggle over culture, and for educating organic intellectuals. In "Questions of Culture," Gramsci argues that acquiring political power must be matched with the "problem of winning intellectual power" (1988, p. 62). If the school is to offer students of the working-class and other subaltern groups the knowledge and skills necessary for political leadership, they cannot be simply, as Hirsch in particular would have it, boot camps for the intellectually malleable. Gramsci is quite clear on this issue:

> A school which does not mortgage the child's future, a school that does not
> force the child's will, his intelligence and growing awareness to run along the
> tracks to a predetermined station. A school of freedom and free initiative, not a
> school of slavery and mechanical precision. The children of proletarians too
> should have all possibilities open to them; they should be able to develop their
> own individuality in the optimal way, and hence in the most productive way for
> both themselves and society. (p. 64)

For Gramsci, any analysis of education can only be understood in
relation to existing social and cultural formations and the power relations
these imply. Gramsci emphasized that schooling constitutes only one
form of political education within a broader network of experience,
history, and collective struggle. Given Gramsci's view of political
education, it is difficult to reduce his view of teaching and learning to a
form of positivist reductionism in which a particular methodology, such
as rote learning, is endorsed without questioning, whether such
pedagogical practices are either implicated in or offer resistance to the
mechanisms of consent, common sense, and dominant social relations.

Hirsch not only enlists Gramsci to justify authoritarian classroom
relations in which students are deprived of the basic right to address
disturbing, urgent questions, but also to foster a sense that the point of
view of the learner is irrelevant. For both Hirsch and Entwistle, schools
are dysfunctional not because they oppress students from subaltern
groups but because the legacy of progressive education emphasizes
"'project oriented,' 'hands-on,' 'critical-thinking' and so-called
'democratic education'" rather than a core curriculum of facts and
information (Hirsch, 1997, p. 7). Hirsch, in particular, endorses a
reductive view of information accumulation in which the critical
relationship between culture and power remains largely unexamined,
except as a pretext to urge working-class and subaltern groups to master
the dominant culture as a way of reproducing the social order. Hirsch
makes this point quite clearly:

> The oppressed class should be taught to master the tools of power and author-
> ity—the ability to read, write, and communicate—and to gain enough traditional
> knowledge to understand the worlds of nature and culture surrounding them.
> Children, particularly the children of the poor, should not be encouraged to
> flourish "naturally," which would keep them ignorant and make them slaves of
> emotion. They should learn the value of hard work, gain the knowledge that
> leads to understanding, and master the traditional culture in order to command
> its rhetoric, as Gramsci himself had learned to do. (1997, p. 7)

The implication here is that any recourse to teaching working-class children about the specificities of their histories, experiences, and cultural memories would simply result in a form of pedagogical infantilism. More importantly, Hirsch misses a central concern that runs throughout Gramsci's work: skills are not universal, and must be addressed within the context that educators, not to mention students, both intervene and attempt to change. Similarly, Hirsch assumes that the poor performance of working-class students results from intellectual sloth and has nothing to do with underfunded schools, a diminished tax base, and urban politics. On the contrary, for Hirsch, overcrowded classrooms, inadequate classroom resources, and broken-down school buildings play no role in whether working-class kids and other subaltern groups do well in schools. The real enemy of student learning, according to Hirsch, is the critical legacy of progressivism (and its failure to endorse rote learning, a core curriculum, and uniform teaching) rather than the force of racial and class bias, poor working conditions for teachers, or poverty.[9]

Of course, while Gramsci was deeply concerned with students learning "facts" and specific forms of knowledge, he did not advocate that the context of such learning was irrelevant. For Gramsci, learning had to be rigorous but meaningful, subject based but related to practical activities. Appropriating Marx's "Theses on Feuerbach" (the educator must be educated), Gramsci believed that "the relationship between teacher and pupil is active and reciprocal so that every teacher is always a pupil and every pupil a teacher" (1971, p. 350). By arguing that the teacher-student relationship leaves no room for elitism or sterile pedantry, Gramsci introduces an important principle into the structuring of classroom social relations. The concept of the teacher as a learner suggests that teachers must help students to appropriate their own histories, and also examine their own roles as public intellectuals, located within specific cultural formations and relations of power. In this instance, Gramsci not only argues implicitly against forms of authoritarian teaching, but he sharply criticizes the assumption that knowledge should be treated unproblematically—beyond the dynamics of interrogation, criticism, and political engagement. Gramsci had no interest in allowing schools to produce a culture that served repressive authority and state power, nor did he have any interest in supporting teachers and intellectuals who were reduced to what he called "experts in legitimation" (in Said, 1983, p. 172).

By ignoring how the imposition of meanings and values distributed in schools are dialectically related to the mechanisms of economic and political control in the dominant society, both Entwistle and Hirsch depoliticize the relationship between power and culture; Hirsch is especially vehement in normalizing the hegemonic role that schools play in defining what is legitimate knowledge and social practice. For Hirsch, this position translates into a call for a common national curriculum that emphasizes the acquisition of core knowledge and standardized testing.[10] Hirsch has no conception that such a position is at odds with the counter-hegemonic project posed by Gramsci—cultural pedagogy as a means to create organic intellectuals whose task is to identify the social interests behind power, challenge traditional understandings of culture, power, and politics; and share such knowledge as the basis for organizing diverse forms of class struggle in order to create a socialist society. Class struggle or the goals of socialism could not be more removed from Hirsch's politics.

Rather than acknowledge the need to revalue the "disrespected identities and the cultural products of maligned groups" (Fraser, 1995, p. 71), Hirsch wants to "save" underprivileged kids by stripping them of their identities and histories while assimilating them into the dominant culture. Curriculum in these terms provides the legitimation for forms of middle-class cultural capital that serves as an institutionally sanctioned bunker against learning and living with differences (Hall, in Lubiano, 1997, p. 297). Hirsch argues that, while teaching multiculturalism may have some value, it is ultimately disruptive to subaltern students because of its approach through "amateur psychological efforts [that] fail because [they result] in lies to children about their achievements [. . .] and lead to further erosion of their self esteem" (1997, pp. 103-04). It appears not to occur to Hirsch that schools may actually systematize failing students through racially motivated models of teaching, tracking, and evaluation. Should we assume that curricular knowledge that represents middle-class cultural capital as the referent against which the narratives of history, identity, and social experience should be judged is unproblematically uplifting for working-class kids? Or that warehousing and tracking, often built into school curricula to the disadvantage of racial, class, and gender minorities, works to their advantage? This position is not merely naive, it is a construct of reactionary politics parading as common sense, and is completely at odds with Gramsci's view of the role that education should play in liberating subaltern groups.

In opposition to Gramsci, neither Entwistle nor Hirsch provides a critical language to deconstruct the basis of privileges that are accorded the dominant culture. There is no attempt to interrogate culture as the shared and lived principles of life, characteristic of different groups and classes, as these emerge within unequal relations of power and struggle.

Nor do Entwistle and Hirsch critically engage how questions of power, history, race, gender, and class privilege work to codify specific ideological educational practices as merely the accumulation of disinterested knowledge "that can be exchanged on the world market for upward mobility" (Mohanty, 1989-90, p. 184). In effect, they de-emphasize unequally valued cultural styles and the ways in which dominant pedagogical practices work to disparage the multiple languages, histories, and experiences at work in a multicultural society.

Hirsch, in particular, ends up legitimating a homogenizing cultural discourse that institutionalizes various policing techniques to safeguard the interests and power of dominant groups. In the end, both Entwistle and Hirsch support a view of culture and knowledge as monolithic: the product of a single, durable history and vision, at odds with the notion and politics of difference. The cultural politics at work in this view of education maintains an ominous ideological silence regarding the validity and importance of the experiences of women, Blacks, and other groups excluded from the narrative of mainstream history and culture. Thus there emerges no critical understanding of Gramsci's focus on culture as a field of struggle, or of competing interests in which dominant and subordinate groups live out and make sense of their given circumstances and conditions of life within incommensurate hierarchies of power and possibility.

Entwistle and Hirsch do more than offer an unenlightened and reductive reading of culture; they appropriate the Gramscian position that schools are agencies of social and cultural reproduction and in doing so defend this position rather than criticize it. Rather than understood as a storehouse of immutable facts, behaviors, and practices, culture is inextricably related to the outcomes of struggle over the complex and often contradictory processes of learning, persuasion, agency, and leadership. Culture is about the production and legitimation of particular ways of life transmitted in schools through overt and hidden curricula so as to legitimate the cultural capital of dominant groups, while marginalizing the voices of the subaltern. If power is related to culture in the discourses of Entwistle and Hirsch, the outcome is a notion of culture cleansed of its own complicity in furthering social relations, and pedagogical practices that reproduce the worst dimensions of schooling. For example, missing from their analysis is any understanding of increasing corporatism and its effects on schools: poverty, racism, and gender bias and the ways in which these forces structure the school curricula, the distribution of financial resources between schools, or the organization of the teaching labor force. While Hirsch's reading of

Gramsci is much more reductive than Entwistle's extensive analysis, both theorists share a conservative ideological project in their reading of the role of intellectuals and the purpose of schooling. Entwistle and Hirsch represent different versions of the same ideology—an ideology that is deeply committed to expunging democracy of its critical and emancipatory possibilities. In what follows, I want to conclude by pointing to aspects of Gramsci's work that might be useful for developing some important theoretical principles for a critical theory of schooling and pedagogy.

Thinking Like Gramsci: Reclaiming the Struggle over Schooling

Given the current assault on schooling, and public life more generally, it is imperative that progressive educators develop a language of critique and possibility along with new strategies for understanding and intervention in order to reclaim and reinvigorate the struggle to sustain public schooling as a central feature of democratic life. Gramsci's work is enormously helpful in this regard because it forcefully reminds us that any attempt to articulate the nature and purpose of schooling must be addressed as part of a broader comprehensive politics of social change. Schooling, in Gramsci's terms, was always part of some larger ensemble "of relationships headed and moved by authority and power" (Said, 1983, p. 169). Hence, the struggle over schooling must be inextricably linked to the struggle against abusive state power, and the battle for "creating more equitable and just public spheres within and outside of educational institutions" (Mohanty, 1989-90, p. 192). Gramsci also makes clear that pedagogy is the outcome of struggles over both the relations of meaning and institutional relations of power, and that such struggles cannot be abstracted from the construction of national identity and what it means to be an active citizen. In this context, the pedagogical is inextricably grounded in a notion of hegemony, struggle, and political education articulated through a normative position and project aimed at overcoming the stark inequalities and forms of oppression suffered by subaltern groups. The theoretical and ideological contours of Gramsci's project offer no immediate solutions to the context and content of the problems faced by American educators. Nor can Gramsci's work simply be appropriated outside of his own history and the challenges it posed. What his vast writings do provide are opportunities for raising questions about what it means to learn from Gramsci at a time that demands theoretical rigor, moral courage, and political boldness.

Gramsci's analysis of the political and social role of culture in establishing and reproducing the power of the modern state represents a crucial theoretical sphere for progressive educators. Central to Gramsci's analysis is not only the important recognition of culture as a terrain of consent and struggle, but also the political imperative to analyze how diverse groups make meaning of their lives within a variety of cultural sites and social practices in relation to, and not outside of, the material contexts of everyday life. For Gramsci, the politics of culture was inseparable from a politics that provided the pedagogical conditions for educators to think critically about how knowledge is produced, taken up, and transformed as a force for social change and collective struggle. The practical relevance of Gramsci's work on culture and pedagogy can be made more clear by commenting further on two issues: the role of basic education and the relevance of Gramsci's call for pedagogical practices that instill young children with an appreciation for self-discipline and an array of intellectual skills. While it is crucial to recognize Gramsci's call for treating various levels of schooling as sites of struggle, it is equally imperative to recognize that education for Gramsci was fundamental to preparing young people and adults with the knowledge and skills that would enable them to govern and not simply be governed, and, equally important, to use civil society as a public enclave from which to organize their moral and political energies as acts of resistance and struggle. While Gramsci did not believe that state sponsored schools alone would provide the conditions for radical change, he did suggest that they had a role to play in nourishing the tension between the democratic principles of civil society and the dominating principles of capitalism and corporate power. The project of liberal education for Gramsci was wedded to the fundamental socialist principle of educating the complete person, rather than the traditional concern with educating specialists, technocrats, and other professional experts. Gramsci was insistent that critical intellectuals had to use their education in order to both know more than their enemies and to make such knowledge consequential by bringing it to bear in all those sites of everyday life where the struggle for and against the powerful was being waged. While Gramsci's work is neither transparent nor merely transportable to different historical and political contexts, it seems reasonable, within the current historical conjuncture, to argue that education for Gramsci was deeply implicated in the project of furthering economic and political democracy, and that such a project is especially important today for articulating a progressive, if not radical, defense of the purpose of public and higher education. In the broadest

sense, this would offer progressives a theoretical rationale for challenging the existing movement on the part of corporate culture, in its various
manifestations, to define public and higher education as a private, rather
than public, good. The purpose of such an education would also serve to
challenge the dominant society's increasing pressure to use the liberal
arts to assert the primacy of citizen rights over consumer rights,
democratic values over commercial values.

Gramsci's emphasis on the importance of culture and pedagogy in
shaping a social subject, rather than an adaptive, depoliticized consuming
subject, provided the context for his insistence on the importance of
skills, rigor, discipline, and hard work. For instance, his often-cited call
for teaching young children skills cannot be read, as I previously argued,
as simply legitimating a conservative pedagogy. Gramsci recognized that
children within the "new" Italian reforms, which argued that children
should simply discover truths for themselves, were being deprived of
basic skills that would enable them to read, write, and struggle over
complex problems, and, therefore, expand their capacities as critical
intellectuals and citizens. For Gramsci, pedagogical approaches that
refused to deal with such issues often reneged on using their authority
self-consciously in the interests of providing the skills and discipline
necessary for young children to assume the role of critical or organic
intellectuals. Gramsci rightly understood that those pedagogies that
focused on the alleged natural development of the child, and devalued
firm classroom authority as antithetical to good teaching, simply offered
a rationale for Mussolini's educational clerks to conceal their own
authority, while simultaneously employing it to limit the intellectual and
political capacities, especially of working-class students, to learn those
skills necessary for resistance, opposition, and, more importantly, civic
struggle. What Hirsch misses in Gramsci's analysis is that rather than
being a call for a depoliticized justification of rote learning, it is an
attempt to both analyze the context for teaching young children the skills
they will need to be active citizens and call into question any pedagogy
that refuses to name the political interests that shapes its own project.

For Gramsci, the learning of skills, discipline, and rigor were not in
and of themselves valuable, they were meaningful when seen as part of a
broader project and performative politics, one that embraced authority in
the service of social change and culture, as the terrain in which such
authority became both the object of autocritique and the basis for social
analysis and struggle. Hence, Gramsci's emphasis on culture as a
medium of politics and power is important for progressive educators
because it challenges theories of social and cultural reproduction that

overemphasize power as a force of domination. Gramsci is extremely sensitive to the productive nature of power as a complex and often contradictory site of domination, struggle, and resistance. Long before Foucault, Gramsci interrogates how culture is deployed, represented, addressed, and taken up in order to understand how power works to produce not merely forms of domination but also complicity and dissent. Gramsci's dialectical analysis of culture and power provides an important theoretical model for linking cultural politics and the discourse of critique to a language of hope, struggle, and possibility. Of course, Gramsci does not provide, nor should we expect him to offer, a blueprint for such a struggle, but his view of leadership and his theory of intellectuals offer a powerful challenge to those conservative ideologues and theoreticians (who currently reduce the function of intellectuals either to their technical expertise, or privilege them unproblematically as the cultural guardians and servants of oppressive state power).

Gramsci's theory of hegemony as a form of cultural pedagogy is also invaluable as an element of critical educational thought. By emphasizing the pedagogical force of culture, Gramsci expands the sphere of the political by pointing to those diverse spaces and spheres in which cultural practices are deployed, lived, and mobilized in the service of knowledge, power, and authority. For Gramsci, learning and politics were inextricably related and took place not merely in schools but in a vast array of public sites. While Gramsci could not anticipate the full extent of the ways in which knowledge and power would be configured within the postmodern technologies that emerged in the age of the high-speed computer and other electronic media, he did recognize the political and pedagogical significance of popular culture and the need to take it seriously in reconstructing and mapping the relations between everyday life and the formations of power. Clearly, Gramsci's recognition that the study of everyday life and popular culture needed to be incorporated strategically and performatively as part of a struggle for power and leadership is as relevant today as it was in his own time. This is especially true for challenging and transforming the modernist curriculum steeped in its celebration of the traditional Western canon, and its refusal to address subordinated forms of knowledge. If critical educators are to make a case for the context specific nature of peda-gogy—a pedagogy that not only negotiates difference, but takes seriously the imperative to make knowledge meaningful in order that it might become critical and transformative—it is crucial that educators expand curricula to include those elements of popular culture that play a powerful role in shaping the desires, needs, and identities of students.

This is not to suggest that students ignore the Western-oriented curriculum, or dispense with print culture as much as redefine the relationship between knowledge and power, and how the latter is used to mobilize desire, shape identities, and secure particular forms of authority. It is not enough for students to simply be literate in the print culture of the humanities, or in the subordinated histories of oppressed groups. Critical education demands that teachers and students must also learn to read critically the new technological and visual cultures that exercise a powerful pedagogical influence over their lives as well as their conception of what it means to be a social subject engaged in acts of responsible citizenship. In addition, they must master the tools of these technologies, whether they be computer programming, video production, or magazine production, in order to create alternative public spheres actively engaged in shaping what Gramsci referred to as a new and oppositional culture.

The questions that Gramsci raises about education, culture, and political struggle also have important ramifications for theorizing about educators as public intellectuals and how such intellectuals might challenge the institutional and cultural terrains through which dominant authority is secured and state power legitimated. Marcia Landy is on target in arguing that one of Gramsci's most important contributions to political change is the recognition that "study of intellectuals and their production is synonymous with the study of political power" (Landy, 1994, p. 26). Gramsci's concern with the formation and responsibility of intellectuals stems from the recognition that they are not only central to fostering critical consciousness, demystifying dominant social relations, and disrupting common sense, but also for situating political education in the context of a more comprehensive project aimed at the liberation of the oppressed as historical agents within the framework of a revolutionary culture.

According to Gramsci, political education demanded that such intellectuals could not be neutral, nor could they ignore the most pressing social and political problems of their times. For Gramsci, the new intellectuals have little to do with the traditional humanist project of speaking for a universal culture or abstracting culture from the workings of power, history, and struggle in the name of an arid professionalism. As cultural critics, the Gramscian intellectuals refuse to define culture merely as a refined aesthetic of taste and civility. On the contrary, the task of Gramscian intellectuals was to provide modes of leadership that bridged the gap between criticism and politics, theory and action, and traditional educational institutions and everyday life. For Gramsci, the role of the engaged intellectual was a matter of moral compassion and practical politics aimed at addressing the gap between theory and practice. This suggests that such intellectuals become what Gramsci calls "permanent persuaders and not just orators," (Gramsci, in Cochran, 1994, p. 153), and that such persuasion takes place not merely in the isolated and safe confines of the universities but in those spheres and public cultures of daily life in which subordinated groups bear the weight of the mechanisms of coercion and domination. Clearly, Gramsci's discourse on the education and political function of "organic" intellectuals provides an important theoretical discourse for questioning the meaning and function of public and higher education at a time when the latter is not only selling its curricula, space, and buildings to corporations but undermining even the humanist understanding of the intellectual as a purveyor of art and culture, now seen as merely ornamental next to the role of the intellectual as servant of corporate interests.

Gramsci's work does more than challenge the reduction of intellectuals to corporate clerks; it also broadens the meaning and role of intellectuals in terms of their social functions and individual capabilities. Changes in the mass media, modes of production, and socioeconomic needs of the state, enlarged the role that intellectuals played in exercising authority, producing knowledge, and securing consent. For Gramsci, intellectuals played a crucial political and pedagogical role in integrating thought and action for subaltern groups as part of a broader project to assert the primacy of political education far beyond the limited circle of party hacks or university academics. Moreover, Gramsci is not just suggesting that marginal groups generate their own intellectuals; he is also broadening the conditions for the production of knowledge and the range of sites through which learning for self-determination can occur. This is an important issue because it legitimates the call for progressives to create their own intellectuals and counterpublic spheres both within and outside of traditional sites of learning, as part of a broader effort to expand the sources of resistance and the dynamics of democratic struggle.

Finally, Gramsci's radical theory of political education provides an ethical language for grounding intellectual work in a project that not only demands commitment and risk, but also recognizes the ethical imperative to bear witness to collective suffering and to provide a referent for translating such a recognition into social engagement. This suggests that intellectuals must be self-critical in order to address the nature of their own locations, self interests, and privileges. Moreover, they must be in constant dialogue with those with whom they deploy their authority as teachers, researchers, theorists, and planners in order to expose and transform those cruelties and oppressive conditions through which individuals and groups are constructed and differentiated. For Gramsci, critical intellectuals must begin by acknowledging their engagement with the "density, complexity, and historical-semantic value of culture," an engagement that grounds them in the power-making possibilities of politics (Said, 1983, p. 171). At the current historical conjuncture, Gramsci's work serves as a reminder that

> democracy requires a certain kind of citizen [. . .] citizens who feel responsible for something more than their own well-feathered little corner; citizens who want to participate in society's affairs, who insist on it; citizens with backbones; citizens who hold their ideas about democracy at the deepest level. (Berman, 1997, p. 37)

Education in this context becomes central to principled leadership, agency, and the ongoing task of keeping the idea of justice alive, while struggling collectively on many fronts to restructure society in the interest of expanding the possibilities of democracy. Gramsci's readings of culture, political education, the role and responsibility of intellectuals, and the necessity to struggle in the interests of equality and justice, are crucial starting points for progressives to rethink and address the current assault on public schooling and the basic foundations of democracy itself.

Notes

*This piece was originally published as "Rethinking Cultural Politics and Radical Pedagogy in the Work of Antonio Gramsci." *Educational Theory,* 49 (1), 1-19.
    1. For a critique of the tendency of theorists such as Todd Gitlin to pit class politics against identity and cultural politics, see Kelley (1998). See especially Chapter 4, "Looking Extremely Backward: Why the Enlightenment Will Only Lead Us into the Dark" (pp. 102-24).
    2. More specifically, "In 1995, 14.7 million children (21 percent of America's children) were living in poverty, 2.1 million more than in 1989" (Children's Defense Fund, 1997, p. 17).
    3. This issue is taken up brilliantly in Aronowitz (1996).
    4. In this case, I am referring specifically to the widely popularized work of Murray and Herrnstein (1994). For three important critical responses to Murray and Herrnstein, see Jacoby and Glauberman (1995),

Kincheloe, Steinberg, and Gresson III (1996), and Fisher, Hout, Jankowski, Lucas, Swidler, and Voss (1996).

5. For some excellent recent sources on the corporatization of the university, see Watkins (1989) and Aronowitz and DiFazio (1994); see especially Chapter 8 of Aronowitz and DiFazio, "A Taxonomy of Teacher Work" (pp. 226-63). See also Nelson (1997).

6. The notion of thinking in Gramscian terms comes from Bové (in Landy, 1994, p. xvi).

7. Joseph Buttigieg is on target in arguing that while Gramsci's writings are fragmentary, there is nothing unclear about his views regarding "the relation between the theoretical work of intellectuals and political praxis" (1991, p. 93).

8. There are a number of instances in his book where Hirsch misrepresents the work of critical theorists in education. For example, he completely misreads the work of the French sociologist, Pierre Bourdieu, claiming that Bourdieu's analysis of "cultural capital" is important because it provides the basis for working-class kids to succeed in schools. Of course, cultural capital for Bourdieu was a class-specific category based on the Marxist notion of exchange value and illuminated how middle-class cultural capital is used in schools to legitimate forms of class inequality. See Feinberg's analysis of Hirsch's distortion of Bourdieu's work (1997, pp. 27-35).

9. For an analysis of schools within a broader political, cultural, and economic context, see Giroux (1997).

10. For in-depth analyses of the work of E. D. Hirsch, see Aronowitz and Giroux (1988), Smith (1990), and Feinberg (1997).

References

Aronowitz, S. (1996). *The Death and Rebirth of American Radicalism.* New York: Routledge.

Aronowitz, S., & DiFazio, W. (1994). *The Jobless Future.* Minneapolis: University of Minnesota Press.

Aronowitz, S., & Giroux, H. A. (1988). Schooling, Culture, and Literacy in the Age of Broken Dreams: A Review of Bloom and Hirsch. *Harvard Educational Review,* 58 (2), 171-94.

Barnouw, E. (Ed.). (1997). *Conglomerates and the Media.* New York: Free.

Berman, P. (1997, May 11). Havel's Burden: The Philosopher-King is

Mortal. *The New York Times*, sec. 6, pp. 32-37.

Bové, P. (1994). Foreword (pp. ix-xxii). In M. Landy, *Film, Politics, and Gramsci*. Minneapolis: University of Minnesota Press.

Butterfield, F. (1997, September 28). Crime Keeps on Falling, But Prisons Keep on Filling. *New York Times*, sec. 4, p. 1.

Buttigieg, J. (1991). After Gramsci. *MMLA*, 24 (1), 93.

Children's Defense Fund. (1997). *Children's Defense Fund, State of America's Children Yearbook 1997*. Washington, DC: Children's Defense Fund.

Cochran, T. (1994). Culture in its Sociohistorical Dimension. *Boundary 2*, 21 (2), 139-78.

Entwistle, H. (1979). *Antonio Gramsci: Conservative Schooling for Radical Politics*. Boston: Routledge.

Feinberg, W. (1997). Educational Manifestos and the New Fundamentalism. *Educational Researcher*, 26 (8), 27-35.

Fisher, C., Hout, M., Jankowski, M. S., Lucas, S., Swidler, A., & Voss, K. (1996). *Inequality by Design: Cracking the Bell Curve Myth*. Princeton: Princeton University Press.

Forgacs, D. (1988). Introduction. In D. Forgacs (Ed.), *An Antonio Gramsci Reader* (pp. 17-25). New York: Shocken.

Fraser, N. (1995). From Redistribution to Recognition? Dilemmas of Justice in a "Post-Socialist" Age. *New Left Review*, 212, 68-93.

Giroux, H. A. (1997). *Pedagogy and the Politics of Hope*. Boulder: Westview.

Giroux, H. A. (1995, July/August). Talking Heads: Public Intellectuals and Radio Pedagogy. *Art Papers*, 17-21.

Gitlin, T. (1995). *The Twilight of Common Dreams*. New York: Metropolitan.

Gramsci, A. (1988). Men or Machines? In D. Forgacs (Ed.), *An Antonio Gramsci Reader* (pp. 62-64). New York: Shocken.

Gramsci, A. (1975). Socialism and Culture. In P. Piccone & P. Cavalcante (Eds.), *History, Philosophy, and Culture in the Young Gramsci* (pp. 20-21). St. Louis, MO: Telos.

Gramsci, A. (1971). *Selections from the Prison Notebooks* (Q. Hoare & G. Nowell Smith, Eds. and Trans.). New York: International.

Grossberg, L. (1996). Toward a Genealogy of the State of Cultural Studies. In C. Nelson & D. P. Gaonkar (Eds.), *Disciplinarity and Dissent in Cultural Studies* (pp. 131-47). New York: Routledge.

Grossberg, L. (1977). *Bringing It All Back Home: Essays on Cultural Studies*. Durham: Duke University Press.

Hacker, A. (1995). *Two Nations: Black and White, Separate, Hostile and Unequal.* New York: Scribner.

Hadjor, K. B. (1995). *Another America: The Politics of Race and Blame.* Boston: South End.

Hirsch, E. D. (1996). *The Schools We Need.* New York: Doubleday.

Holly, D. (1980). Antonio Gramsci: Conservative Schooling for Radical Politics. *British Journal of the Sociology of Education,* 1 (3), 315-19.

Jacoby, R., & Glauberman, N. (Eds.). (1995). *The Bell Curve Debate.* New York: Random House.

Karabel, J. (1976). Revolutionary Contradictions: Antonio Gramsci and the Problem of Intellectuals. *Politics and Society,* 6, 123-72.

Kelley, R. D. G. (1998). *Yo' Mama's Disfunktional: Fighting the Culture Wars in Urban America.* Boston: Beacon.

Kincheloe, J. L., Steinberg, S., & Gresson III, A. D. (Eds.). (1996). *Measured Lies: The Bell Curve Examined.* New York: St. Martin's.

Landy, M. (1994). *Film, Politics, and Gramsci.* Minneapolis: University of Minnesota Press.

Marable, M. (1995). *Beyond Black and White.* London: Verso.

Miller, J. G. (1996). *Search and Destroy: African-American Males in the Criminal Justice System.* New York: Cambridge University Press.

Mohanty, C. T. (1989-90). On Race and Voice: Challenge for Liberal Education in the 1990s. *Cultural Critique,* 14, 179-208.

Murray, C., & Herrnstein, R. J. (1994). *The Bell Curve.* New York: Free.

Nelson, C. (Ed.). (1997). *Will Teach for Food: Academic Labor in Crisis.* Minneapolis: University of Minnesota Press.

Rorty, R. (1998, April 3). The Dark Side of the Academic Left. *The Chronicle of Higher Education,* pp. B4-B6.

Said, E. (1983). *The World, the Text, and the Critic.* Cambridge, MA: Harvard University Press.

Schiller, H. I. (1989). *Culture Inc.: The Corporate Takeover of Public Expression.* New York: Oxford University Press.

Tonry, M. (1995). *Malign Neglect: Race, Crime, and Punishment in America.* New York: Oxford University Press.

Watkins, E. (1989). *Work Time: English Departments and the Circulation of Cultural Value.* Stanford: Stanford University Press.

Williams, R. (1967). *Communications.* New York: Barnes & Noble.

3

Antonio Gramsci:
The Message and the Images

Attilio Monasta

The Truth

Conflict among differing interpretations is the only way of approaching historical truth. Events happen. Actions are undertaken
and achieved. Words are spoken and written. Messages are spread. But
it is only images that are perceived and received. And images, according to Plato, are only a pale, frequently incorrect, representation
of reality. There is no possibility of discovering the "truth." Nevertheless the search for the "true" image, the search for the "true" message, is the unavoidable destiny of human beings and, in particular,
those involved in education.

One method of resolving the unsatisfactory feeling of never
reaching the truth could be the search for misunderstanding, the
search for lies: the exciting game of ever new and differing interpretations. Is all this just a sophisticated game or are we all driven, more or

less consciously, by political interest, i.e., an interest which leads us or drives us toward changing the reality in which we live? Is the final aim of interpretation the understanding (and also changing) of our world?

If it is true that education has a transformative function (Mayo, 1999), the image of a given thought or of the intellectual heritage of a person, regardless of the aim, has an educational and therefore a transformative effect on people, on the consumer. This is the simple mechanism of cultural leadership or hegemony, which Gramsci argued is always a "pedagogical" mechanism.

Gramsci stated that, rather than the thought of an author in itself, what we know will always be the "fortune" of his or her intellectual product, i.e., the image as it is (and as far as it is) diffused. A genuine critical approach and discussion on Gramsci and his "profile" cannot avoid this contradiction, of which Gramsci himself has been one of the most prestigious victims. The challenge, therefore, is not how much we will know of Gramsci's heritage, but rather to compare the different images of his work which have been diffused, and determine what could be the political-educational issue of emphasizing one rather than another.

Many Italian intellectuals who have a place in European history spent their lives and wrote their best essays while in prison or in exile. The more relevant their thoughts and actions were for the people's cultural and educational development, the more repressed and the more deformed were their messages. Just as Tommaso Campanella (1568-1638) wrote the first Italian "Utopia" (*La città del sole*) during his twenty-seven years of incarceration, so also did Antonio Gramsci write in prison the most important draft on the educational and political function of intellectuals: 2,848 pages of handwritten notes which are known today as the *Prison Notebooks* (*Quaderni del carcere*). What should have been, according to his original intention, a critical analysis of the history of Italian intellectuals, became a prophecy on the destiny of his own work, his message, and the way he is perceived by others.

According to Gramsci's analysis, the best-known and the most positive function of many Italian intellectuals has been (and perhaps still is) that of being "cosmopolitan," that is, universal, and, therefore, more relevant to Western (or even global) civilization than to Italy—relevant for the awareness and the growth of the cultural identity of Italian people. The reason for this lies in the historical separation, more evident in Italy than in other European countries, between cultural development, intellectual "work" in a traditional sense, and political leadership.[1]

Education is a field where theory and practice, culture and politics, inevitably merge together, and where intellectual research and achievement combine with social and political action. However, a distinction, if not opposition, between these two aspects of education is not infrequent. The ideological use of culture and science often pushes toward both the "neutralization" of the educational and political effects of cultural development and the "justification" of the political power by domesticated theories, which, therefore, can be defined as "ideologies." It is difficult, within the traditional division and separation of disciplines and fields of cultural research, to define all that constitutes "education," since education is consistently related to the growth of children and the schooling of pupils, including nursery school or university education.

The educational side of Gramsci's writings, however, is not based on the few pages which can be found within his work on school and education in a traditional sense, but rather on the assumption that the core of Gramsci's message—and even the purpose of his writings—is profoundly and largely "educational."

His Life and Politics

The early life and youth of Antonio Gramsci coincide with the early stages of industrial and economic development in Italy. Despite the peculiarities of Italian society (i.e., the marked differences between north and south; the variety of regions, dialects, and traditions; the long domination of different foreign powers; and last, the Rome-centered domination of the Catholic Church), a great effort was made at the beginning of the twentieth century by the industrial and financial world to "modernize" Italian society based on the model of central European countries. Within the "positivistic" approach to science, technology, and education, a parallel development in the "scientific organization of work" (i.e., Taylorism for industrial production) and the scientific organization of culture and education was gradually implemented under the governments of Giolitti.[2] For a short time before the First World War, Italy enjoyed a period of apparent social peace, imposed at the end of the nineteenth century by reactionary governments, justified by the need for colonial conquest, and paid for by a large hemorrhage of southern Italians migrating abroad—to the Americas or to Australia.

Gramsci was born in Sardinia, one of the poorest regions of Italy, which, as is often the case with islands, has maintained its own strong cultural identity. It has its own language, history, and culture, which differ considerably from those of the Piedmontese who ruled the Kingdom of Sardinia from Turin, in the northern part of the mainland. It was to Turin that Antonio Gramsci moved to study at the University. He eventually had to abandon his studies due to lack of money and severe health problems. Turin was, at that time, the center of Italian industrialization and the focus of the first organization of the Italian working-class.

Gramsci started his political and educational apprenticeship during the First World War as a journalist and theater critic, attending frequently in the evening the meetings of the Confederazione Generale del Lavoro (trade union) and the Socialist Party. After the war, within the core of "red" socialist Turin, he created two journals, *Ordine Nuovo* and *Unità*, with an explicit function: to educate the new working class created by industry and the war.

The prevalent theme of *Ordine Nuovo* was the relationship between the "scientific management of work" (Taylorism and Fordism) and the scientific management of education and training. However, this relationship, which has now been recognized by many as the beginning of educational sciences, was not, for Gramsci, intended to be simply an intellectual exercise. A few years before the war, scientific research on Italian education had already been drastically marginalized and repressed by the dominant hegemony of the idealistic philosophers, Benedetto Croce and Giovanni Gentile, who considered this field of studies as a branch of philosophy, ethics, or even religion. In 1923, Gentile, the first Secretary of State for Education of the new fascist government, reformed the whole Italian school system by emphasizing the ideological division between technical and vocational preparation (for work), and cultural and scientific preparation (for the "spiritual" development of persons and, of course, for political leadership).

Gramsci was developing a different approach to these problems, which did not fall into the positivistic arrogance of solving human problems with science and technology, nor into the idealistic illusion of the "independence" of intellectual and cultural life from economic and political determinants. The link between the organization of work and the organization of culture was, rather, envisaged by Gramsci as the new "professional culture," the new technical and professional preparation needed by manpower (from the skilled worker to the manager) to control and lead industrial development, as well as the society which this development inevitably generates.

After 1917, the Russian Revolution captured the attention of working-class movements more than the internal problems of any other nation emerging from one of the worst European wars ever.

The Socialist Party in Italy, as in many other countries, became split not only between the "reformists" and the "communists," but also between the "reformists" and the "nationalists"—with the latter soon becoming the populist section of the Fascist Party.

From 1922 onwards, the fascist regime in Italy brought to a complete halt any attempt to find democratic solutions, not only to economic problems, but also to the social, cultural, and educational growth of the people. In November 1926, Mussolini's government enacted "special legislation" which dissolved the Italian Parliament and all remaining organizations forming the Opposition. It also banned their publications. In the massive series of arrests that followed, Antonio Gramsci was jailed. He was 35 years old, a Member of Parliament, and had been, since 1924, General Secretary of the Italian Communist Party. At Gramsci's trial in 1928, the official prosecutor ended his peroration with the following statement: "We must stop this brain from working for twenty years!"

It was already evident to the fascist regime that the most dangerous opposition would come not just from political action in the traditional sense (i.e., an organization) or from an intellectual protest based on principles, but rather from the blending of both intellectual and political criticism and action.

The Heritage

Gramsci's brain did not stop working in prison. On the contrary, soon after his arrest, he began to make plans to conduct research on what is now considered the most important analysis of "hegemony," that is, of the links between politics and education. In a letter to his sister-in-law, Tatiana Schucht, dated 9 March 1927 (Gramsci, 1965, pp. 57-60), he speaks about a project to write something *für ewig* (for ever), something which would also serve to absorb him and "give a focus to [his] inner life." The first point of the plan refers to a history of Italian intellectuals; then he speaks of studies on linguistics, on the theatre of Pirandello, and on serial novels and popular literary taste. Even if the study plan was meant to be *für ewig*—which means for the sake of knowledge and not for practical or political purposes—the letter already shows a common thread underlying all the different subjects. He defines the history of intellectuals as the process of "formation of the public spirit," and, finally, he writes that the different topics of his plan have a common motif: "the creative popular spirit," that is, the way the hegemony of a certain social group grows up, from the soul of the group, toward its political organization. In fact, in another letter to Tatiana, dated 15 December 1930, he writes: "thinking 'disinterestedly' or study for its own sake are difficult for me [. . .] I do not like throwing stones in the dark; I like to have a concrete interlocutor or adversary." He also refers to the "polemical nature" of his entire intellectual formation (Gramsci, 1965, pp. 389-92).

Gramsci died in 1937, without having had the possibility of completing his work. His thirty-three prison notebooks were saved by his sister-in-law, Tatiana, and smuggled out of Italy. Gramsci had written a good deal before his imprisonment,[3] but his reputation as one of the major Italian thinkers and educators rests on the *Letters from Prison* and the *Prison Notebooks*.

Only after the fall of the fascist regime and the end of the Second World War did a first edition of the prison writings come out, in six volumes, published in Turin by Einaudi, between 1947 and 1951. They were edited by Felice Platone and directly supervised by the General Secretary of the Communist Party, Palmiro Togliatti. The first volume was a selection of Gramsci's letters from prison, which received the "Viareggio Prize," the most prestigious Italian award for literature.

It was in 1947 that an alliance of the two largest and most popular political forces involved in the defeat of the fascist regime—the Christian Democrats and the Communist Party—led the country for a few months: in this context Gramsci became the symbol of fascist persecution and antifascist resistance. However, this period also saw the beginning of a sort of sanctification of Gramsci within the Olympus of traditional intellectuals: Gramsci as a philosopher, historian, political scientist, literary critic, and, quite incidentally, an educator (inasmuch as he wrote on school and education). The structure of the first edition of Gramsci's *Prison Notebooks* reveals how much his work could be "re-absorbed into more traditional forms of thinking" (Paggi, 1970, p. xi). The six volumes of the first edition are a collection of the numerous notes rearranged around different themes: first, philosophy and, above all, "Marxism"; second, culture and intellectuals as a separate subject; third, Italian history, politics, and literature; and last, the remaining, apparently miscellaneous, notes.[4]

The editorial construction of the image of Gramsci was justified and explained by the particular situation in which the notes were written and left. Given the incomplete nature of the work, its "fragmentary" character, and the uncertain nature of Gramsci's intentions, the editors were encouraged to give it a more coherent and readable form. The irony was that frequently, in his notes, Gramsci pointed out the difference between the writings of an author and his or her intentions,

and their "fortune,"—a difference that must be kept in mind by anyone who wants to understand the real "educational" meaning of the
author's message.

It was only in 1975, after important changes in the Italian political and cultural milieu, that a critical edition of the *Prison Notebooks*
appeared, reproducing the complete texts as they were written. In
other words, in Valentino Gerratana's critical edition the notes were
reproduced in the same order and in the different versions Gramsci
himself had written them, sometimes crossed out with a thin penline,
and frequently rewritten in other more "monographic" notebooks.

Critical Ideology

It has been shown, by a philological comparison of the two editions,
that it is possible to have two quite different images of Gramsci (see
Monasta, 1985). The faithful reproduction of his work is much less
"fragmentary" than one would have believed; through the different
themes, which in fact inspired most of the titles of the first edition,
there is a deep unity, a strong common message, insistently repeated.
By giving examples from different fields (philosophy, history, literature, and the organization of culture and schools), Gramsci wished to
discover (and to educate toward the discovery of) the real "intellectual function" within societies, a function which is—always and in-
separably—educational and political. Inasmuch as the first edition
portrays Gramsci as a leading intellectual figure (emphasizing the traditional image of the intellectual, possibly a multifaceted Renaissance
man, finding even in prison the road to spiritual freedom through
reading, studying, and writing for posterity), the center of his image
was missing. In the early 1950s it was probably not possible, either in
the West or in the East, to reveal the truth. The dominating force of
culture, whether conservative or progressive, was not ready to be the
"object" of itself, to let someone reveal its own "material" and political roots.

The central message of Gramsci is that the organization of culture
is "organic" to the dominant power. Intellectuals cannot be defined as
such by the job they do, but rather by the role they play within society; this function is always, more or less consciously, that of the
technical and political "leadership" of a group, either the dominant
group or another, tending toward a dominant position.

> Every social group, coming into existence on the original terrain of an es-
> sential function in the world of economic production, creates, organically,
> together with itself, one or more strata of intellectuals which give it homo-

geneity and an awareness of its own function not only in the economic but also in the social and political fields. (QC, p. 1513; and SPN, p. 5)

The first example of an "intellectual" given by Gramsci is: "the capitalist entrepreneur," who creates

> alongside himself the industrial technician, the specialist in political economy, the organizer of a new culture, of a new legal system, etc. [. . .]. The entrepreneur himself represents a higher level of social organization, already characterized by a certain managerial and technical (i.e., intellectual) capacity.

This is Gramsci's definition of "organic" intellectuals and their function, which is, at one and the same time, technical and political. However, we must understand why many intellectuals "put themselves forward as autonomous and independent of the dominant group," and believe themselves to be a distinctive social group. This is because

> every "essential" social group which emerges into history out of the preceding economic structure [. . .] has found (at least in all of history up to the present) categories of intellectuals already in existence and which, indeed, seemed to represent an historical continuity uninterrupted even by the most complicated and radical changes in political and social forms. (QC, p. 1514; and SPN, pp. 6-7)

Examples of these types of intellectuals, which Gramsci defines as "intellectuals of the traditional type," are the ecclesiastics and a full stratum of administrators, scholars, scientists, theorists, nonecclesiastical philosophers and the like. It is not by chance that, even to this day, many of these intellectuals are defined in English as "clerks," while other similar words, derived from the Latin *clericus*, describe—in many other languages—this traditional form of intellectual work.

If we want to find a "unitary criterion to characterize all the diverse and disparate activities of intellectuals and to distinguish these at the same time and in an essential way from the activities of other social groupings," it is an "error of method" to look only into "the distinctive nature of intellectual activities, rather than at the whole system of relations in which these activities [. . .] have their place within the general complex of social relations."

Criticism of the traditional distinction between "manual" and "intellectual" work is one of the most important steps towards a new theory of education. Following Gramsci, this distinction is ideological insofar as it diverts attention from the real functions within social and working life, to the "technicalities" of working:

In any physical work, even the most degraded and mechanical, there exists a minimum of [. . .] intellectual activity. [. . .] All men are intellectuals, one could therefore say: but not all men have the function of intellectuals in society. [. . .] There is no human activity from which every form of intellectual participation can be excluded: Homo faber cannot be separated from Homo sapiens. (QC, p. 1516)

The educational implications of Gramsci's analysis are developed throughout the twelfth notebook (from which we have taken our quotations). This notebook is a long "monograph" into which Gramsci incorporated several texts taken from other notebooks. His message is not at all ambiguous and finishes with this famous conclusion:

The mode of being of the new intellectual can no longer consist in eloquence, [. . .] but in active participation in practical life, as constructor, organizer, "permanent persuader" and not just a simple orator [. . .]; from technique-as-work one proceeds to technique-as-science and to the humanistic conception of history, without which one remains "specialized" and does not become "directive" (specialized and political). (QC, p. 1551; and SPN, p. 10)[5]

The separation between classical and technical education, which tends to reflect the social division between intellectual and manual work, must be revealed as ideological, hiding the real division, which is between "directive" and "subaltern" roles in society, no matter whether the job that characterizes a group of persons is called intellectual or manual. As far as education, in a strict sense, is concerned, Gramsci suggests that "in the modern world, technical education, closely bound to industrial labor even at the most primitive and unskilled level, must form the basis of the new type of intellectual." This means education for all, therefore, and close links between school and work, and between technical and humanistic education.

Gramsci's analysis of the educational and political levels is not limited to the twelfth notebook—which we consider, however, to be central—but is rather spread throughout all of his prison writings. Notebook nineteen, again a monographic second draft of a collection of texts about the Risorgimento, cannot be considered purely as a historical overview. The longest text of this notebook (twenty-four pages) deals with the "problem of political leadership in the formation and development of the nation and the modern state in Italy" (QC, p. 2010; and SPN, p. 55).[6] There we find the same analysis explicitly based on

the methodological consistency of a criterion of historico-political research: no independent class of intellectuals exists, but every social group has its own stratum of intellectuals, or tends to form one; however, the intel-

lectuals of the historically (and actually) progressive class, in each particular circumstance, exercise such a power of attraction that, in the final analysis, they end up by subjugating the intellectuals of the other social groups;
they thereby create a system of solidarity between all intellectuals, with
bonds of a psychological nature (vanity, etc.) and often of a caste character
(technico-juridical, corporate, etc.).

In his analysis of the development of a new ruling class, Gramsci
makes an important distinction between "direction" and "domination," which had already been made by Lenin, in order to focus on the
differences between the use of force (in the so-called "temporary"
phase of proletarian dictatorship) and the use of cultural hegemony to
obtain the consent of the people. However, this distinction has a different meaning for Gramsci; he speaks about society being "directed"
by a new social class, "before" this class enters the government. The
function of "organic" intellectuals is that of the "intellectual and
moral" leadership of society by means of education and the organization of culture, rather than by the traditional means of legal and
forceful coercion.

Within the tenth and eleventh notebooks, dealing with "philosophy" and the important role played by the Italian intellectual
Benedetto Croce both during the First World War and under the subsequent fascist regime, we find the same analysis and other important
developments. The central theme is "political hegemony" as an educational process:

It is essential to destroy, he says, the widespread prejudice that philosophy
is a strange and difficult thing because it is the specific intellectual activity
of a particular category of specialists or professional or systematic philosophers. It must first be shown that all men are "philosophers," by defining
the limits and characteristics of the "spontaneous philosophy" which is
proper to everybody.

This philosophy is contained in the language itself, in "common
sense" and in popular religion, that is, "in the entire system of beliefs,
superstitions, opinions, ways of seeing things and of acting." The real
problem, therefore, is not one of being a philosopher, but whether

to take part in a conception of the world mechanically imposed by the external environment, i.e., by one of the many social groups in which everyone
is automatically involved from the moment of his entry into the conscious
world [or] to work out consciously and critically one's own conception of
the world and thus, through the labor of one's own brain, to choose one's
sphere of activity, take an active part in the creation of the history of the
world, be one's own guide, refusing to accept passively and apathetically
the molding of one's personality from the outside. (QC, pp. 1375-76; and
SPN, pp. 323-24)

One of the most debated topics within Gramsci's theories of education is the relationship between "spontaneity" and "conformism." Gramsci deals with this problem both in the analysis of the passage from "spontaneous philosophy" to "critical thinking" and in his notes on school, education, and "active education." In acquiring one's conception of the world one always belongs to a particular grouping—that of all the social elements which share the same mode of thinking and behaving. We are all conformists of some conformity or other, always the person-in-the-street or collective human being. The question is: of what historical type is the conformity, the human mass, to which we belong?

A similar, though more crude, analysis of "conformity" can be found in Notebook 22, on Americanism and Fordism. The new Tayloristic organization of work had created, for the first time in history, a radical "massification" of the person at work, and Gramsci seems to consider it a step from the primitive, even animal, condition of humankind, toward a new type of person:

> The history of industrialism has always been a continuing struggle (which today takes an even more marked and vigorous form) against the element of "animality" in man. It has been an uninterrupted, often painful and bloody process of subjugating natural (i.e., animal and primitive) instincts to new, more complex and rigid norms and habits of order, exactitude and precision which can make possible the increasingly complex forms of collective life which are the necessary consequence of industrial development. [. . .] Up to now all changes in modes of existence and modes of life have taken place though brute coercion [. . .] The selection or "education" of men adapted to the new forms of civilization and to the new forms of production and work has taken place by means of incredible acts of brutality which have cast the weak and the non-conforming into the limbo of the lumpen-classes or have eliminated them entirely. (QC, pp. 2160-61; and SPN, p. 298)

The crude and realistic language used by Gramsci to describe the process of "educating" large masses of people for adaptation to the contemporary transformations of the economy, made many scholars believe that he was in favor of an authoritarian pedagogy (see, for example, Entwistle, 1979). On the one hand, he was superficially identified with various trends of Marxist education in the USSR, and, therefore, his "theory of education" was considered near to Lenin's theory of proletarian dictatorship, if not with the Makarenko's methods of re-education for maladjusted young people. On the other hand, Gramsci himself wrote some pieces opposing "some principles of modern education," such as those coming from the "Geneva tradition" of Rousseau and Pestalozzi, for which the "spontaneous development of the child's personality" must not be disturbed or deformed by the intervention of the educator. In some of his letters and in one of the early notes, he criticizes the "illusion" of the "spontaneous development" of the child: from the first moment of his or her life the child is educated to "conform" to the environment, and school is only a small "fraction" of one's life: "Education is always a struggle against the instincts related to the basic biological functions, a struggle against nature, to dominate it and to create the 'actual' human being" (QC, p. 114). And the effort of learning the psychological and physical discipline necessary for studying and for any educational achievement is not "pleasant": "it is a process of adaptation, a habit acquired with effort, tedium, and even suffering" (QC, p. 1549; and SPN, p. 42). While one could have some doubts about Gramsci's actual opinion of "pedagogics" (i.e., teaching methods at school or in the family), because of the relatively small development of these topics within his work, the general theory of education coming from Gramsci's thinking is unequivocal.

Any interpretation of Gramsci's theory of education could be misleading if we do not differentiate between his "descriptive" and his "prescriptive" approaches. The term "conformity" does not mean, for Gramsci, the negative tendency of people to let themselves be driven and conditioned by "fashion," but rather an instrument for the interpretation of the process through which the majority of the population, within any society and under any regime, usually follows tradition and sticks to the rules:

> Conformism, then, means nothing other than "sociality," but it is nice to use the word "conformism" precisely because it annoys imbeciles. [. . .] It is too easy to be original by doing the opposite of what everyone else is doing [. . .]. What is really difficult is to put the stress on discipline and sociality and still profess sincerity, spontaneity, originality and personality. (QC, p. 1720; and CW, p. 124)

The real problem for education is, therefore, an awareness of the different types of "conformism," such as socialization, that are proposed or imposed within a given society, and the struggle for one rather than the other. The real innovation of Gramsci's general theory of education is the "scientific" approach to what education really is, at any level, including political leadership, social "conformism," and the school and family life. However, following the traditional value-oriented approach to education, one could ask some delicate questions. Does Gramsci's theory necessarily imply a cynical perspective on education? Can we have criteria to "prescribe," rather than purely "describe" the type of education that would be preferable? These questions imply the analysis of values and beliefs; that is, the problem of "ideology" and its function in modern society. We can translate our questions in the following way: Can we have education without ideology and, if we cannot, how can we prefer one ideology to another?

In the first step of analyzing ideologies, Gramsci clarifies that "ideologies do not exist in themselves"; they are deformations of theories, resulting when a theory becomes a "doctrine" (that is, not an instrument for understanding reality, but a set of moral principles for "orienting" practical actions and human behavior). This development from theory to doctrine and into ideology is not "spontaneous" (arising from inside the theory itself), but "organic" to the political use of theories—which is, in itself, ideological. "Ideology" is an adjective, one could say, given that we do not have ideologies in a proper sense, but rather the ideological (i.e., educational) use of theories and doctrines.

One of the few notes that remained unpublished before the critical edition of the *Quaderni del carcere*, gives us Gramsci's definition of "ideology": ideology is "a scientific hypothesis which has a dynamic educational character and is verified and criticized by the actual development of history" (QC, p. 507). The critical function of education, which also seems to be essential in Gramsci's thought, could be put at risk if we believe it necessary to relate education to ideology. It is difficult to say what education should be, according to Gramsci, since he seems to be more interested in revealing what education actually is.

Understanding and Misunderstanding

Another "case-study" to which Gramsci frequently refers is that of Machiavelli. His name, as well as the adjective "Machiavellian," still recall the brutal and perverse aspects of political power, because he "described" what politics really was (and, perhaps, always will be), rather than suggesting what politics could be.

Gramsci and Machiavelli leave us with an important question: What is the "educational" function of a precise description of the mechanisms of political power, and, in the case of Gramsci, of the mechanisms of ideology? That of educating people toward a realistic approach and, therefore, toward the political struggle, opposing one power with another, or that of revealing to the people the hidden side of politics, making them diffident towards and independent of political power? Many signals lead us to believe that Gramsci's aim was not purely "descriptive," and that he suggests a strategy for a new type of education.

First of all, Gramsci's interpretation of "Machiavellian policy": when writing about the role played by Machiavelli in the scientific description of "politics," Gramsci poses to himself (and to all of us) two important questions. Who was Machiavelli addressing when writing *The Prince*? What was his aim and his "policy"? It seems evident that Machiavelli did not wish—nor did he need—to teach rulers how to achieve and maintain power. Rather, he wanted to explain and make known the real mechanism of politics. Machiavelli's "policy" is not "politics," according to Gramsci, because the educational effect of a critical understanding of politics made new classes more aware of—and, therefore, more powerful against—the old aristocratic ruling class.

Second, the scientific and "descriptive" process in itself introduces a new conception of "critical thinking." According to common sense, criticism is a sort of opposition against what we do not want; on the contrary, "critical thought" is not, for Gramsci, a theoretical game which opposes one theory with another, one ideology with another, or the "idealistic illusion" that theory, culture, and, therefore, education could be "independent" of their historical "material" base. For Gramsci, critical thinking is the continuous research and discovery of the material bases of theory, that is, criticism of the ideological use of theory. Finally, Gramsci is not "scientifically neutral" in his educational strategy. In his opinion, there is one particular ideological (i.e., educational) approach which is preferable to any other, not for theoretical reasons (one is "true" and the others are "false"), but for practical reasons: the "philosophy of praxis," an ideological instrument for widening popular awareness of the mechanism of politics and culture as well as awareness of the historical and economical determination of ideas, and, therefore, rendering people more able to master their own lives, to "lead their own society and to control who leads."

Here is the focus of different and perhaps opposite interpretations of Gramsci's "profile": "Philosophy of praxis" was identified by the editor of the first edition of Gramsci's notebooks, purely and simply with "Marxism" and "historical and dialectic materialism" (see Gramsci, 1948, pp. xxix-xxx). It was argued that, in his prison writings, Gramsci used to conceal behind key words or paraphrases the names and definitions which might have led the censor to interrupt his work. This is only partially true if we consider that it was not unknown, both inside and outside the prison, that he had been imprisoned as the leader of the Italian Communist Party. In the case of the expression "philosophy of praxis," it is evident that it is not the equivalent of "Marxism."

An analysis of the many points of discord between Gramsci and the "official," "orthodox" doctrine of Marxism, which was being developed in the USSR while Gramsci was in prison, would take up much more space than is available in a "profile" of Gramsci. It is enough to note that Gramsci wrote many notes strongly critical of the vulgarization of Marxism conducted by Bukharin (before Bukharin himself became the victim of Stalinism). Moreover, it is known that, in prison, Gramsci disagreed with many of his Italian Communist Party comrades on the development of Marxism in Europe.

"Philosophy of praxis" is, for Gramsci, an autonomous term to define what he saw to be a central characteristic of Marx's heritage: the inseparable link between theory and practice, thought and action. The originality of "philosophy of praxis" stands, according to Gramsci, in that it is the only "ideology" that could be critical of itself and, hence, that is able to discover the "material" (i.e., economic and political) roots of all doctrines (including, therefore, Marxism itself) and adapt theory and practice continuously to each other.

One of the last ideological uses of theory, science, and information seems to be, at the end of the twentieth century, the widespread message that "ideologies fail" and "ideologies have failed." Within this doctrine, the old image of Gramsci as "one of the major Marxist thinkers"[7] seems to be out of date and may vanish together with all Marxist ideas. We believe, however, that a different image of Gramsci can be found within his great work. He opened up new ways of thinking, of political action, and education during the 1930s—a period of world history when the three movements of dictatorship, social organization, and strong conformity were competing with each other up to the final holocaust of the Second World War. Many differences exist, of course, between Soviet Stalinism, German Nazism, and American Fordism, particularly on the constitutional and political side. However, for the largest part of the population living under these different regimes, their conditions of work, the circumstances of their lives, and the educational conformity of their societies did not allow any particular space for "critical thought" and personal development.

This is why we believe that Gramsci's message, as it now emerges from the shadows of that historical epoch, helps us to discover a new approach to education that is scientifically critical of all kinds of ideological and educational processes.

The New Educational Strategy

The main hypotheses of this theory and practice of education, which we have derived from Gramsci, are the following: Educational processes develop in a large variety of ways, and they must be studied and mastered with particular attention to the educational moments that are not usually considered educational in a strict sense. School, vocational training, adult education, and university could be considered a façade, in which the organization of culture and political power seem to be in conflict, while most of the actions of "permanent persuasion" are occurring behind and outside the formal educational system. Decisions taken by media and the publishing conglomerates, changes made in the organization of work, choices between technologies in industry and services, the system for selecting and appointing trade-union and party officers and leaders (and their function in the daily life of society)—these are the main arenas of the modern educational processes, concealed rather than immediately evident. From Gramsci we can derive both a method of analysis and of educational action that focuses on the types of intellectuals and the type of function they have in society; as well as a new educational strategy that can rejuvenate the educational system in a strict sense (i.e., primary, secondary, and tertiary education).

In keeping with Gramsci's general theory of education, we believe that the new type of intellectual in modern society can be more easily found among the administrators and managers of industry and services, among the upper echelons of state administration, and in central and local bureaucracies, as well as within the teaching profession and the growing sector of vocational and occupational training, rather than among the traditional "academic" intellectuals (who, nevertheless, still seem to be the opinion leaders). The latter are becoming, more or less consciously, an ideological screen for political and cultural operations that are not decided and implemented by them, but through them.

One could disagree with Gramsci's analysis and educational strategy. It cannot be denied, however, that a study of the history of intellectuals and the history of the organization of culture has never been attempted. Intellectuals of the traditional type seem to be experts and specialists on all subjects other than themselves. This is rather meaningful, and it can be explained by the arrogance (and the illusion) of their believing themselves to be the "subject" rather than the "object" of knowledge. However, for the intellectual function in general, and for intellectuals of a new type, the lack of awareness of their real role in society could engender a greater risk for democracy.

It could mean that the real decision-making processes, namely those related to the cultural and political hegemony within society, are displaced from their "natural" (i.e., institutional and constitutional) ground, where popular control could be easily exercised, and are assumed by hidden powers, beyond any democratic control.

Finally, as far as the visible education system is concerned, Gramsci's approach does not mean that school and university education are irrelevant, within the strategy of educating for the development of critical thought. It suggests, rather, innovations in methods, content, and organization of study which should be consistent with the following main points: tighter links between school and work, between theory and practice; greater attention to the history of the organization of work and of the organization of culture, and, therefore, more interest in the study of the "fortune" (namely, the different interpretations) of classics and theories; and, last, an open debate on the aims of education and the values on which educational action is based in a given society.

Moreover, this new educational strategy and method affect the professional status of teachers, insofar as teachers do not perceive themselves as traditional intellectuals and, therefore, as independent of both social and political pressures. Education, as a process of conformity and hegemony, could disturb most teachers, particularly those who work toward helping their students to achieve greater freedom and personal independence. However, the teachers' awareness of political hegemony as an educational process, good or bad, could be the starting point of a new professionality for teachers and educators.

Notes

*A large part of this essay was first published by the UNESCO journal, *Prospects*, 23 (3/4), 597-612.

1. It is interesting to note that the English translators of Gramsci make a number of references to the particular difficulties of translating some of the words that play a central role in Gramsci's analysis, such as:

> the group of words centered around the verb *dirigere* (*dirigente, direttivo, direzione*, etc.). Here, we have in part followed the normal English usage dictated by the context (e.g. *direzione* = leadership; *classe dirigente* = ruling class), but in certain cases we have translated *dirigente* and *direttivo* as "directive" in order to preserve what for Gramsci is a crucial conceptual distinction, between power based on "domination" and the exercise of "direction" or "hegemony." In this context it is also worth noting that the term "hegemony" in Gramsci itself has two faces. On the one hand it is contrasted with

84   Attilio Monasta

"domination" (and as such bound up with the opposition State/Civil Society), and on the other hand "hegemonic" is sometimes used as an opposite of "corporate" or "economic-corporate" to designate an historical phase in which a given group moves beyond a position of corporate existence and defence of its economic position and aspires to a position of leadership in the political and social arena. Non-hegemonic groups or classes are also called by Gramsci "subordinate," "subaltern" or sometimes "instrumental." (SPN, pp. xiii-xiv)

2. The first Italian translation of F. W. Taylor's *The Principles of Scientific Management of Work* dates from 1911. In 1909, Maria Montessori, the first Italian female university graduate in medicine, had published *Il metodo della pedagogia scientifica applicata all'educazione dell'infanzia* (The Method of Scientific Pedagogy Applied to Early Childhood).

3. Most of Gramsci's preprison writings were collected in a series of five volumes, all published by Einaudi in Turin: *L'Ordine Nuovo. 1919-20* (1954); *Scritti Giovanili. 1914-18* (1958); *Sotto la mole. 1916-20* (1960); *Socialismo e fascismo. L'Ordine Nuovo. 1921-22* (1966); *La costruzione del Partito Comunista. 1923-26* (1971).

4. The volumes of the first edition of Gramsci's *Quaderni del cacere* were published by Einaudi of Turin in the following order: *Il materialismo storico e la filosofia di Benedetto Croce* (1948); *Gli intellettuali e l'organizzazione della cultura* (1948); *Il Risorgimento* (1949); *Note sul Machiavelli, la politica e lo Stato moderno* (1949); *Letteratura e vita nazionale* (1950); *Passato e presente* (1951).

5. The central part of Notebook 12 is dedicated to an analysis of the Italian school system and the need for moving away from the old classical "educational principle" to a new one, on which the unified and comprehensive school for all should be based. In the first edition of the *Quaderni*, the notes of Notebook 12 were split up into three different parts: the conclusion was included within the first part as a simple explanation of the definition of the new type of intellectual, whereas the longer texts on the school and "in search of an educational principle" were postponed until after a long series of notes on several examples of "intellectuals." The traditional gap between "intellectuals" and education was, therefore, reinforced.

6. The title of this note in its first version is even more meaningful: "Political leadership before and after the conquest of government."

7. See Grant (1981, p. 97) for his review of Entwistle (1979).

References

Entwistle, H. (1979). *Antonio Gramsci. Conservative Schooling for Radical Politics*. London: Routledge & Kegan Paul.

Gramsci, A. (1965). *Lettere dal carcere* (S. Caprioglio & E. Fubini, Eds.). Torino: Einaudi.

Gramsci, A. (1948). *Il materialismo storico e la filosofia di Benedetto Croce*. Torino: Einaudi.

Grant, N. (1981). [Review of *Antonio Gramsci: Conservative Schooling for Radical Politics* by Harold Entwistle]. *Comparative Education,* 17 (1), 97.

Mayo, P. (1999). *Gramsci, Freire and Adult Education*. New York: Zed.

Monasta, A. (1985). *L'educazione tradita. Criteri per una diversa valutazione complessiva dei Quaderni del carcere di Antonio Gramsci*. Pisa: Giardini edoitore.

Paggi, L. (1970). *Gramsci e il moderno principe. Nella crisi del socialismo italiano*. Rome: Editori Riuniti.

Abbreviated Titles

CW: *Selections from Cultural Writings* (D. Forgacs & G. Nowell Smith, Eds.). Cambridge, MA: Harvard University Press (1985).

QC: *Quaderni del carcere* (V. Gerratana, Ed.). Edizione critica dell' Istituto Gramsci. 4 vol. Torino: Einaudi (1975).

SPN: *Selections from the Prison Notebooks of Antonio Gramsci* (Q. Hoare & G. Nowell Smith, Eds. and Trans.). London: Lawrence & Wishart (1971).

4

Gramsci and the Unitarian School: Paradoxes and Possibilities

Carmel Borg and Peter Mayo

Reference to the work of Antonio Gramsci is *de rigeur* for a number of people who engage the historical materialist tradition to explore educational and cultural initiatives for social transformation. Often referred to as the "Lenin of the Occident" (Morrow & Torres, 1995), Gramsci was mainly concerned, in his work and writings, with the development of a revolutionary strategy for complex Western societies characterized by regional differentiation, uneven levels of development (central to the capitalist mode of production), and a variety of social groups struggling for justice and a greater share of power.

A huge corpus of writings has rendered quite popular such important Gramscian terms as those of Hegemony, the Sorelian concept of a historical bloc, the notion of a Modern Prince, and such distinctions as those between organic and traditional intellectuals, "common sense" and "good sense," and "war of manoeuvre" and "war of position." This paper will therefore not attempt to repeat what so many other works have done, namely, explicating the broader meanings and ramifications of these Gramscian concepts. Such explanations are also to be found in the literature dealing extensively with Gramsci and education (see Broccoli, 1972; Manacorda, 1970; Entwistle, 1979; Ireland, 1986; De Robbio Anziano, 1987; Monasta, 1993; Coben, 1999; Mayo, 1999; and Allman, 1999). Passing references to these concepts will be made, since the reader's acquaintance with them is being assumed. The major focus of this paper will be on the "unitarian school," arguably the most controversial aspect of Gramsci's writings pertaining to education. We argue that, when viewed in the context of Gramsci's larger corpus and, therefore, his overarching view of the workings of power, this element, and other related writings on intellectuals and the organization of culture (Gramsci, 1971a), can easily strike the reader as being full of paradoxes.

Intellectual and Moral Reform

In Gramsci's work, one finds the critical application of Marxist tools of analysis for the study of a specific context—the Italian post-Risorgimento state. It is this specific application which rendered Gramsci's work of great interest to scholars and activists operating in contexts denoting strong cultural affinities with Gramsci's Italy, the Latin American context being a strong case in point (see Ireland, 1987; Aricò, 1988; Coutinho, 1995; Melis, 1995; Morrow & Torres, 1995; and Fernandez Diaz, 1995).

Gramsci's insights were intended to explore possibilities for an "intellectual and moral reform" (see Caruso, 1997) which would emancipate the masses from an old order that was mainly characterized, according to Gramsci, by "a mythological conception of life and the world" (Gramsci, 1975a, p. 495). The new order, the most radical reform since primitive Christianity (Festa, 1976), would accomplish "nationally that which liberalism only managed to gain for restricted sections of the population" (Gramsci, 1975b, p. 1292).

The cultivation of a revolutionary conscience among the deeply religious peasants that would rupture the "reactionary and anti-State bloc made up of the landowners and the great mass of backward peasants, controlled and led by the rich landlords and priests" (Gramsci, 1978, p. 346), was markedly different from Croce's idealism. Gramsci's polemic with Croce centered mainly on the latter's claim of having solved the problems of metaphysics, transcendence, and theology: "Croce takes every opportunity to underline how, in his activity as a thinker, he has studiously tried to eradicate from his philosophy any residual trace of transcendence and theology and hence of metaphysics as understood in the traditional sense" (Gramsci, 1995,

p. 346). For Gramsci, Crocean historicism "is still at the theological speculative stage" (Gramsci, 1995, p. 348). By contrast, according to Gramsci, the "philosophy of praxis is the historicist conception of reality, liberated from any residue of transcendence and theology even in their latest speculative incarnation" (Gramsci, 1995, p. 348).

Religion was central to Gramsci's critique. Gramsci rebukes Croce for accepting religion as a form of primitive philosophy necessary for the people. Croce, according to Gramsci, deepens the gap between the intellectuals to whom he addressed his philosophy, and the people to whom religion is sufficient:

> But Croce has not "gone to the people," has not wanted to become a "national" element (just as the Renaissance men were not, unlike the Lutherans and Calvinists), has not wanted to create a group of disciples who (given that he personally might have wanted to save his energy for the creation of a high culture) could popularize his philosophy in his place and try to make it into an educational element right from the primary school stage (and thus educational for the simple worker and peasant, that is to say for the simple man in the street). (Gramsci, 1995, p. 408)

In response to Croce's elitist stance, Gramsci maintains that one of the main tasks of the philosophy of praxis is that of elaborating a philosophy that tries to weld intellectuals and people together in a historical bloc. The organic rapport that is established between intellectuals and masses is born within the masses themselves: "everyone is a 'philosopher,' even if only in his own way and unconsciously, because even in the minimal manifestation of any intellectual activity, language, there is contained a determined conception of the world" (Gramsci, 1975b, p. 1375).

Within Gramsci's project, historical reality is not something that develops over people's heads. Human beings are not objects, but subjects in the historical process, intervening consciously in reality, of which they are themselves agents. Against this backdrop, Gramsci calls for an analysis of religion as an ideological and historical fact. This analysis forms part of a larger project whereby:

> The dualistic and "objectivity of the external world" conception, as it has taken root in the people through the traditional religions and philosophies that have become "common sense," can only be uprooted and substituted by a new conception intimately fused with a political programme and a conception of history that people recognise as the expression of its absolute necessities. (Gramsci, 1995, p. 409)

Ideology

Gramsci transcends the assumption that social change is affected only by purely structural considerations (Ransome, 1992), maintaining that the "claim [. . .] that every fluctuation of politics and ideology can be presented and expounded as an immediate expression of the structure, must be contested in theory as primitive infantilism" (Gramsci, 1971b, p. 407). It was his sincere hope that the "philosophy of praxis" would undergo a process of emancipation, initially going through a phase marked by crudity, before being elaborated into a "superior culture." This, after all, occurred with the Lutheran reform and Calvinism, both initially giving rise to a popular culture and only much later developing into a "superior culture" (Caruso, 1997, pp. 85-86).

For Gramsci, philosophy constitutes the medium through which a true moral reform can be brought about. Philosophy constitutes an intellectual order "which neither religion nor common sense can be" (Gramsci, 1971b, p. 325). Philosophy, in fact, is "criticism and the superseding of religion and 'common sense.' In this sense, 'philosophy' coincides with 'good' as opposed to 'common sense'" (Gramsci, 1988, p. 327). Within an ideological bloc, philosophy exerts the most profound influence over the conceptions of the world of auxiliaries and subaltern classes.

Unlike traditional philosophy, religion and common sense:

> cannot constitute an intellectual order, because they cannot be reduced to unity and coherence even within an individual consciousness. Or rather they cannot be reduced to unity and coherence within an individual consciousness, let alone collective consciousness. Or rather they cannot be so reduced "freely" for this may be done by "authoritarian" means, and indeed within limits this has been done in the past. (Gramsci, 1988, p. 327)

Gramsci identifies popular religion with common sense, which he describes as the "philosophy of non-philosophers"; that is, "the conception of the world absorbed uncritically by the various social and cultural environments in which the moral individuality of the average man develops. Common sense is [. . .] the folklore of philosophy" (Gramsci, 1975b, p. 1396). While maintaining that the rapport that exists between philosophy and common sense is similar to the one that exists between philosophy and religion, Gramsci clearly identifies common sense with religion: "The principal elements of common sense are provided by religion, and consequently the relationship between common sense and religion is much more intimate than that between common sense and the philosophical systems of the intellectuals" (Gramsci, 1971b, p. 420). To overcome this inorganic and incoherent way of thinking and actualizing a true cultural reform, one has, according to Gramsci, to identify the residues and stratifications in common sense, the legacies of previous philosophers and religions.

Folklore, besides religion and common sense, is another aspect of the subaltern culture that needs to be studied in depth in order to arrive at a real *weltanschauung* and at a real "intellectual order." For Gramsci, folklore is a conception of the world that contains a specific body of beliefs, norms, and values (Salamini, 1981). It can be understood only as a reflection of the people's conditions of life. Folklore is not only unelaborated and uncritical, but also contradictory and ambiguous in its content.

According to Gramsci, a conception of the world is unable to permeate a whole society and become "faith," unless it demonstrates itself capable of replacing preceding conceptions and "faiths" at all levels of social life. Thus, Gramsci's insistence on: "A study of how the ideological structure of a dominant class is actually organised: namely the material organisation aimed at maintaining, defending and developing the theoretical or ideological 'front'" (Gramsci, 1988, p. 380).

Gramsci's writings are to be seen as an ongoing process for the elaboration of a variety of concepts, Marxian and non-Marxian, with the idea of an "intellectual and moral reform" in mind. The quest for agency is a key feature of Gramsci's work as he seeks to break away from the crudity of economic determinism and avoids the imposition that characterizes the Leninist "vanguard" approach, an imposition generating a "passive revolution." The emphasis throughout Gramsci's writings is on ethical agency. Both the Party and the State were regarded as ethical agents and educators. The Party was conceived of as the Modern Prince, unifying the various groupings in society into a "national-popular unity," in the same way that Machiavelli's *Principe* was to unify the nation. While force is not ruled out in any process of hegemony, the emphasis is placed, throughout Gramsci's formulations, on the winning of consent. Writing in his *Note su Machiavelli, sulla politica e sullo Stato Moderno* (Notes on Machiavelli, on Politics and on the Modern State), in the *Quaderni*, Gramsci states: "In reality, the State must be conceived of as 'educator,' in that it tends to create a new type or level of civilisation."[1] Gramsci goes on to argue that, although it functions essentially on the basis of economic forces, the State cannot leave superstructural matters to their own devices, to develop spontaneously, but acts as a means of rationalization, of acceleration, of taylorization, operating according to a plan, exerting pressure, inciting, soliciting, and punishing.[2]

Civil Society

It is through the institutions of *burgherliche gesellschaft* or civil society, conceived of by Gramsci in a manner that is different from Marx (Bobbio, 1987), that much of the educational work (both hegemonic and counterhegemonic) takes place. The concept of the State is one of the most elusive in the social sciences. Gramsci confirms this, using the term differently in different contexts. It assumes a relational sense in his writings on the Factory Councils and workers' democracy (see Gramsci, 1997, pp. 63-73), where the democratic, nonhierarchical social relations he advocates, in this context, prefigure the new socialist state. Here the conception is close to Marx's notion of the State as not being a thing, what Philip Corrigan calls "Thingification" (Corrigan, 1990, p. 264),[3] but a "relation of production" (Corrigan et al., 1980).

On the other hand, in his writings on the State and civil society (cf. the *Quaderni*), Gramsci's conception of the State assumes something akin to Lenin's "armed bodies of men" being surrounded by a network of ideological institutions that form civil society. Gramsci believed that it is in the domain of the party and the institutions of civil society that the organic intellectuals of the subaltern classes (*classi strumentali*) must operate, working to engender an "intellectual and moral reform" suiting the interests of these classes. For Gramsci, and with specific reference to the Italy of his time, these classes were, of course, the industrial working class and the peasant class.

Unlike the way it is used in much of the progressive literature in education, community development, and social activism (see Korsgaard, 1997), civil society is regarded, according to the Gramscian conception, not as "an arena of popular oppositional politics" (see the critique in Mayo, 1999, p. 6), but as the terrain which consolidates the present hegemonic arrangements

> According to this conception, civil society is regarded as an area that, for the most part, consolidates, through its dominant institutions, the existing hegemonic arrangements, but which also contains sites or pockets, often within the dominant institutions themselves, wherein these arrangements are constantly renegotiated and contested. Hegemony is, after all, characterized by its nonstatic nature (Hall, 1996, p. 424). (Mayo, 1999, p. 7)

Education

For Gramsci, education takes place in a broad range of activities beyond the confines of "educational" institutions. Adult Education played a key role in Gramsci's conception of education. His own involvement in a wide variety of projects—ranging from worker education circles, the Factory Councils, and the *Club di Vita Morale*, to the Institute of Proletarian Culture, the Communist Party's (PCd'I) correspondence school, and the *scuola dei confinati* (prisoners' school) at Ustica—testifies to his faith in such a domain of political education (see Adamson, 1980 and Ransome, 1992).

Much has been written on the role of adult education in Gramsci's thinking, as indicated in a review of the English language literature on the subject (Mayo, 1995), and in a number of recently published books (Ledwith, 1997; Coben, 1999; Mayo, 1999; Allman, 1999). There is ample material on the subject of adult education in this volume. While stressing the importance, in Gramsci's conception of counterhegemonic activity, of a wide-ranging educational/cultural action (see Manacorda, in Gramsci, 1972, p. xv) that includes different forms of what can be termed "adult education," it would be pertinent to focus, in the rest of this essay, on his conception of the school, or more specifically, the "unitarian school." This is, after all, the longest and most coherent piece on education to be found in Gramsci's *oeuvre*. We shall start by highlighting some aspects of Gramsci's writings on the subject.

The Unitarian School

Gramsci's writings on the school reflect a concern, on his part, with respect to the means whereby working-class children can gain access to the "cultural baggage," which he felt they needed in order not to remain on the periphery of political life. The piece on education was written partly in reaction to the *riforma Gentile* of 1923, the educational measures introduced by the Fascist education minister and idealist philosopher, Giovanni Gentile, and which were intended to reform the old *Legge Casati* (Gramsci, 1971b, p. 36). The *Legge Casati* antedated the Italian nation-state since it was established in 1859 "as an act of the Kingdom of Sardinia" (Todeschini, 1999, p. 190). The Gentile reforms entailed a two-tier system of education, consisting of grammar and vocational schools. Gramsci felt that these reforms would lead to "juridically fixed and crystallized estates rather than moving towards the transcendence of class divisions" (Gramsci,

1971b, p. 41). The vocational schools were felt to be limited in scope (distinctly utilitarian), likely to commit violence on the working class by mortgaging the children's future ("*ipotecare il futuro del fanciullo*") at such an early age, rendering them "incubators" of "small monsters" programmed for a specific occupation (Gramsci, in Manacorda, 1970, p. 32). They were, therefore, likely to confirm working class members in their social location, denying them access to the kind of knowledge and baggage which would enable them to move in from the margins of political life. Gramsci advocates the creation of an accessible "unitarian school":

> The common school, or school of humanistic formation (taking the term "humanism" in a broad sense rather than simply in the traditional one) or general culture, should aim to insert young men and women into social activity after bringing them to a certain level of maturity, or capacity for intellectual and practical creativity, and of autonomy of orientation and initiative. (Gramsci, 1971b, p. 29)

The common school would consist of two phases. During the first phase, the emphasis would be on discipline, rigor, the acquisition of basic skills, and exposure to what Gramsci regards as a "disinterested" (i.e., for no immediate practical ends) humanistic education. In the second phase, the emphasis would be placed on creativity, discipline, and preparation—not just for university but also for work "of an immediately practical character" (Gramsci, 1971b, p. 32). The school is to be a residential place "with dormitories, refectories, specialised libraries, rooms designed for seminar work etc." (Gramsci, 1971b, p. 30). It is to make up for the working-class child's lack of the stimulating home environment that gives the middle-class child a decisive advantage in access to educational resources. Because it is intended to be an essentially humanist school, emphasis will be placed on traditional academic subjects.

The education provided in the first phase would be rigorous. With regard to this, Gramsci underscores what he regards as having been the virtues of learning such a moribund subject as Latin. He argues that bringing a dead corpse to life—the metaphor he employs to describe the process involved in learning this subject—served the purpose of inculcating certain habits of diligence, precision, poise (even physical poise), and the ability to concentrate on specific subjects (Gramsci, 1971b, p. 37). He also states that, in the process of learning the subject, "logical, artistic, psychological experience was gained unawares, without continual self-consciousness" (Gramsci, 1971b, p. 39). This indicates that Gramsci considered it imperative, regarding working-class children, to "accustom them to research; to disciplined, systematic reading; to setting out their convictions in a clear and objective manner" (Gramsci, in Bellamy, 1994, p. 52). Paradoxically, for someone who loathed the kind of vocationalism introduced by the Gentile reforms, Gramsci seems to be advocating what some authors in Italy have often referred to as the "Taylorisation of schooling." Gramsci's fascination with Taylorism and its ability to generate socially the psychophysical-sexual habits necessary for production is well known. The inculcation of the above learning qualities was not a feature of the kind of education propagated by Gentile that, therefore, favored middle-class children. These children were still capable of acquiring these skills from their home environment. This enables them to enjoy a monopoly over the acquisition of these skills. The acquisition of such qualities was considered essential by Gramsci for a class aspiring to power.

The emphasis on "logic" also reflects a conviction of Gramsci's, namely that the ability to think logically and coherently is not something innate in human beings; it is a skill that has to be mastered. Once again, Gramsci criticizes the Gentile Reform for failing to take this into account; the implication being that, as a result, working-class children are denied access to a skill which he must have considered fundamental for them to be able to convert common sense to good sense. Gramsci also regards as detrimental to working-class interests a curriculum that encourages dialogue and participation without the necessary degree of instruction (Gramsci, 1971b, p. 36). He argues that whereas in the traditional school, the pupils acquired "a certain 'baggage' or 'equipment' (according to taste) of concrete facts," now, the modern teacher fills the child's "head with formulae and words which usually mean nothing to him and which are forgotten at once."

It is fair to assume that Gramsci argued for a pedagogical process characterized by dialogue intertwined with a certain degree of instruction. For Gramsci, if "the nexus between education and instruction is dissolved," the whole would merely constitute an exercise in rhetoric (Gramsci, 1971b, p. 36). In a letter to G. Lombardo Radice, a follower of Giovanni Gentile, Gramsci explains, with respect to the pedagogical strategies adopted by the *Club di Vita Morale*, that:

> The student reads, takes notes and then presents the results of his researches and reflection at a meeting. Then someone—a member of the audience, if someone has prepared, or myself—intervenes to make objections, suggest alternative solutions and perhaps explore the broader implications of a given idea or argument. In this way, a discussion opens up, which ideally continues until all those present have been enabled to understand and absorb the most important results of this collective work. (Gramsci, in Bellamy, 1994, p. 52)

With respect to the issue of instruction and facts, Gramsci stresses that there cannot be a passive learner, a "mechanical receiver of abstract notions" (ibid., p. 34). Information and knowledge are, according to Gramsci, refashioned by children in their consciousness, which, he argues, reflects the social and cultural relations to which they are exposed (ibid., p. 35). All this indicates that Gramsci believed that the transmission of knowledge from educator to educatee is not a mechanistic process but a highly complex one that involves a strong element of mediation and individual appropriation. In Gramsci's view, therefore, people can critically appropriate aspects of the established knowledge (including the "canon") for their own specific ends.

Critical Reaction

Arguably this is the most controversial piece in Gramsci's writings on education and culture. It has excited the interest of scholars because of its apparent advocacy of a "conservative" educational system. Entwistle (1979) argues that, in this piece, Gramsci posits a somewhat paradoxical theory of a conservative schooling for a radical brand of politics—an interpretation that drew adverse criticism from a number of writers, namely Apple (1980), Giroux (1980, 1988, 1999), Holly (1980), and Hoare (1980). Gramsci's advocacy of a strong sense of rigor in his writings on the school, underlined by Entwistle (1979) and, later, also by Senese (1991), as well as by Broccoli (1972), De Robbio Anziano (1987), and Saviani (cf. Da Silva & McLaren, 1993), becomes the focus of much of our commentary on this aspect of his work. There is no denying the fact that, in this piece, Gramsci attaches great importance to a broad humanist education. This somehow reflects his own location with respect to the issue of education as a form of empowerment. Gramsci must have been very reluctant to renounce that very same education which had enabled him to transcend his impoverished environment to emerge as a leading intellectual in the Italian Left. Lest we forget, Gramsci came from a *meridionale* background (facing all the prejudice and patronizing attitudes this generates in the industrialized North). He also had to endure a variety of hardships. There were the great physical hardships: he suffered from what would nowadays be diagnosed as Pott's disease and blamed his parents for giving in to popular superstitions regarding disability, fabricating explanations as to its cause, and not taking the necessary medical measures at the right time.[4] And, of course, the hardships were also social, with his father having been arrested on charges of petty embezzlement (see Germino, 1990 and Lepre, 1998), a situation which led him to prematurely enter the world of hard physical labor (carrying heavy registers) which must have continued to have a deleterious effect on his health. The specific kind of education he acquired, moving through the various *licei*, and eventually his interrupted (because of health and financial reasons) studies for a *laurea in lettere* with a focus (*indirizzo*) on philology (he was expected by Italy's world-class linguist, Bartoli, to become the next great Italian linguist, the "archangel" to defeat the "neo-grammarians") must therefore have meant a lot to him. These personal, psychological factors should, we feel, be borne in mind when considering his pedagogical views. Why deny working-class members the same cultural capital that had enabled him to obtain "by blood and tears" what came naturally to the sons of the Italian ruling class, whom the students of Gramsci's compatriot, Don Lorenzo Milani, would refer to as "*I figli di papà*"?[5] The *figli di papà* are those who, through a class conditioned process of social and cultural reproduction, occupy dominant positions in the Italian power structure (Scuola di Barbiana, 1996, p. 10).

It is, however, precisely this that highlights what, *prima facie*, appears to be a paradox in Gramsci. Few would need reminding that Gramsci is one of the foremost exponents of the theory of hegemony, based on a recognition of the manner in which dominant forms of thought and practice permeate the people's consciousness, including the consciousness of subaltern groups, contributing to the fashioning of their subjectivities. And yet, despite this obvious recognition, Gramsci seems to be, in this particular piece, evoking the virtues of a classical humanist education, predicated on eurocentric knowledge—what today would be termed the "selective tradition" or the "great books" (see Giroux's critique of Bloom and Hirsch on this, in this book and elsewhere); in short, that sort of class-biased curriculum which favors one particular kind of "cultural capital" at the expense of another. Morrow and Torres (1995) provocatively pose the question: are there two Gramscis? Is there not a paradox here? Entwistle underlined the paradox in the title of his very controversial study concerning Gramsci's views on schooling: *conservative* schooling for *radical* politics (our emphasis). Is this what Gramsci is really advocating, given his widely acknowledged tremendous insight into the workings of power, and his explanation of how hegemony is developed? Was he singularly unobservant, failing to spot an important contradiction in his work? Or was he, like John Donne, exploring possibilities that can emerge from apparent paradoxes?

Gramsci was very much concerned with the way a particular class develops its own intellectuals. The piece on education strikes us as constituting an attempt to explore what the "old school" (Gramsci's own term, not ours) offered the ruling class (*classe dirigente*) in terms of producing its own intellectuals. Are there elements of this school that can prove beneficial for a class or group aspiring to power? Does a new group coming into power require a complete overhaul of the educational system? Should the dominant established culture be ignored—a complete break with bourgeois culture, as some would have it? This kind of thinking had been affirmed in Russia following the Bolshevik revolution, and it was strongly opposed by both Lenin and Trotsky (Morgan, 1989, pp. 47-48). Lenin stated unequivocally:

> Proletarian culture is not something that has sprung from nowhere, it is not an invention of those who call themselves experts in Proletarian culture. That is all nonsense. Proletarian culture must be the result of the natural development of the stores of knowledge which mankind has accumulated under the yoke of capitalist society, landlord society and bureaucratic society. (Lenin, in Entwistle, 1979, p. 44; Lenin, in Broccoli, 1972, p. 66)

One of the recurring aspects of much of the radical literature in education is its focus on popular culture as an important terrain wherein hegemony occurs. One might argue that this is as it should be, given the role popular culture plays in enabling one to come into subjectivity. But, as Dennis Haughey (1998) points out with respect to adult education (and we feel this applies to critical approaches to education in general): "largely lacking [. . .] is the ability to function fluently in the language of the dominant culture so as not to be relegated to the periphery of political life" (p. 211). Haughey made this point with reference to what educators—adult educators, in his specific case—can learn from Gramsci. As critical educators, we ignore the dominant culture and intellectual traditions at our peril! Cracking the code, through critical appropriation, must have been considered by Gramsci, and other writers (see Lorenzo Milani), as an important means for members of subaltern groups to enter the corridors of power and begin to transform the existing hegemonic arrangements. No established institution is monolithic, according to the Gramscian conception of power. The textuality that institutions furnish us with can be read against the grain, an insight which Gramsci himself provides (anticipating later post-structural theories). He indicates, in the piece on education, that there is never a passive receiver of knowledge or facts. Texts are open to multiple readings and are "rewritten" or reconstituted in the recipient's mind according to the specific social and cultural relations to which she or he is exposed (see, once again, Gramsci, 1971b, p. 35).

Furthermore, we feel that there is nothing really conservative about Gramsci's advocacy of aspects of a humanistic education for working-class children. There is, after all, a long tradition within the international working-class movement, of negotiations and struggles, some of which were highly successful, intended to secure for workers access to a humanistic education. In his own country, for instance, the trade unions secured educational leave (known as the hundred-and-fifty hours) precisely to provide workers with a humanistic education which, they felt, would be empowering, unlike vocational education which, they believed, primarily served capitalist interests (cf. Yarnit, 1980). The same applies to the United Kingdom where the Workers' Educational Association and the trade union movement in general have been instrumental in securing a humanities education for workers via extramurals provided by the universities or through a variety of programs, including those provided by such residential institutions as Ruskin College, Oxford. Recently, we have witnessed criticism of the U.S. government on the grounds that a humanities education, or an education in the liberal arts, has "always occupied a subordinate position vis-à-vis the dominant languages" (Giroux, 1990, p. 10)—the dominant languages, in this case, being those that promote "the instrumentalist" view of education (ibid.). Gramsci's advocacy of aspects of a humanistic education is therefore well in keeping with a socialist vision that has often found, in this type of education, elements for a logical alternative to an "instrumentalist" education. The "instrumentalist" type of education favors capital (it would normally be inspired by Human Capital Theory). It is the "instrumentalist" type of education that the Gentile Reform was to make available to working-class children through the distinction between "classical" and "vocational" schools. Gramsci's critique of this education and the kind of "streaming" (tracking) which it brought about is also well within the radical tradition of repudiating any kind of differentiation in the quality of schooling claimed to be made on the basis of "meritocracy," when, in effect, the whole process is one of social selection on the basis of class. That Gramsci was capable of making such a critique in the thirties, rather than the sixties, shows remarkable foresight on his part.

Harold Entwistle (1979) argues that the emphasis Gramsci places on the acquisition of a baggage of facts suggests that Gramsci "held a view of learning which is not inconsistent with the notion, now used pejoratively, of education as banking" (p. 47). This would, once again, appear to be quite paradoxical, coming from a man (Gramsci) who denounced the popular universities precisely because their directors and educators filled the stomach with bagfuls of victuals (*"sporte di*

viveri"), which could have also caused indigestion, but did not leave
any trace and did not touch the learners' lives in a way that could
have made a difference (Gramsci, 1972, p. 83). He felt that the
popular universities emulated the old Jesuitical schools, where understanding is fixed and is not regarded as the culmination of a long process of inquiry (Gramsci, 1972, pp. 84-85).

To say, as Entwistle does, that Gramsci favored "banking education" can be somewhat misleading. A close reading of Gramsci's text,
one that devotes great attention to his choice of words, would indicate
that what he was averse to was the encouragement of uninformed
dialogue. For Gramsci, a process of uninformed dialogue is mere rhetoric. It is mere *laissez faire* pedagogy which, in this day and age, would
be promoted under the rubric of "learning facilitation." This is the
sort of pedagogical treachery that provoked a critical response from
Paulo Freire. In an exchange with Donaldo P. Macedo, Freire states
categorically that he refutes the term "facilitator," which connotes
such a pedagogy, underlining the fact that he has always insisted on
the directive nature of education (see, for instance, Freire, in Shor &
Freire, 1987, p. 103; and Freire & Macedo, 1995, p. 394). He insists
on the term "teacher," one who derives one's authority from one's
competence in the matter being taught (see, for instance, Freire, in
Freire & Macedo, 1995, p. 378). As one of us has argued elsewhere,
laissez faire pedagogy "often results in members of an 'in group'
gaining the upper hand, abusing of the pseudo-dialogical process and
silencing others" (Mayo, in McLaren & Mayo, 1999, p. 402).

One may, therefore, justify Gramsci's reservations concerning
such practice on the grounds that it favors middle-class children who
can monopolize the learning activity, silencing other pupils from subordinated groups, by virtue of their possession of the relevant cultural
capital. What Gramsci seems to be advocating is a process of education which equips children with the necessary acumen to be able to
participate in an informed dialogue. This is why Gramsci writes in
terms of a "nexus between instruction and education" (Gramsci,
1971b, p. 36). This immediately brings to mind Freire's statement
that there are moments when one must be fifty percent a traditional
teacher and fifty percent a democratic teacher (Freire, in Horton &
Freire, 1990, p. 160).

The emphasis here is on "authority and freedom," the distinction
posed by Freire (see, for instance, Freire, 1998) but which echoes
Gramsci's constant reference to the interplay between *spontaneita' e
direzione consapevole*—"spontaneity" and "conscious direction" (see,
for instance, Gramsci, 1977a, pp. 70-74). In his piece on the unitarian school, Gramsci calls for a balance to be struck between the kind

of authority promoted by the old classical school (without the excess of degenerating into authoritarian education) and the "freedom" advocated by his contemporary proponents of ideas associated with Rousseau's philosophy as developed in *Emile*. The latter type of education, for Gramsci, had to develop from its "romantic phase" (predicated on unbridled freedom for the learner, based on his or her spontaneity) and move into the "classical" phase, classical in the sense of striking a balance (Gramsci, 1971b, pp. 32-33). This is the balance between freedom and authority (for a useful contemporary discussion on this, see Gadotti, 1996, p. 53).

That Gramsci despised "Banking Education" can be seen from the language used in the following quote: "In reality a *mediocre* teacher may manage to see to it that his pupils become more *informed*, although he *will not succeed in making them better educated*; he can devote a scrupulous and bureaucratic conscientiousness to the mechanical part of teaching" (Gramsci, 1971b, p. 36; our emphasis). Although, for Gramsci, it is better to provide children with information than encourage them to engage in dialogue in a vacuum, he nevertheless regards the teacher who engages in this process, one of instruction, as "mediocre" and one who does not help the children become "better educated." This association between straightforward instruction and mediocrity reflects Gramsci's views concerning "Banking Education." After all, this is a writer who, elsewhere in his writings of the same period, advocated a reciprocal dialogical relationship between intellectuals and masses. It should be a relationship in which "every teacher is always a pupil and every pupil a teacher" (Gramsci, 1971b, pp. 349-50). He repudiates the Leninist notion of a "top-down" vanguardist transmission style and emphasizes the reciprocal basis of consent.

The issue concerning the merits of Greek and Latin also warrants consideration. Here is another paradox and a point of contrast with a position associated with Lorenzo Milani's pupils from the school of Barbiana, who preferred the learning of a contemporary history (say post-World War I) to the learning of a history concerning earlier periods (School of Barbiana, 1996, p. 26), as they found in the former a much greater connection with life (p. 27). And here we have Gramsci apparently advocating the study of two dead languages for the rigor involved in bringing a corpse to life. But is he explicitly advocating the study of Greek and Latin?   Alternatively, as part of an inquiry into how the bourgeoisie creates its own intellectuals, is he exploring the benefits this knowledge offered those who studied the two languages? In highlighting what he considers to have been the merits of the two subjects, Gramsci is merely making the point that there is need for an area or areas in the curriculum which would instill in the pupils a sense of rigor, the sort of rigor which will stand working-class children in good stead when in control of their own environment. This should not, of course, be taken to mean that Gramsci advocates the inclusion of Latin and Greek in a curriculum intended to be beneficial to the working class. On the contrary, he clearly states that:

> it will be necessary to *replace* Latin and Greek as the fulcrum of the formative school, and *they will be replaced*. But it will not be easy to deploy the new subject or subjects in a didactic form which gives equivalent results in terms of education and general formation, from early childhood to the threshold of adult choice of career. (ibid., pp. 39-40; our emphasis)

In an extension of the earlier quote, concerning the need for the pupil to acquire a "baggage" or "equipment of concrete facts" (Gramsci, 1971b, p. 36), Gramsci states that "it *was right to struggle against the old school* but reforming it was not so easy as it seemed" (ibid., our emphasis). Once again, as the Marxist figure accredited with having developed the theory of hegemony, Gramsci must perforce have been fully aware of the implications of certain practices and normalizing discourses associated with the "old school." This explains his being in favor of a struggle against it (Manacorda, in Gramsci, 1972, p. xxix). What he seems to be doing, in this instance, is highlighting the qualities that the "old school" managed to instill and that, he felt, one should not overlook when restructuring the schooling system if such restructuring is to be carried out with the interests of subaltern groups in mind. Critically appropriating elements of the old in order to create that which is new, constitutes a recurring theme in Gramsci's writings, as a number of writers point out (e.g., Giroux, 1980, 1988; Hoare, 1980; Mayo, 1999a). But the old humanistic school, in its entirety, has to be replaced since it no longer serves present realities.

The problem for Gramsci was that the process of reform introduced by Gentile, possibly through the influence of his mentor and predecessor as Minister of Education, Benedetto Croce, was not any better. It struck Gramsci as being more retrograde when measured against the ideal of a fusion between the academic and the technical. The old school had much more merit, Gramsci seems to be saying, with the rider that there are aspects of this institution which can be critically appropriated and, if they are to be replaced, need to be substituted adequately. As Mario Alighiero Manacorda argues, with respect to the note on the unitarian school, what Gramsci has provided is an "epitaph" that celebrates what the humanistic school was and what it can no longer be, since the social reality has changed (Mana-corda, in Gramsci, 1972, p. xxix).[6]

Our focus on these details will hopefully provide the basis for a careful reading of Gramsci's educational writings. We argue, however, that in any attempt to draw sustenance from a writer, for the purpose of a democratizing project in education, one should be wary of a scriptural reading of the texts in question, a point Coben underscores (1998, p. 201). This becomes even more important when bearing in mind what Gramsci tried to do in this note: extol the virtues of the old school to show that the Gentile reforms represent, in contrast, a retrograde step and not an improvement in terms of ensuring social justice.

There are important issues which come to mind in the context of a unitarian school. These are issues that came to the fore in educational debates in the seventies, that is, four decades after Gramsci's death. One issue that arises is: what passes for "humanistic" knowledge? Should such knowledge be deemed problematic? To what extent does it embody the dominant ideology? Does it necessitate the school children's acquisition of a particular "cultural capital," so that those who have access to it possess an advantage over those who do not? Can this problem be overcome simply through the creation of a boarding, unitarian school? Would this unitarian school coexist with other private or church-run humanistic schools? Furthermore, there is nothing in Gramsci's piece to suggest that aspects of working-class life, or the life of any subordinated group for that matter (e.g., peasants), can be included in any of the two phases of the proposed unitarian school. If the proposed school was intended to be an important site for the conversion of "common sense" to "good sense," then the potentially emancipatory elements of this "common sense" (which Gramsci equates with culture), together with elements of the culture of other subordinated social groups, should form part of the curriculum. The emphasis on the ability to crack the dominant culture code is most welcome. But then there should always be room to render popular culture an integral feature of the learning process where the focus does not lie solely on the written word,[7] a limitation in Gramsci's cultural (including popular culture) writings (Forgacs & Nowell Smith, in Gramsci, 1985, p. 345; Mayo, 1999a, p. 108). This would be in the interest of developing a radically democratic education with a "national-popular" character.

This point becomes ever so pertinent in this day and age when we are constantly witnessing the emergence of multiethnic and multiracial societies. This might not have been the case with Italy in Gramsci's time, but it is certainly the case with that country today. Italy is a major recipient of immigrants from various parts of the globe, notably from different areas in Africa, including the Maghreb and Macharek states. That there is the need for a different and more inclusive school, in these circumstances, is a point which is constantly underlined in the various discussions taking place in Italy with respect to the need for a critical multicultural education (see Mayo, 1999b). And yet, ironically, it is to Gramsci that certain authors have resorted to obtain insights concerning the current debate on multiculturalism (Apitzsch, 1992), though certainly not to the noe on the unitarian school.

If one seeks to develop a genuinely multicultural curriculum, then one must break away from the eurocentrism in which Gramsci's thinking seems to be immersed, a feature he shares with many other thinkers in the Marxist tradition, a product of eighteenth-century Cartesian thought. These thinkers would, of course, include Karl Marx. As D. W. Livingstone has stated: "Marx as well as subsequent orthodox Marxists and most critical Western Marxist intellectuals have operated from a eurocentric world view which has regarded European civilisation as the dynamic core of global life" (Livingstone, 1995, p. 64). All told, in his epitaph on the old humanistic school, and his indication as to what is worth salvaging from it and what needs to be replaced adequately, Gramsci presents us with a formidable challenge. We are prompted to address the issue of what really renders the school a genuinely "unitarian" institution, guided by the principles of social justice, equity, and inclusion (in its broadest sense).

Notes

1. Our translation. The original reads: "In realta' lo Stato deve essere concepito come 'educatore,' in quanto tende appunto a creare un nuovo tipo o livello di civilta" (Gramsci, 1972, p. 61).

2. Paraphrased from the original Italian in *Note su Machiavelli, sulla politica e sullo Stato Moderno* (Gramsci, 1972, p. 62).

3. See also Corrigan & Sayer (1985).

4. See Aurelio Lepre's excellent biography (Lepre, 1998, pp. 4-5).

5. Translated literally, this would be: "daddy's children."

6. Literal translation from Mario Alighiero Manacorda's introduction to his anthology of writings on pedagogy by Gramsci (Gramsci, 1972).

7. Gramsci made a substantial contribution to the study of popular culture involving the written word, writing numerous pieces on popular literature (see, for example, Gramsci, 1977b, pp. 121-66).

References

Allman, P. (1999). *Revolutionary Social Transformation: Democratic Hopes, Political Possibilities and Critical Education.* Westport, CT: Bergin & Garvey.

Apitzsch, U. (1992). Gramsci and the Current Debate on Multicultural Education. *Studies in the Education of Adults,* 25 (2), 136-45.

Apple, M. (1980). [Review of *Antonio Gramsci: Conservative Schooling for Radical Politics* by Harold Entwistle]. *Comparative Education Review,* 34 (3), 436-38.

Aricò, J. (1988). *La Cola del Diablo. Itinerario de Gramsci en America Latina.* Buenos Aires, Argentina: Puntosur.

Bellamy, R. (Ed.). (1994). *Gramsci's Pre-Prison Writing.* Cambridge: Cambridge University Press.

Bobbio, N. (1987). Gramsci and the Conception of Civil Society. In R. Bellamy (Ed.), *Which Socialism?* (pp. 139-61). Minneapolis: University of Minnesota Press.

Borg, C. (1995). *Hegemony as Educational Practice: Catholicism, Tradition and the Fate of the Progressive Historical Bloc in Malta—A Gramscian Analysis.* Unpublished doctoral dissertation, OISE.

Broccoli, A. (1972). *Antonio Gramsci e l'educazione come egemonia.* Firenze: La Nuova Italia.

Caruso, S. (1997). *La riforma intellettuale e morale in Gramsci: I Quaderni del carcere. Una riflessione politica incompiuta.* Turin: UTET Libreria.

Coben, D. (1998). *Radical Heroes: Gramsci, Freire and the Politics of Adult Education.* New York: Garland.

Corrigan, P. (1990). *Social Forms/Human Capacities. Essays in Authority and Difference.* London: Routledge.

Corrigan, P., & Sayer, D. (1985). *The Great Arch: English State Formation as Cultural Revolution.* Oxford: Basil Blackwell.

Corrigan, P., Ramsey, H., & Sayer, D. (1980). The State as a Relation of Production. In P. Corrigan (Ed.), *Capitalism, State Formation and Marxist Theory* (pp. 1-25). London: Quartet.

Coutinho, C. N. (1995). In Brasile. In A. A. Santucci (Ed.), *Gramsci in Europa e in America* (pp. 133-40). Rome: Sagittari Laterza.

da Silva, T., & McLaren, P. (1993). Knowledge Under Siege: The Brazilian Debate. In P. McLaren & P. Leonard (Eds.), *Paulo Freire: A Critical Encounter* (pp. 36-46). London: Routledge.

De Robbio, A. (1987). *Antonio Gramsci e la pedagogia del impegno*. Naples: Ferraro.

Entwistle, H. (1979). *Antonio Gramsci. Conservative Schooling for Radical Politics*. London: Routledge & Kegan Paul.

Fernandez Diaz, O. (1995). In America Latina. In A. A. Santucci (Ed.), *Gramsci in Europa e in America* (pp. 141-57). Rome: Saggittari Laterza.

Festa, S. (1976). *Gramsci*. Assisi: Cittadella Editrice.

Freire, P. (1998). *Pedagogy of Freedom. Ethics, Democracy and Civic Courage*. Boulder, CO: Rowman & Littlefield.

Freire, P., & Macedo, D. (1995). A Dialogue: Culture, Language and Race. *Harvard Educational Review*, 65 (3), 377-402.

Gadotti, M. (1996). *Pedagogy of Praxis. A Dialectical Philosophy of Education*. Albany: State University of New York Press.

Giroux, H. A. (1999). Rethinking Cultural Politics and Radical Pedagogy in the Work of Antonio Gramsci. *Educational Theory, 49*, 1-20.

Giroux, H. A. (1990). The Hope of Radical Education. *Education (Malta), 3* (4), 10-15.

Giroux, H. A. (1988). *Teachers as Intellectuals*. Westport, CT: Bergin & Garvey.

Giroux, H. A. (1980). [Review Symposium of *Antonio Gramsci: Conservative Schooling for Radical Politics* by Harold Entwistle]. *British Journal of Sociology of Education*, 1 (3), 307-15.

Germino, D. (1990). *Antonio Gramsci. Architect of a New Politics*. Baton Rouge: Louisiana State University Press.

Gramsci, A. (1997). *Le Opere. La prima antologia di tutti gli scritti* (A. A. Santucci, Ed.). Rome: Editori Riuniti.

Gramsci, A. (1995). *Further Selections from the Prison Notebooks* (D. Boothman, Ed.). Minneapolis: University of Minnesota Press.

Gramsci, A. (1988). *A Gramsci Reader* (D. Forgacs, Ed.). London: Lawrence & Wishart.

Gramsci, A. (1985). *Selections from Cultural Writings* (D. Forgacs & G. Nowell Smith, Eds.). Cambridge, MA: Harvard University Press.

Gramsci, A. (1978). *Selection from Political Writings (1921-1926)* (Q. Hoare, Ed. and Trans.). New York: International.

Gramsci, A. (1977a). *Passato e Presente*. Rome: Editori Riuniti.

Gramsci, A. (1977b). *Letteratura e vita nazionale*. Rome: Editori Riuniti.

Gramsci, A. (1975a). *Sotto la Mole, 1916-1920.* Turin: Einaudi.

Gramsci, A. (1975b). *Quaderni del carcere, Edizione Critica* (V. Gerratana, Ed.). Turin: Einaudi.

Gramsci, A. (1972). *L'alternativa pedagogica* (M. A. Manacorda, Ed.). Firenze: Nuova Italia.

Gramsci, A. (1971a). *Gli Intelletuali e l'organizzazione della cultura.* Rome: Editori Riuniti.

Gramsci, A. (1971b). *Selections from the Prison Notebooks* (Q. Hoare & G. Nowell Smith, Eds.). New York: International.

Hall, S. (1996). Gramsci's Relevance for the Study of Race and Ethnicity. In D. Morley & K. H. Chen (Eds.), *Stuart Hall: Critical Dialogues in Cultural Studies* (pp. 411-40). London: Routledge.

Haughey, D. (1998). From Passion to Passivity: The Decline of University Extension for Social Change. In S. M. Scott, B. Spencer & A. M. Thomas (Eds.), *Learning for Life: Canadian Readings in Adult Education* (pp. 200-10). Toronto: Thompson Educational Publishing.

Hoare, Q. (1980). [Review Symposium—*Antonio Gramsci: Conservative Schooling for Radical Politics* by Harold Entwistle]. *British Journal of Sociology of Education,* 1 (3), 319-25.

Holly, D. (1980). [Review Symposium—*Antonio Gramsci: Conservative Schooling for Radical Politics* by Harold Entwistle]. *British Journal of Sociology of Education,* 1 (3), 315-19.

Horton, M. (1990). *We Make the Road by Walking. Conversations on Education and Social Change.* Philadelphia: Temple University Press.

Ireland, T. (1986). *Antonio Gramsci and Adult Education. Reflections on the Brazilian Experience.* Manchester: Manchester University Press.

Korsgaard, O. (1997). The Impact of Globalization on Adult Education. In S. Walters (Ed.), *Globalization, Adult Education and Training. Impacts and Issues* (pp. 15-26). London: Zed.

Ledwith, M. (1997). *Participating in Transformation: Towards a Working Model of Community Empowerment.* Birmingham: Venture.

Lepre, A. (1998). *Il prigioniero. Vita di Antonio Gramsci.* Bari: Laterza.

Livingstone, D. W. (1995). Searching for the Missing Links: Neo-Marxist Theories of Education. *British Journal of Sociology of Education,* 15 (3), 325-39.

Manacorda, M. A. (1970). *Il Principio Educativo in Gramsci.* Rome: Armando Editore.

108   Carmel Borg and Peter Mayo

Mayo, P. (1999a). *Gramsci, Freire and Adult Education. Possibilities for Transformative Action.* London: Zed.
Mayo, P. (1999b). Towards a Critical Multiculturalism in the Mediterranean. [Reflections on the conference, Il Mare che Unisce. Scuola, Europa e Mediterraneo]. *Mediterranean Journal of Educational Studies*, 4 (1), 117-22.
Mayo, P. (1995). The Turn to Gramsci in Adult Education. A Review of the English Language Literature. *International Gramsci Society Newsletter*, 4, 2-9.
McLaren, P., & Mayo, P. (1999). Value Commitment, Social Change and Personal Narrative. [Peter Mayo interviewed by Peter McLaren]. *International Journal of Educational Reform*, 8 (4), 397-408.
Melis, A. (1995). Gramsci e l'America Latina. In G. Baratta & A. Catone (Eds.), *Antonio Gramsci e il "Progresso Intelletuale di Massa"* (pp. 227-34). Milan: Edizioni Unicopli.
Monasta, A. (1993). *L'Educazione Tradita: Criteri per una diversa valutazione complessiva dei Quaderni del carcere di Antonio Gramsci.* Firenze: McColl.
Morrow, R. A., & Torres, C. A. (1995). *Social Theory and Education. A Critique of Theories of Social and Cultural Reproduction.* Albany: State University of New York Press.
Salamini, L. (1981). *The Sociology of Political Praxis: An Introduction to Gramsci's Theory.* London: Routledge & Kegan Paul.
Scuola di Barbiana. (1996). *Lettera a una professoressa.* Florence: Libreria Editrice Fiorentina.
Shor, I., & Freire, P. (1987). *A Pedagogy for Liberation. Dialogues on Transforming Education.* Westport, CT: Bergin & Garvey.
Senese, G. B. (1991). Warnings on Resistance and the Language of Possibility: Gramsci and a Pedagogy from the Surreal. *Educational Theory*, 41 (1), 13-22.
Todeschini, M. (1999). The University in Italy: Historical Background and Changing Trends. *Mediterranean Journal of Educational Studies*, 4 (2), 187-204.
Yarnit, M. (1980). The 150 Hours—Italy's Experiment in Mass Working-Class Education. In J. L. Thompson (Ed.), *Education for a Change* (pp. 192-218). London: Hutchinson.

5

Gramsci's Theory of Education:
Schooing and Beyond

Stanley Aronowitz

Published under the auspices of the Italian Communist Party after the war—more than a decade after Antonio Gramsci's death in 1937—the celebrated *Quaderni del carcere* (*Prison Notebooks*) have not yet been fully translated into English but have had an illustrious career ever since some excerpts appeared in the late 1950s. The first of the translations was made by the Italian-American trade union and political activist, Carl Marzani, and appeared, under the title *The Open Marxism of Antonio Gramsci*, in the wake of the 20th Congress of the Soviet Communist Party. Upon its publication, Marzani's slim volume, which introduced this previously obscure Italian Marxist thinker to English speaking audiences, was generally regarded as a "revisionist" document by both the orthodox Leninists and by Gramsci's admirers. Gramsci's works seemed to vindicate the anti-Stalinist tenor of Khruschev's main report to the Congress but, more to the point, suggested a departure from the prevailing Marxist-Leninist orthodoxy that had reigned for forty years.

Perhaps most salient was Gramsci's reconceptualization of civil society. Recall that, in the *Philosophy of Right*, Hegel had made the radical argument that in the capitalist epoch every question resolved itself to the cash nexus. Consequently, civil society, rather than constituting a sphere of free discussion among equals, was coterminous with market relations. To the extent that Marx presupposed Hegel's distinction between State and civil society, now transmogrified into the binary categories of infrastructure and superstructure, the Marxist tradition tended to ignore the significance of the public sphere, including such institutions as media, voluntary organizations, educational institutions, and so forth. Gramsci insisted that since all capitalist societies, even the fascist dictatorships, tend to rule primarily by consent rather than by force, the key to the rule of capital was its ability to achieve hegemony over "civil society"—conceived as the sphere of public life that was neither, strictly speaking, of the economy nor of the State. On the contrary, it was precisely the degree to which classes in modern society established their power over "common sense" and, thus, appeared independent from the coercion of economic and State relations that their rule was made possible.

Marzani's slim anthology of Gramsci's writings had little impact in the wake of the breakup of the American and British Communist parties. Gramsci's concepts of revolutionary politics, however, appealed to many in the New Left who sought an alternative Marxist tradition to that of Stalinism and, even, Trotskyism, which they viewed as authoritarian. Despite its fragmentary character, the most widely read volume of English translations of Gramsci is *Selections from the Prison Notebooks*, published in 1971 by Lawrence & Wishart in London and International Publishers in New York. Much longer and better annotated than the Marzani version, it stood alone, until recently, as a definitive scholarly rendition. Edited with a long introduction and copious notes by Quintin Hoare and Geoffrey Nowell Smith, it manages to provide most of Gramsci's central ideas by thematically dividing and synthesizing what are otherwise pithy notes—often provocative but sometimes banal. Despite Hoare's New Left credentials, the volume appeared under the imprint of the U.K. and U.S. Communist Party publishing houses, and remains to this day the primary source of the "popular" reception of Gramsci's thought. A companion volume extracts the large number of entries on culture; also, there now exists *Further Selections*, two volumes of the pre-prison political writings, the prison letters, and two volumes of a projected six-volume edition of the entire *Quaderni*. But the essays that mark Gramsci's most sustained contributions to philosophy; political, social, and cultural theory; and the strategy and tactics of revolutionary struggle are contained in the *Selections*.

Despite the diversity of the topics that occupied Gramsci's interest during his eleven years of confinement (after all, he was himself trained as a "traditional," that is, humanistic intellectual) and the obscurity of many of his references to contemporary Italian writers (most of whom are long forgotten), activists, as much as scholars, still find much to fascinate. Indeed, despite the virtual disappearance of official Communism after the collapse of the Soviet Union, the commentaries (including the present one) continue, on almost every aspect of Gramsci's writings. What can the writings of a General Secretary of the Italian Communist Party, whose major work was done during the fascist era, say to us at a time when the political problematic to which he addressed himself seems surpassed—a condition which perhaps was not evident in the immediate postwar years when the *Quaderni* were first published? For it is not only that the Soviet Union and its satellite states have disappeared from the world stage, or that the Communist Parties of Eastern as much as Western Europe have degenerated into pale imitations of the Social Democratic formations they once despised. Or that what remains of official communism—Cuba, China, and North Korea—are social formations that, to say the least, have proven incapable of sustaining autarchic economies, even as their political systems are, to one degree or another, Stalinist throwbacks—an asymmetry not likely to last. Equally to the point, a strong argument can be made for the historicity of many of Gramsci's formulations, especially his distinction between the war of position and the war of maneuver, where the latter signifies the strategy and tactics of revolutionary struggle. While socialist revolution may not be permanently foreclosed, the prospects for such an event seem dim, at least for the coming decades. What remain, therefore, are the elaborations of the war of position—the long march through institutions, in civil society, and in struggles for intermediate power within the capitalist state, where my term "intermediate" signifies an extension of popular power from the institutions of civil society to the State, but still a capitalist state.

There is much in scholarly terms to commend in Gramsci's writings. Just as Marx was among the greatest of Hegel commentators, so Gramsci must be ranked as a major writer on Machiavelli. His "Notes on Italian History" and, especially, his remarks on the so-called "Southern Question" are landmarks in our collective understanding of why politics, even of an international variety, must always take national and regional specificities into account. Moreover, his contributions to the development of historical materialism, configured as a critique of Nicolai Bukharin's attempt at a "Popular Manual" (i.e., *Theory of Historical Materialism: A Popular Manual of Marxist Sociology*), as well as in other comments on the significance of culture and language in the formation and reproduction of the nation-state (found chiefly in his "Problems of Marxism"), are among the most powerful statements of the nondogmatic Marxism which later transmuted into what Perry Anderson called "western" Marxism. These are contributions that richly deserve the scholarly attention that the *Prison Notebooks* continue to receive, even after the end of official Communism.

There is, of course, a lively debate on Gramsci's ideas about education; and I would argue that his remarks on education and the implicit educational issues addressed in many other places remain the most salient for us. In the United States, the conversation has been conducted mainly among educational theorists and researchers who, given that they are largely ensconced in universities and work—at best—within a reformist environment, tend to focus on schools. Indeed, Gramsci's views on the "common school" could easily be inserted into the contemporary curriculum debate. He insisted that the common school should privilege "formative" (rather than vocational/technical) education on grounds that are familiar today:

> The tendency today is to abolish every type of schooling that is "disinterested" (not serving immediate interests) or "formative"—keeping at most only a small-scale version to serve a tiny elite of ladies and gentlemen who do not have to worry about assuring themselves of a future career. Instead, there is a steady growth of specialised vocational schools, in which the pupil's destiny and future activity are determined in advance. A rational solution to the crisis ought to adopt the following lines. First, a common basic education, imparting a general, humanistic, formative culture; this would strike the right balance between development of the capacity for working manually (technically, industrially) and the development of capacities required for intellectual work. (SPN, p. 27)

Gramsci's discussion addresses not only the existing educational system, but also the question of what an educational system must provide under conditions where the key institutions of the economy and civil society are under popular control. Gramsci remarks that contemporary "deliberative bodies" divide their work into two "organic" spheres: the first are the essential decisions they must make; the second are the "technical-cultural" activities that precede decision-making and are undertaken by "experts." His reference to "deliberative bodies" signifies what popular or workers councils would have to consider in establishing common schools. Far from denigrating technical education, Gramsci calls for a balance, so that those at the top levels of political leadership would possess familiarity with problems of production. While the new society would inevitably require experts and he does not foresee the possibility of abolishing the capitalist division of labor anytime soon, Gramsci insists that "destiny" not be established at the outset of a child's schooling—by what we would now term "tracking"—and that schools play a role in enabling manual and technical workers to engage in the intellectual work required of members of deliberative bodies that direct the system. In short, Gramsci's position on the common school embodies his theory of democratic politics and his social philosophy, in which popular participation as well as representation constitute the twin elements of any future democracy. His educational ideas are directed at improving schools not so much for the sake of reform, but for the sake of making possible a new kind of social rule in every institution of the State and civil society.

Gramsci devotes considerable attention to education, among other institutions, because, even under fascism, schools are primary sites for achieving mass consent for social rule. The great Gramscian, Louis Althusser, argues that among the State's ideological apparatuses, as opposed to the repressive apparatuses (law, courts, police, army, and prisons), educational institutions are the most important. The school is the State institution *par excellence* that prepares children and youth for their appropriate economic and political niches within the prevailing order. It acts as a sorting machine, forming and reproducing the classes of society according to what Bourdieu terms degrees of attainment of cultural capital. Schools transmit the dominant culture, habits of mind, and, perhaps most important of all, they inculcate in a large portion of the society's population the knowledges and values that are deemed appropriate for citizenship within a given social formation. But technical and manual workers are not only formed by specialized curricula. A number of commentators, notably Paul Willis, have argued that school "failure" is a crucial marker of working-class formation at the level of everyday life. Manual or low-level service workers are formed by their refusal (coded as failure) of the standard curriculum that constitutes the basis for the accumulation of cultural capital.

Gramsci-inspired writers on schools in advanced capitalist countries have, with some notable exceptions, taken education to mean schooling. Although many writers have engaged in a sharp critique of the role and function of schooling in terms of what Henry Giroux and I have called "reproductive" theory, there is considerable reluctance to reveal the inner tensions of schools, that is, the degree to which movements within schools have attempted to offer both resistance and alternatives to the dominant program of technicization and the systematic devaluation of formative education. Indeed, there is considerable evidence that many contemporary Gramscians recoil, on populist or libertarian grounds, at Gramsci's call for a curriculum that brings forward some of the features of the "old school of grammatical study of Latin and Greek together with the study of their respective literatures and political histories." Gramsci extols the old school, admittedly reserved for a tiny elite, as a guide for a new common educational program:

> Individual facts were not learnt for an immediate practical or professional end. The end seemed disinterested, because the real interest was the interior development of personality, the formation of character by means of the absorption and assimilation of the whole cultural past of modern European civilization. Pupils did not learn Latin and Greek in order to speak them, to become waiters, interpreters or commercial letter-writers. They learnt in order to know at first hand the civilization of Greece and of Rome—a civilization that was a necessary precondition of our modern civilization; in other words, they learnt them in order to be themselves and know themselves consciously. (SPN, p. 37)

Gramsci defends the old common school for its ability to impart habits of

> diligence, precision, poise (even physical poise), ability to concentrate on specific subjects, which cannot be acquired without the mechanical repetition of disciplined and methodical acts. [...] If one wishes to produce great scholars, one still has to start at this point and apply pressure throughout the educational system in order to succeed in creating those thousands or hundreds or even only dozens of scholars of the highest quality which are necessary to every civilization. (SPN, p. 37)

Clearly, if the criteria of contemporary relevance, of practical scientific and technical knowledge, and of specialization guide the educational system, these scholars are not likely to be produced, and the consequences for civilization would be deleterious. To become a scholar, Gramsci argues, one must master more than one language and civilization, and engage in the "analysis of distincts"—Croce's emendation of the dialectic, enabling signification of difference without contradiction. The student becomes an intellectual—no less than a scholar—by "plunging" into knowledge and life, by subjecting to the discipline of learning.

The old school was intended for the education of the ruling class. Its restriction to the upper reaches of society was intended not only to train succeeding generations of elites, but to subject the subalterns to technical and vocational niches, a "destiny" which deprives them of the means by which any democracy may emerge. For Gramsci, democracy "by definition" means that the distinction between the ruler and the ruled narrows, that "citizenship" (not limited to consent, but extended to participation) is widely instituted. Yet, apart from providing, in his prescription for school reform, a common curriculum of early, disinterested education, Gramsci hesitates to draw the logical conclusion of his own analysis: the mass intellectual education of the subalterns. Or, in another locution of his terminology, the transformation of the masses from spontaneous philosophers to philosophically as well as technically educated social actors.

Gramsci despairs of translating old elite schooling to a mass education system, chiefly because workers and peasants lack the time and the cultural preconditions for study. Until the establishment of a new social order, his recommended strategy is to put education in the service of the formation of an intellectual elite, where the concept of elite is transformed from its class-specific location among the traditional rulers to social groups in whose interest the formation of a new, egalitarian social order may come into being—the historical bloc of discontented social groups led by the working class. But short of an extensive program of formative schooling conducted by the revolutionary party itself, a task which may be necessary under conditions of the surrender of the public schools to occupational priorities, the struggle for reform of the common school curriculum in the direction of formative education is a necessary precondition for producing this elite.

Gramsci's concept of education is, however, only secondarily concerned with schooling. The main goal is the formation of an "intellectual moral bloc" capable of contesting the prevailing common sense and providing in its stead, more or less systematically, a "scientific" understanding of the social world and of politics that can be widely disseminated in the institutions and other social spaces of civil society. Here, the concept of "science" diverges from the common usage of industrial societies in which the object of knowledge is nature or a naturalized social world and the methods of knowing are experimental and mathematical, which strictly exclude intuition and speculation. Gramsci invokes a more traditional idea of science—the preindustrial concept, according to which science signifies only the effort to achieve systematic knowledge, in which philosophy is as legitimate a mode of knowledge acquisition as the traditional natural and social sciences.

Under the censor's gaze, the term Gramsci employed to designate social science was "the philosophy of praxis." For nearly all commentators it stood in for Marxism and, indeed, his texts provide some

confirmation of this view; but there is a sense in which the philosophy of praxis has a specific content, namely, the unity of theory and
practice. Unlike Leninist orthodoxy, where theory is conceived in
"the service" of practice—its "handmaid"—Gramsci understands the
theory-practice unity as two sides of the same totality; there is no
structure of dominance. For—as his essay in "The Study of Philosophy" and the compendium of comments from the *Selections* grouped
under the title "Problems of Marxism" make clear—Gramsci's historical materialism and philosophy are directed principally, and most
polemically, against "mechanical materialism"—the dominant ideology of the Third, Stalinist International—and, especially, against the
ideas of historical inevitability with which Bukharin had identified
himself, as did many in the leadership of the Italian Communist
Party. What mechanical materialism and Catholicism have in common is their fatalism. Gramsci's philosophy, by contrast, emphasizes
the indeterminacy of outcomes. With many others, Gramsci holds
that history presents possibilities, not certainties; and, since outcomes
are up for grabs, it is up to humans to fight for the future at every
level of social life, especially the cultural level.

The philosophy of praxis is the core paradigm, if you will, from
which the intellectual moral bloc needs to be formed to assist the
masses to overcome the simple reductionism of bourgeois or Catholic
common sense, both of which are content to leave them at a "low
level" of understanding. The point of the bloc is "to make politically
possible the progress of the mass and not only of small intellectual
groups" (SPN, pp. 332-33).

> The active man-in-the-mass has a practical activity, but has no clear theo-
> retical consciousness of his practical activity, which nonetheless involves
> understanding the world in so far as it transforms it. His theoretical con-
> sciousness can indeed be historically in opposition to his activity. One
> might almost say that he has two theoretical consciousnesses (or one con-
> tradictory consciousness): one which is implicit in his activity and which
> in reality unites him with his fellow-workers in the practical transformation
> of the real world; and one, superficially explicit or verbal, which he has in-
> herited from the past and uncritically absorbed. But this verbal conscious-
> ness is not without consequences. It holds together a specific social group,
> it influences moral conduct and the direction of will, with varying efficacity
> but often powerfully enough to produce a situation in which the contradic-
> tory state of consciousness does not permit of any action, any decision or
> any choice, and produces a condition of moral and political passivity. Criti-
> cal understanding of self takes place therefore through a struggle of politi-
> cal "hegemonies" and of opposing directions, first in the ethical field and
> then in that of politics proper, in order to arrive at the working out at a
> higher level of one's own conception of reality. Consciousness of being
> part of a particular hegemonic force (that is to say, a political consciousness

in the first stage towards a further progressive self-consciousness in which theory and practice will finally be one. (SPN, p. 333)

It is evident that the crucial educational issue is how to address the political hegemonies, how to bring the practical and theoretical consciousness of the most "advanced" political actors together (i.e., beyond the "masses") to overcome the power of common sense among those who are charged with political leadership within the great social movements. For Gramsci, the intellectuals are not to be conceived of as the technicians of power but as its sinews. No class in modern society, he argues, can organize itself for power—for the war of maneuver, that is, the revolutionary activity—without the participation of intellectuals whose ultimate task is to embody the unity of theory and organization. It is they who contest the institutions of civil society, the trade unions, as well as the universities.

Which brings us to the central question of how to achieve scientific understanding among ever-wider groups of the underlying population. In the "Modern Prince," Gramsci offers a particularly clear formulation of the task. He speaks of the need for "intellectual and moral reform" and suggests that the key to it is the development of a "national-popular collective" which replaces the "divinity and the categorical imperative" by linking moral with economic reform. This is done at the cultural level.

Perhaps, however, Gramsci's major innovation was to have recalled Machiavelli's insistence on the science of politics as an autonomous discourse, and the idea that politics is the main science. Thus, the struggle for a new scientific understanding as a new common sense always entails taking the point of view of "the man of action" rather than that of the scholar—or, in current fashion, the nomadic intellectual. The active intellectual addresses a wide audience and, for this reason, disdains discourses appropriate to small scholarly groups, except when directly addressing them. For Gramsci, how ideas are conveyed is as important as the ideas themselves. For, if the active intellectual does not speak in the national popular vernacular her audience will be self-selected.

Needless to say, this is easier said than done at a time when, in the main, intellectuals are generally coded as "academics" and must observe the rites of passage of institutionalized disciplines in order to get jobs and win promotion and tenure. Moreover, as the distance between universities and civil society remains wide—its increasing corporatization notwithstanding—even those who wish to make politics their principal activity often experience tremendous difficulty adapting their intellectual work to a language that can reach out beyond the

walls of the academy. While inventing new terms and even a new language is often a corollary of creative scientific activity, the refusal of
many otherwise politically-minded intellectuals to subject themselves
to the discipline of good writing becomes self-defeating and a source
of tremendous frustration. It is not a question of dumbing down
thought but of transforming scholarship into education. In short,
Gramsci insists that those who would constitute an intellectual moral
bloc must pay attention to pedagogy:

> the process of development [of the transformative intellectual as a person of
> "action"] is tied to a dialectic between the intellectuals and the masses. The
> intellectual stratum develops both quantitatively and qualitatively, but
> every leap forward towards a new breadth and complexity of the intellectual
> stratum is tied to an analogous movement on the part of the mass of the
> "simple" who raise themselves to higher levels of culture and at the same
> time extend their circle of influence towards the stratum of socialised intel-
> lectuals, producing outstanding individuals and groups of greater or less
> importance. [...] In the process, however, there continually recur moments in
> which a gap develops between the mass and the intellectuals [...] a loss of
> contact, and thus the impression that theory is an "accesssory," a "comple-
> ment" and something subordinate. (SPN, pp. 334-35)

How to close the gap between theory and practice, that is, the gap
between intellectuals, whose task it is to elaborate a new scientific
worldview and understanding, and the mass which, while no longer a
"thing" is not yet a fully conscious social actor? Here, Gramsci invokes the central role of the party as the embodiment of the new
common sense, and the apparatus of popular education. The connection of intellectuals with the party is the best insurance that they will
not lose contact with the masses and lapse into esoterica. For the
party insists that intellectuals teach popular classes, write pamphlets
and articles on cultural as well as political topics, and enter the public
arena in order to disseminate the new scientifically infused counter-
hegemony.

The problem, of course, is that neither the socialist nor communist party formations of the current period nor, indeed, many social
movements, especially the unions, see themselves as a "national
popular collective" on the way to organizing an intellectual moral
bloc whose main task is contesting hegemony. The Left is riven with
anti-intellectualism, a sentiment signified by their subscription to the
view of theory as accessory. To be sure, many intellectuals have
joined these movements and, as people of action, participate in demonstrations and organizational work, or are content to lend their
names as luminaries in order to legitimate a particular issue with which
the party or movement is engaged. The practical work of most intel-

lectuals, however, is scholarship shaped to disciplinary canons; their writings are to be found in appropriate scholarly journals and/or in books published by commercial academic or university presses, and their speeches are confined to scholarly meetings.

Even in their university teaching, many Left intellectuals confine themselves to the traditional classroom and conduct their discourse within the conventional disciplines. American humanistic and social scientific intellectuals have, in the main, assimilated the conventional methodological imperatives of the disciplines. In the social sciences, this adaptation takes the form of keeping a safe distance from the speculative sciences, especially philosophy. Philosophy, like poetry, may have aesthetic value but, for most on the Left, it has little or no scientific value. Science entails an enslavement to method. While many literary scholars read philosophy—particularly in the Nietzschean tradition that includes, among others, Heidegger, Foucault, Derrida, and Deleuze—their readings are rarely addressed to the immanent politics of these thinkers. Even when they are political in the classroom, few Left academics work with students and colleagues in study groups; even fewer see themselves as political actors except in the rituals of Left politics, such as demonstrations, statements, petitions and the like. In the elite schools, almost none of them work with academic unions, although those at third-tier institutions have readily joined and, sometimes, led these unions. Thus, the Gramsci industry is populated, for the most part, by scholars who have taken the term "theoretical practice" literally.

A major arena of popular education, the trade unions, has, to a large extent, been foreclosed by a combination of bureaucratic rot and by the transformation of the unions into business institutions where the labor contract and its administration form the basis of activity and education. While American unions maintain a modicum of educational activities to train shop leaders to administer the collective bargaining agreement, since the unions themselves are part of the prevailing common sense (or, at least, have accommodated it, rather than standing against the dominant worldview), their capacity for counterhegemonic education has withered. Under these circumstances, intellectuals remain the hired hands of the union leaderships, reduced, at best, to technical and advisory roles and subject to the discipline of the main (business) style of the institution.

The current period is, thus, marked by the persistence and the reproduction of the gap between theory and practice, a gap which appears within individuals and not only in the distance between universities, and parties and movements. The reasons for this desperate state of affairs go beyond the notorious collapse of the Left in the wake of neoliberal hegemony. Perhaps more to the point, the movements—ecological, feminist, anticapitalist alike—have abandoned or, to be more exact, renounced struggle at the level of worldviews; they have not yet sought to replace the free market common sense which dominates public discourse, let alone the prevailing technoscientific faith according to which we are on the verge of a new eugenic utopia. Ensconced in small groups and universities, the intellectuals opposed to both discourses are more or less isolated from a significant popular constituency. But, more egregiously, the concept of the totality with its connotations of "integral" connections, as Gramsci terms it, seems to have fallen into the abyss.

We have much more political practice than at any time since the end of the Vietnam War twenty-five years ago. Yet, the philosophy of praxis is not in good condition. The Left sometimes engages in critiques of schooling but, as I have remarked, almost never on the side of a truly formative curriculum. Its interventions are confined, almost completely, to the debate over access to bourgeois education that corresponds, almost merrily, to Gramsci's description of its vocationalization, and its degeneration to the level of surface "breadth." Beyond schooling, the concern of politically oriented intellectuals seems as far from an educational project as ever. It is only partly a problem of the delegitimation of Marxism in the wake of what may be described as "reactionary" postmodernism—the position that all totalizations are totalitarian and struggles over single issues are all that is possible. There are many other factors involved: the pervasive scientism of the Left, its surrender to technoscientific hegemony, its lack of philosophical critique of positivism, and its despair at the possibility of addressing neoliberalism with positions that are worthy of debate. That recent protests against the World Trade Organization and other institutions of the Empire of transnational capital have given hope that effective critique may be on the near horizon does little to overcome my pessimism of the intellect, even if my spirit remains combative.

Abbreviated Title

SPN: *Selections from the Prison Notebooks of Antonio Gramsci* (Q. Hoare & G. Nowell Smith, Eds. and Trans.). London: Lawrence & Wishart (1971).

6

Education, the Role of Intellectuals, and Democracy: A Gramscian Reflection

Joseph A. Buttigieg

> In the present school, the profound crisis in the traditional culture and its conception of life and of man has resulted in a progressive degeneration. Schools of the vocational type, i.e. those designed to satisfy immediate, practical interests, are beginning to predominate over the formative school, which is not immediately "interested." The most paradoxical aspect of it all is that this new type of school appears and is advocated as being democratic, while in fact it is destined not merely to perpetuate social differences but to crystallize them in Chinese complexities. (SPN, p. 40; QC, p. 1547)

Antonio Gramsci expresses this judgement in a relatively long note devoted to "Observations on the School: In Search of the Educational Principle." It is the second of the three notes (composed out of reflections he had articulated earlier in Notebook 4) that constitute the entirety of the "special notebook" that Gramsci entitled: "Notes and Jottings for a Group of Essays on the History of the Intellectuals" (Notebook 12). In spite of its brevity, this particular notebook occupies an especially important place in Gramsci's *ouevre*; indeed, many

careful readers of Gramsci have found in it (specifically in its treatment of the question of the intellectuals) the core, or the central
point of reference, around which the huge and fragmentary ensemble
of the *Quaderni* revolves.

The note from which I extracted the epigraph addresses a very
specific issue (as is typical of Gramsci)—namely, the reform of the
educational system devised by Giovanni Gentile and implemented by
the Fascist government in 1923. It is important to bear this in mind
in order to avoid the temptation and resist the tendency to remove
Gramsci's ideas out of their specific historical context and apply them
simplistically and unproblematically to the present situation. At the
same time, it is equally important to remember that Gramsci's ideas
on education form part of a much broader reflection on a number of
problems and issues that he regarded and inextricably connected—i.e.,
the role of intellectuals in society, modernity and the phenomenon of
Fordism, civil society, subalternity, "common sense," hegemony, and,
above all, the question of how best to prepare the ground for radical
social transformation. The isolation of single propositions or particular observations from the intricate fabric of Gramsci's thought for
the purpose of supporting or refuting a given position in today's
heated debates about education can only lead to distortions, misunderstandings, and cynical instrumentalizations.

I mention this not because I intend to provide a systematic or
comprehensive account of Gramsci's views on education within the
context of his times and of the *Quaderni* as a whole. That would take
too long; and, besides, much of that work has already been done and is
readily available—see, for example, Mario Alighiero Manacorda's excellent study, *Il principio educativo in Gramsci: Americanismo e
Conformismo*, which remains as valid today as when it was first published in 1970 (in fact, it has recently been translated into Japanese).
My motivation, rather, is this: Gramsci's views, properly understood,
can shed valuable light on the questions pertaining to education that
preoccupy us today; they can also help clarify some issues that have
become quite confused in the heated and often vicious debates swirling
around the question of which educational policies and pedagogical
practices are most appropriate for (or adequate to) a modern democracy in the age of globalization. This applies even to the current debates in the United States where the passionate polemics on education
are at the heart of the extremely politicized and divisive "culture
wars" that have been going on for well over a decade—they are, in
fact, one of the most damaging legacies of the Reagan era. Gramsci
has been invoked (positively and negatively) rather frequently in the
course of these debates, but in a manner that has not been very intel-

ligent or fruitful. What I wish to do, then, is offer some observations, from a Gramscian perspective, on certain aspects of the current U.S. debate on education—a debate that is almost always connected, at least rhetorically, with the question of democracy.

The first big salvo in the current debate on education in the U.S. was fired by William Bennett—an ex-Democrat, a repentant convert from the protest movements of the 1960s and early 1970s, who was chosen by Reagan to direct the National Endowment for the Humanities (NEH) and, subsequently, to serve as the Secretary of Education. In a monograph entitled *To Reclaim a Legacy* (published by the NEH in 1984), Bennett lamented the poor state of the nation's educational system and linked it directly with what he considered to be the malaise of society as a whole—a malaise he attributed to the general decline of ethical and moral values and to the fragmentation of the social fabric of the nation as a whole. The first thing that needed to be done to remedy the situation, he argued, was to restore to health and revitalize the country's educational system. His simple prescription: a core curriculum that would expose all students to the great documents of Western civilization, and steep the minds of the young generations in the supposedly universal and timeless values embodied by the "canon" of the Western tradition (that, sometimes, is referred to by different participants in these debates as the Judeo-Christian tradition, or simply as "the great tradition"—by which is meant the tradition of *litterae humaniores*). Bennett quickly found an audience and a following, for a variety of reasons. There is no doubt that in most parts of the country public education, and the schools as such, were and continue to be in a state of crisis. Furthermore, the country was then, as it is now, not only socially fragmented (or, as Gramsci would say, "*disgregata*") but also deeply and dangerously divided, especially along ethnic and religious lines. (See, for example, how easily an incident or an event of a racial, ethnic, or religious nature can polarize the nation, and even spark off violent confrontations within or among communities.)

William Bennett's views coincided with those of certain university academics who were unhappy with and hostile to the theoretical and methodological shifts that had been taking place for some time in the study of the humanities, and most especially in the study of literature. In 1982, a renowned literary scholar, W. Jackson Bate, published an article, "The Crisis of English Studies," in *Harvard Magazine*, excoriating the wave of post-structuralist critical theory which, in his view, fatally exacerbated the "centrifugal heterogeneity" that had been corroding literary studies since at least the 1950s. Once upon a time, Bate maintained, "unity of knowledge [. . .] was taken for granted" (p. 46). That was the time when the values of *litterae humaniores* held sway; it was the time when the study of literature transmitted the glorious tradition that stretches back to ancient Greece and Rome and that "carried Europe through the Renaissance with brilliant creativity, and, in the process, also produced the Enlightenment" (p. 48). Now, however, everything is fragmented; there is no longer a stable center and, consequently, the study of the humanities is no longer of central importance to life. Bate attributes the collapse to two major factors: the tendency towards specialization, and the enormous expansion of the universities that started in the 1950s, which saw an unprecedented increase in the enrollment of students at both the undergraduate and graduate levels. It is important to note that in his analysis of the crisis, Bate evinces only a minimal interest in the world outside the university. He excludes almost completely from his account of the regress of *litterae humaniores* any serious consideration of economic, political, and social factors. He alludes only in passing to the great shortage of teachers in the postwar period that led to the rapid expansion of American universities, and to the subsequent devastating effects of the economic crisis and the public disillusionment with higher education that contributed to the collapse of the academic job market in the 1970s. He makes no mention of the relationships between universities and corporations, the government, the military, and the culture industry; he provides no sense of the changing role of intellectuals in society during the past hundred years; he does not acknowledge the importance of technology, national and international politics, the cold war and the like. What is worse, when Bate encounters evidence of legitimate contemporary sociocultural-political concerns making their mark upon the university curriculum, he considers such evidence indicative of the fragmentation and lack of seriousness that bedevil the humanities. He finds no justification for the introduction of courses in women's studies and "ethnic" literature into the curriculum; they simply pander to "current enthusiasms"; the issues they address would be better treated in the context of the lost tradition of *litterae humaniores*.

Bate's nostalgic lament and Bennett's militant call for fundamental educational reform foreshadowed the publication, in 1987, of Allan Bloom's book, *The Closing of the American Mind: How Higher Education Has Failed Democracy and Impoverished the Souls of Today's Students*. This work, which has a foreword by the Nobel Prize winning novelist Saul Bellow, has had a greater impact than any other book or article on the debate on education and on the cultural polemics in the U.S. during the past decade. One confused and confusing aspect of Bloom's work is its treatment of the relationship between the intellectual/university professor and democratic society. In the opening pages, Bloom describes his monograph as "a meditation on the state of our souls, particularly those of the young and their education" (p. 19). He then states that his assessment of the spiritual and intellectual condition of America is based on his observations of "thousands of students of comparatively high intelligence, materially and spiritually free to do pretty much what they want with the few years of college they are privileged to have—in short, the kind of young persons who populate the twenty or thirty best universities" (p. 22). In other words, for Bloom, the privileged elite represents the entire American population; its spiritual and intellectual well-being or malaise stands for the state of mind of the nation as a whole. The story of this elite is presented as nothing less than the story of the nation, much in the same way as the traditional historians' account of kings, nobles, generals, and so on were presented as descriptions of whole nations and peoples. About the hundreds of thousands of students who frequent the less prestigious universities—not to mention community colleges and other two-year schools—Bloom has nothing to say other than: "They have their own needs and may very well have different characters from those I describe" (p. 22). If Bloom were indeed interested in explaining the current state of higher education in the context of an American society that considers itself democratic, then he would have been led to ask some very complex questions about those "other kinds of students," as he calls them. Questions such as: what exactly are the circumstances that prevent those students from having the freedom to pursue a liberal education? In other words, how has democracy failed them? Such questions never occur to Bloom; worse, he cannot afford to pursue this line of questioning because the very idea of the masses—the *demos*—invading the sacred precincts of the elite university constitutes his worst nightmare. Liberal education must not be wasted on those "other kinds of students"; it is the "advantaged youths" who possess "the greatest talents" that have the most legitimate claim on "our attention and our resources" (p. 22). These "advantaged youths" are the ones most likely "to have the greatest moral and intellectual effect on the nation" (p. 22).

How, then, do these privileged recipients of a liberal education from the elite universities exercise their "moral and intellectual effect on the nation"? They do it, according to Bloom, by spending "their lives in an effort to be autonomous" (p. 21). They need not do anything other than spend their lives in the philosophical pursuit of the good and the untrammeled contemplation of the true. Their contribution to society does not consist in any practical activity; their total freedom to philosophize must not be curtailed by practical worldly involvement or even by concerns regarding family, career and the like. They simply have to be present in society so that they "become models for the use of the noblest human faculties and hence are bene-factors to all of us, more for what they are than for what they do. Without their presence (and, one should add, without their being re-spectable), no society [. . .] can be called civilized" (p. 21).

For Bloom, the intellectual is and deserves to be recognized as an aristocrat. Therefore, his real complaint in *The Closing of the Ameri-can Mind* is not that higher education has failed democracy but, rather, that democracy has failed higher education by seducing the intellectuals. The failure of higher education, as Bloom sees it (and here he echoes the views of Jackson Bate), consists in its inability to protect itself from the incursion of the *demos*, and its capitulation to the demands of the less privileged and marginalized members of soci-ety. Much of the resentment that underlies Bloom's jeremiad stems from his sense that the intellectuals have lost their privileged status because many of them have betrayed their own class—a new kind of *trahison des clercs*. Bloom's concept of the intellectuals as a special, privileged class has a long history; nonetheless, at first sight, it might seem odd that this concept was so readily accepted and endorsed by Bloom's American readers. After all, there has been a long and power-ful tradition of anti-intellectualism in the United States. But, in fact, it is precisely because many Americans are suspicious towards intellec-tuals that Bloom's book was so successful. The conservatives were able to argue, following Bloom, that university professors had be-trayed their vocation by: (a) failing to inculcate in their students the values of the great tradition of *litterae humaniores*; and (b) becoming involved in social and political issues, and especially by advocating the causes of minorities, women, and other marginalized groups. The cor-rosion of American society, the conservatives maintained, citing Bloom, was taking place on university campuses. Some right-wing commentators, such as Michael Novak and Rush Limbaugh, perceived in all this a Gramscian plot to bring about revolution by an assault on the cultural (instead of the economic and political) front.

Gramsci, however, is pertinent to this discussion for a very differ-ent reason. A reading of Gramsci's discussion on the intellectuals (which, we must not forget, is intertwined with his reflections on edu-cation) would: (a) bring into relief the undemocratic thrust of Bloom's views; and (b) reveal how Bloom's concept of the role of the intellec-tual in society fails to take into account the realities of the modern world. Whereas Bloom starts by establishing a sharp distinction be-tween intellectuals and nonintellectuals, Gramsci asserts that "all men are intellectuals [. . .] but not all men in society have the function of intellectuals" (SPN, p. 9; QC, p. 1516). To be an intellectual, for Gramsci, is a job. Bloom's concept of the intellectual as a kind of aristocrat is antithetical to Gramsci's. To illustrate what I mean I will quote a few lines from the last section of Notebook 12:

> When one distinguishes between intellectuals and non-intellectuals, one is referring in reality only to the immediate social function of the professional category of the intellectuals [. . .]. This means that, although one can speak of intellectuals, one cannot speak of non-intellectuals, because non-intellectuals do not exist. [. . .] Each man, finally, outside his professional activity, carries on some form of intellectual activity, that is, he is a "philosopher," an artist, a man of taste, he participates in a particular conception of the world, has a conscious line of moral conduct, and therefore contributes to sustain a conception of the world or to modify it, that is to bring into being new modes of thought. [. . .] The traditional and vulgarized type of the intellectual is given by the man of letters, the philosopher, the artist. (SPN, p. 9; QC, pp. 1550-51)

Gramsci also makes us realize that Bloom's vision of intellectuals as a restricted group has been rendered obsolete by modernity: "In the modern world the category of intellectuals [. . .] has undergone an unprecedented expansion" (SPN, p.13; QC, p. 1520). Bloom remains attached to the idea of what Gramsci calls the "traditional" intellectual so that he can defend the notion that the intellectual is (or should be) autonomous. As Gramsci explains, the traditional intellectuals constitute a

> noblesse de robe, with its own privileges [. . .]. Since these various categories of traditional intellectuals experience through an esprit de corps their uninterrupted historical continuity and their special qualification, they thus put themselves forward as autonomous and independent of the dominant social group. (SPN, p. 7; QC, p. 1515)

This self-conferred autonomy, however, is an illusion—and a dangerous one. Among other things, this illusion perpetuates the separation of the intellectuals from the people. There is not enough space here to recapitulate Gramsci's extensive discussion of this issue in various sections of his notebooks. For the sake of brevity, I will quote just one observation of Gramsci's; it consists of an attack on Croce, but here one can substitute the name of Bloom for that of Croce:

> What matters to Croce is that the intellectuals should not lower themselves to the level of the masses [. . .]. The intellectuals must govern and not be governed; they are the ones who construct the ideologies with which to govern others [. . .]. The position of the "pure intellectual" becomes either a real and proper form of retrograde "Jacobinism" [. . .] or a despicable "Pon-

tius Pilatism" or first the former, then the latter, or even both of them simultaneously. (QC, pp.1212-13)

Like Pontius Pilate, those who pose as "pure intellectuals" are un-
willing to assume any real responsibility and do not want to be subjected to the judgement of the people. Their professed detachment
from politics is merely a pose; in reality, they play a fundamental political role.

The primary role of the traditional intellectuals in society, Gramsci explains, is to produce consensus—hence their work is carried out
in the context of civil society rather than political society, but their
work is not for that reason any less political. Hence, Bloom's posture
of detachment from the worldly political scene is disingenuous at best.
In fact, what lies behind Bloom's fear of what he calls the "relativism" of our times is an awareness of the unraveling of consensus. The
principles that once generated consent are no longer seen as self-
evident; the authority of the permanent and universal truth upon
which the legitimation of the current hegemony depends is no longer
authoritative. Social groups and classes with different needs and different concepts of the social order have found a voice—i.e., they have
their own intellectuals, they have produced their own version of the
worldly reality they inhabit. It is not the case, as Bloom would have
his readers believe, that the intellectuals have betrayed their class by
presenting themselves as defenders and spokesmen of marginalized
social strata in order to enhance their own status. Rather, the subaltern "others" have finally started to produce their own defenders and
spokesmen so that their "otherness" is now hard to ignore. It is this
otherness (which a true democracy should have a place for) that so
profoundly troubles and threatens Allan Bloom that he wants to close
the American mind against it. His bastions are the great books; or,
rather, not so much the great books as his way (and only his way) of
reading and interpreting the great books.

Allan Bloom, William Bennett, and Jackson Bate are convinced
that American society has lost its cohesion because the intellectuals in
the universities have failed to transmit the eternal verities of the
Western tradition of *litterae humaniores*. Gramsci, by contrast, believed that the educational crisis of his time was not the cause but,
rather, a consequence and a reflection of a much broader moral, social, and cultural crisis. Yet, even those who are familiar with Gramsci
often fail to grasp this fundamental point. This is the case, for example, with E. D. Hirsch. Hirsch has written two influential books on the
crisis of the schools in the U.S. The first book, *Cultural Literacy*, was
first published in 1987 (the same year as Bloom's *Closing of the*

American Mind); the second book, *The Schools We Need*, appeared much more recently (1996). Many of Hirsch's admirers and critics have regarded his work and the positions it espouses to be in the same mold as Bloom's. Hirsch himself, however, has repeatedly tried to distance himself from the political conservatism of Bennett and Bloom. He has argued that his socio-political agenda is liberal and progressive; but at the same time he has maintained that progressive social goals can only be achieved through conservative forms of schooling. "I would label myself a political liberal and an educational conservative" (1996, p. 6), he writes. As if to reinforce this point, he dedicates his second book to William Bagley (a scholar in the field of education, and a contemporary of John Dewey's) and to Antonio Gramsci—describing them as "two prophets who explained in the 1930s why the new educational ideas would lead to greater social injustice." Hirsch contends that American education is in ruins because the dominant pedagogy is inspired by a Romanticism which seeks to foster the "natural" aptitudes of the child and has a "deep aversion to and contempt for factual knowledge" (1996, p. 54). The teaching of literacy has become a contentless teaching of skills. But literacy, Hirsch maintains, "is far more than a skill and [. . .] requires large amounts of specific knowledge" (1987, p. 2). The goal, then, is not literacy pure and simple, but "cultural literacy." In other words, Hirsch wants to make sure that all students in the course of their schooling from kindergarten through high school acquire a "cultural baggage," a "national vocabulary," and "a whole system of widely shared information" (1987, p. 103). He calls for a return to the "Ciceronian ideal of universal public discourse" (1987, p. 109). Hirsch is convinced that a common school system (i.e., a national system of education with a common curriculum that is based on the acquisition of shared/common knowledge and not just pure skills) would "create a literate and independent citizenry" (1996, p. 17), and by doing so reinforce democracy. These views, as one can see, are quite similar to some of the ideas expressed by Gramsci in his critique of the *riforma Gentile* (that is, the Fascist overhaul of the Italian educational system implemented by Mussolini's minister of public instruction in 1923).

Why then do leftist critics reject Hirsch's views? The answer is provided by Hirsch himself: "Some have objected that to publish the contents of our national vocabulary would have the effect of promoting the culture of the dominant class at the expense of minority cultures" (1987, p. 103). Hirsch rebuts these criticisms with the following affirmations: "To regard a standardized cultural instrument as a class culture is a facile oversimplification. [. . .] mainstream culture is not a class culture and [. . .] outsiders and newcomers influence its forms as much as they are influenced by it" (1987, p. 104). Here, Hirsch reveals that his knowledge of Gramsci is partial and selective. Nobody familiar with Gramsci's writings on hegemony and subalternity would say that "mainstream culture is not a class culture." Even the so-called "facts" of history are not established and transmitted in a "neutral" manner—on this one can see Gramsci's notes on the Risorgimento, or even his remarks on the history of subaltern social groups. (As Walter Benjamin reminds us, history and tradition in general are always in danger of becoming a tool of the ruling classes.) Nor is this simply a question that concerns the schools. Gramsci has shown us how powerful hegemony is, how it penetrates every aspect of life. The power relations that constitute hegemony cannot be reversed simply through the correction of teaching methods.

Leftist theorists of education are opposed to any form of curriculum based on a uniform canon of "great books" or on a "common cultural vocabulary." They want to discover educational methods that would not result in the uncritical transmission, reproduction, and hence the perpetuation of dominant values and interests. Some of the alternative approaches they offer are sensible. Henry Giroux, for example, has proposed the development of "a critical pedagogy [that] rejects a discourse of value neutrality" (1990, p. 127). In practice, critical pedagogy would do the following: (a) study "the privileged texts of the dominant or official canons" in order to arrive at a better understanding of "the important role they have played in shaping, for better or worse, the major events of our time"; (b) study the "noble traditions, histories and narratives that speak to important struggles by women, blacks, minorities and other subordinate groups that need to be heard so that such groups can lay claim to their own voices as part of a process of both affirmation and inquiry" (p. 126).

The problem is: how does one achieve all this? How does one plan the various stages of the educational process in order to attain this goal? In order to answer these questions, it would help to turn to Gramsci's plan for the common school. There is one point in particular that Gramsci insists on and that needs to be underlined. The basic problem with the educational system, Gramsci observes, is that

> Each social group has its own type of school, intended to perpetuate a specific traditional function, ruling or subordinate. If one wishes to break this pattern one needs, instead of multiplying and grading different types of vocational school, to create a single type of formative school (primary-secondary) which would take the child up to the threshold of his choice of job, forming him during this time as a person capable of thinking, studying, and ruling—or controlling those who rule. (SPN, p. 40; QC, p. 1547)

In most debates on education, there is an underlying assumption that the basic problem identified by Gramsci has been overcome. That is why the main debates have focussed on curricular issues. On the surface, it appears that everyone goes to the same type of school. The reality, however, is different, at least in the United States. There are big disparities between one school and another. Some schools are well funded, others are not. Some schools are almost entirely made up of young people from more or less affluent families. These schools may adopt the same pedagogical methods as the schools populated by the poor and other subordinate groups. Yet, in the rich schools the general atmosphere is infinitely more conducive to learning, for a variety of reasons that need hardly be spelled out. The remedy to this situation cannot be found in curricular reform. It requires a radical transformation of social relations in the nation as a whole. But the will to confront the issue at its basic level is missing. And things are getting worse. The source of the problem, in fact, is the current fashion of exalting civil society—i.e., the drive to dilute the power of intervention of the State. How can the State ensure equal education for all, when it is deprived of the means to do so—both the financial means that come from taxation, and the political means that come from investing the State with a measure of authority?

Our current educational system still educates the few to become the leaders of the future, and the many to become productive, efficient workers. To be sure, many workers in post-Fordist society are in some sense or other "professionals"; they are certified as such by diverse educational institutions. This is a travesty of the concept of "education" as such; and yet even the universities have become for the most part professional schools. What does this mean in a democracy? Gramsci's reflections on this matter are quite disturbing:

> The multiplication of types of professional school tends to perpetuate traditional social differences; but since, within these differences, it tends to encourage internal diversification, it gives the impression of being democratic in tendency. The labourer can become a skilled worker, for instance, the peasant a surveyor or petty agronomist. But democracy, by definition, cannot mean merely that every "citizen" can "govern" and that society places him, even if only abstractly, in a general condition to achieve this. Political democracy tends towards a coincidence of the rulers and the ruled (in the sense of government with the consent of the governed), ensuring for each non-ruler a free training in the skills and general technical preparation necessary to that end. But the type of school which is now developing as the school for the people does not tend even to keep up this illusion. (SPN, pp. 40-41; QC, p. 1547)

According to Gramsci's criteria, we are still a long way from an educational system worthy of a true democracy.

References

Bate, W. J. (1982). The Crisis of English Studies. *Harvard Magazine,* 85 (1), 46-53.

Bennett, W. J. (1984). *To Reclaim a Legacy: Report on the Humanities in Higher Education.* Washington, DC: National Endowment for the Humanities.

Bloom, A. D. (1987). *The Closing of the American Mind: How Higher Education Has Failed Democracy and Impoverished the Souls of Today's Students.* New York: Simon & Schuster.

Giroux, H. A. (1990). Liberal Arts Education and the Struggle for Public Life: Dreaming about Democracy. *South Atlantic Quarterly,* 89 (1), 113-38.

Hirsch, E. D. (1996). *The Schools We Need and Why We Don't Have Them.* New York: Anchor/Doubleday.

Hirsch, E. D. (1987). *Cultural Literacy: What Every American Needs to Know.* Boston: Houghton Mifflin.

Manacorda, M. A. (1976). *Il principio educativo in Gramsci: Americanismo e Conformismo.* Rome: Armando Editore.

Abbreviated Titles

QC: *Quaderni del carcere* (V. Gerratana, Ed.). Edizione critica dell' Istituto Gramsci. 4 vol. Torino: Einaudi (1975).

SPN: *Selections from the Prison Notebooks of Antonio Gramsci* (Q. Hoare & G. Nowell Smith, Eds. and Trans.). London: Lawrence & Wishart (1971).

7

On "A Dog Chasing Its Tail": Gramsci's Challenge to the Sociology of Knowledge

John Baldacchino

Introduction

This essay proposes that a Gramscian analysis of education must take into account those cultural necessities by which the School becomes contingent to what will be referred to as "the parameters of possibility." Within these parameters, education is prefaced by the individual moments of art, so that human expression—and, consequently, education—is distanced from the sociology of knowledge and its simplistic logic.

I will first draw on Croce's distinction between art and the philosophy of history, and how Gramsci's theory of culture runs parallel to it. This is essential to the understanding of Gramsci's stance against economic determinism and its productivist offshoots in art, culture, and, ultimately, education. Gramsci's discussion of art and literature also draws our attention to the sociology of knowledge where, it will be argued, there is a parallel between Adorno's critique of the sociology of knowledge and Gramsci's notion of the representation of history as a series of moments that gain personality on the grounds of individuality and autonomy. This is further tied to Benjamin's philosophy of history and its doubts of any determinist view of progress.

The implication of autonomy in the moments of history takes the argument into the questions of individual makings, as opposed to socialized forms of production. This distinction lies at the heart of Marx's analysis of the alienation of "living labor" and how this analysis goes against the commonplace "progressivist" thread that nurtures the false hopes that such an alienation could be reversed. At this point, this essay forwards Gramsci's notion of an autonomous educational construct and his theory of the disinterested school (*scuola disinteressata*) wherein any hope of mechanistic reversal is confronted and denounced as a tautological illusion.

Representation, Judgement, and Totality

Somewhere in his *Notebooks*, Gramsci raises the issue of literary crisis and the criteria by which an epoch makes its mark. Being an epoch—*essere un'epoca*—is another way of trying to explain the making of an age as something that gains autonomy for those who live the age in question: "The absence of an artistic order [. . .] tallies with the absence of a moral and intellectual order; that is, with an absence of an organic historical development. Society turns on itself like a dog chasing its tail, but this impression of movement stands for no development" (Gramsci, 1975a, p. 25).

Gramsci's comment is set against Arturo Calza's and Roberto Forges Davanzati's laments over what they saw as a crisis in Italian literature at the beginning of the twentieth century. Their laments merely prompted Gramsci's ironic remark: "*Quante parole inutili tra il Calza e il Forges Davanzati.*" In view of Gramsci's other literary observations, this was most typical. He concludes that Calza and Davanzati were missing the forest for the trees because they could not see the link between the arts and what makes an epoch as culture, as history—and, we may dare add, as education. The absence of an artistic order places no fault of its own on literature or any other forms of representation, because this absence cannot be found within literary or artistic parameters. The "fault" is not found in the arts but in the lack of an organic development in history. Without this form of development, art has no autonomy and could never signify its specificity. The crisis is primarily symptomatic of this absence and not the other way around. Failing to make it as an age implies, by default, society's failure to stop chasing its tail.

To be able to argue this case, Gramsci places his judgement on the parameters of the possible: a possibility that claims its own forms of autonomous development. One also notes that Gramsci's argument echoes Croce, who wrote that:

> Art is not mere representation, but a representation that can judge and bring together pace and value to things, charging them with the light of the universal. This theory may still face a single, yet uttermost difficulty, from which it emerges intact: where judgmental representation is no longer art, but historical judgement—or better, history. Indeed history could not be maintained anymore as it used to—as a mere and base assertion of facts; but here, judgement, or judgmental representation, is identifiable with philosophy, the so-called "philosophy of history," and never with art. (1994, p. 150)

In Croce's mind, there were two pitfalls to avoid: (a) the confusion between art and the philosophy of history, and (b) the mistake by which romantic aesthetics took judgement away from art and consigned it to the fantasies of feeling *per se*. Croce rightly concluded that if art's judgmental act mimicked those of the philosophy of history, it would not only become ahistorical but would lose its ability to mediate the subject with the object. In other words, human forms of representation would be ancillary to the objective world, and would either be expected to do miracles (as some kind of immanent magic)—so as to leap into being an epoch; or remain secondary to the historic necessities of the time—by relying on the epoch to give them being. Croce argued that while the problem of romantic aesthetics was partly solved by the recognition of art's judgmental nature via history, submitting art to "epistemological simplicity" (*semplicismo gnoseologico*) and "exclusive logicism" (*esclusivo logicismo*) remained a dangerous prospect.

Gramsci followed a similar line of thinking when he argued that the artistic process demonstrates "especially in the philosophy of praxis, the fatuous idiocy of parrots who believe that their little stereotypical formulae hold the key to all doors. Two authors may well represent the same sociohistorical moment, but while one may be an artist, the other's work may be nonsense." If one tries to solve the problem by "limiting oneself to a description of what they both represent or express socially" and by trying to itemize the characteristics of a common social-historical moment, this would leave us nowhere nearer to the problem of art (Gramsci, 1975a, p. 4). Which brings us back to Croce when he says: "It is intrinsically inconceivable that in artistic representation one could ever affirm mere particularity, individual abstraction, or finitude in its finality. When it looks as if this could happen—and in some ways it really happens—representation is not artistic, or at least not entirely" (Croce,

1994, pp. 152-53). When it comes to explaining the intrinsic relationship between the particular and the universal within the contexts of art, Gramsci's stand is clearly in favor of the specificity of the arts and their autonomous relationship with culture. In his analysis one can see with what care he maintains a balance between the totality partaken by art, and how art is appraised in its autonomous specificity. Gramsci unequivocally maintains that it would be absurd to struggle for the creation of new individual artists "because artists cannot be created artificially." Instead, "one must speak of the struggle for a new culture, that is, for a new moral life which cannot but be tied to a new intuition of life *until it becomes a new way of feeling and seeing reality* and thus a world intimately made natural with 'possible artists' and 'possible works of art'" (Gramsci, 1975a, pp. 8-9, my emphasis).

Gramsci operates on a line of thinking that is distinct from both idealism and materialist historicism. This may explain why he often shared a platform with secularists and liberals like Piero Gobetti. Yet, one hastens to add that Gramsci's engagement in the struggle for a new culture remained at a distance from that of liberals and secularists. Be that as it may, Gramsci's opposition to those who equated literary activity with political activity, was as secularist as it could be:

> Insofar as the political person exerts pressure so that the art of the time becomes an expression of a determined cultural world, it is a political act, and not artistic critique: if the cultural world for which one struggles is at all a living and necessary fact, there will be no resistance to its outcome. It will itself see to its own artists. (Gramsci, 1975a, p. 12)

It is by now clear that Gramsci never could have proffered a productivist view of art, culture, or education. This is confirmed by his active engagement with the works of authors like Luigi Pirandello and Italo Svevo, sharing a secularist view that was not at all distanced from Gobetti's. This understanding emerged from Gramsci's recognition of the relationship between history, culture, and the arts, pretty much in the way Croce reasserts art's specificity and the relationship between form's autonomy and its intrinsic historicity.[1] Where Gramsci parts with the Liberal view is in the polity by which the (historic) totality actively partakes of historical change. However, Gramsci's critique of Croce is never prompted by any productivist obligation. Rather, it is charged by his quest for a historic (read also: *revolutionary*) realization of human potentiality.

Though incisively critical of the Liberal and Catholic traditions, Gramsci could never dismiss the centrality of these narratives. This is where the emancipatory nature of his critique lies. As Berlinguer reminds us, Gramsci's Marxist stance is genuine and rigorous precisely because, while contesting other ideas, he always kept in mind that in the other's stance there was always a nucleus of truth which one needs to recognize in order to reach a full understanding of society and history (1985, pp. 276-77). This will come as no surprise to those who, like Berlinguer, have always recognized the autonomous evaluation and participation of knowledge, and kept their views at a considerable distance from simplistic epistemologism.

Knowing History

An analysis that claims a Gramscian ground needs to be precise in how to go about the business of citing Gramsci as "Gramscian." This is no play of words, especially when "post-Marxism" has more than one lesson to teach in similar respects vis-à-vis "the Marxists" and their tradition. If this has managed to highlight anything with respect to the "historicist" argument, it is that the historicization of discourse needs to distinguish between dialectics and sociology:

> A dialectical theory is bound—like Marx's, largely—to be immanent even if in the end it negates the whole sphere it moves in. This contrasts it with a sociology of knowledge that has been merely brought up from outside and is powerless against philosophy, as philosophy was quick to discover. (Adorno, 1990, p. 197)

If knowledge were to be taken away from a sociology whose "type of positivist economics" brought society into "nothing but the average value of individual reactive modes" (Adorno, 1990, p. 198), where would one place history? In other words, if one accepts Adorno's distinction between dialectics and the sociology of knowledge, how would one start to define history? In attempting to find an answer, I propose to employ two (related) notions of history: Gramsci's and that of Walter Benjamin.

Gramsci argues that "every determined socio-historical moment is never homogeneous, but rich in contradictions." It acquires personality and becomes a moment of development "by the very fact that in it certain fundamental activities in life predominate over others, representing a historical 'peak' (*una 'punta' storica*)." In all this, Gramsci holds one major reservation: If one were to recognize history as a series of historical peaks, then one has to presuppose "a hierarchy, a contrast, a struggle." Gramsci's difficulty with a supposition of this sort lies in how to judge other activities that are equally represented in history, even when it is evident that history is a series of representative moments that give it personality. Indeed, aren't all moments representative of history? And isn't it also true that a historical moment may well be reactionary and anachronistic? (cf. Gramsci, 1975a, p. 5). With these questions, Gramsci challenges those who would readily align progress with history, as if the latter could presuppose the former and vice versa. If one were to accept this interchangeable equivalence, then one would also have to accept that a reactionary moment (which is undeniably a moment of history) could be absolved *a priori* (and consequently "justified") as some determined function of progress.

As in his resistance to any determinist equivalence between art and a presumed political act, Gramsci could never accept any interchangeable equivalence between a "hierarchy" of historical moments and a presumed teleology. Even when a reactionary moment in history remains representative of a particular time and place, it cannot be redeemed by an act of sociological equivalence. Like Adorno, Gramsci could never agree with sociological determinism.

In his fourteenth thesis on the philosophy of history, Walter Benjamin cites Karl Kraus's maxim: "Origin is the goal." Benjamin goes on to propose that "history is the subject of a structure whose site is not homogeneous, empty time, but time filled by the presence of the now" (1973, pp. 252-53). This is anticipated by his ninth thesis on the philosophy of history, which figures Paul Klee's *Angelus Novus* as the angel of history by whose open mouth and spread wings he contemplates history, "his face turned towards the past":

> Where we perceive a chain of events, he sees one single catastrophe which keeps piling wreckage upon wreckage and hurls it in front of his feet. The angel would like to stay, awaken the dead, and make whole what has been smashed. But a storm is blowing from Paradise; it has got caught in his wings with such violence that the angel can no longer close them. This storm irresistibly propels him into the future to which his back is turned, while the pile of debris before him grows skyward. This storm is what we call progress. (1973, p. 249)

A storm of debris could only produce further debris, even when the historicist claim may well be that it represents history as a homogenous moment above all others. Conversely, in the heterogeneous realization of its quantity, the storm could become "common sense" because it is representative of a historical moment, but in its representation it cannot retain a hierarchical domain over other moments of history. One may remark that while a sociology of knowledge would take an average of history's diverse moments as an identitarian moment of history, the dialectic of knowledge makes such an apparent homogeneity impossible. What Gramsci terms the heterogeneity of the historical moment, also figures in Benjamin as a structure of a time "filled by the presence of the now." Here, the now is the moment; it gains personality; it is representative; and it figures a historical peak—but, unlike any sociological averaging, its individuality is assumed on the ground of a diversity of such moments, of such "nows." This gives ground to a hypothetical dialogue between two points of view, where both Gramsci and Benjamin construe history as preclusive of any sociological imperative.

In seeing a homogeneous site as "empty," Benjamin also recalls history as a site where the now distils the distance between origin and end, between *arché* and *telos*. When *arché* becomes *telos,* history would be rightly seen as that rejection of history—negatively dialecticized, one may say—and thrown at the feet of the debris which positive historicists accumulate, rationalize, and assume as progress. Benjamin's contestation of this form of certainty turns political:

> One reason why Fascism has a chance is that in the name of progress its opponents treat it as a historical norm. The current amazement that the things we are experiencing are "still" possible in the twentieth century is *not* philosophical. This amazement is not the beginning of knowledge—unless it is the knowledge that the view of history which gives rise to it is untenable. (1973, p. 249)

In its functionalist equivalence, the sociology of knowledge makes the excuse "that the truth or untruth of philosophical teaching has nothing to do with social conditions." Adorno shows how, in this excuse, the sociology of knowledge attempts to conceal the fact that, backstage, "relativism allies itself with the division of labor" (Adorno, 1990, p. 198). It is interesting to note that in both Gramsci's and Benjamin's definitions of history, this alliance is precluded. As to why and how this happens, one needs to go back to Marx and identify a further distinction which challenges any linear notion of change—that between making and production.

Making *contra* Production

I have distanced Gramsci's view of art and history from the productivist assumption of progress in anticipation of my assessment of his challenge to the sociology of knowledge vis-à-vis his *pedagogic* vision. Here, I emphasize the word "pedagogic" in its continental, not Anglo-Saxon, sense. In its Greek original meaning as *paideía* and *agogí*, pedagogy carries an ontological implication, which is not found in the Anglo-Saxon operative meaning of "pedagogy" as "*a technique of teaching.*" As "a technique of teaching" pedagogy operates on the polity of the School, and functions to the School's epistemological standardization. In every effect, the positivist objectives of "efficiency" in the current jargon of the School are still

measured by a Benthamite apriorism of need. As in the early notions
of utilitarian planning, the modern School operates on a selection of
knowledge and ability that responds to an economic interest falsely
presented as some kind of "personal and individual need." What this
really implies in the contemporary School is a profile of education
that tallies with predetermined and fixed schemata as assumed and
canonized by the polity's educational blue-print.[2]

It is interesting to note how the School's socialization of knowledge is promoted by liberal conservatives and social democrats alike
in their efforts to eradicate what they see as "a crisis in education"
(which they back by statistical evidence of low achievement in
literacy and numeracy skills). It is also tacitly accepted that a "historical" fault lies with "radical" and "progressive" forms of pedagogy
which, according to the postmonetarist wise men of education, lost
their focus on what is now quantified as "target-attainments" or
"levels of competence."

Beyond this argument, one could conclude that in both cases the
issue of pedagogy in its ontological—and entelecheic—senses has
been sidelined. To put it in Gramscian words, the hegemonic assumption of education today is still alienated by the fact that in the main,
state education is operated by an interested form of schooling that is
socially engineered by a supply-oriented curriculum. On the other
hand, it has always been a tacit understanding that academic disinter-
estedness would be preserved for those who enjoy its privileges—whether in free grammar schools and so-called "Beacon
Schools," or, indeed, in fee-paying private schools.[3]

However, one hastens to add that as far as the "classical" argument against elitism and selectivity can go, it adds nothing to the
critique of educationist functionalism by which the School currently
consolidates productivist standardization. One must note that the
constant panegyrics against selectivity by the grand apostles of
comprehensive schooling have blatantly failed to recognize that what
they offered as a "solution" to selectivity was founded on a sociology
of knowledge geared to a view of progress whose Saint-Simonist
imprint—though now virtually invisible—is equally sustained by the
Benthamite *raison d'être* which nurtures the educational policies of
Tories and New Labour in contemporary Britain. Indeed, the tautological predicament of any "progressive" educational thinking remains such that it is still played on the same functionalist and conservative score.

This takes us to the relevance of Gramsci's pedagogical discourse,
and how it invites us to a leap of faith as far as the organization of
culture and the school are concerned. More importantly, it challenges
our very understanding of knowledge in its pedagogical relationship

with history. Let us reconsider pedagogy as *agogí*—as "a manner of life," "a direction," and a "way of leading." This incremental notion of pedagogy takes learning into the organizational strategies adopted by the understanding of the world in its fulfilment. Furthermore, because it operates on a notion of history as making and not as a linear development of production, it takes a dialectical view of history where knowledge is perceived as a ground for possibility. The Aristotelian character of this pedagogical process and of history as making, must be set squarely behind Marx's theory of labor, especially when Gramsci's works are read in the light of Marx's *Grundrisse* where the theory of labor is presented in its entelecheic origin.

Labor as making—as opposed to labor as production—provides a focus by which one can distinguish between the identitarian dialectic of the sociology of knowledge and the recognition of a possible nonidentitarian dialectic. Here, I draw attention to Marx's discussion of the alienation of what he calls *living labor*:

> The objective conditions of living labor appear as *separated, independent* values opposite living labor capacity as subjective being, which therefore appears to them only as a value of *another kind* (not as value, but different from them, as use value). Once this separation is given, the production process can only produce it anew, reproduce it, and reproduce it on an expanded scale. [. . .] What is reproduced and produced anew is not only *the presence* of these objective conditions of living labor, *but also their presence as independent values, i.e. values belonging to an alien subject, confronting this living labor capacity.* The objective conditions of labor attain a subjective existence *vis-à-vis* living labor capacity—capital turns into capitalist; on the other side, the merely subjective presence of the labor capacity confronted by its own conditions gives it a merely indifferent, objective form as against them—it is merely a *value of* a particular use value *alongside* the conditions of its own realization as *values* of another use value. Instead of their being realized in the production process as the conditions of its realization, what happens is quite the opposite: it comes out of the process as mere condition for *their* realization and preservation as values for themselves opposite living labor capacity. (1973, pp. 461-62)

This is Marx's argument for labor as making—i.e., as living labor. Living labor is the direct opposite of productively subjectified labor—i.e., labor accumulated as capital. Elsewhere, Marx (1973, p. 297) argues that capital "confronts the *totality* of all labors *dunámei*"—i.e., all different forms of labor in their potentiality. This is possible because as potentiality, living labor is a representation of labor in its totality. Capital confronts and ultimately alienates living labor by appropriating its potentiality. Capital appropriates labor's productive actuality and realizes it for itself as external accumulation. In this process, the realization of labor is not only hegemonized as (and turned into) production, but capital turns the fulfilment of human labor into a subjectivity that is deprived of its object. In this way, capital transforms the dialectic of living labor into a tautological cycle. It also fixes the vitality of living labor into a functional sociology that backs the totality. The antinomic vitality of labor's potentiality (originally found in labor's potentiality as a subject-object antinomy) is reduced to an identitarian construct where labor functions as a subject-*qua*-subject. Thus, Marx concludes: "the objective conditions of living labor appear as *separated, independent* values opposite living labor capacity as subjective being" (Marx, cit.).

The Left's classical "sociological" solution has always proposed the reversal of this alienation—whether by the Welfare State's amends, or (more unlikely) via a revolution. Indeed, had this been an identitarian process of alienation, the potentiality of living labor could well be retraceable to its origin (as a making) and re-emancipated. However, Marx has shown that contrary to what the sociology of knowledge purports, labor cannot be reassembled positively, because the tautological subjectification of living labor by capital forecloses any retraceable origin: "the merely subjective presence of the labor capacity confronted by its own conditions gives it a merely indifferent, objective form as against them" (Marx, cit.).

As the origin of this foreclosure, the indifference of subjectified labor is attained by the same indifference with which capital confronts labor's potentiality where "the particular one it confronts at a given time is an accidental matter" (Marx, 1973, p. 296). This contingent nature of capital's confrontation may sound contradictory in itself, only if one forgets that, as a totality, capital encompasses labor across all of its specific moments by foreclosing labor's mediational capacity. Marx's analysis argues that capital reroutes the fulfilment of labor as a making (as living value) and takes it into the productive particularity of use value. The making becomes a product, and living value is sold as use value. Moreover, the foreclosure of the making's entelecheic process is not done quantitatively and selectively. To the contrary, what power of fulfilment living labor may have had for itself in full freedom and power, before its value became subjectified use-value, is cut off qualitatively by dint of capital's totality. Here the antinomic origin of living labor (as a subject-object antinomy) is posited and identified with the tautological socialization of its value. Ultimately, the hegemony—be it economic, cultural, social, and even pedagogical—is founded on a truth-value whose identitarian origin bears all the hallmarks of capital's tautology.

Because the dialectic by which capital has alienated labor was seen by the Left as a quantitative hegemonic mechanism, the tautological nature of capital was wrongly assumed as a reversible process whose identitarian mechanism could re-emancipate living labor with its original potentiality. Here lies the trap of the dialectical tautology of capital: the assumption of hegemonic alienation and the equal hope that it could be unravelled by its own rules is itself further fuel to the productive subjectification of living labor by its own object—capital. To put it mildly, capital made sure that the assumed implements of revolution—be they communist, social democratic, reformist, or other—would guarantee the positivity of its dialectic, so that it could secure the tautological implements by which it confronted labor's entelecheic individuality.

Gramsci's Nonidentitarian Challenge

It is with this process in mind that I finally come to Gramsci's notion of "the disinterested school." Here, I would argue that Gramsci's notion of hegemony with respect to education is contradictory by dint of the assumption that any argument for a "common schooling" (una *scuola unica*) must emerge from the recognition of knowledge as entelecheic—i.e., as a form of knowledge that has to address the process between potentiality and actuality. Contrary to a sociology of knowledge, an entelecheic consideration of knowledge necessitates a pedagogic construct that would originate from the idea that the potentiality of labor as making can only be realized if it has the understanding of its autonomy. As with the arts, the autonomy of this understanding could only emerge when, among other forms of social mechanisms, education is founded on the universal right to a disinterested school.

As a young socialist, Gramsci had already matured in his humanist understanding of the revolutionary praxis of education when he argued that "it is necessary for the proletariat to have a disinterested school" (*"al proletariato è necessaria una scuola disinteressata"*) (Gramsci, 1964, p. 227), which John Mathews mistranslates as "What the proletariat needs is an educational system that is open to all" (cf. Gramsci, 1977, p. 26). The difference between a "disinterested school" and a "school open to all" lies in the qualitative context which, as we have seen above, is often missed when the question of reform is taken into account. If the question was that of an equal right to schooling, then the argument is one for comprehensiveness and against selection—a quantitative right for which New Labour makes the case when the British Prime Minister, Tony Blair, rightly argues that all children should be able to read, write, and be numerate.

Gramsci's call for a right to a disinterested school, however, is concerned with more than an ability to meet standardized quantities. The call for a disinterested school is a qualitative right that attaches its strategies to an immanent form of knowledge that could confront (and short circuit) the alliance between relativism and division of labor. In Gramsci's account, a disinterested school is meant as a humanist school: "a school which does not mortgage the child's future, a school that does not force the child's will, his intelligence and growing awareness to run along tracks to a predetermined station" (Gramsci, 1977, ibid.). Indeed, in this statement, Gramsci is precluding any equivalence between a quantitative moment of education (as prescribed in a National Curriculum) and a sociological prescription of knowledge (as articulated by academic and vocational qualifications). Gramsci calls for a heterogeneous and, hence, an individualized view that responds to the child's own individual needs—i.e., a form of living knowledge that is entelecheically construed. In this distinction, there could be no clearer argument against the alliance between relativism and division of labor where education becomes itself a hegemonic contradiction where the quality of capital is confronted by the (diametrically opposed) quality of entelecheic knowledge. In his Aristotelian understanding of education, Gramsci—unlike contemporary sociologists of knowledge—fights fire with fire, quality with quality.

The question of education is becoming ever more critical in the face of the draconian measures by which, at least in Britain, schooling and teacher training have been functionalized and knowledge depreciated. Had this been just a matter of standardization, then those who are opposed to its productivist sociology would be able to sabotage and secure its reformation. But, here, we are talking of a process that is tautologically foreclosed by a system where the entelecheic meanings and application of pedagogy are sealed forever into the triumphal quantum which Fukuyama (1992) hailed as capital's last word on history.

If we are at all interested in Gramsci's ideas, we have at hand a situation that Gramsci had a lot to comment about; something he anticipated when he witnessed how epistemological freedom was abolished in education and left to "only few versions reduced to the service of a tiny elite of ladies and gentlemen with no worries about a future career" (Gramsci, 1975b, p. 126). The thriving of private schooling surely does not lie solely with the power to buy intellectual capital for the select few who can afford it. If this were the case, then the Welfare State was a failure from the start by not seeing how simple it would be to throw money and achieve results (and, indeed, some still harbor that illusion). The issue goes deeper.

What freedom the money of the wealthy could buy is that of retaining the entelecheic fulfilment of living labor for themselves, while playing the game of sociology with the rest. Indeed, "the rest" were often keen to oblige in their fideist assaults on anything they deemed "conservative" or "selective" and failed to see that by doing so they were merely consolidating the elite's privilege. While liberals and socialists, armed with the fallacy of the sociology of knowledge, waged war on what they saw as a reversible selectivity, the elites were spared from curricular engineering, keeping for themselves the right to a humanist notion that their "opponents" happily denounced as "bourgeois." The failure to perceive how lost was the cause of those who fruitlessly fought for a standardized (misread as an "egalitarian") system, could only prove that Gramsci's judgement remains valid to this day: that the dog's attraction to its tail remains a source of "progress" could only confirm that society still basks in its own tautological illusions.

Notes

1. It is not the purpose of this essay to ascertain whether Gramsci was a Crocean in this context, but it is very relevant to note that he placed a high value on Croce's stand in this respect. This is evident when he quotes Croce on the pedagogic role of art and comments that this fits well within the remit of historical materialism (cf. Gramsci, 1975a, p. 10). The same is true of Gramsci's appraisal of De Sanctis's notion of culture as a "concept of life and man" that was coherent, unified, and intended to be spread on a national scale. Unlike the exclusivist concept of the Right, De Sanctis's notion of culture was intended to organize the cultured classes of Naples and bring them nearer to the people (cf. Gramsci, 1975a, pp. 3-4). For Gramsci, De Sanctis's valorization of culture was not intended as a levelling down of all into one form of "popular culture," but a recognition of the various trends that have to come together, without neutralizing each other as the conservative Right, and later Fascist corporativism, intended.

2. In Britain, the blueprint culture is epitomized in the power wrenched by *Quasi Autonomous Non-Governmental Organisations* (Quangos) whose jurisdiction often supersedes that of the Civil Service by directly responding to Secretaries of State, who, by their own initial appointment, are hardly inclined to oppose any Quango decision. The quangoist legacy in Education is one of the most authoritarian—the *Office for Standards in Education* (Ofsted), flanked by other Quangos like the Teacher Training Agency (TTA), holds immense power over all Educational Institutions, from childcare, nurseries, schools, up to Teacher Training at the University level (for which it sets specific standards that it defends as sacrosanct blueprints of progress). It will take time to assess appropriately how much the TTA's standardization will impoverish the teaching profession and education in general.

3. Although paying lip service to the antiselectivity lobby in the Labour and Liberal parties, the New Labour Government is currently proposing the development of what are being called "Beacon Schools," which are meant (in theory) to be "Centres of Educational Excellence." Beacon Schools would serve as models for teachers and pupils in other schools, setting "high standards" for everyone to see. Given that these schools will have extra funding and direct support, and in view of the fact that they mainly correspond to middle-class areas, it has been argued that Beacon Schools are no different from the old Grammar Schools, and that, in its promotion of such schools, the New Labour Government is introducing selectivity by stealth.

References

Adorno, T. (1990). *Negative Dialectics*. London: Routledge.

Benjamin, W. (1973). *Illuminations* (H. Arendt, Ed.). Glasgow: Fontana/Collins.

Berlinguer, E. (1985). La lezione di Gramsci. *Critica Marxista*, 2-3, 274-86.

Croce, B. (1994). *Breviario di estetica. Estetica in nuce*. Milano: Adelphi.

Fukuyama, F. (1992). *The End of History and the Last Man*. New York: Free.

Gramsci, A. (1977). *Selections from Political Writings (1910-1920)* (Q. Hoare, Ed. and J. Mathews, Trans.). London: Lawrence & Wishart.

Gramsci, A. (1975a). *Letteratura e vita nazionale*. Torino: Editori Riuniti.

Gramsci, A. (1975b). *Gli intellettuali*. Torino: Editori Riuniti.

Gramsci, A. (1964). Uomini o macchine? In G. Ferrata & N. Gallo (Eds.), *2000 Pagine Di Gramsci* (Vol. 1, pp. 226-28) Milano: Il Saggiatore.

Marx, K. (1973). *Grundrisse* (M. Nicolaus, Trans.). New York: Vintage.

8

The Specter of Gramsci: Revolutionary Praxis and the Committed Intellectual

Peter McLaren, Gustavo Fischman, Silvia Serra, and Estanislao Antelo

Introduction

The posthumous birth of Antonio Gramsci in the works of the British and North American New Left theorists over the last twenty years has left an impressive and important legacy. The contemporary debates that it has provoked—about the saliency of the term "articulation"; the conceptual status of the term "ideology" in relation to that of discourse; the political import of the "new times" project of analyzing and regulating capitalism via the flow of finance and post-Fordist capitalist formations and the concomitant changes these formations have brought about in social, political, and cultural life; the rise of the metropolitan service class and the overall decomposition of social class as the main axis of politics; the question of whether the social totality is an open field or structured by the determining lines of force of material relations; the positionality of politics within a network of strategies and powers and their articulations—are as variable as they are important (see Harris, 1992). However, it is not the purpose of this chapter to map the shifting trajectories of these debates, except to note a general one that has emerged from them: Given current structural and conjunctural conditions such as the capitalization of global culture, the privatization of subjectivity, and the moral collapse of social democracy after the defeat of communism, should the role of Gramsci's "organic" intellectual primarily be restricted to practicing "cultural politics," or should the Gramscian agent challenge the pernicious power of capital? In other words, to what extent has Gramsci's work remained at the level of methodological idealism with respect to a neo-Gramscian privileging of culture over structure? To what extent have the entire dynamics of subjectivity been commodified, including those very faculties of self-reflexivity that might enable the masses to disturb official culture and rebel against such commodification? In this essay, we shall argue that (in the face of the global restructuring of accumulation, the financescape of "high octane" capitalism, and the blandishments of "free market authoritarianism," and in the midst of the current embattlement of the culture/ideology of consumerism and individualism within neocapitalist technoculture) revisiting Gramsci's ideas can provide important resources and inspiration for teachers as they attempt to transform schools into sites of radical reform within "real existing capitalist societies."

Today's commodity culture provides an urgent backdrop for revisiting Gramsci, especially his work on the role of the intellectual. De Azua (1996) has described the intellectual as someone who consults the dead. However, in the light of current metropolitan life, does this not necessarily imply several paradoxes? Haven't present-day intellectuals spent more time and energy trying to get an "advertising" spot in tabloids, instant sound-bite news commentary, and television talk shows instead of using those media as forums for critique and analysis? A second paradox results from the rather simple observation that talking with the dead is impossible. It is impossible because death implies closure and ending. Death "does not conceal any mystery, does not open any door. It is the end of the human being. What survives [. . .] is what is given to other human beings, what remains in their memories" (Elias, cited in Eribon, 1992, p. 100). Yet, what is not considered in Elias's remark is the presence of the dead through their ability to haunt and influence the living, and thus the tremendous and tremulous power of their spectral essence. What do we make of such specters haunting us as intellectuals, teachers, and activists, as we struggle with the limitations of contemporary social theory and social activism?

Haunting and Talking to Specters

In *The Communist Manifesto* (1848), Karl Marx and Friedrich Engels write that "the specter" of communism is haunting Europe; 148 years later, Jacques Derrida (1996) defines the term "specter" as the frequency of a certain visibility—the visibility of the invisible, as if the specter were projected on an imaginary screen (for our purposes this screen is composed of the pedagogical discourses of the contemporary educational left). The specter sees us before we see it. It pre-exists our consciousness, puts us under surveillance, and can violently repay us a visit. It occupies a social mode or style of haunting that demands to be understood in the singularity of its temporality or historicity (which for us seems too eerily close to Nietzsche's eternal return of the same).

Whereas Marx and Engels call for the specter of communism to become a living reality, a concrete presence on the stage of world history, Derrida examines the "specters of Marx" as "the persistence of a present past, the return of the dead which the worldwide work of mourning cannot get rid of, whose return it runs away from, which it *chases* (excludes, banishes, and at the same time pursues)" (1995, p. 101). For Derrida, Marxism is a discourse whose finality is interrupted by its own haunting of the present. Derrida believes that Marx wanted to replace the ghost of communism with the living presence of communism. Just as capitalist states feared the ghosts of communism, so Marx apparently fears the ghost of communism's "other." In *Specters of Marx*, Derrida accuses Marx of fearing spectrality, of wanting to rid society of its ghosts altogether in order to raise his own philosophy to the status of ontology (Lewis, 1997). Derrida wishes to replace Marxist ontology with hauntology—yet, paradoxically, the entire project of *Specters of Marx* is to exorcise the ghost of Marx, to blast Marx from the rock of living history. In this deconstruction as exorcism, Derrida disavows class struggle and establishes an International built on the unfinalizability of discourses and the impossibility of political coordination. It is here that Derrida betrays a voguish dissidence, a fashionable apostasy, an insurgent posturing in his preoccupation for celebrating the incommensurability of discourses. Uninterested in class politics, Derrida forecloses the possibility of mounting a program of anticapitalist struggle. Marx saw vividly in a way that Derrida does not that discourses always converge and pivot around objective labor practices and that global capitalism has a way of reshaping, reinflecting, and rearticulating dissent. Consequently, Derrida's cosmopolitan deconstructionist efforts to establish a "hauntology" fit securely within the manageable compass of business interests and a corporate-sponsored rebellion. And, while they unsettle and decenter the dusty elitism of canonical tomes of Western Enlightenment thinking, aloof and posturing on varnished bookshelves, the conditions of life and action that structure our everyday lives through exchange value and labor are rarely, if ever, deeply challenged.

Fixation on the dead can embalm the spirit of the living and often signals the other face of the cynicism we harbor about the living. We need not be impeccably reverential in our role as translators of the dead since our unswerving loyalty is neither to the dead nor to the living; our role is to disinter the unsaid so as to provoke an awakening of critical self-consciousness. Avery Gordon (1997) develops a "spectral sociology" that takes such "structuring conditions" of everyday life more seriously than Derrida. She maintains that "haunting" is a "constituent element of modern social life," a "generalizable social phenomenon of great import." Hers is a spectral sociology or hauntology that "looks for a language for identifying haunting and for writings with the ghosts any haunting inevitably throws up" (p. 7). For Gordon, ghosts are the remains of a history of unaddressed social injustices that have been spectacularly and systematically suppressed in mainstream sociological thinking. Gordon describes haunting in a haunted society as an objective force. It is the moment of mediation that she believes exceeds both psychoanalysis and Marxism. She writes:

Haunting [. . .] is precisely what prevents rational detachment, prevents your willful control, prevents the desegregation of class struggle and your feelings, motivations, blind spots, craziness, and desires. A haunted society is full of ghosts, and the ghost always carries the message—albeit not in the form of the academic treatise, or the clinical case study, or the polemical broadside, or the mind-numbing factual report—that the gap between personal and social, public and private, objective and subjective is misleading in the first place. That is to say, it is leading you elsewhere, it is making you see things you did not see before, it is making an impact on you; your relation to things that seemed separate or invisible is changing. This is not to say that the gap or the reification is not an enormously powerful real experience. Nor is it to say that haunting somehow transcends the actually existing social relations in which we live, think, and think up new concepts and visions of life. Quite the contrary. But these questions remain: what effectively describes the gap as an organized and elaborate symptom, and what describes the moment when we understand that it is, in fact, misleading us? (p. 98)

Hauntings, as we intend the term, have little to do with the ectoplasm of Ouija board conjurers in rhinestone turbans, but rather refer to dangerous memories that live in the structural unconscious of humanity. It is the task of the intellectual to set these ghostly memories on fire so that they irrupt to haunt the social consciousness of the living. That is, the intellectual does not function to exorcise ghosts but to give ghosts the necessary materiality so that we recognize them and have the opportunity to understand their meaning. An intellectual is an artisan and a laborer who works with inherited memories, recollections of that stuff of which we are constituted. Yet, death and memory only speak about heritage. Heritage, however, has been described by Derrida (1994) as something not related to what is given and easily transmitted but is a neverending labor. Heritage involves infinite operations of acquisition. We agree with Derrida on this point. But let us now bring the conversation closer to our main theme: that of education. We recognize that if heritage implies intellectual labor and operations of acquisition, these tasks must, at the same time, be eminently pedagogical. In this sense, then, an educator is a carrier of culture, a dealer, a "smuggler of memories" (Hassoun, 1996)—a smuggler who testifies, gives testimonies, and shapes words. An intellectual speaks through the lips of the dead and serves as the medium through which subjugated histories are released into the present. Yet, it is precisely the intellectual who is most at risk for failing to give voice to the specters of history. This is because, for Derrida, scholars feel that looking is sufficient and are singularly incapable of entering into a dialogue with a ghost. Derrida writes:

> As theoreticians or witnesses, spectators, observers, and intellectuals, scholars believe that looking is sufficient. Therefore, they are not always in the most competent position to do what is necessary: speak to the specter. [. . .] A traditional scholar does not believe in ghosts—nor in all that could be called the virtual space of spectrality. (1995, p. 11)

The dead are not only visited by us; their ghosts also attempt to be hauntingly present among us. To talk to the dead is not to visit them and reverentially offer their ghosts our most sincere homage. It is to press them for answers, for explanations; it is to demand that they give us reasons for why they haunt us. The dead to whom we wish to speak—not as scholars but as social agents who care about education—are the spirits of Antonio Gramsci, for it is certainly true that Gramsci is not one but many spirits. There are the Gramscian spirits that haunt the cultural Marxists, the orthodox "manifesto Marxists," the "post-Marxists," and the "other than Marxists" who occupy the North and South American educational Left. The ghosts of Gramsci haunt teachers working in public schools who have been reduced to a fetishized form of hypostasized public service clerks. And they haunt us, the educators of the educators, those of us who are paid by the State to teach the clerks of the new internal colonies of hegemonized memory. For some of us, the surviving ideas of Gramsci become the ghosts of memory that we must confront in order to understand our own histories. For others, they represent a ghoulish voice from the past that threatens the foundations of our moral, ethical, and political lives and our studied complacency as citizens. As critical educators, we are concerned with speaking to both the ghosts and the ghouls of Gramsci on specific issues surrounding the role of the educator as intellectual, as activist, as someone engaged in organic praxis, and in revolutionary struggle.

Talking to the Specter of Gramsci

Gramsci studied historical linguistics at Turin University, but abandoned his studies in favor of working full time on the paper *Avanti!* Inspired by the Russian Revolution, he became involved with the Turin factory council movement (at a time when thousands of workers from Italian industrial cities occupied their factories), and was greatly influenced by the work of Italian idealist philosopher Benedetto Croce. In 1919, he helped to found the socialist paper *L'Ordine Nuovo*, with its motto: "Pessimism of the intellect, optimism of the will." Determined to break with the Second International Marxism and social Darwinism, Gramsci became involved with rethinking Marxist philosophical formulations that were developing from the Third International. He spent the 1920s involved in the Italian revolutionary movement as leader of the Communist Party. In 1922, he was an Italian Communist Party delegate on the Executive Committee of the Communist Third International in Moscow. In 1922, Mussolini took power, began arresting Communist leaders, and, in a relatively short time, defeated the Italian proletariat drive for a Soviet-style revolution. In the general election of April 1924, Gramsci was elected parliamentary deputy and eventually became the general secretary of the Italian Communist Party. He worked from the conviction that the greatest potential for overthrowing fascism lay with the peasantry and helped to organize the party on the basis of workplace cells. His inaugural speech in 1924 exhibited an uncompromising and fearless commitment to antifascist struggle, and several years later, in November 1926, he was arrested along with other Communist deputies on charges of conspiracy, insurrection, agitation, inciting class war, and subverting the State. Sentenced on June 4, 1928, to over twenty years of imprisonment, he spent the 1930s—"the long Calvary of Antonio Gramsci" (Fiori,

1973)—in Mussolini's prison. His prosecuting attorney, Michele Isgro, is reported to have exclaimed, "For 20 years we must stop this brain from working" (cited in Ledwith, 1997, p. 84). Moving from Rome, to exile on the island of Ustica, to Milan to await trial, back to Rome for sentencing in May 1928, to a special prison in Bari in July 1928, and then to a clinic in Formia in 1933, Gramsci remained a prisoner of the State until his death from a cerebral hemorrhage on April 27, 1937. It is a testament to his indomitable will and fearless optimism that his brain did not stop functioning during his confinement in prison, which saw him produce thirty-three notebooks or 2,848 dense pages of writing that constitute his *Quaderni del carcere* or *Prison Notebooks* (Ledwith, 1997, p. 84).

Throughout his intellectual life, Gramsci sought ways to oppose the idealist conception of consciousness common to neo-Hegelian and neo-Kantian philosophy through an encounter with Saussurean linguistics and Russian formalism (Brandist, 1996, 1996a). Perhaps the two Gramscian concepts that have exercised (and exorcised) the North and South American educational Left the most over the last two decades have been those of ideology and hegemony. For Antonio Gramsci, as well as for many of his followers (Aronowitz, 1992; Eagleton, 1991), there exists a continuous interplay—a dialectical reinitiation of sorts—between the workings of ideology and hegemony. Terry Eagleton (1991) indicates that for the Italian revolutionary, the concept of "ideology"—based on Marx's "solidity of popular beliefs"—refers to the way that power struggles are developed in any given society at the level of signification. The view of ideology presented by Stuart Hall and James Donald (1986) is quintessentially Gramscian. For Hall and Donald, ideology refers to

> the framework of thought which is used in society to explain, figure out, make sense of or give meaning to the social and political world [. . .] without these frameworks, we could not make sense of the world at all. But with them, our perceptions are inevitably structured in particular directions by the very concepts we are using. (pp. xi-x)

For this reason, it is possible to say that ideologies serve as a collective embrace or cajolery that seductively corrupts the civic culture, or that is perhaps imposed upon the people (an obvious condition of any colonial project), such as in the case of white supremacist ideologies in South Africa or national security doctrines that predominated during long periods of dictatorial rule in Latin America, Asia, and Africa. These historical examples illustrate what Gramsci meant when he stated that "the function of 'domination' without that of 'leadership': dictatorship without hegemony" (1971, p. 106) occurs when a dominant class resorts to coercive means of control rather than adopting a strategy of hegemonic consensus building.

Hegemony is a broader concept than ideology, as it requires the use of ideological forms but at the same time cannot be reduced to them. Hegemony invents a coincidence among four relevant sites of ideological production: identity politics, "imagined" communities, the State administration, and social relations of production. Hegemony points to the essential caducity of ideology. Not only does hegemony eluviate over time, it also enlists new forms and assemblages; it is able to permute new social relations and formations; it functions as a public regulatory agency that embargos certain ideas and promotes others. In other words, hegemony points to the constitutive nature of ideology.

The relationship between ideology and hegemony is further elucidated in Dick Hebdige's (1996) discussion of the two dominant and potentially opposed tendencies that have emerged from debates (primarily among the British Left) surrounding Gramsci's work. First, there exists the tension between populism and the national-popular. Second, there exists the tension between ideological discourse in the shaping of historical subjectivities and the world outside of discourse (sites of extradiscursivity). The imaginary community of the "we" has itself become a reflection of these tensions. Stuart Hall's use of the term "articulation" is heralded as a theoretically fecund means by which the "double emphasis" of Gramsci—that is, the emphasis on culture and structure, on ideology and material social relations—can be linked together. What this "double movement" through the concept of articulation has achieved has been to conceptualize class and cultural struggles as interwoven and complexly articulated as a "range of competing populisms" (Hebdige, 1996). According to this formulation, groups and classes exist in a shifting and mediated relationship, in a structured field of complex relations and ideological forces stitched together out of social fragments and privileging hierarchies, in structured asymmetries of power, in contending vectors of influence, and in emergent, contingent alliances. When one examines ideology, one does not look for smooth lines of articulation; rather, one conceives of a regime of culture not stitched together as a set of canonical ideas but rather existing as a palimpsest of emergent and residual discourses. Hebdige offers a summary of the Gramscian conception as follows:

> From the perspectives heavily influenced by the Gramscian approach, nothing is anchored to the "grand recites," to master narratives, to stable (positive) identities, to fixed and certain meanings: all social and semantic relations are contestable hence mutable: everything appears to be in flux: there are no predictable

outcomes. Though classes still exist there is no guaranteed dynamic to class struggle and no "class belong": there are no solid homes to return to, no places reserved in advance for the righteous. No one "owns" an ideology because ideologies are themselves in process: in a state of constant formation and reformation. In the same way, the concept of hegemony remains distinct from the Frankfurt model of a "total closure of discourse" (Marcuse) and from the ascription of total class domination which is implied in the Althusserian model of a contradictory social formation held in check eternally (at least until "the last (ruptural) instance") by the work of the RSAs and the ISAs. Instead hegemony is a precarious, "moving equilibrium" (Gramsci) achieved through the orchestration of conflicting and competing forces by more or less unstable, more or less temporary alliances of class fractions. (1996, p. 198)

In order to grasp the nuanced relationship between ideology and hegemony, we recommend that they be seen in parallax, that is, from the perspective of the positionality of the social agent at the present moment, with the understanding that this location or site of enunciation is in itself dialectically conditioned by this interplay. Gramsci underscored the fact that to obtain hegemonic power, a dominant class or class alliance necessarily requires two forms of control: coercion (sustained by politically regulated repression) and consent. These forms of control work together to stipulate an ethical domain tied to the forces of production. According to Gramsci,

every State is ethical in as much as one of its most important functions is to raise the great mass of the population to a particular cultural and moral level, a level (or type) which corresponds to the needs of the productive forces for development, and hence to the interest of the ruling classes. The school as a positive educative function, and the courts as a repressive and negative educative function, are the most important State activities in this sense. (1971, p. 258)

Not only are hegemonic relationships ethical, but they are also pedagogical. Gramsci (1971, p. 350) clearly stated that "every relationship of hegemony is necessarily a pedagogical relationship" because

a class is dominant in two ways, i.e. leading and dominant. It leads the classes which are its allies, and dominates those which are its enemies [. . .] one should not count solely on the power and material force which such position gives in order to exercise political leadership or hegemony. (Gramsci, 1971, p. 57)

These perspectives stress the importance of cultural, political, and pedagogical aspects in the construction of hegemonic orders. However, as a Marxist intellectual, Gramsci never failed to stress the importance of economic relations, because he insisted that the economy determines (in the last instance) the extent of the compromises and agreements that can be achieved among the dominant groups and the popular sectors. He further clarifies this point as follows:

> Undoubtedly the fact of hegemony presupposes that account be taken of the interests and the tendencies of the groups over which hegemony is to be exercised, and that a certain compromise equilibrium should be formed—in other words, that the leading group should make sacrifices of an economic-corporate kind. But there is also no doubt that such sacrifices and such a compromise cannot touch the essential; for though hegemony is ethical-political, it must also be economic, must necessarily be based on the decisive function exercised by the leading group in the decisive nucleus of economic activity. (1971, p. 161)

Richard Brosio (1994, p. 48) emphasizes Gramsci's realization that "hegemony must be ultimately anchored in economic strength—and ultimately physical power." Brosio also reminds us that while the State uses a combination of force and consent in order to maintain hegemony, we must not forget "that the exercise and maintenance of hegemony over subaltern groups is still a variation of class struggle." Brosio further cautions us not to forget the relationship of power to the educative aspects of hegemony: "There is a tendency to stress Gramsci's important development of hegemony, the role of persuasion and consent, the seemingly willing participation by subaltern groups in their own domination; however, he was not naive about the relationship of power to this persuasive hegemony" (1994, p. 49). The characteristics of consent and coercion that underwrite Gramsci's model of hegemonic domination are fundamentally dynamic categories. Because they are dynamic and not static relationships, they admit the possibility of rearticulation into alternative or counterhegemonic practices. We must not forget Gramsci's firm conviction that "ordinary men and women could be educated into understanding the coercive and persuasive power of capitalist hegemony over them" (Brosio, 1994, pp. 49-50). One of the merits of Gramsci's framework is that it makes a vital departure from the conception of ideology as a somewhat outdated system of static and fixed ideas—such as in Althusser's conceptualization that is often recited by orthodox leftists with great condescension toward the very possibility of new forms of resistance—to ideology as embodied, lived, dynamic sets of social practices that are constructed and carried out by individuals as well as institutions.

The notion of hegemonic rule, however, was not well developed in Gramsci. Walter Adamson notes that the relationship among hegemony, State power, and forms of political legitimization was at times ambiguous and was used in several different (and sometimes contradictory) senses:

It is used, first of all, in a morally neutral and instrumental sense to characterize those bourgeois regimes that have proved capable of organizing mass consent effectively. But it is also used in an essentially ethical sense to characterize the functioning of a proletarian regulated society. Here is another instance in which the attempt to incorporate Machiavellian and ethical state traditions raises perplexing and unresolved questions. Is the sort of consent being obtained the same in both cases? Or is consent in a bourgeois hegemony somehow passive and noncritical, while under proletarian auspices it would be active, participatory, and philosophical? If so, what more fully is the institutional basis of this latter sort of control? (1980, p. 242)

We find that the Gramscian dichotomy of force and consent is not nearly sufficient or comprehensive enough to allow us to examine the complex character of hegemonic rule since these two terms do not permit a detailed and nuanced analysis of forms of political legitimization. Consequently, it makes more sense to view the terms "force" and "consent," in Adamson's terms, as "endpoints of a continuum that includes such intermediate positions as constraint (e.g., fear of unemployment), cooptation, and perhaps even Arendt's category of 'authority'" (Adamson, 1980, p. 243).

Whereas Gramsci often stressed as a defining attribute the spirit or the will, Marx gave pride of place to production. Gramsci emphasized human consciousness as a defining attribute of humanity. Consciousness was akin to spirit, which was linked to the notion of history as a form of "becoming." Organized will becomes the basis of his philosophy. While Gramsci acknowledges the link between humanity and production, he does not sufficiently emphasize the most important aspects of humanity's "complex of social relations": the satisfaction of human needs and the human necessity to produce (see Hoffman, 1984). The satisfaction of human needs is the primary historical act, and must be satisfied before men and women are in the position to make history. The human necessity to produce thus underwrites all social relationships. For Gramsci, humanity is defined by concrete will (will plus historical circumstances); for Marx, will is a response to social and historical circumstances independent of human will. Human relationships thus exist independently of the way in which people understand them (Hoffman, 1984, p. 112). Here we agree with Brosio (after Mandel) that "classical Marxism examined closely the repressive function of the class State, and that Gramsci and Lukacs stressed the integrative function" (1994, p. 50).

Eagleton (1991) points out that Gramsci, "with certain notable inconsistencies," associates hegemony with the arena of civil society, a term used by the Italian revolutionary to indicate an extensive range of institutions that serve as intermediaries between the State and the economy: the church, schools, press, family, hospitals, political parties, and so on. In this regard, Perry Anderson (1977) asserts that Gramsci was wrong when he exclusively located hegemony within the realm of civil society, because, by doing so, he diminished the importance of the capitalist State as a vital organ of hegemonic power. However, Torres (1992), also referring to Anderson's work, points out that Gramsci's distinction between civil society and political society is basically methodological. In addition, Gramsci's attention to culture and the relatively autonomous institutions of civil society enabled him to reject the pitfalls of a monodeterministic base-superstructural model:

> Although Gramsci did adhere to the Marxist premise of one hegemonic center (i.e., the social relations generated by the mode of production), his attention to culture and to the relatively autonomous institutions of civil society amounted to a rejection of the monodeterministic base-superstructure argument of classical Marxism. Unlike Leninism, which ignored the democratic forms of culture needed to sustain autonomous movements, Gramsci's focus on a "war of position" resonates with the efforts of social movements to create new political spaces within civil society and alter the content of hegemony. The Gramscian concept of "historic bloc" has its counterpart in the coalition-building notions prevalent in NSM [New Social Movement] theory. The emphasis on the unification of class with popular-democratic struggles can be viewed, positively, as offering an analytic basis for exploring historical continuities between "old" and "new" social movements, a continuity otherwise obliterated by the atemporality of identity politics. (Carroll & Ratner, 1994, p. 21)

For our own purposes, it should be stressed that hegemony is as much related to antagonistic processes as it is to consensual individual and social practices of negotiation and/or exchange that take place, not only in the realm of the civil society but also in the everyday actions of families, the State, and the various political arenas. Ernesto Laclau and Chantal Mouffe (1985) explain that the concept of hegemony was originally tied to an essentialist logic in which only one authentic historical subject, "the working class," was able to develop truly counter-hegemonic policies and practices. Such a logic, rather than advancing the project of social change and social justice, covered over and obstructed multiple forms of struggles developed by several groups and social movements (such as those developed by indigenous peoples, ethnic groups, women, ecologists, human rights activists, and the like), which could not be reduced or categorized on the exclusive basis of the class position of their members. However, instead of throwing the baby out with the bathwater, Laclau and Mouffe propose to free "hegemony" of any kind of essentialism and reappropriate the potentially emancipatory characteristics of the concept. Best and Kellner maintain that, for Laclau and Mouffe, "hegemony entails a detotalizing logic of articulation and contingency that refuses the conception of the a priori unity or the progressive character of the working class or any other subject position. Rather, cultural and political identities are never given in advance, but must be constituted or articulated, from diverse elements" (1991, p. 195).

Similar to the position articulated by Laclau and Mouffe, Stuart Hall situates the Gramscian challenge as the struggle for a new social order. Hall's eloquent summary is worth quoting at length:

> Gramsci always insisted that hegemony is not exclusively an ideological phenomenon. There can be no hegemony without "the decisive nucleus of the economic." On the other hand, do not fall into the trap of the old mechanical economism and believe that if you can only get hold of the economy, you can move the rest of life. The nature of power in the modern world is that it is also constructed in relation to political, moral, intellectual, cultural, ideological and sexual questions. The question of hegemony is always the question of a new cultural order. The question which faced Gramsci in relation to Italy faces us now in relation to Britain: what is the nature of this new civilization? Hegemony is not a state of grace that is installed forever. It is not a formation that incorporates everybody. The notion of a "historical bloc" is precisely different from that of a pacified, homogeneous, ruling class. It entails a quite different conception of how social forces and movements, in their diversity, can be articulated into strategic alliances. To construct a new cultural order, you need not to reflect an already-formed collective will, but to fashion a new one, to inaugurate a new historical project. (1988, p. 170)

Contemporary social scientists such as Hall and Laclau and Mouffe have developed a conception of hegemony as an ever-evolving political, economic, ideological, and cultural set of processes by which the dominant social sectors (hegemonic bloc) elicit consent from the popular sectors. And yet, hegemony is inseparable from conflicts and struggles over it. In this process, the struggle for control over the symbolic and economic means of any given society and the role the State plays in such struggles cannot be diminished. Nevertheless, we have some reservations about the analysis advanced by Laclau and Mouffe, as well as by Hall, in terms of their penchant for de-emphasizing the totalizing power and function of capital. In their inauguration of a new collective will, postmodernists and post-Marxists such as Laclau and Mouffe often theorize or abstract out of existence the working class, even as they seek new positions of popular will from which to struggle and wage war against the hegemonic order. We believe this is a major mistake and misappropriation of hegemony. In our view, Gramsci's work can help us in understanding the class contradictions that structure the subjectivities of oppressed classes. Such an understanding enables us to resist the formation

of the comprador intellectual, who simply (and often unwittingly) rese-
cures the consent of the subaltern classes for the relations of domination
that structure and exploit them. It is a major error, we contend, to use
Gramsci's concept of hegemony in such a way as to depotentiate class
analysis by reducing class to a series of unstable "negotiations" among
all and every political position. Hegemony does not take place in an indeterminate terrain (Katz, 1997). The concept of hegemony as articulated
by many post-Marxists often serves as a type of *trompe d'oeil* whereby
forces of domination are willfully misrecognized as the structured equa-
nimity of inevitability, fate, chance, or irreversibility. Built into a number
of theories of hegemony is the notion of the "reversibility" of cultural
practices, as if such practices are asocial or ahistorical or have otherwise
been severed from the chains of class determination. According to Katz
(1997), this is clearly a misunderstanding of Gramsci and evacuates the
entire problem of domination. Misappropriations of Gramsci's work
have caused domination, in effect, to virtually disappear into a storm of
relational "negotiations" in which certain ideological positions are "won"
through "consent." Here we need to be reminded that intellectuals themselves are always the products of new forms of collective labor power
brought about and consolidated by the forces of late capitalism.

From Resistance to Agency

In Gramsci's work, the distinctive presence of the notions of collective
will and consciousness are closely related to the concepts of resistance
and agency. Gramsci described resistance as largely passive and unconscious, and suggested that as a political movement develops, agency replaces resistance:

> if yesterday the subaltern element was a thing, today it is no longer a thing but a
> historical person, a protagonist; if yesterday it was not responsible because "re-
> sisting" a will external to itself, now it feels itself to be responsible because it is
> no longer resisting but an agent, necessarily active and taking the initiative. But
> even yesterday was it ever mere "resistance," a mere "thing," mere "non-
> responsibility"? Certainly not. (1971, p. 337)

Gramsci also argued that some intellectuals, particularly those that
may be described as traditional, mistakenly understand the popular sectors as merely resisting hegemonic processes, "when they don't even expect that the subaltern will become directive and responsible" (1971, p.
337). Gramsci deeply understood the importance of the articulation of

knowledge with passion and commitment. He reminds us that:

> The intellectual's error consists in believing that one can know without under-standing and even more without feeling and being impassioned (not only for knowledge in itself but also for the object of knowledge): in other words that the intellectual can be an intellectual (and not a pure pedant) if distinct and separate from the people-nation, that is without feeling the elementary passions of the people, understanding them and therefore explaining and justifying them in the particular historical situation and connecting them dialectically to the laws of history and to a superior conception of the world, scientifically and coherently elaborated—i.e., knowledge. (1971, p. 418)

For Gramsci, "resistance" was a sign of (subaltern) discontent, rather than a conscious effort to promote social change. How is it possible, then, to turn mere resistance into agency? The organic intellectual (specialized intellectuals that each class develops), was Gramsci's answer. According to Carl Boggs, Gramsci helped to synthesize Lenin's Marxist Jacobinism (harnessing the State apparatus to the task of social reconstruction) and the radical spontanaeism of Luxemburg and Lukács.

It was Kautsky who first set forth the rationale for an intellectual vanguard. He argued that "since socialist ideas were first coherently articulated within the bourgeois intelligentsia, mass revolutionary consciousness depended upon the tutelary function of an educational and politically committed elite" (Boggs, 1993, p. 41). Boggs affirms that

> Kautsky's thesis, inspired by a naturalistic and positivist view of consciousness, justified a rigid separation between the "scientific" knowledge of intellectuals and the limited, partial ideology of the average worker. It follows that only when the proletariat finally grasps the necessary "laws" of historical development (as formulated by intellectuals) can it become an active revolutionary force. (1993, p. 42)

Lenin similarly felt that the ideology of the worker, confined to the realm of production, could only be partial and that workers needed intellectuals to teach them the laws of historical development and disseminate among them the socialist ideals necessary to move beyond the logic of bourgeois reformism and towards a class political consciousness. This could be achieved most productively through the efforts of a disciplined and highly organized vanguard party that, through forms of bureaucratic centralism, would serve as a repository of political knowledge and the agency of collective will capable of seizing State power. Unmediated popular self-activity was flatly rejected. According to Boggs (1993),

> Leninism, therefore, was able to "resolve" the problem of mass consciousness that had troubled Marxism for so long: a centralized, professional, and disci-

plined party would be the main repository of political knowledge. Intellectuals, fiercely dedicated to the party's historical mission, impose their own conception of totality upon the chaotic flow of disparate popular experiences and struggles. (p. 43)

Yet, Lenin's vision of intellectual leadership demanded coercion, force, and manipulation in order to be successful. More than this, it demanded the type of instrumental rationality and rationalizing ethos based on an internal division of labor that was constitutive of the very logic of capitalism. This situation was as precarious as it was perilous:

Leninism found itself trapped in a dilemma. As it strove to consolidate power in a way that was bound to turn the masses it claimed to "represent" into manipulated objects, it was sure to gravitate toward an instrumental rationality wherein the methods and tools of politics took precedence over ultimate objectives. This suppression of the teleological element permitted Lenin to employ the very logic of capitalism in the service of its overthrow: hierarchical organization, mass assembly-line production, material incentives, strict forms of labor discipline. It also meant that socialist goals would be deferred to a "future" that bore little resemblance to the actuality of the present. Ultimate aims were scarcely discussed or questioned, meaning in effect that organizational methods became ideological ends. (Boggs, 1993, p. 45)

Marxists such as Rosa Luxemburg, Emma Goldman, and Georg Lukács supported a more voluntarist or spontaneous approach, as did the worker-centered syndicalism of Sorel. From the spontaneist perspective, radical consciousness was immanent and organic to proletarian social relations. Boggs writes:

Luxemburg, like Lukács a few years later, sought to locate her critique of Jacobinism squarely within a Marxist framework: pitting Marx against Lenin, she anticipated massive worker upheavals growing out of the ever-widening global crisis of capitalism [. . .] Luxemburg waged a protracted fight against elitism, bureaucracy, and authoritarian manipulation that, in her view, was too often justified by appeals to "scientific" truth and the need for an intellectual vanguard. She understood democracy as being central to the revolutionary process, following the 1905 Russian model of the mass strike. Both the social Democrats and Bolsheviks had erred seriously in their tendency to dismiss mass spontaneity and in their fetishism of leadership. (1993, p. 51)

Gramsci took up the challenge of articulating the extent to which the working class could generate its own intellectual force, building on his well-known conviction that "All men are intellectuals [. . .] but not all men have in society the function of intellectuals" (1971, p. 9). His solution—the "organic intellectual"—took a collective character within a working-class formation in which the role of theory was organically linked with the ebb and flow of daily proletarian life. In this view, intellectuals should become an elaborate, historical expression of traditions, culture, values, and social relations. As Boggs (1993) notes, quasi-Jacobin ideological functions were still important intellectual tasks but now were required to be centered within the proletarian milieu (factories, community life, and culture). In this regard, intellectuals would be organic to that milieu only if they were fully immersed in its culture and language. Intellectuals, therefore, carried out "universal" functions that situate social activity within local and specific class struggles and in the defense of class interests. In effect, Gramsci was able to transcend the mechanical separation between the intellectual and popular realms that was upheld by both spontaneism and vanguardism. According to Gramsci:

> The popular element "feels" but does not always know or understand; the intellectual element "knows" but does not always understand and in particular does not always feel. The two extremes are therefore pedantry and philistinism on the one hand and blind passion and sectarianism on the other. Not that the pedant cannot be impassioned; far from it. Impassioned pedantry is every bit as ridiculous and dangerous as the wildest sectarianism and demagogy. [. . .] One cannot make politics-history without this passion, without this sentimental connection between intellectuals and people-nation. In the absence of such a nexus the relations between the intellectual and the people-nation are, or are reduced to, relationships of a purely bureaucratic and formal order; the intellectuals become a caste, or a priesthood. (1971, p. 418)

In a similar fashion, Paulo Freire also proposed transcending the antimony of populism and vanguardism through a synthesis of various types of demands and the development of reflective knowledge. Aronowitz remarks:

> Freire's solution to [the] antimony of populism and vanguardism is to find a "synthesis" in which the demand for salaries is supported but posed as a "problem" that on one level becomes an obstacle to the achievement of full "humanization" through workers' ownership of their own labor. Again, workers pose wage increases as a solution to their felt oppression because they have internalized the oppressor's image of themselves and have not (yet) posed self-determination over the conditions of their lives as an object of their political practice. They have not yet seen themselves subjectively. (1993, pp. 16-17)

Aronowitz describes the role of the Freirean intellectual as sharing the power over knowledge. He writes:

> Reporting on a conversation with workers' leaders in São Paulo, Freire defines class consciousness as the power and the will by workers and other oppressed and exploited strata to share in the formulation of the conditions of knowledge and futurity. This demand inevitably alters the situation of power: intellectuals

must be consistent in the translation of their democratic visions to practice. In other words, they must share the power over knowledge, share the power to shape the future. (p. 21)

Gramsci, like Freire, urged intellectuals to develop a relational knowledge of and with the masses in order to help them become self-reflective. His unsurpassed understanding of the relationship between theory and practice stipulated an active participation in their quotidian struggles and an investment in their future well-being. Hence, Gramsci enjoined intellectuals to live intellectual life praxiologically, that is, in a state of ongoing praxis: "The mode of being of the new intellectual can no longer consist in eloquence, which is an exterior and momentary mover of feelings and passions, but in active participation in practical life, as constructor, organiser 'permanent persuader' and not just a simple orator" (1971, p. 10). In other words, Gramsci believed that intellectuals need to develop not only intellectual capital to distribute to the masses, but also the social capital of trust and collective will necessary to bring about community-based liberatory praxis (Richards, 1998).

Gramsci was concerned that popular revolt would be absorbed into the prevailing hegemony or else mobilized into the direction of reactionary fascism. Gramsci did not believe, as did the anarchists and syndicalists, that common sense was innately rebellious. For Gramsci, mass consciousness was contradictory and rather formless by necessity, and the construction of a collective political will is always gradual, uneven, and part of a counterhegemonic movement where intellectuals play an increasingly important role (Boggs, 1984). Leadership was indirect, as spontaneity was refracted through cultural formations and organizational and institutional sites. The challenge for Gramsci "was how to move beyond social immediacy without at the same time destroying spontaneous impulses" (Boggs, 1984, p. 208) to a point where common sense became good sense and spontaneity was transformed into critical consciousness. Boggs describes the democratizing character of the organic intellectual as follows:

It seems clear that Gramsci, with the Turin council movement of 1918-1919 always in mind, saw the organic intellectual as a democratizing force who, virtually indistinguishable from the average worker in many ways, could articulate the values and goals of proletarian revolution. It was in this spirit that Gramsci could refer to theory as a "popular" enterprise and could champion the subversive idea that all persons are in some sense intellectuals insofar as they carry out certain forms of mental activity, enter into social relations, express opinions and make cultural choices. (1993, pp. 58-59)

Intellectuals: From Organic to Committed

For Gramsci, organic intellectuals were a fundamentally important expression of working-class life, an interrogation of emergent patterns of thought and action, the radicalization of the subaltern strata, the translation of theory into strategy, and the creation of revolutionary subjectivity through the formation of continuous and multifaceted counterhegemonic activity and the development of a revolutionary historical bloc where divergent interests converge and coalesce around shared visions and objectives. Gramsci did resign himself, however, to a commitment to some form of mass party, given the conjunctural events within Italy. Boggs writes:

> Gramsci's anti-Jacobinism gave way to certain historical pressures: he soon concluded that the Communist party ought to be the repository of theory, with its leadership the final arbiter of strategy. Gramsci himself was a founder and leading figure in the Italian Communist party. Yet his view of the party, like his concept of intellectuals, differed profoundly from Lenin's in many ways, beginning with Gramsci's emphasis on the ideological-cultural role of the party (the "myth prince") in contrast to Lenin's zeal for organization and power. Gramsci's idea of a "national-popular" movement required jettisoning the strict Leninist boundary between political and social realms best exemplified by the professional cadre—the hallmark of Bolshevik-type parties. Even in his later Jacobin phase, Gramsci approached critical consciousness as the product of an ongoing dialectical relationship between intellectuals and masses. This synthesis, however flawed, did go beyond the polarities of Marxist theory in the period 1890-1930: it was more compatible with the aims of popular self-emancipation than was vanguardism, more attuned to the indeterminate nature of mass consciousness than spontaneism, and more suitable to the condition of advanced capitalism than either. (1993, pp. 59-60)

While Gramsci considered all individuals to be intellectuals, not all of them had the function traditionally assigned to and developed by intellectuals (1971). Most importantly for Gramsci, organic intellectuals of the working class not only resist hegemonic processes, but attempt to displace the old hegemonic order by leading their class or popular front into more elaborated forms of understanding of the capitalist system of exploitation. At the same time, organic intellectuals serve as role models that open the horizons of their class or popular front in order to secure a more equitable system of societal organization, which Gramsci believed must take the form of a socialist society.

The role of the organic intellectual was to mediate between the good sense of subaltern groups and the formation of a counterhegemonic con-

sciousness able to read the contextually specific and historically conjunctural contradictions that suffuse the social formation. According to
Carroll and Ratner, Gramsci

> held that all people are intellectuals in capacity, if not function. He believed that
> counter-hegemonic leadership emanates from intellectuals whose organic ties to
> subaltern groups enable them to achieve a unity of theory and practice and of
> thinking and feeling, thus mediating between the abstract and concrete in a
> manner foreign to traditional scholastic, ecclesiastic, and political elites. For
> Gramsci, the role of the intellectual is that of organizer and facilitator: instead of
> bringing correct consciousness to the masses "from without," the organic intel-
> lectual facilitates the practical movement from "good sense" (which resistant
> subordinates already possess) to a broader, counterhegemonic consciousness
> that is sensitive to the specific conditions of a social formation at a given con-
> juncture. (1994, p. 12)

In the search for the limits of what it means to be an intellectual, there
exists a lucid mistrustfulness in Gramsci's materialism. He maintains that
an intellectual activity is not outside of a relational logic; therefore, to
think about the role of an intellectual is to think about its very limits. If,
as Ernesto Laclau (1993) points out, to see the limits of something is to
see what is beyond those limits, then the criterion of distinction of what
is and what is not, in strict terms, an intellectual task becomes constitu-
tively opaque.

Gramsci knew that to say "all men" or "everyone" is the same as
saying "no one." He was more concerned with the intellectual "function"
than the function of the intellectual. Laclau (1993) has pointed out that
"the intellectual for Gramsci is not a segregated intellectual group but
one that establishes the organic unity among a group of activities that, if
left to themselves, would remain fragmented and dispersed. A union activist, in that sense, would be an intellectual" (p. 204). As Laclau emphasizes, this is not about the function of the intellectual but about the intellectual function. It is not focused on a class; it cannot be the exclusive
place of an elite: it emerges at all points of the social net—and consists
of the practice of articulation. Priests, physicians, notaries, lawyers,
teachers, nurses, dropouts, and gang members; schools, court, houses,
hospitals, churches, and streetcorners: once we accept the intellectual
task as a function, does it matter who and what they are? For Gramsci
(and also for Paulo Freire), political-pedagogical actions are not an exclusive problem of having the right knowledge, but also of faithfulness to
the event; in other words, to be in the right place at the right time.

Let us remember a passage of a rural educator's tale, which Freire
mentions in his *Pedagogy of Hope*: "We need to tell you, friend, some-

thing very important. If you came here thinking you were going to teach us that we are being exploited, you do not need to, because we know that very well. Now, what we want to know about you is whether you are going to be with us at the time we are hit" (Freire, 1995, p. 67). Is this a popular expression of the rejection of intellectual tasks? Not necessarily. It deals with the ethical privilege of being "there" over being "something." By focusing on the relationships developed through hegemonic and counterhegemonic practices, Gramsci highlights the paradoxical practices in which the popular sectors engage, showing only one way out of this paradox. The organic intellectuals of the popular classes have the knowledge and the solutions that must be exercised if society is to become democratic. Gramsci saw democracy as essentially a dialectical movement between individual agency and structural location.

> But democracy, by definition, cannot mean merely that an unskilled worker can become skilled. It must mean that every "citizen" can "govern" and that society places him, even if only abstractly, in a general condition to achieve this. Political democracy tends towards a coincidence of the rulers and the ruled (in the sense of government with the consent of the governed) ensuring for each non-ruler a free training in the skill and general technical preparation necessary to that end. (1971, pp. 40-41)

On the one hand, Gramsci believed that the popular classes are the only historical subjects able to effectively resist, challenge, and transform the hegemonic position of the bourgeoisie—even though the working class and the peasants (i.e., popular classes) have developed a contradictory consciousness which ultimately does not allow the elaboration of autonomous decisions. On the other hand, organic intellectuals, on their own merits, are able to construct other models of consciousness in political and cultural arenas, and it is this process that, for Gramsci, constitutes the key to overcoming the shortcomings of the popular classes:

> Critical self-consciousness means, historically and politically, the construction of an élite of intellectuals. A human mass does not "distinguish" itself, does not become independent in its own right without, in the widest sense, organizing itself; and there is no organization without intellectuals, that is without organizers and leaders, in other words, without the theoretical aspect of the theory-practice nexus being distinguished concretely by the existence of a group of people "specialized" in conceptual and philosophical elaboration of ideas. (Gramsci, 1971, p. 334)

One of the main challenges of Gramsci's framework, and one that is repeated by many in the field of education, is that there exists a categorical assumption that organic intellectuals must develop some sort of su-pranatural level of consciousness, avoiding or overcoming the contra-dictory personal and social struggles present in everyday life. At the same time, this hypervalorization of the role of one small group of lead-ers and organizers replicates the heroic myths of romantic idealism of the last century, which in turn reflects its positivistic heritage, and a firm belief in the existence of a normal and teleological line of progress for all societies (i.e., from backward societies, to capitalistic forms, to socialist and finally communist societies). Additionally, it is worth noting that ideology, hegemony, and resistance are also concepts that have been de-veloped and employed in deeply gendered frameworks. For this reason, the important criticisms of feminist scholars must be taken seriously (i.e., Alcoff & Potter, 1993; Butler, 1993; Hill Collins, 1990). Margaret Led-with (1997) points out that Gramsci's work often "fell foul of the public-private divide" (1997, p. 91). For example, Gramsci largely overlooked the support of his sister-in-law, Tatiana Schucht, during his prison years, especially in relation to her assistance with his prison notebooks. Gram-sci's thinking, however, did capture at least some of the issues confront-ing gender equality. Ledwith notes that Gramsci

> was not confronted with the feminist awareness that has developed over the last few decades. There seem to be some contradictory issues here: Gramsci ac-cepted as natural the roles of the women in his personal life without recognizing their political implications. However, there is a glimpse that he was aware at some deeper level of the complex subordination of women. In his discussion of Americanism and Fordism [. . .] he not only acknowledges women's exploita-tion in the public domain, but also recognizes our vital function in the reproduc-tion of the workforce, thereby identifying sexuality as a focus of oppression. [. . .] he saw economic independence as only part of the story; true emancipation involves freedom of choice in relation to sexual relationships. What he referred to as a "new ethic" [. . .] is the transformative moment gained from a war of po-sition, which frees women in a truly liberatory way. Gramsci's feminist con-sciousness therefore connects women's sexual rights not only with women's lib-eration, but also with the total transformation of society as a whole. (1997, p. 91)

Some Gramscian scholars and activists have pointed out that the very distinction between domination and resistance has often been misunder-stood by contemporary social scientists, because it is only when resis-tance is performed as a violently explicit act, or as an act of direct oppo-sition, that it is given validity or conceptualized as the true voice or will of subjects expressing their agency. Yet, counterhegemonic practices do not necessarily result in violent acts. They partake of many genres and modalities of "performance," ranging from decentering dominant dis-courses in a spectrum of public practices (such as political journalism, political theatre, insurrectionary artistic endeavors, or acts of scholarship) to actively resisting repressive State apparatuses (through strikes, walkouts, political demonstrations, armed struggle and the like). Furthermore, counterhegemonic resistance among feminist intellectuals carries its own set of special challenges. Boggs notes that feminist intellectuals

> are immersed in the world of collective action, in the language and values of women struggling to change their lives. The gulf between intellectual work and everyday life, between thought and action, is greatly narrowed where it is not eliminated altogether. With few exceptions, feminist intellectuals of this sort carry no Jacobin illusions, no global or "imported" theories, no fixation on a single privileged agency of change. Nor do they adhere to prevailing technocratic norms. At the same time, the always shifting social bases and fortunes of women's movements and projects means that long-term organic attachment of intellectuals to local communities is problematic. In this sense the "organic" character of intellectuals in new social movements can be expected to have a provisional status. (1993, p. 178)

Perhaps the main problem in this Gramscian inspired framework is that it presents a categorical assumption that agents of change (organic intellectuals, teachers, or social activists) should be able to develop a supranatural level of consciousness.

Rethinking Critical Pedagogy in the Spirit of Gramsci

While we agree with Boggs (1986) that today's critical intellectuals also embody some elements of Gramsci's organic model, we are concerned about the lack of interest in class politics and class struggle on the part of the emerging strata of postmodern intellectuals and their relationship to new social movements, including global movements. We further believe that Gramsci's appropriation by educational postmodernists has too often emphasized the priority of language and representation in the hegemonic processes of identity formation to the detriment of acknowledging how the social construction of race, class, and gender are implicated in the international division of labor. Postmodern educators have not sufficiently grasped the importance of understanding and challenging the totalizing power of capitalism. Capitalism totalizes like nothing else—it is its totalizing character that renders capitalism unique (Carroll & Ratner, 1993). According to Marx:

> [I]t is not values in use and the enjoyment of them, but exchange value and its augmentation, that spur [the capitalist] into action. Fanatically bent on making value expand itself, he ruthlessly forces the human race to produce for production's sake [. . .]. Moreover, the development of capitalist production makes it

constantly necessary to keep increasing the amount of the capital laid out in a given industrial undertaking, and competition makes the immanent laws of capitalist production to be felt by each individual capitalist, as external coercive laws. It compels him to keep constantly extending his capital, in order to preserve it, but extend it he cannot, except by means of progressive accumulations [. . .]. To accumulate, is to conquer the world of social wealth, to increase the mass of human beings exploited by him, and thus to extend both the direct and the indirect sway of the capitalist. (Marx, 1967, p. 592, cited in Carroll & Ratner, 1994, p. 17)

We argue for a counterhegemonic coalition of social formations composed of committed intellectuals whose political links are connected and articulated through the unification of demands in heterogeneous, multifaceted, yet focalized anticapitalist struggles. This is not to limit counterhegemonic struggles to the productivist framework of unilinear labor struggles or Marxist "workerism," but rather to forge new links between labor and new social movements without dismissing the potential of "politically" unorganized social sectors (such as the growing numbers of the unemployed and homeless) (Boggs, 1986).

One of the main goals of these multivaried coalitions should be to suffocate the authoritarian power of the State and curb its ability to support other structures of oppression. This demands moving beyond the radical autonomy of localized struggles or the creation of a network of micropolitical struggles. It does not mean that we reject community-based multiform politics; rather, we need to coordinate our single-issue and micropolitical efforts so that the power of State apparatuses are not underestimated and can be effectively challenged. Of course, we also acknowledge that the State is not the all-encompassing structure of domination that orthodox Marxists have often made it out to be. But we recognize that State formations, while more fluid in the context of global markets and the internationalization of capital, have not become obsolete. Too often radical pluralism does not sufficiently acknowledge the extent to which relations of subordination are connected to State formations, through which capitalist power circulates and becomes legitimate.

While we agree with Boggs that "a reconstituted definition of organic intellectuals emphasizes movement as opposed to class or social identity" (1993, p. 179), we worry that such a renovated dialectic between intellectuals and social forces or movements is unlikely to overturn the highly integrated power structures of global capitalism associated with the economic exploitation of the masses, ecological genocide, and bureaucratic domination. We maintain that it is imperative to move beyond a monodeterministic base-superstructural argument. Consequently, we reject, as did Marx (in the *Grundrisse*), the establishment of a mechanical one-to-one "mimetic" relation of determination between the social relations of production and cultural formations. Yet we still urge the recognition of the priority of labor relations in social processes and the "logic" inherent in the productive processes of capital—the expropriation of the labor of the many by the few.

While it is surely the case that economic and cultural relations can be—and often are—decoupled within capitalist society, we call for the need to acknowledge that objective surplus labor grounds cultural practices and social institutions. Here we follow Hoffman (1984) in arguing that to avoid a mechanical hypostatization and organic splicing apart of the Gramscian couplet of coercion and consent, all political action must be premised on the idea of the coercive character of all social relationships. Failure to do this has led post-Marxists who champion the new social movements to overemphasize contingency at the expense of structural determination. The cabaret avant-gardism of many postmodernist critics confirms rather than contests the authority of the sovereign discourses in a way that reduces the desired exchange with the specters of the unsaid. While their gravitational center constitutes a cultural politics that attempts to locate culture as a terrain where social justice is contested and where victory for the subaltern needs to be won, it is too often the case that dominant images, symbols, and representations are portrayed as establishing the most fundamental conditions of daily action, structuring daily life in the most immediate and important ways. This is not to say that cultural discourses are secondary to economic relations, or to maintain that symbolic production (as in the work of Walter Benjamin) has no revolutionary significance or potential; nor are we suggesting that resistance at the level of culture is merely epiphenomenal (we are thinking, for instance, of the Chicano school walkouts in East Los Angeles over Proposition 187, the art of Barbara Kruger, and project ACT-UP). What we are saying is that in much postmodern criticism, the world of class struggle linked to the social division of labor and relations of production is theoretically dissolved into a world composed of unstable constellations of meanings and indeterminate and incommensurable discourses that appear severed from the messy terrain of capitalist social relations. In this scenario, class struggles are too often rewritten as a political economy of conjunctural antagonisms or a type of crosshatching of determinations that do not intersect neatly in terms of class location.

Post-Marxist or postmodernist critics do not see consent as a moment conceived within social coercion brought about by productive practices. By contrast, the committed intellectual recognizes that so-called autonomous acts of consent are always already rooted in the coercive relationships of the realm of necessity. Since coercion is the "ethical expression of the fact that people have to produce" (Hoffman, 1984, p. 212), it makes sense to view the dialectical relationship between coercion and consent as a unity in distinction. Hoffman asserts that "consent has to respond to coercion in order to 'negate' it. We have to avoid [. . .] a fatalistic social determinism [. . .] and a voluntaristic postulation of situations in which 'social' pressures are non-existent" (1984, p. 210). Without acknowledging coercion, we are faced with a pedagogy grounded in an antipolitics of free-floating critique. As Carroll and Ratner remark: "Politics becomes an anything-goes adventure—as exhilarating as it is strategically rudderless" (1994, p. 14).

Towards a Critical Pedagogy of the Committed Intellectual

We wish to extend the role of the organic intellectual by suggesting that the resisting, hegemonized, and fragmented subaltern needs to function not only as a critically superconscious "organic intellectual," but also as a committed one (Fischman, 1998). The committed intellectual is sometimes critically self-conscious and active, but at other times is too confused about, or even unaware of, his or her limitations or capacities to be an active promoter of social change. Or, as Paulo Freire has noted: "Conscientization is not exactly the starting point of commitment. Conscientization is more of a product of commitment. I do not have to be already conscious in order to struggle. By struggling I become conscious/aware" (Freire, 1988, p. 114).

Consciousness always implies that the subject has some awareness of the immediate world that concerns him or her. As Freire (1989) came to recognize, a deep understanding of the complex processes of oppression and domination is not enough to guarantee personal or collective praxis. What must serve as the genesis of such an understanding is an unwavering commitment to the struggle against injustice. Only by developing an understanding that is born of a commitment to social justice can such an understanding lead to the type of conscientization necessary to challenge the hegemonic structures of domination and exploitation. The globalization of capital can be challenged and defeated not only by understanding its formation but also by developing the will and the courage—the commitment—to struggle against it.

The committed intellectual is not someone who is interested only in resisting and defeating forms of cultural domination, but rather someone for whom the end of all forms of exploitation is the focal point of his or her commitment to transform the world. We do not endorse the view that conflicting or competing claims are ultimately, or "in the last instance," unsolvable, nor do we wish to articulate a view of the intellectual that merely invites the subaltern to add his or her recipe to the existing pot so that the clenched fists of history can label them into an apocalyptic melt-down of final consensus. This would be a politically ambiguous stance, as well as an intellectually dishonest one.

The point is not to initiate a "face off" between two equally dogmatic assertions: between advocates of structural determination and proponents of universal contingency; or between supporters of Leninist reflectionism and those who support a poststructuralist relativism. We believe that a better strategy is to follow Gramsci's stress on acquiring a critical under-standing of the hegemonic structures (civic, social, and State) that con-strain human action, while at the same time emphasizing a commitment to revolutionary agency that will permit collective re-definitions of social change and enable freedom from capitalist exploitation. Following Carroll and Ratner (1994), we need a more dialectical view of revolu-tionary praxis that acknowledges that systems of intelligibility and rela-tions of signification (i.e., cultural politics) are reciprocally reenacted in social relations in the material world.

We recognize, of course, that the situation today is far different from the milieu of Turin in which Gramsci struggled. With the pervasiveness of ideological and social diversity that exists today, and with the lack of an integrated working class, it is more likely that intellectual labor for the cause of social justice will take place outside a single global system of thought (such as Marxism), although we believe such a system to be in-dispensable for achieving the conditions of liberation of which Gramsci spoke. Boggs remarks on the growth of critical, free-floating intellectuals that has accompanied the pluralization of social life-worlds and political opposition. As we noted in the case of feminist intellectuals, the new "critical intellectual" associated with the new social movements and the struggle for radical democracy

articulates oppositional values but does so in something of a free-floating man-ner, alone or in small groups, removed from the sphere of popular movements or constituencies. The organic type, on the other hand, engages in a more collec-tive, transformative activity where the old distinction between intellectuals and masses is broken down, so that "theoretical" and other mental functions are no longer imported from the outside, in Jacobin style. From a Gramscian stand-point, organic intellectuals are counter-hegemonic precisely to the extent that their contribution takes place within a democratized struggle for social change. (Boggs, 1994, p. 175)

The committed intellectual recognizes that self-reflexivity (or the capacity to engage in critical self-consciousness) is not enough to resist both the repressive and integrative functions of hegemony. It is necessary to find ways to actively intervene in the capitalist world order. Such strategies entail combining aspects of the free-floating intellectual with those of the organic intellectual. In other words, the committed intellectual works in diverse spheres, in which new social movements intersect with more organically traditionalist socialist movements. What links the two groups of intellectuals is a common commitment to anti-capitalist struggle and a provisional model of socialist democracy. As Brosio warns:

> The fact that working-class consciousness has not yet overcome this hegemony in the West causes one to think that becoming aware may not be enough, when one considers the advances which have been made by capital in its colonization of the quotidian, lived experiences of the masses since the time in which Gramsci wrote. Moreover, there are many persons in Gramsci's native country and elsewhere who understand the nature of their sophisticated oppression, but are unable to muster the power to stop it and finally overcome it. (1994, p. 50)

Legacies of Gramsci's Specter: Revolutionary Patience and Committed Intellectuals

The figure of the committed intellectual that we are developing never forgets that we live in a world of messy material relations that not only structures our consciousness and shapes our subjectivities but frequently exploits human labor and strips subaltern subjects of their fundamental humanity and self-worth (McLaren, 1995, 1997). Exploitation not only alienates, it also destroys; it forces people to work and live in dangerous workplace environments, it pollutes the earth with toxic, life-threatening chemicals, it forces people to endure long hours of indignity, job insecurity, and low wages.

The objective world produces our social intelligibilities and our discourses about it. These discourses often function in ways that naturalize and legitimize objective labor practices (Ebert, 1997). They help to win approval for the extraction of surplus labor from the working class. The textuality of the world enables us to know it primarily through narratives. Our engagement with the discourses of everyday life are relational because knowledge is never pristine or stable. Discourses themselves have a materiality about them by the very fact that they are uncontainable by any theory or explanation. As narratives, they are immune from ultimate closure. Even though the arena of signification is always already an undecidable social text, this is not the same thing as claiming that meanings constitute nothing more than the relations among signs or the free play of significant difference. The committed intellectual does not view these discourses as seamless but rather views all discourses as fundamentally contradictory and conflictual; further, discourses are never immune from the larger context of objective labor practices or disentangled from social relations arising from the history of productive labor. Recognizing that the international division of labor is refracted through race, class, and gender antagonisms, the committed intellectual confronts the capitalist world order with a race, class, and gender consciousness and a politics of respite and renewal. The committed intellectual does this without succumbing to a right-wing anti-statism of backlash populism (as in the case of agrarian fascists or Christian militia movements), an organic communitarianism, populist nostalgia, possessive parochialism, or militant cultural particularism.

Walter Adamson remarked that although Gramsci's world "is no longer our world, his experience remains a critical moment in the development of Western Marxism from which we can all continue to learn" (1980, p. 246). Gramsci's work is highly suggestive for understanding how the regime of capital functions through historically specific ethnic and gender differentiation, and for understanding how the law of value is refracted through the culturally specific character of labor power. His work on the contradictory aspects of ideological formations can give us a much needed critical understanding of the nature of "the 'subjection' of the victims of racism to the mystifications of the very racist ideologies which imprison and define them" (Hall, 1996, p. 440). His concept of the organic intellectual offers a fecund beginning for understanding the possibilities inherent in critical agency. We have attempted to build on these potent ideas in our nascent formulation of the committed intellectual. We believe that Gramsci's conception of the relationship between the role of the intellectuals and ideology and hegemony provides contemporary educators with a basis to forge a critical pedagogy capable of meeting the challenges of the new millennium.

References

Adamson, W. L. (1980). *Hegemony and Revolution: A Study of Antonio Gramsci's Political and Cultural Theory.* Berkeley: University of California Press.

Alcoff, L., & Potter, E. (Eds.). (1993). *Feminist Epistemologies*. New York: Routledge.

Anderson, P. (1977). *Las Antinomias de Antonio Gramsci*. Barcelona: Fontana.

Aronowitz, S. (1993). Paulo Freire's Radical Democratic Humanism. In P. McLaren & P. Leonard (Eds.), *Paulo Freire: A Critical Encounter* (pp. 8-24). London: Routledge.

Berger, J. (1988, January 4). How to Live with Stones. An Open Letter to Subcommandante Marcos in the Mountains of Southeast Mexico. [Book Review]. *Los Angeles Times*, 3.

Best, S., & Kellner, D. (1991). *Postmodern Theory: Critical Interrogations*. New York: Guilford.

Boggs, C. (1996). *Social Movements and Political Power*. Philadelphia: Temple University Press.

Boggs, C. (1993). *Intellectuals and the Crisis of Modernity*. Albany, NY: State University of New York Press.

Boggs, C. (1984). *The Two Revolutions: Gramsci and the Dilemmas of Western Marxism*. Boston: South End.

Brandist, C. (1996). Gramsci, Bakhtin and the Semiotics of Hegemony. *New Left Review*, 216, 94-109.

Brandist, C. (1996a). The Official and the Popular in Gramsci and Bakhtin. *Theory, Culture & Society*, 13 (2), 59-74.

Brosio, R. A. (1994). *A Radical Democratic Critique of Capitalist Education*. New York: Peter Lang.

Butler, J. (1993). *Bodies that Matter: On the Discursive Limits of "Sex."* New York: Routledge.

Butler, J. (1990). *Gender Trouble: Feminism and the Subversion of Identity*. New York: Routledge.

Carroll, W. K., & Ratner, R. S. (1994). Between Leninism and Radical Pluralism: Gramscian Reflections on Counter-Hegemony and the New Social Movements. *Critical Sociology*, 20 (2), 3-26.

De Azua, F. (1997). Para que leer? *Cuadernos de Pedagogia*, 1 (1).

Derrida, J. (1994). *Specters of Marx: The State of the Debt, the Work of Mourning, and the New*. London: Routledge.

Donald, J. (1992). *Sentimental Education: Schooling, Popular Culture, and the Regulation of Liberty*. London: Verso.

Eagleton, T. (1991). *Ideology. An Introduction*. London: Verso.

Ebert, T. (1997). (Oc)Cult of the Post-al. *Rethinking Marxism*, 9 (3), 103-18.

Eribon, D. (1992). *Foucault*. Barcelona: Editorial Anagrama.

Fischman, G. (1998). Donkeys and Superteachers: Popular Education and Structural Adjustment in Latin America. *International Journal of Education.*

Fiori, G. (1990). *Antonio Gramsci: Life of a Revolutionary* (T. Nairn, Trans.). London: Verso.

Fraser, N. (1997). Heterosexism, Misrecognition, and Capitalism: A Response to Judith Butler. *Social Text,* 52-53, 279-89.

Freire, P. (1989). *Education for the Critical Consciousness.* New York: Continuum.

Freire, P. (1988). *Pedagogia, Dialogo y Conflicto.* Buenos Aires: Ediciones Cinco.

Freire, P., & Gadotti, M. (1995). We Can Reinvent the World. In P. McLaren & J. Giarelli (Eds.), *Critical Theory and Educational Research.* New York: State University of New York Press.

Gordon, A. (1997). *Ghostly Matters: Haunting and the Sociological Imagination.* Minneapolis: University of Minnesota Press.

Gramsci, A. (1971). *Selections from the Prison Notebooks.* New York: International.

Hall, S. (1996). Gramsci's Relevance for the Study of Race and Ethnicity. In D. Morley & K-H Chen (Eds.), *Stuart Hall: Critical Dialogues in Cultural Studies.* London: Routledge.

Hall, S., & Donald, J. (Eds.). (1986). *Politics and Ideology: A Reader.* Philadelphia: Open University Press.

Harris, D. (1992). *From Class to Class Struggle to the Politics of Pleasure: The Effects of Gramscianism on Cultural Studies.* London: Routledge.

Hassoun, J. (1996). *Los contrabandistas de la memoria.* Buenos Aires: Ediciones de la Flor.

Hebdige, D. (1996). Postmodernism and "the other side." In D. Morley & K-H Chen (Eds.), *Stuart Hall: Critical Dialogues in Cultural Studies* (pp. 174-200). London: Routledge.

Hill Collins, P. (1990). *Black Feminist Thought.* New York: Routledge.

Hoffman, J. (1984). *The Gramscian Challenge: Coercion and Consent in Marxist Political Theory.* Oxford: Blackwell.

Katz, A. (1997). Postmodern Cultural Studies: A Critique. *Cultural Logic: An Electronic Journal of Marxist Theory and Practice,* 1 (1).

Laclau, E., & Mouffe, C. (1986). *Hegemony and Socialist Strategy.* London: Verso.

Laclau, E., & Mouffe, C. (1990). *New Reflections on the Revolution of Our Time.* London: Verso.

178 McLaren, Fischman, Serra, and Antelo

Ledwith, M. (1997). *Participating in Transformation: Towards a Working Model of Community Development*. Birmingham: Venture.

Lewis, T. (1996/97). The Politics of "Hauntology" in Derrida's *Specters of Marx. Rethinking Marxism*, 9 (3), 19-39.

McLaren, P., & Lankshear, C. (Eds.). (1994). *Politics of Liberation: Paths from Freire*. London: Routledge.

McLaren, P. (1995). *Critical Pedagogy and Predatory Culture*. London: Routledge.

McLaren, P. (1997). *Revolutionary Multiculturalism: Pedagogies of Dissent for the New Millennium*. Boulder, CO: Westview.

Richards, L. (1998). *The Heart of Knowledge: An Epistemology of Relationship*. Unpublished doctoral dissertation, The Fielding Institute, Santa Barbara.

Torres, C. A. (1992). *The Church, Society and Hegemony*. London: Praeger.

9

Gramsci and Popular Education in Latin America: From Revolution to Democratic Transition[1]

Raymond A. Morrow and Carlos Alberto Torres

> If the philosophy of praxis affirms theoretically that every "truth" believed to be eternal and absolute has had practical origins and has represented a "provisional" value (historicity of every conception of the world and of life), it is still very difficult to make people grasp "practically" that such an interpretation is valid also for the philosophy of praxis itself, without in so doing shaking the convictions that are necessary for action. (Gramsci, 1971, p. 406)

1. Introduction: Gramsci, Education, and Popular Movements

The writings of Antonio Gramsci (1891-1937), a founder of the Italian Communist Party who died in 1937 after eleven years of captivity in a Fascist prison, are increasingly acknowledged—along with the early Frankfurt School—to be the most important contributions to Marxist theory in the first half of this century (Adamson, 1980). The distinctiveness of Gramsci's contributions are linked to a number of now relatively well-known concerns, e.g., the subjective side of praxis, the cultural dimensions of politics (hegemony), the significance of popular culture, the multiple forms and bases of struggle, and the need for historical specificity. Central to all of these preoccupations were pedagogical problems, both in the narrower sense of the school and in broader notions of political learning in relation to his strategic concern with revolutionary transition.

We would like to address how the reception of Gramsci in Latin America poses three fundamental questions about the significance of Gramsci's theory and its relevance at the present time. First, this reception points to the problematic of Marx's "Eurocentrism" and Gramsci's "historicism," and the extent to which the Gramscian model inspired distinctive transformative strategies that have had a significant impact in Latin America. Second, the waning of the Marxist revolutionary project in general poses questions relating to problems of historically reconstructing Gramscian themes in a radically different context defined by the intersection of globalization, democratic transition, and social movements that cannot be understood within the framework of classic revolutionary theories of transition. Third, these first two questions shed light on the tensions within Gramsci's approach to education—in particular, *popular education*—which was torn between a particularistic, class-based conception of revolutionary political learning and a universalistic model of cultural appropriation. In the Latin American context, these issues cannot be interpreted without reference to Paulo Freire's conception of critical pedagogy which had a significant impact on popular education prior to the general reception of Gramsci in the late 1970s and early 1980s.

Before turning to the reception of Gramsci in Latin America, however, we would like to address the question of the "radical" versus "conservative" aspects of Gramsci's pedagogical theory—a theme that has influenced his reception in recent educational theory.

2. Conflicts of Interpretation: Two Gramscis on Education? Radical or Conservative?

A consequence of Gramsci's conception of the learning processes required for effective working-class cultural mobilization is that his overall approach to change is centered on how all politics is educational and all education political. There is, nonetheless, a fundamental tension in his thinking with profound implications for "popular" education. A comparison of Entwistle's (1979) and Adamson's (1980) books on Gramsci's theory points to two apparent logical alternatives in Gramsci's work: either a "conservative" position which uses education to promote workers' acquisition of universal cultural baggage (cognitive and practical skills), or a "radical" stance that privileges the development of the revolutionary political consciousness of workers.

This issue is not only of interest with respect to understanding Gramsci, it also relates to ongoing debates in educational policy in Latin America. Moreover, it has also been introduced in an even more problematic way in the context of American educational debates. The well-known advocate of "cultural literacy," E. D. Hirsch, has recently exploited Gramsci's ostensible "conservative" approach to education (citing Entwistle) by contrasting it with Freire's unrealistic "progressivism":

> Like other educational progressivists, Freire rejected traditional teaching methods and subject matter. [. . .] He called for a change of both methods and content—new content that would celebrate the culture of the oppressed, and new methods that would encourage intellectual independence and resistance. [. . .] Gramsci took the opposite view. He held that political progressivism demanded educational conservatism. The oppressed should be taught to master the tools of power and authority—the ability to read, write, and communicate—and to gain enough traditional knowledge to understand the world and culture around them. Children, particularly the children of the poor, should not be encouraged to flourish "naturally," which would keep them ignorant and make them slaves of emotion. They should learn the value of hard work, gain the knowledge that leads to understanding, and master the traditional culture in order to command its rhetoric, as Gramsci himself had learned to do. (Hirsch, 1999, p. 3)

Entwistle's argument builds on what he takes to be Gramsci's paradox: "the pursuit of a radical political education through a traditional curriculum and pedagogy. If schools are a major hegemonic instrument of existing class rule, how can counter-hegemonic change occur except through radical reform and a liberal pedagogy?" (1979, p. 16). For Entwistle, Gramsci concluded that "to emphasize discipline, intellectual order and the authoritative transmission of the 'thought of the past' is to inoculate the learner against political authoritarianism, as well as to transmit the skills and knowledge necessary for the pursuit of radical social change" (p. 86). Entwistle's assumption is that "the impetus towards a person's political orientation of one kind or another owes little to the ideology of schooling" (p. 89). In short, school knowledge is neutral and empowering—thus the need for a disinterested school; and it is up to the individuals to put their knowledge or skills to the service of status quo or its transformation (p. 91).

The second and more sustained preoccupation of Gramsci's pedagogical thought, however, is the political education of adult workers. But, for Entwistle, there is a paradoxical relationship between the school and worker education which can only be resolved by recognizing that "the key to his theory of political education lies in the education of adults, especially as workers within an occupational context" (p. 111). This is fundamental for Gramsci's distinction between traditional intellectuals and the working class, or organic intellectuals who are to lead the process of working-class self-education outside official educational institutions.

Reframing the Issue

We would argue that there are three basic problems in assessing these tensions in Gramsci's educational theorizing.[2] First, attention needs to be directed to the different contexts of his comments. His comments are frequently directed—often without clear indications—to quite different contexts (fascist Italy, the Soviet Union, a future socialist society, and different types of capitalist society), each of which poses distinctly different issues. In the case of Italy's corrupt parliamentary system threatened by fascist takeover, Gramsci holds out no hope for democratic educational reform. What he might have advocated under a more democratic regime requires a historicist rethinking of Gramsci of the type proposed by Henry Giroux's defense of public education in the U.S. (Giroux, 1999).

Second, the question of the relative emphasis on traditional skills-oriented content versus the formation of a political consciousness must address the specific types of schools and social order in question. In a context where a process of democratization is effectively allowing dominated groups to take advantage of educational opportunities, the technical content of education becomes of crucial importance. However, there is a profound gap between the rhetoric of "standards" and the complex realities of educational reproduction in the Latin American context. Does it make sense to expose children to "universal" knowledge, which is transmitted by badly paid and poorly trained teachers who will exert authority in the classroom? In such contexts, attempts at knowledge appropriation by the working class may result simply in an exposure to authoritarian education of low quality that is rarely completed. These "dropouts" would have been exposed to the "right" knowledge and the wrong authoritarian hidden curriculum, contributing directly to the reproduction of educational inequality.

Third, we think this notion of the "two Gramscis" on education—and Hirsch's related construal of Gramsci and Freire as opposites—involves a false dichotomy between a "radical" and "conservative" position in this context.[3] Gramsci's position with respect to public schools—whether in quasi-democratic or post-revolutionary societies—cannot be neatly labeled "traditional" or "conservative." It is only "conservative" in the sense of not embracing either a dogmatic "Rousseauean" free school model or reducing instruction to the socialization of children into a preconceived, Marxist "proletarian" worldview. With respect to the relation between freedom and discipline, some of Gramsci's remarks stem primarily from reacting to the Gentile reforms in Italy on the grounds that the "spontaneism" they sought to encourage gave a decisive advantage to those who entered the school with high levels of cultural capital. At the same time, he is generally critical of traditional education built on the teaching of Greek and Latin civilization as the foundation for humanist schooling, though appreciative of its ability to inculcate a capacity for discipline (even if at the price of creativity and autonomy). In short, his pragmatic position with respect to variable relations between spontaneity and discipline can be easily reconciled with contemporary cognitive research of the type associated with Piaget and Vygotsky.

Following his criticism of Rousseauean type voluntarism, Gramsci advocates a unified school that attempts to achieve a balance between creativity and discipline. Despite the need for the school to be built around a core curriculum reflecting the needs of society, as well as providing the context for cultivating intellectual "discipline" in the sense of study habits and standards of achievement, Gramsci's common school is not "conservative" in the more traditional sense:

> In fact, the common school should be organised like a college, with a collective life by day and by night, freed from the present forms of hypocritical and mechanical discipline; studies should be carried on collectively, with the assistance of the teachers and the best pupils, even during periods of so-called individual study, etc. (Gramsci, 1971, p. 31)

A key aspect of the common school as a "creative school," therefore, would be to provide a smooth transition from dependent to autonomous learning with maturation, rather than the abrupt shift from the authoritarian school to the university or professional work where a capacity for self-direction is required:

By contrast, therefore, the last phase of the common school must be conceived and structured as the decisive phase, whose aim is to create the fundamental values of "humanism," the intellectual self-discipline and the
moral independence which are necessary for subsequent specialisation—whether it be of a scientific character (university studies) or of an
immediately practical-productive character (industry, civil service, organisation of commerce, etc.) [...] This phase of the school must already contribute to developing the elements of independent responsibility in each
individual, must be a creative school. (p. 32)

The radical character of Gramsci's educational theory lies in its
subtle understanding of the links between culture and power, as well as
critical reflection and practice. His position, however, is not "radical"
(either in the "free school" sense or in the simplistic revolutionary
perspective of the school as imposing a party ideology on the masses
on the Soviet model) because he does not conceive such political educational activity in primarily propagandistic terms. As he puts it in
justifying the formation of a cultural association in Turin in 1917,
party mobilization had raced ahead of the members' understanding:

Consequently, when they do follow the strategy established, they do so out
of a spirit of discipline and out of the trust which they have in their leaders,
more than out of an inner conviction, out of a rational spontaneity [...] This
also explains the phenomena of idolatry, which are a contradiction in our
movement, letting back in through the window the authoritarianism that
was kicked out of the door. (Gramsci, 1985, p. 22)

In short, Gramsci's views on education cannot be located in terms of
the spectrum of a vague notion of "radical" as opposed to "conservative" education based on contemporary debates. If anything, his basic
intuitions coincide most clearly with aspects of John Dewey's philosophy of education, though radicalized in that Gramsci's specific
focus—like that of Freire—is on adult education as a context of political conscientization.

At the heart of Gramscian pedagogy—whether as an account of
political learning or of more general cultural appropriation—is a very
basic thesis with profound implications: that the mobilization of subaltern groups requires the cultivation of what today would be called, in
Freirean terms, a "critical literacy" (Lankshear & McLaren, 1993;
Morrow & Torres, forthcoming). Such a position resists propaganda
or indoctrination as the basis of radical politics. Only those who can
rationally grasp and reflect upon their social and political everyday
lives—as reflective citizens—will be able to form an effective democratic movement, let alone an autonomous personal identity (Torres,
1998). With these issues in mind, we can now turn to the distinctive,

uneven, and contested reception of Gramsci in Latin America, especially in the context of the prior reception of Paulo Freire.

3. The Reception of Gramsci in Latin America
The Latin American Left

Internationally, the most visible versions of the Latin American Left have been revolutionary, as represented by the models of the Cuban revolution and the guerilla strategy of Che Guevara, and by momentary revolutionary successes elsewhere. At the same time, however, official communist parties were ambivalent about such insurrectionary strategies and opted for biding their time awaiting the ripening of capitalist crises. These two versions of the revolutionary Left can be identified with a series of pivotal events: the Cuban Revolution in 1959; the deaths of Che Guevara in 1967 and Salvador Allende in Chile in 1973; the victory of the Nicaraguan Revolution in 1979 and the subsequent defeat of the Sandinistas in the elections of 1990. However, even before the decline of the revolutionary Left in the 1980s, the complexity of the less visible Latin America Left was considerable. In ideological and political terms, four basic groups have been identified: "traditional Communist parties, the nationalist or populist left, the political-military organizations, and the region's reformists. Functionally, two groups can be added: the grass roots and the intellectual left" (Castañeda, 1993, p. 19). The last two decades have been marked by the decline of both the traditional Communist parties and the armed political organizations, coupled with the renewal of the populist Left (especially in response to diverse, multi-class grassroots movements).[4] It is in these latter contexts that Gramsci has played an important and distinctive role.

Discovering Gramsci: Historical Specification

Following the marginalization of Latin America in Hegel's model of world history, Marx and Engels' scattered, often deprecatory, remarks on this region reflected a problem of "Eurocentrism." From a peripheral perspective, "the historical subject 'Latin America' in fact signifies recognizing the limits of a theory for understanding a reality to a great extent 'unclassifiable' in the terms in which Marxism historically was configured as the predominant ideology within the socialist movement" (Aricó, 1980, pp. 37-38). Though the effects of such misunderstandings were already evident in the Second International, they became even worse with Soviet hegemony following the Russian Revolution. In contrast, Gramsci was the first European Marxist theorist to open the way for a creative adaptation of historical materialism to Latin American historical realities.

Though it is not well known, the most substantial and earliest publications of Gramsci's writings (other than Italy) appeared in Argentina and Brazil.[5] This early reception took place primarily on the margins of the Argentinean Communist Party by a group that was eventually expelled (Aricó, 1988, p. 62). Moreover, Gramsci was virtually ignored by the leaders of the Cuban Revolution (Aricó, 1988, p. 137n7). What Marxists in Latin America initially found captivating was the "national" character of Gramsci's thought (Aricó, 1988, p. 54)—that is to say, the fact that Gramsci's Marxism provided a serious and profound reflection on the specific conditions of the Italian social formation, rather than a tedious repetition of the Communist slogans of the Third International. Moreover, Gramsci even made some brief comments on the peculiarities of Latin American societies; i.e., "a situation in which the secular and bourgeois element has not yet reached the state of being able to subordinate clerical and militaristic influence and interest to the secular politics of the modern State" (Gramsci, 1971, p. 22). Most importantly, the conditions of Gramsci's Italy related fairly directly to Latin American questions of "late" development (Aricó, 1988, p. 89). But various factors undermined the possibility of Gramsci having a major impact on the Left from the 1950s to the middle 1970s: the resistance of Latin American Communist parties; periods of dictatorship in Argentina, Brazil, and elsewhere; and the apparent success of the Cuban Revolution and new possibilities for Guevarist-type guerilla insurrections.

Therefore, the current influence of Gramscian thinking reflects a second reception—a virtual Gramsci explosion—beginning in the mid-1970s. Three key factors can be cited for this revival, which was more political than academic. First, the rise of Louis Althusser's structuralist Marxism in the late 1960s and early 1970s brought new attention to Gramsci who was credited with the theory of hegemony, though castigated for his idealist and historicist epistemology. In this context, Gramsci was viewed primarily as a creative successor to Lenin. With the rapid decline of Althusserianism in the late 1970s, however, theorists began to read Gramsci independently, as an alternative to both Althusser and Marxism-Leninism. Second, this new reception was also facilitated by the reprinting, in Mexico, of the long out-of-print Gramsci texts published earlier in Argentina, as well as the initiation, in 1981, of a complete translation of the *Prison Note-*

books. The turning point was marked by an international conference held in Morelia, Mexico in 1980 (Labastida Martín del Campo, 1985) and the publication of a collection of Juan Carlos Pontantiero's essays dating from 1975 onwards (Portantiero, 1981b). A parallel reception also took place in Brazil (Coutinho, 1981; Coutinho & Nogueira, 1985). Third, Gramsci provided insights into the new turn of historical events in Latin America. Beginning in the mid 1970s, the continuing failure of revolutionary movements, the emergence of various middle-class and popular grass roots movements not tied to classic party organizations, and greater knowledge of the historicist origins and implications of Gramsci's thinking contributed to a fundamental rethinking of Marxist theory. An important context for this rethinking was the convergence of the new understanding of Gramsci with Freirean models of popular education.

4. Gramsci and Popular Education:
Popular Education

The theory and practice of "popular education"—an original educational experience in part specific to the region—has had a significant impact in Latin America, both in the domains of nonformal (adult) education and public schooling. Gramsci's work has had a diffuse, somewhat belated, but little clarified impact on this tradition. The paradigm of popular education originated in the early contributions of Paulo Freire in Brazil in the early 1960s, but there are a number of subsequent elaborators of such issues (Gadotti & Torres, 1994). The notion of "popular education" is closely linked with the concept of "popular movements" which have been described as follows:

> By popular movement we understand all of the forms of mobilization of all people from popular classes directly linked to the production process, either in the cities or countryside. Popular movements include neighborhood associations (barrio) in the periphery, clubs of mothers, shantytown (favela) associations, groups of illegal land settlements, (Christian) base communities, groups organized around the struggle for land, and other forms of struggle and popular organizations. Due to their very nature, these movements have a definite class character given the occupational categories of their members. (Documento de São Bernardo, cited in Brandão, 1984, p. 115)

However, this representative formulation points to a number of theoretical ambiguities—and confusions—with respect to the relationships between popular education, popular movements, and classical Marxist revolutionary theory. Despite the "class character" of these movements, their diversity in other respects is striking. In any case, the basic principles of popular education can be summarized as follows:

(1) It has an explicitly political and social intentionality (rationale), which is to work in favor of the poor and socially dominated classes of Latin America societies;

(2) It attempts to combine educational research with processes of education and popular participation;

(3) It understands knowledge both as popular—or common sense—knowledge, and as elitist knowledge, as an instrument of social transformation, thus criticizing any attempt to separate theory from practice, or to dichotomize knowledge as popular wisdom and educated (scientific) thought;

(4) It assumes the need to have, at the outset of any educational practice, a vision of the concrete totality, therefore questioning the effects of technocratic reformism;

(5) It aspires not only to develop critical consciousness (e.g., conscientization á la Freire), but also to construct concrete alternatives for the organization and mobilization (participation) of the poor to overcome the conditions of their own poverty and powerlessness (Centro de Estudios Educativos, 1982);

(6) Finally, it seeks to link popular education to the social movements in Latin America, especially through identification of local basic needs, focusing initially on rural areas but later extending this strategy to urban areas (Gajardo, 1982).

Paradoxically, the essential features of popular education in Latin America emerged during the late 1960s and early 1970s, hence prior to the general reception of Gramsci in the late 1970s and early 1980s.[6] In other words, the initial impact of Paulo Freire was crucial in providing an existential and phenomenological pedagogical foundation that allowed a wide variety of progressive groups—Christian, Marxist, populist, social democratic, and so forth—to find common cause in diverse projects of popular education. But the very flexibility of Freire's pedagogy as a psychosocial method of conscientization did not facilitate addressing what Marcel Gajardo—one of his closest collaborators in Chile—referred to as the question of "the relation between conscientizing education and the different political and ideological projects of the social classes struggling for power" (cited in Austin, 1997, p. 341).

Gramsci and Popular Education

The reception of Gramsci in the 1980s opened the way for a series of debates relating to the reconciliation of Freirean and Gramscian perspectives. Given the intrinsic openness of Freire's thinking as a practical pedagogy and its enormous influence on popular education, his approach has been used in a number of different ways and linked up with diverse social theoretical positions. Paraphrasing Adriana Puiggrós (1994, pp. 15-16), these diverse strategies of "Freirean" popular education can be differentiated as follows:

(1) A more or less literal replication of the principles and methods of literacy training proposed in *The Pedagogy of the Oppressed* and *Education as the Practice of Freedom.*

(2) The selection of privileged social subjects or sectors (e.g., campesinos, marginal urban groups, and women) as the focus of pedagogical action.

(3) The mythification of the creative spontaneity of the masses, thus disqualifying the role of the educators and accumulated cultural traditions.

(4) An "assistentialist," or technocratic strategy that uses Freirean terminology essentially for "banking" purposes as part of social control and reform.

(5) The reduction of "conscientization" to "politicization" by militants in political organizations who re-establish banking relations as part of transmitting political doctrines.

(6) The articulation of popular education with political strategies of social transformation, without reducing it to the political.

With the reception of Gramsci in the 1980s, Freirean popular educators were confronted with fundamental splits over how to appropriate his work for Latin America. On the one hand, three of the first four Freirean alternatives were theoretically ruled out by linking him with Gramsci: ritualistic literacy training in isolation from other practices; pure spontaneism; and an "assistentialist," or manipulative, top-down type reformist strategy.

Debate centered instead around issues related to the other three options: the selection of privileged groups; the reduction of conscientization to political indoctrination; and, the linking of popular education with popular movements in civil society. Discussion of Gramsci in this context was complicated by his self-understanding as a Leninist who attempted to work out the implications of Marxism for the "West." Similarly, those Latin American Leninists inspired by Gramsci could see themselves as doing the same for a peripheral region. From this perspective, it was possible to justify the selection of the working class as a privileged group, even though the significance (even if secondary or derivative in character) of other oppressed subject positions was also acknowledged. At the same time, this Leninized Gramsci implied a direct politicization of conscientization, and its reduction to the strategic logic of party organization.

This injection of a Freirean and Gramscian moment in Leninism, however, did little to overcome the inherent limitations of such strategies in the Latin American context, especially given the division within and between urban and rural sectors, the weakness of civil society, the authoritarian character of the State, and the threats of external intervention (Arnove, 1986; La Belle, 1986; Torres, 1991). Though postrevolutionary Nicaragua provided a fruitful context for the application of Freirean principles, it also revealed the contradictions of linking Freire with Leninism. With the collapse of the Somoza regime and the emergence of a Sandinista revolutionary government in Nicaragua (1979-1989), the paradigm of popular education was used not only to guide educational reform at the level of nonformal education, but also to inspire the principles of the "new education" proposed by the revolutionary state where "the revolution is, in and of itself, an immense and continuous 'political workshop' where revolutionary politics become a sort of pedagogy of the masses and the leadership" (Torres, 1990, p. 111). But these revolutionary intentions must be read in light of authoritarian educational practices that contributed significantly to the subsequent failure of the Sandinistas in the elections of 1990 (Arnove, 1994). In the rather different case of El Salvador, however, the failure of revolutionary forces to gain an outright victory contributed to a pragmatic strategy that allowed popular educational initiatives to remain an ongoing project for bringing literacy training to populations not served by public education (Hammond, 1997). The outcome was Gramscian in spirit, even if based on an ad hoc adaptation of Freirean principles to specific historical conditions rather than a systematic reflection on the failures of Leninism.

On the other hand, the more enduring impact of Gramsci was to provide a theoretical basis for the link between popular education and mobilization within civil society, as well as for questioning class essentialism and the use of Freirean techniques for purposes of political indoctrination. Those who read Gramsci more systematically in historicist terms and independently of the Marxist-Leninist revolutionary model, elaborated pedagogical practices informed by a general—vaguely defined—model of social transformation linked with grassroots movements, democratization, and the building of civil society (Alvarez, Dagnino, & Escobar, 1998; Escobar & Alvarez, 1992).

Within this increasingly dominant framework on the Left, it was possible to accommodate a focus on various privileged groups, as long as this was conceived pluralistically, i.e., not excluding other groups.

Tensions: The Brazilian Debate

The impact of Gramsci on popular education has been especially significant and visible in Brazil and provides important insights about debates within the Left (Gadotti, 1990; Junqueira Paoli, 1981; Tavares de Jesus, 1989). Brazil has also provided the most significant confluence of Freirean and Gramscian influences in the context of popular educational projects oriented toward radical democratization (O'Cadiz, Wong, & Torres, 1998; Stromquist, 1997). As Moacir Gadotti concludes in his comprehensive study of Brazilian education: "The itinerary suggested by Gramsci is very current not only in terms of educational content, but also in the theme of struggle for democracy (democratization), the only way possible to successfully overcome what Gramsci calls 'groups or castes' of privileged people" (1990, p. 69). However, this kind of optimistic reading, linking popular movements and democratization as part of a socialist project, remains an internally diverse position that is at odds with classical Leninist revolutionary theory.

The polarized reception of Gramsci in popular education in Brazil is reflected in two conflicting Left positions that parallel in some respects the "two Gramscis" debate with which we began: a "dialectical" perspective represented in Brazil in the work of Freire and Gadotti, as opposed to a more "technocratic" perspective that emphasizes the critical and social appropriation of universal knowledge on behalf of the popular sectors—by improving the popular sectors' access and control of public schooling. The latter argument—initially developed by Dervermal Saviani (1983, 1991), partly in the name of Gramsci as a critique of Freire—shifts the focus away from politics to the content of education. Therefore, though the political character of education is not denied, political practice and educational activity are differentiated on the grounds that the relationship between student and teacher is not antagonistic. Moreover, following Gramsci (in an interpretation similar to Entwistle's), it is argued that the content of education—as universal knowledge and a form of cultural capital—is the crucial empowering aspect of the school. From this perspective, though the existing tradition of knowledge may be contaminated by its relation to the system of cultural hegemony, students must pass through it to criticize it: "In fact, they can criticize that knowledge and improve it. How can it be improved without passing through it?" (Namo de Melo, 1985, p. 58). In short, from this perspective, the school is defended as the principal (if not exclusive) environment for guaranteeing universal education: an education that allows the popular and subaltern sectors a more competent participation in the world of work, culture, and politics (Namo de Mello, 1985, p. 255).

Critics of this approach see it as a depoliticization of education, hence unable to clearly differentiate itself from liberal technocratic perspectives (Silva & McLaren, 1993). From the dialectical perspective,

> only the popular tendency sees the political education of the working classes as essential for the exercise of hegemony. It privileges politics (of contents) over the technical (reform), insisting on an education that emerges with a popular organization, with the educational projects that the people-nation have. (Gadotti, 1990, p. 161)

Passing through the contents of hegemonic knowledge can only undermine working-class resistance:

> The more that hegemonic discourse penetrates the common sense of subjects (members of the dominated classes), the more it saturates their world-view, their moral and life world, and the more it will increase the power of the dominant classes, who will thus consolidate themselves also as hegemonic classes. (Tamarit, 1990, p. 37)

This controversy does not lend itself to easy answers, either with respect to strategies for educational reform in Brazil and elsewhere, or the implications of Gramsci's pedagogical stance. A crucial factor would appear to be whether, and to what extent, the critical-appropriation position allows one to contest aspects of existing systematic knowledge, as opposed to uncritically taking it for granted. Paradoxically, this is not an issue that Gramsci's thought is always well prepared to deal with since he does not provide a critique of science and technology—a point reflected in his uncritical acceptance of "Fordist" work relations. On the other hand, for the dialectical position, the decisive question is whether a more direct politicization of education—and the resulting risk of the dogmatic imposition of agendas by intellectuals, organic or not—will in fact serve the longer term interests of subordinate groups.

These questions bring us back to the problem of Gramsci's position: are we again confronted with postulating "two Gramscis," though in a different sense than suggested by Entwistle and Hirsch? The crucial issue would appear to be whether it remains plausible, as

Gramsci assumed in his time, that a working class could constitute itself through the formation of a new worldview that breaks decisively with the "leading" hegemonic classes. In its strong form, such a "dialectical" position postulates the possibility of a revolutionary transcendence, hence sustaining the claim that such a technical, organizational, and moral alternative exists and could become hegemonic.

If this classic revolutionary working-class model is no longer plausible (as implied by post-Marxist readings of globalization and postmodernity), then the critical-appropriation position is on strong ground in suggesting that the most realistic strategy is to prepare subordinate classes as well as possible to participate in a worldsystem that can at best be redirected, not overthrown. In this instance, Gramsci's remarks on the "creative school"—though envisioned primarily for a socialist society—become relevant to a radical democratic reformist strategy. But Gramsci's conception of the relation between culture and power—which tends to uncritically accept the organizational imperatives of Fordism and its inevitable effects on workers—needs to be supplemented with a more critical conception of the technical "knowledge" that is to be appropriated in the creative school. Here the critical theory traditions represented by the Frankfurt School and Foucault provide insightful points of departure.

5. Rethinking Gramsci: Popular Movements and Democratic Transition

What kinds of lessons can be learned from the Latin American reception of Gramsci, especially in light of issues such as the Brazilian debates on popular education and the more general question of popular movements and "democratic transition"?

The Brazilian case points to intrinsic dilemmas that defy hard and fast theoretical resolutions based directly on either Gramsci's texts or a projection of their contemporary meaning in Brazil. The most obvious lesson is that the complexity of domination, the multiple roles of education, and the ambiguity of future possibilities will necessarily engender debates among progressive educators that cannot be resolved merely with logical argumentation; nor can empirical research provide much help in the short run. Furthermore, the differences between the "dialectical" and "critical-appropriation" perspectives, like the related tensions between Gramscian and Freirean perspectives on popular education and culture,[7] should not be viewed as impossible to mediate.

The more fundamental issues, perhaps, lie elsewhere. As Mexican political theorist Carlos G. Castañeda has argued, the Gramscian reception in Latin has been confronted with a dilemma:

> behind this ideological and political bewitchment lay a theoretical misunderstanding and a facile solution to real problems. The fact was that most of the movements that burgeoned throughout Latin America during the sixties and seventies only appeared to be "exterior" to the state because the states they faced were typically authoritarian ones, in contrast to previous movements that had been totally incorporated by the state. (Castañeda, 1993, p. 199)

With movement towards democratic transition, however, Latin American societies have been confronted with the same dilemmas found elsewhere: the interpenetration of the State and civil society. At the same time that Latin Americans became enamoured with civil society, European social theory came under the spell of Foucault's conception of the all-pervasiveness of State power. As Castañeda warns, without calling for a return to Leninism, the Latin American reaction runs the danger of a "substitutive wishful thinking" which holds—without altogether persuasive argument or evidence—that a "new left emanating from the plural, proliferating popular movements could succeed where others had failed" (1993, p. 200).

In any case, the resulting split between the "party Left" and the "movement Left" has redefined oppositional organization: "Indeed, from this perspective, the left's most important successes of recent years are all of the 'movement' variety. Lula's coalition in Brazil in 1989, Cárdenas's broad front in Mexico in 1988, the Coalición del NO in Chile in 1988 constitute examples of this" (Castañeda, 1993, p. 202). A key theoretical question is whether this movement strategy, though not fully consistent with Gramsci's specific stance in the 1930s, could be reconciled with a fundamental reconstruction of his approach in light of the new historical circumstances.

A decisive problem for a conventional Gramscian analysis today is that "organic" intellectuals have not followed his revolutionary script. Revolutionary neo-Gramscians have assumed that the emergence of "organic" intellectuals within the working class would provide the catalyst for linking theory and praxis. But the history of urban labor, rural campesino, and indigenous movements has provided contradictory support for this thesis: intellectuals rooted in "working-class" social relations have taken a variety of positions linked to diverse factors, but never consistently from a classic "revolutionary" perspective. It was not by accident that Lenin saw as the only alternative a theoretical avant-garde led by bourgeois "traditional" intellectuals. Much neo-Gramscian theory, in short, has not completely freed itself from the mystique of revolution or fully embraced the consequences of Gramsci's absolute historicism. Writing more than two decades ago, at the height of the revival of revolutionary neo-Marxism in the mid-1970s, Perry Anderson—implicitly drawing upon Trotsky and Gramsci—concludes his otherwise insightful survey of Western Marxism with a renewed appeal to the theoretical mystique of the revolutionary "masses," noting that while the conditions for revolutionary Marxism had been absent since the Second World War:

> The prospects for their reappearance are now, however, at last increasing. When a truly revolutionary movement is born in a mature working class, the "final shape" of theory will have no exact precedent. All that can be said is that when the masses themselves speak, theoreticians—of the sort the West has produced for fifty years—will necessarily be silent. (1976, p. 106)

This "optimistic" projection now appears misguided. The theoretical problem with this formulation is that "masses" do not speak. A revolutionary democratic public sphere can only be constituted by concrete groups with diverse identities necessarily articulated by new types of "organic" theoreticians in dialogue with various types of "traditional" and "independent" intellectuals. Although the resulting theory may have "no exact precedent," it has not taken the shape presumed by Anderson's philosophy of history. Though Gramsci may have identified with this vision in his own time, his absolute historicism would today push him to rethink his own project along lines that would have to confront the democratic theory of current "post-Marxism" (Laclau, 1990; Laclau & Mouffe, 1985). His own method would force him to admit the complexity of the task and the necessity to return to concrete historical experience. From this perspective, no totalizing theoretical solution can be found in any given understanding of "correct" praxis, and no single modus operandi (or praxis per se) will safely lead theory through the labyrinths of logical appraisals of the complexity of reality. For better or worse, popular movements and participatory educational and community projects provide the primary source of inspiration for the transformative processes that sustain the Left in contemporary Latin America. Whether the contribution of such popular movements will culminate in something more than a formal "democratic transition" remains more a question of practice than of theory. In any case, Gramsci would have methodological grounds for taking seriously the implications of the post-Soviet decline of working-class revolutionary ideology. He would be confronted, in short, with the question of whether, and to what extent, these new grass roots popular movements possess the "rationality and historicity" that respond to the new "demands of a complex organic period of history."

> It is evident that this kind of mass creation cannot just happen "arbitrarily," around any ideology, simply because of the formally constructive will of a personality or a group which puts it forward solely on the basis of its own fanatical philosophical or religious convictions. *Mass adhesion or non-adhesion to an ideology is the real critical test of the rationality and historicity of modes of thinking.* Any arbitrary constructions are pretty rapidly eliminated by historical competition, even if sometimes, through a combination of immediately favourable circumstances, they manage to enjoy a popularity of a kind; whereas constructions which respond to the demands of a complex organic period of history always impose themselves and prevail in the end, even though they may pass through several intermediary phases during which they manage to affirm themselves only in more or less bizarre and heterogeneous combinations. (Gramsci, 1971, p. 341)

Notes

1. The translations from the Spanish and Portuguese are our own unless otherwise indicated.

2. For a similar argument we encountered only after completing this essay, see Giroux (1999).

3. For a more elaborate critique of Hirsch, see Giroux (1999).

4. Though the Chiapas Zapatista movement in Mexico is armed, its strategy is implicitly that of a democratic, grassroots movement based in civil society, echoing Gramsci even though his name is not used (Bruhn, 1999).

5. José Aricó, one of the early representatives of Gramsci's thought in Latin America, notes that the *Quaderni del carcere* were partially published in Buenos Aires, Argentina, between 1958-1962; in Brazil, Portuguese editions appeared between 1966-1968: "both editions were the more numerous and complete produced in any languages other than Italian" (1988, p. 135).

6. For example, in the early 1970s, in Argentina, Barreiro's influential Marxist interpretation of Freire only alludes to Gramsci in passing, drawing instead upon social phenomenology and Poulantzas' structuralism to construct a problematic agency-structure dialectic (Barreiro, 1974). The turning point was the reception of Gramsci in the late 1970s, and the appearance of Manacorda's Italian selection of Gramsci's writings on education (Gramsci, 1981). Hence, until then, Gramscian theory remained a peripheral (even if emergent) influence on leftist educational theory. For example, the first edition of

the comprehensive anthology by Rivera and Torres included an expository essay on Gramsci (Portantiero, 1981a), but his work remains peripheral to the volume as a whole. Discussion of Althusser's problematic impact is more prominent. Though Carlos A. Torres mentions Gramsci in an extensive discussion of the sociology of education, his sources are all non-Latin American (Torres, 1981, p. 78). Only Puiggrós demonstrates some broader implications by drawing upon Gramsci as part of her critique of French structuralism; she cites the work of Chantal Mouffe (Puiggrós, 1981). Nor is there any extensive engagement with Gramsci in the adult education literature before the 1980s (e.g., Torres, 1982).

7. See especially Peter Mayo's suggestive discussion of a Gramsci-Freire synthesis (Mayo, 1999, p. 126).

References

Adamson, W. L. (1980). *Hegemony and Revolution: A Study of Antonio Gramsci's Political and Cultural Theory*. Berkeley: University of California Press.

Alvarez, S. E., Dagnino, E., & Escobar, A. (Eds.). (1998). *Cultures of Politics/Politics of Cultures: Re-Visioning Latin American Social Movements*. Boulder, CO: Westview.

Anderson, P. (1976). *Considerations on Western Marxism*. London: NLB.

Aricó, J. (1988). *La cola del diablo: Itenerario de Gramsci en América Latina*. Caracas: Nueva Sociedad.

Aricó, J. (1980). *Marx y América Latina*. México, D. F.: Alianza Editorial Mexicana.

Arnove, R. F. (1994). *Education as Contested Terrain: Nicaragua, 1979-1993*. Boulder, CO: Westview.

Arnove, R. F. (1986). *Education and Revolution in Nicaragua*. New York: Praeger.

Austin, R. (1997). Freire, Frei, and Literacy Texts in Chile, 1964-1970. In C. A. Torres & A. Puiggrós (Eds.), *Latin American Education: Comparative Perspectives* (pp. 323-48). Boulder, CO: Westview.

Barreiro, J. (1974). *Educación y proceso de conscientización*. Mexico, D. F.: Siglo Veintiuno.

Brandão, C. R. (1984). *Pensar a prática*. São Paulo: Edições Loyola.

198   Raymond A. Morrow and Carlos Alberto Torres

Bruhn, K. (1999). Antonio Gramsci and the *Palabra Verdadera*: The Political Discourse of Mexico's Guerrilla Forces. *Journal of Interamerican Studies & World Affairs*, 41, 29-56.

Castañeda, J. G. (1993). *Utopia Unarmed: The Latin American Left after the Cold War*. New York: Knopf.

Centro de Estudios Educativos. (1982). *La educación popular en América Latina. ¿Avance o retroceso?* México, D. F.: Centro de Estudios Educativos.

Coutinho, C. N. (1981). *Gramsci*. Porto Alegre: L&PM Editores.

Coutinho, C. N., & Nogueira, M. A. (Eds.). (1985). *Gramsci e a América Latina*. Rio de Janeiro: Paz e Terra.

Entwistle, H. (1979). *Antonio Gramsci: Conservative Schooling for Radical Politics*. London: Routledge & Kegan Paul.

Escobar, A., & Alvarez, S. E. (Eds.). (1992). *The Making of Social Movements in Latin America: Identity, Strategy, and Democracy*. Boulder, CO: Westview.

Gadotti, M. (1990). *Uma só escola para todos*. Petrópolis: Vozes.

Gadotti, M., & Torres C. A. (Eds.). (1994). *Educação popular: Utopia Latino-Americanada*. Sao Paulo: Cortez Editora/Editora da Universidade de São Paulo.

Gajardo, M. (1982). *Evolución, situación actual y perspectivas de las strategías de investigación participativa en América Latina*. Santiago: FLACSO.

Giroux, H. (1999). Rethinking Cultural Politics and Radical Pedagogy in the Work of Antonio Gramsci. *Educational Theory*, 49, 1-19.

Gramsci, A. (1985). *Antonio Gramsci: Selections from the Cultural Writings* (D. Forgacs & G. Nowell Smith, Eds. and W. Boelhower, Trans.). Cambridge, MA: Harvard University Press.

Gramsci, A. (1981). *La alternativa pedagogica* (M. A. Manacorda, Ed. and C. Cristos, Trans.). Barcelona: Editorial Fontamara.

Gramsci, A. (1971). *Selections from the Prison Notebooks* (Q. Hoare & G. Nowell Smith, Trans.). New York: International.

Hammond, J. L. (1997). Popular Education and the Reconstruction of El Salvador. In C. A. Torres & A. Puiggrós (Eds.), *Latin American Education: Comparative Perspectives* (pp. 349-71). Boulder, CO: Westview.

Hirsch, E. D. (1999). Reality's Revenge: Research and Ideology. *Arts Education Policy Review*, 99, 3-16.

Junqueira Paoli, N. (1981). *Ideologia e hegemonia. As condições de produção da educação*. São Paulo: Cortez Editora-Autores Associados.

La Belle, T. J. (1986). *Nonformal Education in Latin American and the Carribbean: Stability, Reform, or Revolution?* New York: Praeger.

Labastida Martín del Campo, J. (Ed.). (1985). *Hegemonía y alternativas políticas en américa latina (Seminario de Morelia)*. México, D. F.: Siglo Veintiuno.

Laclau, E. (1990). *New Reflections on The Revolution of Our Time*. London: Verso.

Laclau, E., & Mouffe, C. (1985). *Hegemony and Socialist Strategy: Towards a Radical Democratic Politics* (W. Moore & P. Cammack, Trans.). London: Verso.

Lankshear, C., & McLaren, P. L. (Eds.). (1993). *Critical Literacy: Politics, Praxis, and the Postmodern*. Albany: State University of New York Press.

Mayo, P. (1999). *Freire and Adult Education: Possibilities for Transformative Action*. London: Zed.

Morrow, R. A., & Torres, C. A. (forthcoming). *Critical Social Theory and Education: Freire, Habermas and the Dialogical Subject*. New York: Teacher's College Press, Columbia University.

Namo de Melo, G. (1985). *Las clases populares y la institución escolar: una interacción contradictoria. Educación y clases sociales en América Latina*. México, D. F.: DIE.

O'Cadiz, M., Wong, P. L., & Torres, C. A. (1998). *Education and Democracy: Paulo Freire, Social Movements, and Educational Reform in São Paulo*. Boulder, CO: Westview.

Portantiero, J. C. (1981a). Gramsci y la educación. In G. G. Rivera & C. A. Torres (Eds.), *Sociología de la educación: Corrientes contemporáneas* (pp. 221-28). México, D. F.: Centro de Estudios Educativos.

Portantiero, J. C. (1981b). *Los usos de Gramsci*. México, D. F.: Folios Ediciones.

Puiggrós, A. (1994). Historia y prospectiva de la educación popular latinoamericana. In M. Gadotti & C. A. Torres (Eds.), Sao *Educação popular: Utopia Latino-Americanada* (pp. 13-22). São Paulo: Cortez Editora/Editora da Universidade de São Paulo.

Puiggrós, A. (1981). La sociología de la educación en Baudelot y Establet. In G. G. Rivera & C. A. Torres (Eds.), *Sociología de la educación: Corrientes contemporáneas* (pp. 279-302). México, D. F.: Centro de Estudios Educativos.

Saviani, D. (1991). *Pedagogia histórica-crítica. Primeras aproximações*. São Paulo: Cortez-Editoria Autores Associados.

Saviani, D. (1983). *Escola e democracia*. São Paulo: Cortez-Editoria Autores Associados.

200   Raymond A. Morrow and Carlos Alberto Torres

Silva, T., & McLaren, P. (1993). Knowledge Under Siege. In P. McLaren & P. Leonard (Eds.), *Paulo Freire: A Critical Encounter* (pp. 36-46). London: Routledge.

Stromquist, N. P. (1997). *Literacy for Citizenship: Gender and Grassroots Dynamics in Brazil.* Albany, NY: State University of New York Press.

Tamarit, J. (1990). El dilema de la educación popular: entre la utopía y la resignación. *Revista Argentina de Educación,* 8, 7-45.

Tavares de Jesus, A. (1989). *Educação e hegemonia no pensamento de Antonio Gramsci.* São Paulo: Editora Unicamp-Cortez.

Torres, C. A. (1998). *Democracy, Education, and Multiculturalism: Dilemmas of Citizenship in a Global World.* Lanham, MD: Rowman & Littlefield.

Torres, C. A. (1991). The State, Nonformal Education, and Socialism in Cuba, Nicaragua, and Grenada. *Comparative Education Review,* 35, 110-30.

Torres, C. A. (1990). *The Politics of Nonformal Education in Latin America.* New York: Praeger.

Torres, C. A. (Ed.). (1982). *Ensayos sobre la educación de los adultos en América Latina.* México, D. F.: Centro de Estudios Educativos.

Torres, C. A. (1981). Materiales para una historia de la sociología de la educación en América Latina. In G. G. Rivera & C. A. Torres (Eds.), *Sociología de la educación: Corrientes contemporáneas* (pp. 77-107). México, D. F.: Centro de Estudios Educativos.

10

Antonio Gramsci's Contributions to Radical Adult Education

Paula Allman

There are many variants of radical education. When I use this term I mean forms of education, political engagement, and other forms of cultural action which aim, in the first instance (i.e., within capitalist social relations), to prepare people to totally transform their social and economic mode of existence. These forms of engagement involve a struggle to challenge and transform the given social and epistemological relations of such encounters as we currently experience them. Antonio Gramsci offers many important contributions to developing this type of radical education.

To interpret Gramsci's contribution within the type of radical projects I have defined I must begin by establishing that there are two essential ingredients which we need in order to inform our "reading" of Gramsci. First, Gramsci's analysis and his ideas are firmly grounded in an understanding of Marx's dialectical theory of consciousness, and I will begin by briefly explaining this theory. The second ingredient pertains to our own approach to studying Gramsci. This is the approach Gramsci himself advocated, and it will be discussed in greater detail later. It involves a critical attempt to grasp the *leitmotiv*, or guiding thread, of Gramsci's thought that develops and links his thinking about revolutionary tactics and strategy. (My references and notes provide a guide to his *leitmotiv* for readers who wish to follow it in more detail than I can offer here.) I must note that, unfortunately, I can only attempt this with reference to his works available in English translation; others, hopefully, will have the linguistic competency to take this attempt much further than I can. I begin with Marx, the first ingredient, because his thinking is so fundamental to Gramsci's own thought and, therefore, an accurate indication of the meaning that Gramsci is trying to convey.

In the nineteenth century, Marx's theory of consciousness was both philosophically and practically revolutionary, and it remains so today. Marx always began every analysis from a dialectical conceptualization of the material or real world, a world that was never static but historically and dialectically dynamic. This conceptualization derives from his understanding of a dialectical contradiction. Marx offers his definition with reference to a specific example; others, such as Colletti (1975), have more recently offered general definitions. I will begin with my own general definition, one that draws on Colletti as well as "the philosophy of internal relations" (Ollman, 1976, 1991), in order to generalize Marx's definition. A dialectical contradiction is the unity, or relation, of two opposites, which are internally related such that they could not exist, or have existed historically, outside of the way in which they are related. Therefore the historical development, or change, within each opposite depends primarily on the nature of the relation rather than factors external to the relation. Marx in *The Holy Family* (1844), which he coauthored with Engels, offered his definition of a dialectical contradiction by reference to the specific relation between the proletariat and capital (Marx & Engels, 1975, pp. 34-38 —according to the "Table of Contents," Marx wrote this section). He portrayed the proletariat and capital as two opposites within an antagonistic/oppressive dialectical social relation. Using the philosophical language which is more prevalent in his early writings, Marx says that one of the opposites (capital) is the "positive," in that it is in the interest of the capitalist class to preserve this type of relation; therefore, it is positive only in the sense of the relation and its preservation. The other opposite, in this case the proletariat, is the "negative." It is in the interest of this class to abolish the relation, and in so doing to abolish itself as a separate and oppressed class, to create a classless and totally nonoppressive social formation.

Again using philosophical terms, this is called the "negation of the negation"; the negative opposite ceases to exist as an oppressed group by abolishing an antagonistic relation and creating an existence and a history, where all people live in harmony. Needless to say, throughout the historical development of this particular relation, the negative opposite has been, at best, a restless negative—one which struggles for gains of a type within the relation rather than one which devotes its energies, in the first and continuous instance, to abolishing the antagonistic relation that is the bedrock of this dialectical contradiction—to devote its energies to the "negation of the negation."

This definition or conceptualization of a dialectical contradiction underpins Marx's dialectical theory of consciousness; and it is this theory of consciousness that underpins Gramsci's analysis of his own conjuncturally specific context and his ideas for challenging it. Marx's theory of consciousness posits a dialectical unity between social being (active sensuous experience) and consciousness. This can be difficult to grasp because it seems obvious that we are born into a world where consciousness, ideas, and thought already exist. However, Marx insists that these forms of consciousness also arose from social being or in unity with people's active engagement in their social conditions of existence—an existence prior to our own. This dialectical unity of thought and "being" is called praxis. One could say that Marx's theory of consciousness is actually a theory of praxis (Allman & Wallis, 1990; Allman, 1999).

Although Marx never used these terms, he discussed two very different forms of praxis. One could be called limited or reproductive praxis; the other is critical or revolutionary praxis. People engaged in reproductive praxis are born into certain social relations, modes of existence, which they accept as natural, even inevitable. They fail to question these and, therefore, reproduce the type of consciousness and conditions of social being that are already in existence. Minor changes or reforms may be attained, but these are not of a type that challenges or threatens the fundamental social relations—that is, the dialectical contradictions that make the capitalist social/economic formation possible. Critical/revolutionary praxis involves becoming critically aware of these fundamental social relations and actively planning and engaging in the various forms of action that could lead to their abolition (Allman, 1999). I must stress again that it is not the people who constitute opposite groups or classes whom those engaged in critical praxis seek to abolish, but the relation that constitutes the opposites in an antagonistic or dehumanizing manner.

I turn now to the second ingredient that we need to inform our "reading" of Gramsci. As I mentioned previously, it was Gramsci who suggested to us how we should formulate an interpretation of his ideas. In discussing how we should interpret Marx's writings, Gramsci says that we should search for his "guiding thread" or *leitmotiv* as it develops throughout his writings (SPN, p. 383); and this is an approach that is equally applicable to Gramsci's own work. It is Gramsci's guiding thread which I have attempted to identify and upon which I have based my interpretation of his ideas.

Gramsci, like many other communists of his time, was attempting, in his prison notebooks, to analyze why proletarian revolutions had not occurred in the West in the aftermath of the 1917 Bolshevik Revolution in Russia. His analysis appears to draw heavily upon Marx's analysis of the bourgeois democratic state. From this analysis, Gramsci concluded that there had to be two phases of revolution in the West. He explains that in Western democracies power is experienced and consent engineered not just through the political State, as it was in pre-Revolutionary Russia, but also within the various organizations of civil society, e.g., the family, church, trade unions, and education (which falls within both the State and civil society) (SPN, II, 2). He uses the term hegemony, or moral ethical leadership, to describe the means by which consent is organized. According to Gramsci, however, hegemony as a form of leadership can either work primarily through domination or direction. In his analysis of hegemony in bourgeois civil society, Gramsci describes how it works primarily through domination or the imposition of ideological systems of belief, as well as through the absorption of radical elements into the existing framework (SPN, pp. 57-59). On the other hand, when he uses the term hegemony with reference to "the war of position" or the socialist project to establish hegemony prior to the "war of movement," or revolution, he suggests a type of leadership which involves direction, vision, and collaboration with the people rather than domination.[1] Of course, once political power is achieved, there would be the necessary domination of the enemies of the new order. Therefore, Gramsci conceptualizes hegemony as a combination of moral ethical direction and domination, or a unity of consent and force. With socialist hegemony, however, consent is not manipulated or managed, but arrived at through critical choice.

I think that one of the greatest sources of confusion in Gramsci's prison notebooks comes from his use of terms or concepts in two different senses. This is particularly true with his use of the terms hegemony and ideology. This is why it is so essential to follow his *leitmotiv.* I will begin by first analyzing a brief section of the notebooks wherein readers would expect to find the meaning he attributed to the term ideology. Then, I will return to a discussion of this problem in relation to his use of the term hegemony. Counter-hegemony, a term so often attributed to him, was never used, to my knowledge, by Gramsci. However, this term is extremely useful, and I hope the reason why will become clear in this discussion.

Before undertaking my own in-depth study of Gramsci and when I was attempting to arrive at a critical theorization of ideology, I had read many current Marxist theorists' explanations of ideology (see, for example, Simon, 1982 and Hall, 1982). These authors encouraged me to think that the concept of ideological struggle they had drawn from Gramsci involved the transformation of ideology—the replacement of an inferior ideology by a better, more comprehensive, socialist ideology. When I began to read Gramsci for myself, however, I could not agree. To start with, I could not agree, in particular, with one thing that Simon claims:

> In reading the *Prison Notebooks* it is helpful to bear in mind that Gramsci uses a variety of terms which for him are broadly equivalent to ideology, such as culture, philosophy, or world outlook or conception of the world as well as the phrase "moral and intellectual reform" when he is dealing with the transformation of ideology required for the advance to socialism. (1982, p. 59)

On the contrary, I thought Gramsci was struggling to draw distinctions between ideas, particularly those that had to do with political strategies, and was not just using them interchangeably. My reading of Gramsci also indicated that he was using his prison notebooks to clarify his thinking. He was not just criticizing other people's ideas but also his own previous thought and political practice (e.g., SPW). Most importantly, however, I did not think that he was trying to transform ideology in order to come up with an ideology appropriate for socialism. I think he was trying to transform the meaning of ideology, the meaning of the word itself, when he used it in connection with Marxism or revolutionary strategy. In fact, he goes so far as to suggest this strategy even in the context of a post-revolutionary situation (SPN, p. 453). He felt that even radical social change could not transform the external aspect of language, the word. Nevertheless, he stresses that "the content of the language must be changed." In a few places, Gramsci signals that he is changing the meaning or content of the term ideology, by referring alternatively to "ideology in the bad sense" or "ideology in the highest sense" (e.g., SPN, pp. 328 and 407). However, he is not very consistent in doing so, and this makes any definitive interpretation of what he is saying in one place or another impossible. Therefore, Gramsci uses ideology to refer to both something that is negative and something that is positive; however, Gramsci's distinction arises from changing the actual meaning of ideology whenever he uses it to mean something positive,[2] rather than from contrasting competing explanations or systems of belief. Whether or not either of these tactics leads to an appropriate socialist strategy is a question to which I will return later. First, I want to consider whether Gramsci's attempt to change the meaning of ideology was successful.

In a section entitled "The Concept of 'Ideology'" (SPN, pp. 357-77), Gramsci comes closest to a definition of this term. The only problem is that he offers two definitions; and it is open to interpretation as to which one he considers "the bad sense." He starts off with the observation that in the context of eighteenth-century French materialism, ideology meant the science of ideas; and, since science meant analysis, ideology actually meant "'the investigation of the origin of ideas' [definition one]" (p. 375). Rather than rejecting this definition, he dismisses the assumption of French materialism that ideas are derived from sensations. He seems to imply that the origin of ideas was being sought in the wrong place. Gramsci then offers a second definition by suggesting that there should be an investigation of the historical process through which the meaning of ideology changed from an "'analysis of the origin of ideas' to meaning specific 'systems of ideas' [definition two]" (p. 376).

At this point, then, Gramsci has suggested two definitions; but, in his next paragraph, it is not clear which of these he is referring to—he actually seems to use both. First he says that Freud was the last of the "Ideologues"; and just after this he says that Bukharin in his *Popular Manual* (a popular guide to Marx's ideas) had remained "trapped in Ideology" (SPN, p. 376). One must assume that the reference to Freud pertains to his psychoanalysis of the "origin of ideas." However, if we consider that later in the *Notebooks* Gramsci accuses Bukharin of dispensing a mechanical, dogmatic, undialectical presentation of Marxism, then the reference to his entrapment seems to refer to a "system of ideas" (SPN, pp. 471-72). The lack of clarity, here, is extremely unfortunate because in the next sentence Gramsci says:

> the philosophy of praxis [this is the term Gramsci uses to refer to Marx's philosophy] represents a distinct advance [. . .] in opposition to Ideology. [. . .] Marxist philosophy implicitly contains a negative value judgement and excludes the possibility that for [Marx and Engels] the origin of ideas should be sought for in sensations [. . .] (SPN, 376)

It is important to remember that these are Gramsci's notebooks, not a finished exposition. Considering this together with his *leitmotiv*, it seems to me he is saying that Marx and Engels's theory of ideology was a theory of the origin of ideas but not one which attributed that origin to sense impressions or any other physiological or psychological source. However, just when you think you might be reaching a clear idea about how Gramsci is changing the content of the term from "system of ideas" to the "analysis of the origin of ideas," he begins to discuss distinctions between different "systems of ideas." He says that in assessing the worth of an ideology there can be a problem because "the name ideology is given both to the necessary superstructure of a particular structure and to the arbitrary elucubrations of particular individuals" (SPN, p. 376). Immediately before this he has said: "Ideology itself must be analysed historically, in terms of the philosophy of praxis, as a superstructure." These passages could be read in two ways. One reading encourages the interpretation that ideology, including the "philosophy of praxis," is a system of ideas, but more precisely a system of ideas that is organically necessary to a particular structure. The ideologies of individuals are of no serious concern unless they are mistaken for organically necessary ones. So, liberal-democratic ideology would be necessary to British capitalism, and Marxist ideology would be organically necessary to socialism. This seems to be the way that many Marxist and neo-Marxist writers interpret what Gramsci is saying. My reading or interpretation of these passages, however, is quite different.

Although it may appear that Gramsci is reverting to definition two, "a system of ideas," I think he is actually developing his discussion of the real origin of ideas. The origin is either material reality, the structure, or "arbitrary elucubrations of individuals." So these are not refinements of definition two. The task for the "philosophy of praxis" is to analyze the origin of ideas in the structure—to grasp the relations from which these ideas emerge. Marxist ideology, rather than being a system of ideas, would involve an analysis of reality, a way of conceiving or understanding the structure that would enable people to change it. Therefore, the use of ideology would entail the type of radical education project previously defined. Of course, my interpretation is only feasible if you accept that Gramsci changed the content of the term ideology when he used it in connection with Marxism (or the "philosophy of praxis"), but retained its "bad sense," a system of ideas, when referring to bourgeois ideology.

Unfortunately, no one can offer a definitive interpretation of these three pages because Gramsci simply is not clear. Nevertheless, the two interpretations have important implications for strategy, especially for interpreting what Gramsci was advocating as a revolutionary strategy and the process of education that would be involved in that strategy.[3] Before leaving these points about interpretation, one further comment is necessary. From what Gramsci has said, we can see that he thought ideologies were the organically necessary superstructure of a particular structure. We also know that he thought the "philosophy of praxis" was a more advanced form of thinking than existing ideologies. Furthermore, the structure he is referring to is a capitalist one. So if, as he claims, Marxism is "an advance," he clearly cannot be referring to it as "a system of ideas" or a superstructure because it arose prior to the existence of any socialist structure and is certainly not a superstructure organically linked to capitalism. On the other hand, Marx's analysis is organically linked to capitalism in the sense that it is historically specific to the capitalist mode of production; but, as Gramsci makes clear, there is an important difference between "analysis" and "a system of ideas." His use of ideology in connection with Marxism must refer to a way of understanding the origin of the existing "system of ideas," viz., bourgeois ideology. This, in fact, is what Marx's critique or critical analysis of capitalism does (Allman, 1999). It is fortunate for those of us trying to interpret Gramsci that he had a great deal more to say about ideology than what he says on these three pages. In fact, you need to consider every other reference he makes to this term in the notebooks in order to interpret this section and to contextualize these references in respect to his *leitmotiv*. I think that my later discussion of Gramsci's revolutionary strategy, in particular, will add further weight to the interpretation I have just given of his concept of ideology. Furthermore, Marx's theory of consciousness contains a critical, negative concept of existing ideologies or systems of belief; and, as I have suggested, Gramsci's thinking is fundamentally grounded in that theory.

Another concept in Gramsci's writings, one essential to his strategy for revolution and the educational relations necessary to that strategy, is his notion of what it currently means, and what it could mean, to be a human being. Once again, he seems to hold an idea very similar to, if not identical with, the one that can be culled from Marx's writings. In a section of the *Notebooks* entitled "What is Man?," Gramsci says that it is important to think of people as beings who exist in "active relationships"—with one another and with nature. He also suggests that our "individuality" is the result of the "ensemble of these relations" (p. 352). In other words, what we are like as human beings does not exist before our relationships with other people and our natural and social circumstances. Furthermore, we can become conscious of the historically specific nature of our current relations and can actively, in association with other people, create new relations within which we could realize our human potential to plan and direct our historical future (Allman, 1999). Taking into consideration the limitations which the current ensemble of relations places on our consciousness (limited praxis), Gramsci reminds us that so far in history, human beings have not been united by their capacity for thought but rather by what they think and how they think; and, of course, this has differentiated as well as united us (SPN, p. 355). He also stresses that the current ensemble of relations is based on dialectical contradictions. "Indeed social relations are expressed by various groups of [people] which each presupposes the others and whose unity is dialectical not formal. Man is aristocratic in so far as man is a serf, etc."

Gramsci clearly states that Marx's thinking was the most advanced form of thinking—even more advanced than Hegel's dialectical philosophy. He stresses that it is "a new way of philosophising which is more concrete and historical than what went before"—that is, other forms of philosophy, including Hegel's (p. 448). The last quote comes from a section of the notebooks where Gramsci, in criticizing Bukharin's *Popular Manual*, offers his clearest articulation of his own understanding of Marx's ideas. When read in its totality, this section makes it clear that Gramsci had fully understood that Marx's materialism was epistemologically revolutionary and was entirely distinct from past forms of materialism. Besides trying to evade the prison censor, I suspect that Gramsci's use of the expression "philosophy of praxis," rather than "dialectical" or "historical materialism," was also part of his polemic with deterministic and mechanical interpretations of Marx, such as those contained in the *Popular Manual* (see SPN, pp. 419-72).

Gramsci also recognized that, according to Marx, there are different types or levels of consciousness. Gramsci emphasizes the difference between common sense, ideology, and the philosophy of praxis. He stresses that all people are philosophers in that they hold some conception of the world. Common sense, however, is fragmented due to the limitations and contradictions we experience in our daily lives. Ideologies (in the bad or negative sense) draw upon these fragments, offering partial explanations; but they do so with a coherence that is able to organize people and cement the hegemony of a particular ruling group (see SPN, pp. 197-98, 324-25, 404-05).

As I mentioned, Gramsci thought the "philosophy of praxis" was a new form of thinking or "philosophizing," and that it was the pinnacle of philosophical achievement—the most advanced form of thinking ever achieved by human beings. It was a "superior conception of the world" because it had been elaborated in a "scientific" and also a "coherent way" (SPN, p. 418). Therefore, the "philosophy of praxis" provides a coherence, as does ideology; but, instead, it is a scientific—that is, a nonideological or dialectical —coherence. In fact, as noted before, he insists that the "philosophy of praxis [. . .] is precisely in opposition to ideology" (p. 376).

In terms of socialist political strategy, it seems to me that Gramsci is saying that political leaders should use ideology—the analysis of the origin of ideas—to problematize people's already existing thought (common sense), so that all people can become philosophers of praxis. This suggests that Gramsci's political strategy is based on, or requires, a radical educational process. Before discussing the passages in the notebooks that imply such a strategy, it is important to note that the strategic implication deriving from the idea of three different levels of thought or consciousness can be, and frequently is, interpreted differently. For readers who do not accept that Gramsci uses the term ideology in two different senses (i.e., for those who maintain that for Gramsci "ideology" means only a coherent system of beliefs), the "philosophers of praxis" are only the "organic intellectuals"[4] of the working class or the vanguard political leaders. It is they who engage in the dialectical analysis of reality and who translate it into a coherent system of beliefs (ideology) capable of organizing the consent and the action of the people. Given some passages in the notebooks, this interpretation is entirely feasible. I would argue, however, and I think experience has also indicated, that this leads to an inappropriate strategy—the type of strategy that would contradict Gramsci's guiding thread.

In discussing what an accurate theory of the "philosophy of praxis" would entail, Gramsci says it would have to work out: "the relationships between ideologies, concepts of the world and philosophies" (p. 425). His editor/translators comment that Gramsci is attempting to answer questions pertaining to those relationships in the philosophical sections of the notebooks. In those sections, Gramsci stresses that it is important to challenge the idea that philosophy is of interest and comprehensible only to intellectuals or specialists (p. 323). After arguing that everyone is a philosopher because he or she holds a conception of the world, he suggests that we all need to move away from thinking in the fragmented way, which is characteristic of common sense, and that we should never accept uncritically ideas imposed on us by external sources. What we think should be the result of what we have worked out for ourselves—consciously and critically (pp. 323-24). Later, he establishes the relationship between philosophy and common sense. He says that philosophy (and it is clear that he is talking about the "philosophy of praxis") involves the critique of common sense; it is, in this respect, "good" sense rather than "common" sense (p. 326).

Frequently, Gramsci stresses that this type of philosophy must be the preserve of everyone. For example, if a great number of people can be enabled to think coherently about their present reality, then this is of even greater importance than "the discovery by some philosophical 'genius' of a truth which remains the property of small groups of intellectuals" (p. 325). Although the "philosophers of praxis" may, at first, be a small group, their task is to help or lead others so that they might develop this way of thinking about or understanding their world. To do this they would need to encourage others to criticize their current perceptions of reality, and by doing so they would come to think in terms of a "coherent unity"—their thought could become as advanced and as insightful as Marx's (p. 324).

He goes on to argue that if intellectuals form a dialectical unity (nonantagonistic) with the people, they will be "organic" intellectuals. After criticizing the "Popular Universities" (Italian institutions somewhat similar to the British Workers' Educational Association) for failing to be organic, he says "organic" intellectuals must persuade people that the "philosophy of praxis" is a more advanced form of thinking. However, they must begin with common sense in order to demonstrate to the people that they are already thinkers—philosophers. "[I]t is not a question of introducing from scratch a scientific form of thought into everyone's individual life, but of renovating and making 'critical' an already existing activity" (SPN, pp. 330-31).[5]

This passage may well be one of self-criticism. In his writings between 1921 and 1926, Gramsci stressed the need for the party to educate the working class and the peasants in terms of Marxist theory. At that time, he actually advocated the use of Bukharin's manual (SPW, pp. 283-92) which, as I mentioned before, is extensively criticized in the *Prison Notebooks* (SPN, pp. 419-72) for its dogmatic, undialectical positivism. In his years of active political life, Gramsci insisted that the revolution would only succeed in containing the forces of counterrevolution if it had the solid support of the majority of the working class behind it; and he also stressed that they had to establish their hegemony (leadership) with the poor peasants (see SPW, pp. 441-62). However, I think that through his self-critical reflections in the prison writings, Gramsci was struggling to develop a more complex strategy for working with people in a way that could forge a collective will for revolution. I would suggest that Gramsci's self-criticism is most strongly reflected in such phrases as: "To criticise one's own conception of the world" (SPN, p. 324), as well as in the last phrase of the preceding quotation: "renovating and making 'critical' an already existing activity." Clearly the intellectuals or original philosophers of praxis are not the "renovators" or the "makers," but rather everyone is. At least, that is how I read these passages. The leader's or radical educator's role is to persuade and encourage people to undertake these renovations and to help them question their already existing activity (common sense thinking) until it becomes "critical" activity (dialectical thinking).

I concede that my interpretation may be influenced by the fact that I find striking parallels between Gramsci's educational ideas and those of Paulo Freire (especially Freire, 1972; see Allman, 1999; Mayo, 1999). The educator or political activist begins with people's concrete perceptions of the world (their limited praxis) and helps them to come to a critical, scientific, or, in other words, dialectical perception. Freire offers greater detail than Gramsci on how to learn and think with the people, but Gramsci advocates the same sort of transformed relations between teachers and students as Freire does. Gramsci also gives an indication of just how expansive and deeply rooted the socialist hegemonic project must be when he says that it must be accomplished by "collective man," and for that to be possible a considerable degree of social cohesion would have to have been attained. More precisely, after suggesting that people will have a variety of needs and desires, or "wills," and also different objectives or "aims," he says that these must be "welded together with a single aim, on the basis of an equal and common conception of the world [creating an] intellectual base so well rooted, assimilated and experienced that it becomes passion" (p. 349). In this regard, he refers to what he considered to be Marx's educational doctrine; namely, that "the relation between teacher and pupil is active and reciprocal so that every teacher is always a pupil and every pupil a teacher." He also felt that this relationship was not one that pertained only to formal education, but one that existed throughout the whole of society; it pertained to every individual's relationship with every other individual. "Every relation of 'hegemony' is necessarily an educational relationship."

In this instance, Gramsci places the term hegemony in inverted commas. It could be that he was highlighting his distinction between hegemony primarily through direction and reciprocity as opposed to hegemony by domination. It is certainly clear that he is referring throughout this passage to socialist rather than bourgeois hegemony. Gramsci appears to realize that a social-historical movement aimed at abolishing classes demands an entirely different type of educational relationship. This is because it demands a new type of person—one who is constituted within an entirely different "ensemble of social relations." Here he has stressed the teacher/pupil and the leadership relations. Moreover, if we consider what he has said in an earlier passage about the critique of common sense, which he later extends to include "all previous philosophy" (p. 350), it appears that he (and once again this is something he shares with Freire) also advocates a changed relationship to knowledge (Allman, 1994, 1999). In fact, in several places in his notebooks, Gramsci indicates that Marx offered an entirely new theory of knowledge—i.e., epistemology (e.g., SPN, p. 456)—and, as I have argued elsewhere (especially Allman, 1999), this new theory would necessarily demand a new relation to knowledge. It should not be surprising that Gramsci advocates a changed relation to knowledge. Marx's theory of consciousness/praxis marked both an epistemological and an ontological revolution—revolutions in the way we think about "knowledge" and "being," and the relation between them.

The idea that a period of preparation or prefiguration is necessary to revolutionary struggle is central to Gramsci's thinking. In fact, he is often credited with this original contribution to Marx's thought. It is, perhaps, more accurate to say that his contribution was an elaboration of Marx's thought. In a letter to German socialists, Marx too had stressed the need for preparation. He warned:

> The point of view of the minority is dogmatic instead of critical, idealistic instead of materialistic. They regard not the real conditions but a *mere effort of will* as the driving force of revolution. Whereas we say to the workers: "You will have to go through 15, 20, 50 years of civil wars and national struggles not only to bring about change in society but also to change yourselves, and prepare yourselves for the experience of political power." (Marx, 1979, pp. 402-03)

Gramsci stresses the importance of will, but not the solipsistic type that Marx is criticizing. For Gramsci, will must be rational and not arbitrary (SPN, p. 345). He says that the relationship between the "leaders and the led" is created by a cohesive unity that develops within the relation—becomes organic to it; and when this is the case, the passion that the people feel is turned into an understanding and knowledge of the world. It is only through these kinds of relations that a shared life is created—one that is solid enough to form a social force and ultimately a "historical bloc" (p. 418).

A further contribution by Gramsci to Marxism was the idea of "forming alliances." I think this idea is often interpreted naively, or generalized far beyond what he intended. For Gramsci, the main alliances to be forged were between poor peasants, agricultural wage laborers, and the industrial workers. Also included were intellectuals of bourgeois origin who realigned themselves with the interest of socialist revolution. However, he was adamant, as were most members of the Italian Communist Party during the 1920s, against forming alliances with other antifascist forces who had reformist tendencies, such as those exhibited by the Italian Socialist Party. Despite concerted Comintern pressure, the Italian communists stood firmly opposed to either fusing or forming a "United Front" with the Socialist Party. Their tactic was a united front from below, which involved the creation of organizations that all workers could participate in, regardless of party or union affiliation. Through argument, leadership, or example, they hoped to encourage the majority of the working class to affiliate with the Communist Party (see SPW, pp. 287ff and 400-11).

Gramsci (in a way similar to Paulo Freire) contributes something new to Marx's thought by discussing in detail how socialist educators, political activists, or any other cultural workers should work with people prior to the moment of revolution. There are parts in Gramsci's writings which have led some interpreters to view him as a rigorous, no-nonsense "authentic revolutionary" with a specific ideology or "truth" that must be delivered to the people. I can only suggest that such interpretations ignore the *leitmotiv* of Gramsci's writings and do him a great injustice. The consequence of ignoring Gramsci's *leitmotiv* is worse still; because the broad based movement that we need to develop for socialism will be denied a theoretical mode of action for working together with people for a socialist or communist future. It also bars us from engaging in an analysis, based on our own context, of whether the initiator of that broad-based movement should be a political party, as Gramsci advocated (see SPN, II, 1), or some other form of organization that might initially ally Marxists who are members of different political parties. The need for this analysis is urgent.

There is one aspect of Gramsci's strategy that raises important questions concerning just how extensive prefiguration must be for revolution to be successful. Unfortunately, once again, we are faced with the problem of Gramsci's lack of clarity. Not only is his concept of the extensiveness of prefigurative work not entirely clear, but it also may have been so intimately linked to his own conditions that it cannot be generalized to others.

In discussing the "war of position," Gramsci equates it with a formula for "civil hegemony" (p. 243). Earlier in the notebooks where he is analyzing the nature of bourgeois hegemony, he insists that a "social group [. . .] must already exercise 'leadership' before winning governmental power. [There] must be a 'political hegemony' even before the attainment of governmental power" (p. 57). He seems to imply that socialism must become the "good sense" of the vast majority of people prior to the revolutionary moment of taking power. The party, or, in other contexts, the broad based movement that allies all Marxists or socialists, would have to have attained a position of leadership in all sections of civil society. From a current perspective, this appears to be an extremely extensive prefigurative project; but just how extensive, actually hinges upon Gramsci's definition of civil society. Once again, we are faced with an unclear definition. Hoare and Smith, his editor/translators, point out that sometimes he includes the mode of economic behavior in civil society, following Marx's usage of the term, but at other times he locates civil society as standing between the economic structure and the state (pp. 207-09). However, Gramsci says, at least in one place, that such distinctions between structures are not organic but merely methodological (p. 160). Again, we must consider his "guiding thread" which on balance appears to include the mode of economic behavior as part of civil society. Gramsci's proposed strategy simply seems too ambitious to realize in most contexts. Hoare and Smith also point out that this is one of the most fundamental paradoxes in Gramsci's thinking—one to which he never found an answer. They point out that his discussion ignores the difference between the situation of the bourgeoisie and that of the proletariat. Capitalist relations were able to develop within the feudalism without directly creating conflict because the serfs, not the bourgeoisie, were the dialectical opposite of the feudal lords. They argue that it is impossible for socialist relations of production to develop within capitalism (SPN, p. 47).

I would not deny that, with appropriate organization, a great deal could be done and must be done to infuse a majority of people with socialist "good sense," or a critical perception of capitalism and a will for socialism. I also think, though, that every advance made in that direction will of necessity create movements in capital's bourgeois hegemony and ideology. These movements will alternate between concession or conciliation and force; therefore, our own movements will have to be based on a critical reading of the situation. It seems to me, then, that in every instance prior to revolution, our project must be an oppositional one, a critique of existing conditions, a counter-hegemonic project, rather than a predominantly hegemonic one. In fairness, there are parts of Gramsci's notebooks that also seem to suggest this and to question the degree to which "civil hegemony" can be accomplished prior to revolution.

I have raised these points about the extent to which Gramsci was suggesting the project for "civil hegemony" should be taken because I think they have important implications for a socialist strategy in the new millennium. In Britain, in the 1980s, a great deal of intellectual work was devoted to using Gramsci's concept of hegemony to analyze both the appropriate strategy for socialism as well as neo-conservative's success in establishing a new hegemonic consensus.[6] In my opinion, these hegemonic projects need to be analyzed dialectically because they relate back to two of the most fundamental dialectical contradictions of capitalism—the contradictions between productive labor and capital, and between production and exchange. The neoconservative or neoliberal hegemonic project that has been in place at least since the early 1980s is aimed at safeguarding the interests of the most advanced, and, in capitalist terms, progressive capitalist organizations. Therefore, it is incumbent upon us to consider, in a more dialectically conscious way, what the strategy of the restless negative should be vis-à-vis that of its opposite. Moreover, that consideration must also include an analysis of just who the restless negatives are.

Gramsci's ideas are important to struggles for a socialist future. But in the last analysis, I would urge that these ideas are used not to dictate strategies but to inform and guide the development of a revolutionary praxis based on a dialectical understanding of our present conditions. Surely, Gramsci, or any other critical (dialectical) thinker, would never advise otherwise.

Notes

1. See SPN (pp. 133, 238-39, 241-43, 263, 267-68, and 418).
2. For example, see SPN for the positive use (p. 356) as well as the negative use (p. 445).
3. The most crucial implication pertains to the type of relationships that are to exist between the revolutionary leaders, any organic intellectual or radical educator, and the people.

4. This is Gramsci's term. For an in-depth study of the SPN, it is instructive to use the excellent index to follow everything he has to say about how these intellectuals differ from traditional intellectuals.

5. See also SPN (pp. 332-35 and 345-46).

6. See in particular the excellent articles written by Stuart Hall for *Marxism Today*.

References

Allman, P. (1999). *Revolutionary Social Transformation: Democratic Hopes, Political Possibilities and Critical Education*. Westport, CT: Bergin & Garvey.

Allman, P. (1994). Paulo Freire's Contributions to Radical Adult Education. *Studies in the Education of Adults*, 26 (2), 141-61.

Allman, P., & Wallis, J. (1990). Praxis: Implications for "Really" Radical Education. *Studies in the Education of Adults*, 22 (1), 14-28.

Colletti, L. (1975). Marxism and the Dialectic. *New Left Review*, 93 (4), 3-29.

Freire, P. (1972). *Pedagogy of the Oppressed*. Harmondsworth: Penguin.

Hall, S. (1982). Managing Conflict, Producing Consent. *Conformity, Consensus and Conflict, D102 Social Sciences: A Foundation Course* (unit 21, block 5). Milton: The Open University Press.

Marx, K. (1979). Revelations Concerning the Communist Trial in Cologne. In *Karl Marx and Frederick Engels Collected Works* (Vol. 2, pp. 402-03). Moscow: Progress.

Marx, K. (1977). On the Jewish Question. In D. McLellan (Ed.), *Karl Marx: Selected Writings* (pp. 39-62). Oxford: Oxford University Press.

Marx, K. (1976). Theses on Feuerbach, Thesis I, Appendix I. *The German Ideology*. Moscow: Progress.

Marx, K., & Engels, F. (1975). The Holy Family (1844). *Karl Marx and Frederick Engels Collected Works (1844-1845)*. London: Lawrence & Wishart.

Mayo, P. (1999). *Gramsci, Freire and Adult Education: Possibilities for Transformative Action*. London: Zed.

Ollman, B. (1993). *Dialectical Investigations*. London: Routledge.

Ollman, B. (1976). *Alienation: Marx's Conception of Man in Capitalist Society*. Cambridge: Cambridge University Press.

Simon, R. (1982). *Gramsci's Political Thought*. London: Lawrence & Wishart.

Abbreviated Titles

SPN: *Selections from the Prison Notebooks of Antonio Gramsci* (Q. Hoare & G. Nowell Smith, Eds. and Trans.). London: Lawrence & Wishart (1971).

SPW: *Selections from Political Writings (1921-26)* (Q. Hoare, Ed. and Trans.). London: Lawrence & Wishart (1978).

11

Working-Class Learning, Cultural Transformation, and Democratic Political Education: Gramsci's Legacy

D. W. Livingstone

Culture is [. . .] the mastery of one's personality; the attainment of a higher awareness, through which we can come to understand our value and place within history, our proper function in life, our rights and duties. [. . .] And this awareness has [. . .] developed through intelligent reflection, first on the part of a few, then of a whole class, on the reasons why certain situations exist and on the best means of transforming what have been opportunities for vassalage into triggers of rebellion and social reconstruction. Which means that every revolution has been preceded by a long process of intense critical activity, of new cultural insight and the spread of ideas through groups of men (sic) initially resistant to them, wrapped up in the process of solving their own, immediate economic and political problems, and lacking any bonds of solidarity with others in the same position. (Gramsci, 1994a, pp. 9-10)

[T]here is no reason why the proletariat, as it seeks to add one more link to that chain [of human efforts to overcome privileges, prejudices and idolatry], should not know how and why and by whom it has been preceded, and how useful that knowledge can prove. (Gramsci, 1994a, p. 12)

Introduction

From his early years, Antonio Gramsci had affinities with the stand-points of oppressed and marginalized people, based on his own physical disability, Sardinian regional inferiority, and his family's déclassé status following his father's imprisonment. These affinities facilitated his recognition of the centrality of working-class self-activity in both the reproduction of existing civil society and any movement toward democratic socialism. His attraction to Marxism as a practical world-view, or "philosophy of praxis," was probably similarly based on its critical analytical capacity to enable the contesting of conditions of oppression through the actions of the oppressed themselves (see Germino, 1990). This paper will attempt to draw on Gramsci's con-tributions in order to further contemporary understanding of: (1) the character of working-class learning practices; (2) some of the com-plexities of the role of organic working-class intellectuals in current cultural change; and (3) the prospects for more democratic forums of political education in advanced capitalist societies. I will present evi-dence from the Working Class Learning Strategies project (WCLS), case studies conducted in Canadian labor union contexts in coopera-tion with progressive labor movement educators and informed by Gramsci's general approach (Livingstone, Hersh, Martin, & Stephen, 1994).

Working-Class Learning

Gramsci was distinctive among prominent early-twentieth-century socialist leaders in his positive but nuanced appreciation of intellectual activity among the mass of humanity. As he concluded in his prison writings:

> There is no human activity from which every form of intellectual participa-tion can be excluded: *homo faber* cannot be separated from *homo sapiens*. Each man, finally, outside his professional activity, carries on some form of intellectual activity, that is, he is a "philosopher," an artist, a man of taste, he participates in a particular conception of the world, has a conscious line of moral conduct, and therefore contributes to sustain a conception of the world or to modify it, that is, to bring into being new modes of thought. (1971, p. 9)

The validity of this perspective is confirmed by a wide array of em-pirical research on adults' informal learning (Tough, 1979), as well as by a recent Canadian national survey (NALL, 1998) that provides unprecedented documentation of the typically ignored sphere of informal learning. This recent survey has found that Canadian adults, by their own self-reports, are now spending an average of over fifteen hours per week in explicit informal learning projects. This pattern occurs across all occupational classes as well as most other socio-demographic statuses. While such estimates undoubtedly ignore a great deal of tacit learning activity, they also dwarf the amount of time that adults generally spend in the organized educational activities of formal schooling and further education courses. There are important class differences in the extent to which this informal learning is focused on and recognized as connectable with current jobs, with working-class people less likely than capitalists and the professional-managerial strata to be so preoccupied, as well as being much more likely to be underemployed. In fact, whether or not they are able to utilize much of this knowledge in paid workplaces, adults in advanced capitalist societies are now spending greater amounts of their discretionary time than ever before in pursuit of new knowledge (see Livingstone, 1999). But the central point is both a strong confirmation of Gramsci's claim that we all continue to actively engage in intellectual activities and a rejection of dominant elitist notions of working-class incapacity or disinterest in learning activities. A more specific comparative perspective on working-class learning is provided by Table 1, which is derived from the same national survey (see Livingstone, 2000). While most people of working-class origins now graduate from high school, universities remain very effective reproducers of class-based credentialed knowledge privileges. Corporate capitalists and professionals are at least eight times more likely than industrial workers to have a university degree. Participation in further education courses is now less strongly related to the level of prior schooling and occupational class than it used to be, but the more affluent classes are still much more likely to participate than industrial workers and the unemployed.

As Table 1 also shows, the gap between current and desired participation in organized education is much greater for working-class people than for corporate executives, professionals, and managers. Industrial workers and the unemployed would double their participation if they could receive recognition for their prior informal learning experience. The pent-up demand for further education that recognizes and assists in developing already established learning competencies among the working class may have been ignored almost as much as their extensive informal learning activities. There is a massive egalitarian informal learning society hidden beneath the pyramidal class-structured forms of schooling and further education. Nevertheless, the high and increasing levels of participation found in most forms of learning strongly suggest that we are living in a society full of intellectually active people (see Livingstone, 1999). Our case studies of the learning practices of labor union members in the Toronto area have further documented the diversity of individual and collective informal learning activities among working people, including the development of high levels of competency in many areas of knowledge not directly related to their present jobs, such as computer learning (Sawchuk, 1996).

Table 1: Schooling, Further Education, Interest in PLAR Credit and Incidence of Informal Learning by Class, Canadian Labor Force, 1998

Occupational Class	University Degree (%)	Course Workshop Last Year (%)	Interest in Courses if PLAR* (%)	Informal Learning (Hrs/week)
Corporate executives	70	71	61	17
Small employers	40	52	58	16
Self-employed	28	52	69	14
Managers	52	72	62	13
Professionals	76	76	69	15
Service workers	12	54	73	17
Industrial workers	8	37	73	17
Unemployed	16	38	82	20
Total	26	50	70	15

*Prior Learning Assessment and Recognition
Source: Livingstone (2000).

The educational hegemony of schooling and the prevalence in schooling of forms of knowledge most familiar to the affluent classes continues to obscure these less visible forms of working-class knowledge and competency. Contemporary social researchers have documented these discriminatory school practices in extensive detail (e.g., Bourdieu & Passeron, 1977; Bernstein, 1990; Curtis et al., 1992). Gramsci himself suggested a similar "cultural capital theory" of schooling:

> In a whole series of families, especially in the intellectual strata, the children find in their family life a preparation, a prolongation and a completion of school life; they "breathe in," as the expression goes, a whole quantity of notions and attitudes which facilitate the educational process properly

speaking. They already know and develop their knowledge of the literary
language. [. . .] The individual consciousness of the overwhelming majority
of children reflects social and cultural relations which are different from and
antagonistic to those which are represented in the school curriculum. [. . .]
There is no unity between school and life [for the majority], and so there is
no automatic unity between instruction and education. (1971, pp. 31, 35)

Current cultural capital theorists have been preoccupied with deline-
ating the cultural reproduction of inequality within fixed educational
forms; they fail to comprehend the creative cultural practices, independent education and learning activities, or collective cultural agency
of the organized working class (see Livingstone & Sawchuk, 2000).
Gramsci never made this error. Even in his critical analyses of Italian
schooling, he was insistent on reorganizing the institution along poly-
technical lines to enable the full development of the denied intellectual and practical abilities of all children:

A rational solution to the crisis [of chaotic differentiation] ought to adopt
the following lines. First, a common basic education, imparting a general,
humanistic, formative culture; this would strike the right balance between
development of the capacity for working manually (technically, industri-
ally) and development of the capacities required for intellectual work. From
this type of common schooling, via repeated experiments in vocational orientation, pupils would pass on to one of the specialized schools or to productive work. [. . .] For the learner is not a passive and mechanical recipient.
[. . .] The relation between these educational forms and the child's psychology is always active and creative, just as the relation of the worker to his
tools is active and creative. (Gramsci, 1971, pp. 27, 42)

A good example of how the creative abilities of working-class
children have continued to be either denied or only partially recognized by established forms of schooling is provided by the educational
career of one of the young trade union activists in the WCLS project,
whom I will call "Pete Jones." Pete is an assembly line worker in a
large auto plant. He is in his late twenties and has worked in the auto
industry most of his adult life. His parents were both union members
in other industries. He has a European ancestry and his relatives have
lived in Canada for many generations. Pete is very active in his local
union. His views will be referred to extensively throughout the following sections. Pete was also an active and creative youth, but at
least some of his teachers saw him as just another working-class kid
with limited prospects:

I remember painting in kindergarten. [. . .] I was really hyper when I was
younger, but just very curious. In school, I was a bad student, a horrible
student. [. . .] It was always a struggle. I either had teachers who understood

or ones that didn't, but if I liked something I'd get right into it. In grade one
or two, I could tell you all the names of the dinosaurs, where they lived, all
that stuff. Later, I wanted to be a cartoonist because I liked to draw. [. . .] In
grade eight, the guidance counselor told me that I should take basic English
because I was a failure at English, mainly because my spelling was bad. So I
went to a different high school than the rest of my grade eight class and
took commercial art and advanced English. When you got to high school,
all of a sudden they assume you could read and had to read books,
like Shakespeare or whatever, guess what? They're interesting. I could understand the story and it was all very logical if you read it, it was easy. So
that guidance counselor in grade eight? There are kids that need a little different attention. [. . .] Then I had a math teacher who said why don't you just
skip if you have no interest in participating. [. . .] As soon as I could get out
of high school, I did. [. . .] I have grade 12 and then I went to community
college where I took graphic design for one year. Then I dropped to go to
work. I took night classes for a while but pretty soon everything went under.

In contrast, Pete's informal adult learning activities are much more
coherent and sustained, and clearly linked to his own social and political interests:

I'll spend time learning anything to be better, music, computers, but the union is the big passion for me, like I feel like that's the thing where I can have
the most opportunity to do things. For me, it's like that's what I want to do,
you know. I'd love to play music too, but realistically, if I had to choose, I'd
have to take the union because you can always listen to music and you can
always play it, and it doesn't matter whether people know who you are or
not. But with the union, there's so much potential to change and to do
things and let's face it, the pendulum has swung back. You know, I think we
made a lot of progressive gains and it's swung back the other way where
we're getting stripped of things that we bargained for. We're losing things
that we achieved forty and fifty years ago and those things are being challenged, and the movement is an exciting place to be right now. Let's face it,
because we haven't, you know, we've had struggles, like, no question all the
way through. But now we're at a real pivotal point where the corporations
are really saying to hell with the trade union movement, let's go global.
Let's set up shop some place in the Pacific Rim where the human rights are
ignored. I want to learn about issues like East Timor. Things go hand in
hand because Nike, you know, they're operating in that country, you know.
Their global workforce makes shoes and clothing and bags and hats and
what not. And they paid Michael Jordan last year more money than they
paid for the people that work in each of their factories around the world in a
year's salary. If you took all those people who make the products themselves, they paid Michael Jordan more. He got paid forty million dollars,
like, for Nike ads. I mean, it's horrible.
    When you think about it, I mean, how can you support a system like
that?

The WCLS case studies generally reveal a wide array of informal
learning activities and related further education courses and workshops

among trade union members (Livingstone, Sawchuk, & contributors, forthcoming). There is a very substantial amount of working-class learning capacity here, being applied in many diverse ways. Our specific evidence from the auto plant where Pete Jones works suggests that a growing involvement in organized union courses and political education programs, such as their paid educational leave program (PEL), along with workers' continuing informal learning, are contributing to the building of a grassroots social movement (Roth, 1997; Livingstone & Roth, 1998). As one PEL graduate told us:

> The way it [PEL] really contributes would be [reflected in] the idea of humanity that I try to show to the people that I work with. [. . .] We have a lot of [visible] minority cultures. I try to openly show them some kind of a welcome. That's another thing from PEL too, I tended to [believe] "all trade unionists are the same." So I ended up spending some time on the picket line [at another plant], I talked with those people, and I dropped into the plant demonstration because it was a labour strife issue and I felt [. . .] I wanted to be there. I sort of have this sympathy [. . .] They've been jerked around by a corporation that's making a lot of money and there's no reason for it. I can't see the underdog go like that.

This trade union local constitutes one of the largest, most concentrated, and well-organized working-class communities in Canada. At this union local, and more generally in the Canadian Auto Workers Union (CAW), there is extensive engagement in political education. Political education programs like PEL have now produced hundreds of social movement activists within the auto plants. As a fall 1996 strike and plant occupation demonstrated, this local represents a fertile site for critical social learning and the further development of a working-class-based community that includes "the hope of more profound change in the nature of society" (Gindin, 1995).

Pete Jones has taken the PEL program as well as other recent union-sponsored courses related to employment benefits and job assessment issues. But most of Pete's learning, and especially his union-related learning, is done in informal collective settings by drawing on the knowledge of more experienced colleagues:

> Most of my learning is done with other workers. Whether it's fighting a production standard or whether it's a problem in a certain area, if it's an [employment] insurance problem or whatever, you know. You seek out the advice of somebody else and there's always something to learn about a different part of the collective agreement or a different approach to how to handle a certain job or, you know, a specific problem that somebody's come to you with. So talking to other workers is a good way to do it.

Pete's current learning practices, in fact, exemplify the kind of active, engaged learning related to life experience that Gramsci advocated as a new model for high school education. Gramsci (1971, pp. 26-43) was greatly concerned to reorganize the common school to instill the self-discipline that would ensure intellectual and moral development in young working-class children. Pete has clearly achieved a high level of self-discipline in spite of his schooling, probably in large part through his upbringing in a union family, including his mother who was a union militant, a "real fighter." But very little of the extensive political, legal, and technical work knowledge of working-class activists like Pete is valued or recognized outside the labor movement, and he knows it:

> You can be intelligent and not be an engineer or a lawyer, you know. Take the case of Bob White [President of the Canadian Labour Congress], you know, a grade 8 education took him to the top of the labour movement and you'd be hard pressed to find somebody that's more qualified to speak for workers and to negotiate their issues against a group of lawyers from Detroit or the captains of industry. So, I think that's proof enough. We have people that have succeeded in the labour movement, specifically in the Canadian Auto Workers, that have limited formal education. We have other ones that are highly educated. The bottom line is that intelligence can't be proven simply by a piece of paper saying that you've successfully completed grade 8, grade 12, university. That's all well and good but the bottom line is that if you don't understand the issues on the shop floor and aren't able to approach management and have communication skills, well [. . .] It's all about communication. If you can read that collective agreement and understand the way it applies, you could have a degree or you could not have a degree.

Most working-class people do not have university degrees, but they have plenty of useful knowledge and many like Pete are actively engaged in trying to transform the everyday cultures of their societies.

Complex Cultural Change and Organic Intellectuals

Gramsci was always fascinated with the complex forms of cultural life and with agencies of cultural change. With the influence of French writers on democratic educational and cultural reforms, he developed a broad conception of culture—including popular ideas, habits, and folklore, the common sense of the masses—that went far beyond the established notions of elite culture (Boggs, 1984, p. 44). The common sense of the masses was, therefore, a complex combination of many elements:

Common sense is not a single unique conception, identical in time and space. It is the "folklore" of philosophy, and like folklore, it takes countless different forms. Its most fundamental characteristic is that it is [. . .] fragmentary, incoherent and inconsequential, in conformity with the social and cultural position of those masses whose philosophy it is. At those times in history when a homogenous social group is brought into being, there comes into being also, in opposition to common sense, a homogenous—in other words coherent and systematic—philosophy. [. . .] None the less the starting point must always be that common sense which is the spontaneous philosophy of the multitude and which has to be made ideologically coherent. [. . .] There is [. . .] the necessity for new popular beliefs, that is to say a new common sense and with it a new culture and a new philosophy which will be rooted in the popular consciousness with the same solidity and imperative quality as traditional beliefs. (Gramsci, 1971, pp. 419, 421, 424)

But popular culture and the new philosophy of praxis, Gramsci's version of Marxism, also included the best of dominant intellectual and moral cultural forms:

The philosophy of praxis presupposes all this cultural past: Renaissance and Reformation, German philosophy and the French Revolution, Calvinism and English classical economics, secular liberalism and this historicism which is at the root of the whole modern conception of life. The philosophy of praxis is the crowning point of this entire movement of intellectual and moral reformation, made dialectical in the contrast between popular culture and high culture. [. . .] It is still going through its populist phase: creating a group of independent intellectuals is not an easy thing; it requires a long process, with actions and reactions, coming together and drifting apart and the growth of very numerous and complex formations. (Gramsci, 1971, pp. 395-96)

The central problem for democratic cultural transformation was the sustained emergence of organic intellectuals from the working class, ideologically prepared and organizationally capable to lead the collective emancipation of the oppressed masses (Gramsci, 1971, p. 397). Organic intellectuals continue to emerge in working-class life. The creative works of some, such as the plays of Trevor Griffiths or the songs of Billy Bragg, have met sufficient commercial success to become internationally known. Some have periodic regional showcases for their cultural projects, such as the Mayworks festivals of worker-produced visual and performing arts that now occur annually across Canada. Most working-class intellectuals continue to labor within the relative obscurity of their local communities. Pete Jones, for example, composes and plays music to express many of his thoughts on a variety of political and social issues, drawing inspiration both from his own experiences and other cultural sources that resonate with these experiences:

A couple of years ago I bought a used synthesizer and I learned to play pi-
ano, simple small stuff but not a virtuoso. So that's opened up stuff in
songwriting and augmenting when I do four-track recording. I'm always ex-
perimenting and writing. [. . .] So I noodle around until I find something
that I think sounds good but it's different. Then you get inspired, one
thought leads to another and then all of a sudden it's like your brain kicks
in and then you get like maybe one word and that's usually how I write my
lyrics. I always write the music and the lyrics together. The music will kick
in an image and I'll start to think of words. It's a struggle sometimes but
other times it's really quick and it just happens. [. . .] I draw on my own experience, fellow local musicians, beat poets, folk singers like Dylan, country
singers like Steve Earle, a post-punk band from California called "Bad Religion," anything I can find.

Gramsci's major contribution to understanding the complex processes of progressive cultural transformation was probably his theory
of ideological hegemony (Livingstone, 1976; Boggs, 1984, pp. 153-
98). In response to the evident failure of mechanistic and reductionist
versions of Marxism, he developed a wide-ranging analysis of the active role of dominant ideologies and of intellectuals aligned with
dominant classes in the reproduction of capitalism. He recognized
that revolutionary class consciousness would not merely unfold in response to economic conditions, but would likely remain variable and
contradictory as long as bourgeois ideological claims of universal
truth—such as equating private corporate profits with the common
good—prevailed in public sphere discourse. Of course, Gramsci wrote
prior to today's proliferation of the corporate capitalist-controlled
mass media, which are characterized by the pervasion of commercial
products into most spheres of everyday cultural life, and through
which only the most fragmentary and limited portrayals of economic
and political alternatives to established institutional forms occur. Organic working-class intellectuals attempting to convey such alternative worldviews can hardly ignore these massive barriers. Pete has a
clear appreciation both of the barriers that the dominant ideology of
free market exchange between buyers and sellers presents to building
workers' class consciousness, and of the role of the mass media in reproducing this ideology:

> People in the labour movement if they have a protest, it's easy [for the me-
> dia] to marginalize, "Oh, here we go, there's a picket sign and a bunch of
> people singing 'Solidarity Forever,' or shouting with their fists in the air."
> But no one has a problem with a board of directors meeting every week and
> finding out new ways to screw people out of their employment and some-
> how extracting more money and gaining more wealth. [. . .] People have
> bought into the idea that a few have to succeed and they're allowed absolute

free reign and that you can't question. They say they're doing what's best
for the company but they're doing what's best for themselves. [. . .] If you
watch TV, it's like the theory of that professor at MIT, Noam Chomsky, his
idea of using the medium to ingrain a political ideal or a role or a form,
sending a message or watering down things. It's primarily the media driving
these things. An issue like social welfare, folks are losing over 20 percent of
their benefits [a recent move by the neo-conservative government of On-
tario] and the media are talking about *Jerry Maguire*; when they say "show
me the money," they're caring about [movie star] Tom Cruise, not caring
about the government cutting people's income.

However, as Gramsci understood more deeply than most later Western Marxist intellectuals (who remain remote from the everyday cultural life of working-class people), the lived experiences of exploitation and oppression continually come into contradiction with the
universalist claims of the dominant ideology. In addition, the socialization of the forces of knowledge production (e.g., the availability of
voluntary forms, including public libraries, trade union schools, and
electronic information networks) represent a major source for
autonomous cultural production by subordinate social groups. The increasing availability to working-class people of such socialized forces
of knowledge production represents a continual challenge to private
capitalist efforts to appropriate creative control of the social relations of knowledge production via such means as conglomerate own-
ership of mass media and commodified information packages. Pete
Jones both appreciates the potential power of new information technologies to enhance popular creativity and actively uses these means
for his own progressive ends:

I think electricity changed everything because, at the start of the century,
people still had to do things in a manual way. They didn't have machines to
do it. Then, when technology came in, there was a huge boost in creativity, a
massive boost in creativity. [. . .] If there's a piece of legislation coming,
you know, I'll look at a copy at the library where they have all the pieces of
legislation, and I'll look up legal language on the Internet. [. . .] There's always something new going on on the Internet, you know. I do my leaflets
and stuff usually on my computer. There's learning stuff on how to take a
picture, producing union logos and filing off web pages. [. . .] With the
computer, there's a little bit of a struggle involved and you'll make a mistake and something bad happens, but when you figure out how to do it,
there's more of a sense of achievement than if you just read it.

Pete's creative impulses in his music and his daily activities with
his workmates are frequently driven by his sense of the social injustices in capitalist society, as the earlier quote about Nike suggests. He
has developed a very concrete understanding of the central exploita-
tive relations of capitalist production systems:

Management is screwing my people day after day [. . .] ruining our lives, screwing up our jobs, eliminating work, adding the remaining work onto everybody else. We're working harder than we ever have before and these guys can sit and laze around. There's whole days when they don't do anything but yak [. . .] They're overpaid, we actually earn our money and more profits for the company. We're assets, they're expenses. [. . .] We had a guy fired recently for breaking a piece of equipment. A door got jammed and he got fired for restricting throughput because he couldn't work it. If the recourse is to fire somebody like that for having a broken piece of equipment, well, what happens if the company breaks my equipment, my hands, say with carpal tunnel syndrome which is no longer listed as a workplace accident? You're going to be thrown on the scrap heap.

But Pete also understands, as deeply as Gramsci did, the imperative of engaged dialogue with other rank-and-file workers to sustain any democratic cultural and political transformation:

You've got to understand. If there's an agenda that you want to put across to people and you want to build a movement, you have to have some knowledge on what the issues are. You have to be able to explain them on the shop floor if you want the support because as a union we're only going to move forward or push an agenda if we have the support of the people.[. . .] We're going to have to pave the road before they'll drive down it. It's a dirt road and they're not ready to drive down some of these roads yet, but they will, or we're going to lose. We're at a bit of a crossroads. We have to change. We can't stay the same, but we can't forget our past and we can't give up the gains we've made. So this means new ways of fighting for things and sometimes the new ways of fighting things are going back and doing the old way. For example, young guys who've never been on strike have to learn how to picket and how prior strikes contributed to increased workers' and civil rights.

Gramsci fully appreciated that sustainable progressive cultural transformation would also involve critical appropriations from the dominant forms of popular culture through what he came to see, with Machiavelli, as a long "war of position." He saw popular religion as of central import in this regard (Gramsci, 1971, pp. 325-43, 388-99). So does Pete Jones, as social majorities continue to profess Christian beliefs in most advanced capitalist societies:

I use it when people, especially on the Right, will quote The Bible with just absolute authority like they own it and quote it as law. [. . .] People say, "well, it says in The Bible this." Yeah but, it also says the opposite in another verse in another chapter in another book, so it's too complex a book for certain issues to simply say that this is the law. My leaning towards The Bible is that it evolved. I remember that there was a debate on capital punishment and they brought up the famous "an eye for an eye." And, you know, I thought I seem to remember reading that more than once so I checked it out and it appears three different times in three different contexts in three different rules of law. If you want to go by the route, the initial law of God is that if you kill, okay, you would be killed as equal punishment. The second one is a little more vague and that's in the Old Testament as well. Then the third time was in the New Testament and it was Jesus speaking and he says, you've all heard an eye for an eye and a tooth for a tooth, but I tell you to turn the other cheek. So what's the message? If the Christian Right wants to say that there's a new covenant with God, that the old covenant was thrown aside and the new covenant is when Jesus Christ was resurrected and this is what they believe as Christians and that's their faith, if they want to quote The Bible using an Old Testament verse, then they've got to make sure that they're not trying to extract the meaning for their own political agenda, when I would take it as Christ is saying you should have mercy on those that sin against you or those that sin against God, just as God will. So, you know, it's a philosophy that I find very interesting because you can't escape Christian philosophy in our society, you know, the founding of the country. The very first sentences say, you know, they recognize God right at the very beginning of the formation of the country as being the supreme ruler [. . .] and it's the same with the United States. Our rule of law is Judeo-Christian. They talk about the work ethic and things like that. It's intertwined with everything in our society and it's far too fascinating a book to ignore and it's far too easy to take somebody else's word for what it actually says [. . .] I believe that my image of a Christian value is somebody that champions the underdog, somebody that doesn't fight for the corporation, somebody that doesn't fight for the rich, they've already got enough.

Especially after the demise of the factory council movement, Gramsci was very cautious about the immediate prospects for political revolution. Again and again, he emphasized the necessity of a long preparatory cultural process, the formation of strategic alliances among diverse groups into a "historical bloc," and the imperative of continuing dialogue among prospective leaders and the social majority to ensure a democratic transition. For example:

> It is a question of more or less long processes of development and rarely of sudden, "synthetic" explosions. [. . .] The formation of a collective historical movement [. . .] in all its molecular phases [. . .] is made up of an endless quantity of books, pamphlets, review and newspaper articles, conversations and oral debates repeated countless times and which in their gigantic aggregation represent this long labour which gives birth to a collective will. (Gramsci, 1971, p. 194)

Pete Jones recognizes the need for a similar process of patient democratic dialogue both in his engagement on the shop floor and in his community, as well as to make the connections between these spheres required for social transformation:

I'm constantly involved with a lot of folks and there's always issues that are broader than my own workplace. [. . .] I believe in social unionism 100 percent. I believe I'm a social democrat. I believe that there should be a certain form of socialism that at its root is very democratic. It is the only way to be fair. There has to be a democracy. There is no democracy when people aren't informed on issues. How do you do that, how do you make them all aware? You can't force them into education camps or re-educate people. You can't force them to learn. You can't force them to understand or even agree with what you're talking about, but there's a lot of information that only a few people know about and they're driving the whole agenda. They're not telling the public what the issues are and there's no room for debate. You know, effectively, the type of parliament we have, the opposition parties have been reduced to a role of being very ineffective, I believe. [. . .] It's going to take a long time if it ever happens totally.

There is a fundamental understanding of social change shared by Gramsci and organic working-class intellectuals like Pete Jones. First, cultural transformation from the ideological hegemony of the currently dominant social groups in advanced capitalist societies is an extremely complex and time-consuming process. It will require concerted challenges to many ruling myths and "common sense" cultural beliefs before seriously challenging established forms of political power. Second, sustaining such challenges will require the development of more democratic forums for popular dialogue on all the issues of potential political importance in everyday life.

Democratic Forums of Political Education

Gramsci was both strongly committed to developing democratic cultural and political forums and fearful of intellectual leaders' desertion of them in tough times:

In the history of cultural developments, it is important to pay special attention to the organization of culture and the personnel through whom this organization takes concrete form. [A book] on Renaissance and Reformation brings out the attitude of very many intellectuals, with Erasmus at their head: they gave way in the face of persecution and the stake. The bearer of the Reformation was therefore the German people itself in its totality, as undifferentiated mass, not the intellectuals. It is precisely this desertion of the intellectuals in the face of the enemy which explains the "sterility" of the Reformation in the immediate sphere of high culture, until, by a process of selection, the people, which remained faithful to the cause, produced a new group of intellectuals culminating in classical philosophy. Something similar has happened up to now with the philosophy of praxis. The great intellectuals formed on the terrain of this philosophy, besides being few in number, were not linked with the people, they did not emerge from the peo-

ple, but were the expression of the traditional intermediary classes, to which
they returned at the great "turning points" of history. (1971, p. 397)

The historical failure of progressive intellectuals to remain linked
with the people and to critically engage with their popular culture that
was observed by Gramsci has been a persistent tendency both in Italy
(e.g., Behan, 1997) and in other advanced capitalist societies (e.g.,
Lidtke, 1985; Fuller, 1999). Gramsci's own practice of cultural politics was quite different. Gramsci's engagement with the Turin factory
council movement during 1919-20 was his most substantial experience in popular education work. In the wake of growing popular protests in Italy, many unofficial "internal committees" emerged to deal
with working conditions in Turin factories. Gramsci's first editorial in
the weekly newspaper, *L'Ordine Nuovo*, on 21 June 1919, proposed
their transformation into worker-controlled soviets. Gramsci and his
editorial colleagues were quickly invited by many workmen's circles
and internal committees to discuss this proposal, which gained many
supporters. By the end of the year, more than 150,000 Turin workers
were organized into factory councils which were intended to be more
inclusive than established unions and to enable the entire working
class to educate itself not only for self-management of production but
for state power. The elected council leaders organized labor schools
for increasing workers' technical skills. *Ordine Nuovo* established a
"School of Culture and Socialist Propaganda" for workers and university students at which Gramsci gave frequent lectures and conferred
regularly with workers in developing his ideas. As he said, in later reflection on this process:

> At that time, no project was undertaken unless first tested by reality and
> until we had sounded out in many ways the opinions of the workers. Con-
> sequently, our projects almost always had an immediate and broad success
> and appeared as the interpretation of a widely felt need, never as the cold
> application of an intellectual scheme. (Gramsci, 1924, cited in Cammett,
> 1967, p. 94)

Both during the rise and after the fall of this workers' movement,
Gramsci was actively involved in the creation of grassroots educational forums with workers. This included founding the Club of Moral
Life in 1917, the Institute for Proletarian Culture in 1921, and party
schools after the founding of the Communist Party and until his imprisonment in 1926 (see Bellamy, 1994). These initiatives typically
developed in dialogue with a wide range of workers. This close engagement dispelled any romantic notions of how sustainable such explosive developments as the factory councils could be. From the fac-

tory occupation in 1920 through his reflective prison writings, Gramsci recognized that material conditions favoring working-class revolt were not sufficient to ensure a socialist transformation and that a long process of engagement in open dialogue and popular education would be needed (see Bellamy, 1994, pp. 112-13). As Boggs (1984, p. 13) observes: "This spirit of engagement [with working-class politics and culture] dominated every phase of Gramsci's intellectual output."

But the enduring significance of the factory councils was that they provided a practical concrete form for the expression and further development of working-class consciousness. As Gramsci noted six years after the Turin defeat:

> [T]he occupation of the factories has not been forgotten by the masses, and this is true not just of the working-class masses but also of the peasant masses. It was the general test of the Italian revolutionary class, which as a class showed that it was mature; that it was capable of initiative; that it possessed an incalculable wealth of creative and organizational energies. If the movement failed, the responsibility cannot be laid at the door of the working class as such, but at that of the Socialist Party which failed in its duty; which was incapable and inept; which was at the tail of the working class not at its head. (Gramsci, 1926, cited in Boggs, 1984, p. 107)

Gramsci saw both socialist parties and trade unions as initially reactive organizations responsive to capitalist market dynamics rather than autonomous expressions of working-class interests and desires (see Cammett, 1967; Williams, 1975). Trade unions were social organizations founded with the emergence of industrial capitalism by people who shared a concern to improve working conditions and wages. Gramsci realized that defensive trade unions would continue to be necessary as long as society remained based on the principle of private property and workers had to bargain with employers. But labor unions also took up a mandate to challenge established conditions in pursuit of greater economic justice for members and other workers who were potential members. Gramsci's basic instinct in his popular education work appears to have been to engage with already organized workers to extend these challenges to capitalist hegemonic forms. In my view, many union locals now constitute communities, in the sense that they are social organizations of people in immediate contact based on shared territory, economic life, and language, as well as a common working-class culture (see Lovett et al., 1983; Newman, 1993; Martin, 1995; Livingstone & Roth, 1998). In Canada and the U.S., unions have always had a public image problem. Membership has remained a minority of the workforce. The employer-dominated mass media have largely ignored the community-building activities of the unions, focusing instead on strikes and other events of resistance. Progressive intellectuals have often justly been strong critics of trade union leaders' opportunism (see Mills, 1948; Gaspasin & Yates, 1997). Arguably, however, no other social organization offers as much transformative potential in advanced industrial societies. Labor unions are among the most democratically structured organizations. Leaders are regularly elected and subject to recall by their membership, and frequent meetings of the general membership provide real opportunities for interested workers to present alternative motions to the entire body. Labor unions can appeal to the interests of the vast majority of people because they are intimately linked with the paid work activities that are still necessary to our subsistence and central to our identities. Labor unions generate sufficient resources from members' dues to construct and sustain organizational vehicles for popular social change, including their own extensive educational programs. The capacity of labor unions to transform capitalist society remains as limited as in Gramsci's time (see Seccombe & Livingstone, 1999), but they also remain the organizations with the greatest potential to nurture such alternative forms as workers' councils.

The fact is that the collective memory of themes of workers' control and grassroots democratization of everyday life remain alive in advanced capitalist societies mainly via the militant working-class political cultures that exist within some labor unions (e.g., Livingstone & Mangan, 1996). Consider, for example, Pete Jones' views on workers' control of production, views that have been nurtured almost exclusively through his activities within the labor movement:

> There should be greater worker control in the workplace in order to allow employees to make fuller use of their knowledge. Look at Algoma Steel [Canada's third largest steel company, now worker-owned]. The workers turned it around. The company lost money for what, a decade, or whatever it was. The workers took control of the company. The union took control of the company. They hired a new board, they set out to specialize. The workers knew what they could do the best, the union had a good idea and the people that they brought in weren't driven by a straight profit ideology. They were looking after the workers now because the workers were the shareholders. Before, the shareholders weren't the workers, so they didn't give a shit if they took a loss because they might be part of a parent company where you want one division to take a loss so you can slough off and write off for the part of the business that you want to drive at that point. So there's no more games. Now the shareholders are the employees, so you have to look after your shareholders, that's your obligation to the board. [. . .] You know, anybody will say utilizing people is the most important part of the success of a corporation, of a union, of any kind of organization, is fully utilizing people, you know. We can argue about the tools that fully utilize, whether they're adding more work or not, but to fully allow people to participate us-

ing their skills is I think a dream for most people, to be able to do what you do best or want to do and to be able to do it and function and perform in society, I think.

Pete's views on a shorter work week and redistribution of paid employment, as well as his understanding of actual trends, offer basic elements for a broader democratization of work:

> I think the German autoworkers got the right idea, they got a 32-hour work week with a 40-hour pay. They took full advantage of a political opportunity. The Berlin wall came down, it's as simple as that. Somehow they had to employ people, somehow they had to have people in there so it made sense. You know, governments are only willing to do things when they have an absolute crisis and they really do have to move. Government has the power to create jobs. When they say they don't, it's a lie because they do. [. . .] I learned about that in Port Elgin [CAW workers' education centre], I believe, two years ago where we were discussing, you know, different labour unions and different strategies, and we were talking about employment. [. . .] I mean when we got a 40-hour work week, we set our sights on a 20. [. . .] Remember, you know, like, back in the 50s and 60s they had projections that by today we'd be working 20 hours a week, didn't they? Progress and technology was going to make for more leisure time for people. People bought in. Now some people are working 60 hours for 40 hours pay. There's people that are doing that that don't realize that they have a right. They don't have to work for free and any company that tells you that you will not be employed unless you go by the program is breaking the law. And they go, well, you know, I have to do it so why shouldn't you? Well, put it this way pal, if I wasn't basically holding the fort, everybody'd be working 60 hours a week for 40 hours pay. So, the capitalist takes a full advantage of high unemployment. [. . .] Well, maybe the incentive should be to tell business "you're not going to get a tax break," or "we're not going to give you a deal unless you employ people." Let's set a target. [. . .] If we can do it with the deficit which is a hell of a harder problem, obviously there's no shortage of money. With all the record profits being made, why aren't we employing people?

The point here is that although revolutionary conceptual alternatives to capitalism, such as economic democracy and guild socialism, may be fully elaborated in leftist academic literature, critical oppositional ideas to capitalist hegemony continue to be actively developed in everyday life within the educational forums and informal community life of progressive labor unions. These settings are generating the organic working-class intellectuals who can also sustain popular democratic dialogue.

The Canadian survey cited earlier (NALL, 1998) also found that unionized workers spend a greater amount of time in employment-related informal learning than nonunionized workers (7 hours versus 4.5 hours per week). This suggests the existence of previously unexplored links between knowledge and power in workers' learning practices. Where worker-controlled education programs are readily available, workers may be more likely in both material and motivational terms to integrate their further education and informal employment-related learning. More generally, the sites where subordinated groups have the greatest control over their social practices are the places where their own cultural knowledge reproduction and generation may be most frequent. The contemporary site where the working class is most concentrated and most fully self-organized is the labor union. Those who wish to align themselves with working-class interests in contemporary societies should attend closely to these contexts.

Conclusion

Antonio Gramsci's worldview suffered from many of the limitations of the dominant modes of thought of his times. His political analyses tended to be overly focused at the point of production while paying scant attention to household and other community spheres of working-class life. He accepted uncritically many of the assumptions of Eurocentric modernism, including the inevitability of material progress, man's mastery over nature and patriarchal power. Whether provoked by a commitment to dialectical inclusiveness or fears of prison censorship, his conceptual legacy remains replete with ambivalent, vague, or fragmented formulations. Contemporary ethnographic research suggests that working-class political consciousness is often even more variable and complex than Gramsci posited (e.g., Seccombe & Livingstone, 1999). But Gramsci's insistence on the centrality of working-class self-activity and of responsive engagement with this self-activity by organic intellectuals, and his equal insistence on the massive difficulties posed by bourgeois ideological hegemony, continue to offer a fruitful starting point for contributing to the democratic transformation of capitalist societies.

As the evidence presented above should suggest, working-class and other subordinated groups continue to exercise their own creative and critical learning capacities both within and outside dominant class forms of knowledge. The knowledges that they produce and reproduce continue to constitute oppositional cultural forms as they probably have throughout the history of industrial capitalism (e.g., Sharp et al., 1989). The above illustrations only begin to suggest the real richness and complexity of actual working-class learning and cultural practices in contemporary everyday settings, and do not even hint at the many important ways in which gender, race, and generational relations interact with such class-based practices (see Livingstone, Sawchuk, &

contributors, 1999). The working-class culture expressed in these settings should not be romanticized; it remains full of contradictions and reactionary aspects. But, in spite of much academic opinion to the contrary, it is from these most concentrated and independent sites of collective expression of working-class culture that struggles against bourgeois cultural hegemony and for participatory democracy and economic justice are likely to be sustained. This is the cultural process that Raymond Williams (1975, p. 241), one of the most able developers of Gramsci's conceptual legacy in the past generation, aptly called the "long revolution":

> I believe in the necessary economic struggle of the organized working class. I believe that this is still the most creative activity in our society. But I know that there is a profoundly necessary job to do in relation to the processes of cultural hegemony itself. I believe that the system of meanings and values which a capitalist society has generated has to be defeated in general and in detail by the most sustained kinds of intellectual and educational work.

Contrary to the prevalent impression conveyed by current postmodernist academic theory, which portrays the oppressed in terms of a bewildering and bewildered diversity of disembodied voices (see Seccombe & Livingstone, 1999), many working-class people are actively engaged in the work of this long revolution. Progressive scholars, popular educators, and labor movement activists need, once again, to follow the example of Gramsci and the factory council movement by working together patiently and responsively to promote rank-and-file mobilization in strategic alliances for social transformation. As Pete Jones says, we are only going to move forward if we have the support of the people.

References

Behan, T. (1997). *The Long Awaited Moment: The Working Class and the Italian Communist Party in Milan, 1943-1948.* New York: Peter Lang.

Bellamy, R. (Ed.). (1994). *Antonio Gramsci: Pre-Prison Writings.* Cambridge: Cambridge University Press.

Bernstein, B. (1990). *Class, Codes and Control. Vol. 4: The Structuring of Pedagogic Discourse.* London: Routledge.

Boggs, C. (1984). *The Two Revolutions: Gramsci and the Dilemmas of Western Marxism.* Boston: South End.

Bourdieu, P., & Passeron, J. C. (1977). *Reproduction in Education, Society and Culture.* London: Sage.

Cammett, J. (1967). *Antonio Gramsci and the Origins of Italian Communism.* Stanford: Stanford University Press.

Curtis, B., Livingstone, D. W., & Smaller, H. (1992). *Stacking the Deck: The Streaming of Working Class Kids in Ontario Schools.* Toronto: Our Schools/Our Selves Educational Foundation.

Fuller, L. (1999). *Where Was the Working Class? Revolution in Eastern Germany.* Urbana: University of Illinois Press.

Gaspasin, F., & Yates, M. (1997). Organizing the Unorganized: Will Promises Become Practices? *Monthly Review,* 49 (3), 46-62.

Germino, D. (1990). *Antonio Gramsci: Architect of a New Politics.* Baton Rouge: Louisiana State University Press.

Gindin, S. (1995). *The Canadian Auto Workers: The Birth and Transformation of a Union.* Toronto: Lorimer.

Gramsci, A. (1994a). Socialism and Culture. In R. Bellamy (Ed.), *Antonio Gramsci: Pre-Prison Writings* (pp. 8-12). Cambridge: Cambridge University Press.

Gramsci, A. (1994b). Workers' Democracy. In R. Bellamy (Ed.), *Antonio Gramsci: Pre-Prison Writings* (pp. 96-100). Cambridge: Cambridge University Press.

Gramsci, A. (1971). *Selections from the Prison Notebooks* (Q. Hoare & G. Nowell Smith, Eds.). New York: International.

Lidtke, V. (1985). The Alternative Culture: Socialist Labor in Imperial Germany. New York: Oxford University Press.

Livingstone, D. W. (1999). Exploring the Icebergs of Adult Learning: Findings of the First Canadian Survey of Informal Learning Practices. *Canadian Journal for the Study of Adult Education,* 14 (1), 49-72.

Livingstone, D. W. (1999). *The Education-Jobs Gap: Underemployment or Economic Democracy.* Boulder, CO: Westview.

Livingstone, D. W. (1976). On Hegemony in Corporate Capitalist States: Material Structures, Ideological Forms, Class Consciousness and Hegemonic Acts. *Sociological Inquiry,* 46 (3-4), 235-50.

Livingstone, D. W., Hersh, M., Martin, D., & Stephen, J. (1994). *Working Class Learning Strategies in Transition.* SSHRC research project proposal.

Livingstone, D. W., & Lake, D. (1977). Preferred Images of the Future: Twentieth Century Bourgeois and Socialist Visions. *McGill Journal of Education,* 12 (1), 95-110.

Livingstone, D. W., & Mangan, J. M. (Eds.). (1996). *Recast Dreams: Class and Gender Consciousness in Steeltown.* Toronto: Garamond.

Livingstone, D. W., & Roth, R. (1998). Workplace Communities and Transformative Learning: Oshawa Autoworkers and the CAW. *Convergence*, 31 (3), 12-23.

Livingstone, D. W., & Sawchuk, P. (2000). Beyond Cultural Capital Theory. *Review of Education, Pedagogy and Cultural Studies*, 22 (2), 121-46.

Livingstone, D. W., Sawchuk, P., & contributors. (forthcoming). *Working Class Learning*. Toronto: Centre for the Study of Education and Work.

Lovett, T., Clarke, C., & Kilmurray, A. (1983). *Adult Education and Community Action*. London: Croom Helm.

Martin, D. (1995). *Thinking Union: Activism and Education in Canada's Labour Movement*. Toronto: Between the Lines.

Mills, C. W. (1948). *The New Men of Power*. New York: Harcourt, Brace.

NALL (Research Network on New Approaches to Lifelong Learning). [On-line.] *Lifelong Learning Profiles: Preliminary Findings of the First Canadian Survey of Informal Learning Practices*. Available: http://nall.oise.utoronto.ca.

Newman, M. (1993). *The Third Contract: Theory and Practice in Trade Union Training*. Sydney: Stewart Victor.

Roth, R. (1997). Kitchen-Economics for the Family. *Paid-Education Leave in the Canadian Region of the United Auto Workers*. Unpublished Master's thesis, University of Toronto, Ontario.

Sawchuk, P. (1996). *Working-Class Informal Learning and Computer Literacy*. Unpublished Master's thesis, University of Toronto, Ontario.

Seccombe, W., & Livingstone, D. W. (1999). *"Down to Earth People": Beyond Class Reductionism and Postmodernism*. Toronto: Garamond Press.

Sharp, R., Hartwig, M., & O'Leary, J. (1989). Independent Working Class Education: A Repressed Historical Alternative. *Discourse*, 10 (2), 1-26.

Tough, A. (1979). *The Adult's Learning Projects*. Toronto: OISE.

Williams, G. (1975). *Proletarian Order: Antonio Gramsci, Factory Councils and the Origins of Italian Communism*. London: Pluto.

Williams, R (1975). You're a Marxist, Aren't You? In B. Parekh (Ed.), *The Concept of Socialism*. London: Croom Helm.

12

Antonio Gramsci and Raymond Williams: Workers, Intellectuals, and Adult Education[1]

W. J. Morgan

Introduction

[E]very teacher is always a pupil and every pupil a teacher [. . .] This form of relationship exists throughout society [. . .] Every relationship of hegemony is, necessarily, an educational relationship [. . .]. (Gramsci, 1971, p. 350)

We must emphasize not the ladder but the common highway, for every man's ignorance diminishes me and every man's skill is a common gain of breath. (Williams, 1989b, p. 15)

It is obvious that there is a relation between autobiography and sociological reflection in the work of both Antonio Gramsci and Raymond Williams. Yet the relation is, in both cases, complex, intimate, and of necessity, historically and culturally specific. The former makes comparison of the two, the communist and Sardinian, the socialist and Welshman, internationalists both very tempting. The latter makes such a comparison potentially misleading. Gramsci and Williams were, of course, both born into a subaltern people, conscious of the domination—political, economical, and cultural—of an imperial neighbor; members of small peripheral nations swallowed up, as it were, yet refusing stubbornly to be digested.

Points of Departure

The Sardism of Antonio Gramsci's youth was to be expected in someone growing up isolated in a closed rural community, speaking the local dialect, sharing in the common village life, and absorbing the islanders' indigenous fear and suspicion of "the continent." When he first went to school he was taught traditional songs about the historical resistance of the Sards to "haughty Aragon," about the defeat of exploiters and the deeds of local folk heroes; though nothing, of course, about the oppression of the contemporary Italian State (Davidson, 1977, p. 9).

The only essay that has survived from Gramsci's schooldays in Cagliari repeats, as he recalled in 1924, the favorite slogan of his schooldays: "Throw the mainlanders into the sea!" This essay also shows, interestingly enough, the development of an internationalist opposition to colonialism in an equally vehement attack on European policy towards China (Gramsci, 1971, p. xix). When Gramsci first left the island in 1911, at the age of twenty, his attitude was strongly Sardist, as he himself stated (and confirmed by those who knew him at that time).[2] However, this Sardism, though rooted in experience and family attachment, was not a narrow, exclusive nationalism, as his literary preferences of the time indicate. The Sard national writer was commonly accepted as Deledda,[3] the novelist of the peasantry, while Gramsci inclined to the poems of Satta,[4] which described the conditions of the incipient Sard proletariat of the coal mines. Sardinia, he commented, was not merely sheep and folklore, but also miners exploited by an anonymous capital (Davidson, 1977, p. 50). He realized that the problems of Sardinia were connected to those of the broader Italian society, something soon to be confirmed by personal observation.

The crossing of the sea to attend the University of Turin was a symbolic as well as a physical act for Gramsci. He did not reject his Sardinian origins, but informed himself about them, becoming known (together with a fellow student and Sardinian, Palmiro Togliatti) as the campus expert on the island and its problems. During the elections of 1913, the first under universal suffrage, Gramsci noted how the property owners of Sardinia made an alliance with the ruling class "of the continent," subordinating their Sardism to their class interests. He realized that the problem of Sardinia and the Italian South required a different solution. By July 1913, he made the decisive moral and intellectual step, by applying for membership in the Italian Socialist Party.

Raymond Williams' account of his early life recalls that he was brought up in a border area of Wales that had been anglicized in the 1840s (Morgan & Preston, 1993, pp. 3-8). This process had been carried through by an intense and conscious pressure in the schools to eliminate the Welsh language, with the "Welsh Not" sign marking punishment for those children who dared to speak it. The result was a minority of families who were bilingual and a majority who spoke only English. Yet Welsh poems and songs continued to be learned by heart for use on special occasions, a romantic view of early Welsh history was revived in the elementary schools, and a sense of Welsh identity persisted. As Williams observes, this "often happens in border districts, which produce a conscious nationalism" (1979a, p. 25).

Williams won a scholarship to the local grammar school that was named, ironically enough, the King Henry VIII School, Abergavenny.[5] What he did not understand at the time but came to see later was that such grammar schools had been implanted in the towns of Wales for the purpose of Anglicization (Jarman, 1950, p. 85). The result, combined with his growing hostility to the moral norms of the Welsh nonconformist community, was to be a rejection of his Welshness, which he says he did not work through until he was well into his thirties and "began to read the history and understand it" (Morgan & Preston, 1993, p. 5). Williams' schooling left him, as he says, in some uncertainty about "the identity of the enemy, to say nothing of the identity of our own side." It left him also without much clue to the "very odd world" he had started noticing outside school. There were, he realized, gaps in the history that he had been taught of the four centuries after the Acts of Union with England, and in the history which had brought the tramway and the railroad through the valley where he had been born. And, as he observed later in a broadcast talk on "Welsh Culture" (published by Plaid Cymru),[6] where there were gaps there was not only the need for inquiry but also the making of myths (Williams, quoted in Morgan & Preston, 1993, p. 4).

In October 1929, thanks to the initiative of his headmaster and the support of his railwayman father, Raymond Williams entered Trinity College, Cambridge. Like Antonio Gramsci, in entering the university, he made a cultural as well as a physical crossing of a border. Later he was to ask: "Why didn't my headmaster send me to a university in Wales? That would have been an orientation which would have suited my life much better. It is no use going back over it, but it would have. But that is what he was there for . . . to find boys like me and send them to Cambridge" (1979a, p. 25).

Culture and Class

Culture is not merely a container for life's activity, as a barrel is a container for beer. Rather, it is something constantly shaped, reshaped, produced, and reproduced according to the demands of material life. Among the conditions of this material life are concepts and sets of ideas, together with the language of their expression, which are themselves historical products and which, in turn, act as material forces. As Raymond Williams said of Marx's celebrated base and superstructure metaphor, the problem is not that it is too materialist, but that it is not materialist enough; it fails to see that culture is itself material (Roseberry, 1992, p. 29). Culture also has a dual character in that while the lives of individuals are conditioned by their cultural perceptions, fresh circumstances may allow one to see those understandings extended or changed. Yet the individual, having acquired an immediate and intimate understanding of the native, familiar world in which he or she is brought up, is unable to acquire easily or fully the cultures of the world that lie beyond. Access to culture begins with a specific culture that is internalized and becomes subconscious.

Moving across the cultures of class and nation, as Gramsci and Williams did, carried with it obvious tensions. Their formal education presented them with a new culture and was a process of increasingly knowing participation and acquisition. This was quite different from the direct familiarity with the native cultures in which they had their origins and to which they constantly referred, both emotionally and intellectually. This was done, as Marx observed, in the same way as "the beginner who has learned a new language always re-translates it into his mother tongue" (Roseberry, 1992, p. 29). Such cross-referencing assisted Gramsci in his development of the concept of hegemony, and Raymond Williams in his similar notion of a dominant culture. By these terms they understood the existence and use of a complex web of ideas, associations, and meanings, together with the forms of language and expression in which they are transmitted. Further, this cultural web, a product of history, is presented as a common sense, even a natural condition. In class societies it serves to hide the realities of inequality and domination, or to present them as necessary and even desirable.

Power over the means of cultural production is obviously crucial, while such a hegemonic process is not simply ideological in that it must succeed in having real meaning for those people who do not have power over or access to such production. For example, an important feature of such a dominant culture is the presentation of a partisan version of history, which Raymond Williams refers to as selective tradition. The invention of tradition also plays a significant role (Hobsbawm & Ranger, 1983). Such a version is based upon events and personalities significant to the dominant class and evolves meanings, attitudes, and forms of discourse that are conveyed successfully to the subaltern classes whose own experience is profoundly different. The key concept here is the apparently successful separation of meaning from experience.

In practice, cultural attitudes are not acquired so coherently and systematically. Social classes are rarely so tightly knit and homogenous as to exclude the possibilities of internal gradations, tensions, conflicts, and splits. One thinks, for instance, of Edmund Husserl, who, observing that he had received the education of a German and not that of a Chinese, added that "it was also that of the inhabitant of a small town, with a home background, attending a school for children of the lower middle class, not that of a country land owner's son at a military college" (Bourdieu, 1971, p. 182). Further, one should not dismiss as hopelessly passive and ignorant those who appear to absorb the dominant culture, even when they do not share in its production. They too are individuals who "possess among other things consciousness and therefore think" (Marx & Engels, 1970, p. 64; Roseberry, 1992, p. 32), as the personal histories of Gramsci and Williams illustrate so powerfully. The separation of meaning from experience is not always successful. Though this may not necessarily be significant, it may prove to be so at moments of crisis or when its realization has reached a critical mass. It is then that the hegemonic culture may falter, its class basis exposed to view.

Commercial Culture and Mass Communications

Antonio Gramsci's interest in the persistence of folklore, and of oral traditions and their effect on popular conceptions of contemporary reality is well known. However, as Raymond Williams also did years later, Gramsci gave considerable attention to "commercial culture" and to "mass communications." In both cases, their analyses are scattered over an eclectic range of writing, including theoretical works and journalism. Gramsci was the theatre critic of *Avanti!* and Williams was the television critic of *The Listener.*[7] Both men realized that capitalist control over a commercial culture designed specifically to simultaneously appeal to, influence, and exploit the masses was an essential part of a greater hegemony. Analyses of such culture (and of what today we would call "the media") were necessary if that hegemony was to be challenged effectively. Their analyses provided the essential theoretical basis for understanding the informal education of the mass of people and the opportunities and alternatives for a counterculture through informal education presented from a working-class and socialist perspective. Such "cultural studies" have become fashionable in the developed world since the 1960s with Raymond Williams regarded as a pioneering intellectual influence.[8] A generation earlier, Antonio Gramsci, himself influenced by what he knew of the Proletkult in Soviet Russia and of the workers' movement in the German speaking countries, emphasized the importance of the informal education of workers and their families to their cultural and ideological development (Mally, 1989; Morgan, 2001). It is, however, doubtful that the "cultural studies" of the second half of the twentieth century have had much political impact of the kind that Gramsci and Williams intended—whatever the ideological preferences or political affiliations of its theorists who have been (as, of course, Raymond Williams was) professional academics. The sad irony is that their work, if it has had any cultural effect, may have made the capitalist hegemony of popular culture and the media more effective. Such criticism is not meant to imply any lack of sincerity, but to point out the crucial difference between the revolutionary and the academic worlds.

Gramsci was particularly interested in the popular theatre, at that time drawing sizeable audiences in Italy's urban centers. He wrote enough on Pirandello between 1915 and 1920 "to form a book two hundred pages long" (Gramsci 1985, p. 136). He also considered popular novels (including detective stories), newspapers, and magazines. During his imprisonment in Milan in 1927 and 1928, he borrowed many commercially successful novels from the prison library. They were of interest, he wrote to his sister-in-law Tania Schucht, if one asked the question "why are these books always the most read and the most frequently published?" (p. 342). The emerging media of radio and cinema received less of his attention, although he recognized that as a means of ideological diffusion they had a rapidity and emotional immediacy that "beat all forms of written communication, including books, magazines, newspapers and newspapers posted on walls;" but, he then adds, "superficially, not in depth" (pp. 382-83). Gramsci was concerned particularly with the commercial commodification of culture which in the example of the theatre, and its rival the cinema, had "become quite simply a business, a shop dealing in cheap junk" (p. 53). There was also the hegemonic effect of commercial culture illustrated by the popular success of the serial novel which Gramsci regarded as "a powerful factor in the formation of the mentality and morality of the people" (pp. 54-55). In a comment on Paul Nizan, a French intellectual and member of the French Communist Party, Gramsci observes that "he does not know how to deal with so called 'popular literature,' that is with the success of serial literature (adventure stories, detective stories, thrillers) among the masses, that is assisted by the cinema and the newspapers" (p. 101). Yet, as he continues, "it is this question that represents the major part of the problem of a new literature as the expression of moral and intellectual renewal" (p. 102).

Sports is the one important aspect of popular culture that is almost completely neglected by both Gramsci and Williams, though it has certainly been a concern of recent cultural studies (Tomlinson, 1999). This is significant given the importance attached to it both by the fascists and by organized religion, and the massive growth of sports as a leisure and consumer activity during the first half of the twentieth century. Gramsci's comments on sports are relatively few, though he did remark that "Football is a model of individualistic society. It demands initiative, competition and conflict. But it is regulated by the unwritten rule of fair play" (Avanti!, 27 August 1918). It is also a team game capable of arousing strong feelings of enthusiasm, solidarity, and partisanship. This was understood very clearly by his political opponents. Sports and organized recreation have been integral parts of modern welfare capitalism, with employers sponsoring representative teams and providing recreational facilities for their workers (Morgan, 1990, pp. 199-211). In Fascist Italy, sporting and recreational activities were brought under the control of the "Dopolavoro" ("After Work") organization (De Grazia, 1981). On 5 December 1926, the following declaration appeared in the national

press: "The secretary-general of the Fascist Party has ordained that
the Italian National Olympic Committee shall be considered a dependent organ of the Party, which will supervise all activities concerning physical education and sport" (Salvemini, 1936, p. 364). Two
weeks later, in response to national and international criticism, the
secretary-general of the Party commented: "We must not forget that
sport not only develops the race physically, but gives rise to moral
and political phenomena which must be followed and watched" (pp.
364-65). The Nazi Party in Germany followed suit with the formation of the "Kraft durch Freude" or "Strength through Joy" organization. As is well known, Fascist and Nazi ideology placed great emphasis on the regimentation of youth and especially young workers
(Grunberg, 1979, pp. 239-60). Socialist organizations and labor
movements have also owed much of their support to their capacity to
provide workers with opportunities to both relax together and to develop solidarity through organized and competitive sporting activities
(Prynn, 1976, pp. 65-78). The Soviet regime certainly recognized
their importance throughout its history, as did the various socialist
governments which emerged after the Second World War in Europe,
Asia, and the Americas (Riordan, 1978). In the second half of the
twentieth century, however, sports and recreation have become a
major part of the entertainment industry and big business on a global
scale. Over the same period, participation in independent sporting
associations of the working class has declined in proportion with the
influence of the organized labor and socialist movements and of the
State socialist societies. It is clearly an important aspect of popular
education, culture, and hegemony. How, then, does one explain its
relative neglect by Gramsci and Williams? Was it simply personal in-
clination, a preference for the cerebral over the physical? Although
Gramsci's physical condition excluded him from direct participation
in sports, this is unlikely. Williams had been a rugby player both at
school and at the university and, as an army officer, would have continued physical education into early manhood at least. Indeed, he
comments that on entering the university he put his name down for
everything that he was interested in, "for example rugby, because it
was a continuation of school" (1979a, p. 39). The personal is not, of
course, a complete answer and such neglect of the importance of
sports in the development of a hegemonic culture deserves further
investigation and comment.

The critique of capitalist systems of mass communication and the
development of an authentic popular counterculture were also
recurrent themes in the extensive writing of Raymond Williams.
They are seen not only in his professional engagement with literary

criticism, but in his analyses of the press, film, radio, and television and in his work as an adult educator (Williams, 1962, 1974). In mapping popular cultural taste in their respective societies, both he and Gramsci explored the historical and contemporary relations between dominant and subaltern forms of cultural production. Both opposed the mass commercial culture commodified by capital and serving its hegemony. Gramsci recognized that "the people themselves are not a homogeneous cultural collectivity, but present numerous and variously combined cultural stratifications" (1985, p. 195). People have the capacity to create an autonomous culture, but also, as we would say today, to "customize" what they are given and to make it authentically their own. For instance, in a comment on what characterizes a popular song, Gramsci claims that what gives it authenticity is "the way in which it conceives the world and life in contrast with official society" (p. 195).

Raymond Williams echoes this when he asserts that "We should not seek to extend a ready made culture to the benighted masses" (1993c, p. 100), and that "culture and education are ordinary" (p. 102). Values, he argues, in an allusion to the medieval Gresham's Law,[9] are not some kind of externally determined gold standard, but emerge from the experience of ordinary people as "living affirmations and conclusions" (p. 88). The objectives are to eliminate cultural class distinctions and to build an authentically popular counter-culture in opposition to the commercialism of capitalism. This requires a political strategy, which "if it doesn't take account of cultural questions is living in the past" (Williams, 1979b; McGuigan, 1993, p. 184); an assertion with which Gramsci would have been in complete accord. As McGuigan shows, it recognizes that "cultural production is situated within a model of relations in a whole social process; what Williams, following Antonio Gramsci, increasingly came to conceptualize in terms of 'hegemony'" (1993, p. 170).

Workers and Intellectuals: Gramsci

Antonio Gramsci was concerned ultimately with the preparation of the Italian working class for a process of hegemonic displacement, not doubting that the proletariat was the primary agent of human liberation. Socialism, which he saw as in the objective interests of the working class, was in conflict with the hegemonic culture which served bourgeois interests. Yet this was not subjectively perceived by the mass of the people. Socialism was not only a minority ideology within

Italian society but also within the Italian working class. Gramsci agreed that to change this a "long revolution" would be necessary, the complex and long range task of a political and cultural "war of position." Like the Hegelian Marxists George Lukács and Karl Korsch (Kann, 1980, pp. 250-66), Gramsci argued that while economic circumstances set the context of historical change, human consciousness can comprehend that context and must act on this understanding if it is to be altered. In "The Revolution Against *Capital*"—which, in Kann's view, is perhaps Gramsci's single most important article—Gramsci asserted:

> The Bolsheviks are not "Marxists," that is all: they have not compiled an external doctrine of dogmatic, indisputable statements on the basis of the Master's works. They live the Marxist thought that never dies, which is a continuation of Italian and German idealistic thought, which in Marx was contaminated with positivist and naturalistic encrustations. And this thought always sees man—not brute economic facts—as the supreme factor in history. (Cavalcanti & Piccone, 1975, p. 123; Kann, 1980, p. 252)

The false consciousness which characterized the proletariat, enveloped as it was in a hegemonic bourgeois culture, represented a failure of comprehension; a fatal separation of meaning from experience. These had to be reunited through a systematic process of political and cultural resistance. Critical understanding comes through such a contest of political hegemonies of opposing directions, first in the field of ethics, then of politics culminating in a higher elaboration of the conception of reality. Yet the mass of people can only liberate themselves through a process of collective action which, because it changes social relations, forms a revolutionary praxis. In considering the formation and function of intellectuals, a central concern of the *Prison Notebooks* (1971, pp. 3-23), Gramsci analyzed how people have been prevented, by the structural division imposed by capitalism, from remedying the separation of "those who know" from "those who don't know." Marx had realized this when he observed that "When communist artisans form associations, teaching and propaganda are their first aims, but their association itself creates a new need, the need for society and what appeared to be a means has become an end" (Avineri, 1968, p. 42).

Gramsci's strategy rested on the creation of such autonomous class organizations through which people could affirm control over their daily lives. But, unlike Georges Sorel or Rosa Luxemburg, Gramsci did not believe that they could or should be left to emerge spontaneously, and he commented critically on Sorel's syndicalism and Luxemburg's theory of the mass strike (1971, pp. 160, 233). Organization and leadership were the responsibilities of the "Modern Prince," the Communist Party, and the vanguard of the working class. Gramsci wrote: "In fact, if it is true that parties are only the nomenclature for classes, it is also true that parties are not simply a mechanical and passive expression of those classes, but react energetically upon them in order to develop, solidify and universalise them" (1971, p. 227; Kann, 1980, p. 256). The Party should commit itself to a massive effort of political education of a genuinely popular kind; through its own schools, publishing, broadcasting, film, and through the development of study circles and independent learning. The aim should be to encourage working people to take charge of their own lives rather than rely on bourgeois experts—whose contacts with the working class, Gramsci wrote, were reminiscent of the first meetings between European traders and the natives of Africa when "trashy baubles were exchanged for nuggets of gold" (1971, p. 330). He recognized that the creation of organic intellectuals of the working class would be an immensely difficult and long-range task: "If our aim is to produce a new stratum of intellectuals, including those capable of the highest degree of specialization from a social group which has not traditionally developed the appropriate attitudes, then we have unprecedented difficulties to overcome" (p. 43).

Gramsci's personal practice was exemplary, resting on his double conviction that theory which could not be translated into terms of fact was useless abstraction, while political action not guided by theory was fruitless and impulsive. His characteristic method, particularly notable in his journalism, has been described as "obstetric" or "Socratic." It envisaged mass education as a process of dialogue rather than a series of rhetorical statements or Party edicts delivered from the platform or committee room. A member of a discussion circle for young militants recalled: "Gramsci let us talk [. . .] he never acted like a theoretical know all; he set great store by other people's opinions and was a good listener [. . .] When he finally said something and summed up the discussion, we usually saw our mistakes and corrected them ourselves" (Fiori, 1973, p. 113). The strategic objective was the creation of a socialist hegemony in Italy. Gramsci saw education as an essentially critical and collective activity of the working class, judging it by its capacity to create autonomous class organizations and worker intellectuals who would be in an organic relationship with the vanguard Party. But, it was the Party alone which could organize the decisive taking of power and bring about revolutionary social change. This was, he recognized, of necessity a totalitarian politics, which must: (a) ensure that the members of a certain party find in this one party all the satisfaction they formerly found in a multiplicity of organizations; (b) destroy all other organizations or incorporate them in a system of which the party is the sole governor. This happens when the given party is a vehicle of a new culture.

> The modern Prince, as it develops revolutionizes the whole system of intellectual and moral relations, in that its development means precisely that any given act is seen as useful or harmful, as virtuous or as wicked, only in so far as it has as its point of reference the modern Prince itself, and helps to strengthen or to oppose it. (1971, p. 133)

Workers and Intellectuals: Williams

As is obvious from the title of his most important early work, Raymond Williams too was concerned with the effects and direction of a "long revolution," defining his objective as the interpretation of a cultural revolution and recognizing

> the aspiration to extend the active processes of learning, with the skills of literacy and other advanced communication, to all people rather than to limited groups, as comparable in importance to the growth of democracy and the rise of scientific industry. This aspiration has been and is being resisted, sometimes openly, sometimes subtly, but as an aim it has been formally acknowledged, almost universally. (Williams, 1965a, p. 11)

Although profoundly influenced by the social criticism of the Leavisite school[10] (Williams, 1965b, pp. 246-57, 1993a, pp. 102-05), the emphasis in Williams' own interpretation of modern British history was on a critique of capitalism rather than industrialism. He argued that the interaction between industrialism and parliamentary democracy had produced simultaneously a cultural revolution, manifested by the development of literacy, numeracy, and general public education, together with a rapidly expanding network of communications. This raised with it the notion of mass cultural production. As Williams observes of the early nineteenth century, "Once one begins to break economic production down into its specific processes, it is not so surprising that in a society at that stage of historical development what was also being produced was popular literacy, political order, public opinion or entertainments" (1979a, pp. 144-45). Faced by this process, the critical problem he identified was how to tap the enormous potential created by this cultural revolution free from the limitations set by its historical context, the capitalist economy and society. It is here, Williams argues, that the major achievement of the working class may be seen. It lies in the social institutions that developed from the core values of equality, solidarity, and collective struggle which formed the moral heart of the labor movement—the friendly and cooperative societies, the trade unions, and the Labour Party. They appeared to provide an alternative model of social organization to the individualistic, competitive, and hierarchical model of the dominant bourgeois order.

An important element of this alternative was the practice of an autonomous and democratic education. It is an illuminating history, Williams observes, of a long struggle by working people to get an education that answered their needs. Though dependent on people like himself, who through opportunity and training knew the things they wanted to know, generation after generation insisted on sharing in the essential decisions about what was to be studied and how. Education, Williams insisted, was ordinary and consisted above all else in providing for ordinary members of society—and this is crucial—"its full common meanings," and the skills to "amend these meanings in the light of their personal and common experience" (1993c, p. 98). This is illustrative of Williams' deeply felt antielitism and his resistance to any argument that presented people as a mass, failing to recognize their individual autonomy and right to equality of treatment. In his view,

> Popular education [. . .] begins from a conception of human beings which, while recognizing differences of intelligence, of speed in learning and of the desire to learn, which is clearly affected by differences of environment, nevertheless insists that no man can judge for another man, that every man has a right to the facts and skills on which real education is based, and that in this sense all education depends on the acknowledgement of an ultimate human equality. (1993, pp. 121-26)

Williams' extensive experience as an adult education tutor, coupled with his personal sensitivity towards his students, ensured that he came to understand this in a direct, concrete way. His scholarship and theoretical reflections allowed him to relate that understanding to the broader social and political issues with which he was concerned. He was conscious of himself as a professional intellectual and educator and reflected carefully on the meaning of this for his students many of whom, but by no means all, were working class. He asserted with conviction that the practice of adult education rested upon successful communication, a genuine cultural conversation among autonomous and equal individuals, commenting that

The use of television, broadcasting and cheap books, for the real
improvement of our society depends on an approach to communication
which has nothing to do with "personalities" and "masses," but with
genuine interchange between people. The great virtue of traditional adult
education is that don and miner, specialist and layman, have seen again and
again that they can learn from each other. (1979a, p. 78)

Yet the tutor still carries the responsibility of scholarship and should
not, from the outset, assume mutual understanding and common purpose. This is not achieved by some pretense that the relationship between tutor and student is even, balanced, and unproblematic. The
student demands recognition of individuality, opinions, and experience. But the point of the relationship is learning, and what the tutor
knows and can give is fundamental. Yet no learning can take place
until these positions are reconciled. As Williams observes, "the most
significant moments in working-class education came precisely when
people were willing to declare in a situation of trust that even the
most basic intellectual tools had to be learned" (O'Connor, 1989, p.
212). This may be compared with an observation of Gramsci's, which
is itself an allusion to a passage from Engels' *Anti-Duhring*, that
"even ways of thinking are acquired and not innate and that, once
acquired, their correct use corresponds to a professional qualification"
(1985, p. 383).

This problem was aggravated by the limitations imposed by the
institutional setting in which Williams' adult education work was
carried out. The Workers' Educational Association (WEA) was
appropriated more and more by the middle classes as a means of
educational recreation. This imposed a quite different cultural
atmosphere than that of working-class students and usually resulted in
their exclusion. Consequently, classes with working-class people
became increasingly classes for working-class people, concentrating
on a narrow range of trade union skills and ideologically neutered. All
the time, he says, there was constant pressure from the university;
"you must improve academic standards, you must get written work [. .
.] the effect was to eliminate people without secondary education"
(1979a, p. 80). Yet he had taken up the work with optimism after the
Second World War, commenting that "increasingly what for me
became the decisive world was adult education. Virtually every WEA
tutor was a socialist of one color or another [. . .] If there was a
group to which *Politics and Letters* referred it was adult education
tutors and their students," or what he believed was "this very hopeful
connection to the working class movement" (p. 69). Later he was to
recall the social historian G. D. H. Cole saying at a meeting of the
Oxford University Delegacy of Extra Mural Studies, "I am damned

well not interested in adult education, I am interested in workers' education" (p. 78). That was the conflict, said Williams, with Cole a minority voice who lost, though it has been argued that the battle had been fought and lost long before (Morgan, 1988, pp. 38-48). Indeed, Williams' years in the Oxford University Delegacy of Extra Mural Studies were noted for their internal political conflict and ideological pressure on those tutors with a communist or left-wing affiliation or even perspective. As he remembered, in a lecture given in memory of his colleague Tony Maclean,[11] the very notion that adult education was contributing to the process of social change became suspect. This was so, especially in the period of the forties and fifties, "when almost everybody put their intellectual resources well under cover. For it was a politically dangerous time" (1989a, p. 158), although one thinks of the comparison with Fascist Italy in the 1920s. Williams' view was that "in the end you cannot be financed and academically controlled by those kinds of universities and carry out a program of education of the working class. The WEA had the same ambiguity as the program of *Politics and Letters*. There is no denying that" (1979a, p. 82). By 1960 he felt that "adult education ceased to have enough meaning" (p. 81), and he moved on, returning to Cambridge the following year.

Conclusion

Considerable claims have been made for the standing and significance of both Antonio Gramsci and Raymond Williams. Ralph Miliband was not alone in 1969 when he argued that, since Lenin, "the only major Marxist contribution to the theory of the State has been that of Antonio Gramsci" (1973, p. 6). Similarly, Francis Mulhern has found many echoes to his assertion in 1988 that Raymond Williams was "the outstanding intellectual in British culture this century" (1988, p. 49).

Antonio Gramsci was, of course, a communist revolutionary and not a professional educator. Nevertheless, his work contains, implicitly and explicitly, many insights into the nature of education. His explicit writings on education concentrate on the schooling of children and have been criticized for their conservatism. It should be noted, however, that his comments on education were made in response to the Fascist educational reforms of 1923, introduced by Giovanni Gentile.[12] These reforms emphasized spontaneity, neglecting what Gramsci believed to be the necessary intellectual diet in favor of a menu of sports activities and the banal sloganizing of Italian history. Against this, Gramsci counterposed the educational benefits of disciplined study, sustained concentration, and rational reflection as a guide to action. Paradoxically, this may explain, at least in part, his relative neglect of sports and of physical education as a factor in hegemonic domination.

Gramsci's Sardinian origin helped him to better understand the political and social contradictions caused by uneven economic development and aggravated by cultural divisions among what he called the subaltern classes. Furthermore, he was convinced of the capacity of working people, flesh and blood men and women, to educate themselves into a position of cultural and political autonomy. The objective was the creation of a collective and decisive belief in the possibilities of revolutionary change. Finally, despite the many apparently consensual elements within his political strategy, at its heart lay the necessity for a vanguard party, with the capacity to apply the revolutionary force needed if bourgeois society was to be thoroughly dismantled and replaced by socialism. Gramsci's work and the concepts it elaborates have taken on a heuristic value which continues to have a powerful attraction. It has been suggested, for instance, that one of the best examples of a creative use of Gramsci's ideas is to be found in Eugene D. Genovese's *Roll Jordan Roll*. In this study of the interrelations between American masters and slaves, Gramsci's notion of hegemony provides a basis for analyzing and structuring a mass of crude data. Genovese writes:

> the fashionable relegation of law to the rank of a superstructural and derivative phenomenon obscures the degree of autonomy it creates for itself [. . .] for no class in the modern Western world could rule for long without some ability to present itself as the guardian of the interests and sentiments of those being ruled. (p. 25; Kann, 1980, p. 266)

Raymond Williams was, of course, a professional educator, as well as a committed socialist. Yet, even in the closing chapter of *The Long Revolution*, he moves away from the optimistic perspectives of his earlier historical analyses. The real achievement is now regarded as highly problematic; the labor movement is seen to be in clear moral and political decline, the unions narrow and sectional in outlook, the cooperatives mere traders, and the Labour Party struggling to present itself as an alternative government. This was, of course, in the 1960s. Insofar as he sought to account for the declining prospects of socialism in terms of a weakening working-class consciousness, Williams did so not by reference to affluence, or to changing conditions and residence, but to more diffuse cultural influences. In particular, he focused on the fact that most of the country's modes of cultural production are directly or indirectly under capitalist control. When asked to state what his own alternative cultural perspectives had been after the war, he replied:

> I still believe that the failure to fund the working class movement culturally when the channels of popular education and culture were there in the forties became a key factor in the very quick disintegration of Labour's position in the fifties. I don't think you can understand the projects of the New Left in the late fifties unless you realize that people like Edward Thompson and myself, for all our differences, were positing the recreation of that kind of union. Perhaps by that date it was no longer available. (Williams, 1979a, pp. 73-74)

Yet, despite this pessimism, Raymond Williams' work, like that of Gramsci, has its heuristic value, perhaps even especially so in the cold climate of socialist retreat. As a recent commentator has observed: "As the long revolution in culture and democracy gathers force in eastern Europe, the values that Williams steadily extended stand more persuasively than ever as a humane vision of a possible—perhaps our best collective future" (Moglen, 1993, p. 66). The intention of this chapter has been to suggest some points of origin and cultural and political concern that Antonio Gramsci and Raymond Williams have in common, without, of course, ignoring the clear differences in social and political circumstances and in personal experience and destiny. It is difficult to estimate the direct influence that the older Sardinian may have had on the younger Welshman. It certainly should not be exaggerated, as the specific references to Gramsci in Williams' writings are few.[13] However, in the essay, "You're a Marxist, Aren't You?," first published in 1975, Williams does say that what the New Left saw emerging in the 1960s was a new form of corporate State, and the emphasis on culture, which was often taken as identifying its position, was (at least in his case) an emphasis on the process of social and cultural incorporation. He goes on to say:

> Indeed, in seeking to define this, it was possible to look at certain important parts of the Marxist tradition notably the work of Gramsci, with his emphasis on hegemony. We could then say that the essential dominance of a particular class in society is maintained not only, although if necessary, by power, and not only, although always, by property. It is maintained also and inevitably by a lived culture. (Williams, 1989b, p. 74)

This is an important statement of continuity and development that has been recognized by, for example, Roseberry who quotes the well known passage from Marx's *The German Ideology* on the ideas of the ruling class being in every epoch the ruling ideas, and goes on to connect it with both Gramsci's concept of hegemony and with Williams' notion of a dominant culture (1992, pp. 32-33). Certainly the work of both men will continue to attract and to inspire both political and scholarly controversy. As Perry Anderson observed of Antonio Gramsci, "the price of so ecumenical an admiration is necessarily ambiguity: multiple and incompatible interpretations of the themes" (1976, p. 5; Kann, 1980, p. 256). This concluding remark may serve for both of their works.

Notes

1. Originally given as a paper to the conference, "Culture, Community, Democracy," University of Wales, Swansea, 10-11 September 1993. It was published first in *Convergence*, 29 (1), 61-74 and translated into Spanish for *Estudios*, 10 (July 1998), 117-30. It has been revised and extended for this book.

2. For instance, Palmiro Togliatti commented that "at that time, as a very young man, his outlook was frankly and proudly pro Sardinian, even Sardinian nationalist" (quoted in G. Fiori, 1973, p. 77). Togliatti was in the *Ordine Nuovo* movement with Gramsci and was a founding member of the Italian Communist Party. He became the leader after Gramsci's arrest in 1926 and was Secretary General from 1945 until his death in 1964.

3. Grazia Deledda, a Sardinian novelist who won a Nobel Prize for Literature in 1927.

4. Sebastiano Satta, a Sardinian poet, nationalist, and folklorist.

5. Ironically, as it was Henry VIII (a Tudor King of Welsh descent) who forced the integration of Wales into England through the Act of Union of 1536, which decreed that "English was to be the sole official language of all legal and government business in Wales." See Jarman (1950, p. 85).

6. Plaid Cymru, or the Party of Wales, is the Welsh nationalist party.

7. *Avanti!* was the newspaper of the Italian Socialist Party. *The Listener* was a very influential magazine that was devoted to broadcasting and published by the British Broadcasting Corporation.

8. It is worth noting that English critical analysis of "commercial culture" and "mass popular culture" has a longer pedigree than is often realized. William Hazlitt and Charles Dickens are examples, while George Orwell's essays, "Boys' Weeklies" (1938), "The Art of Don-

ald McGill" (1941), "Raffles and Miss Blandish" (1944), and "Decline of the English Murder" (1946) are from the period before, during, and after the Second World War.

9. Gresham's Law is a proposition in economics which claims that "bad money drives out good," if both are in circulation at the same time.

10. See Leavis (1972) and Leavis and Thompson (1933).

11. "Adult Education and Social Change" was first given as The Tony McLean Memorial Lecture in 1983. McLean, a veteran of the International Brigade in Spain, had been a colleague of Williams' at the Oxford University Delegacy of Extra Mural Studies.

12. Giovanni Gentile was Fascist Minister of Education and Culture in 1923. He was responsible for the Education Law of that year and for the Manifesto of the Fascist Intellectuals in 1925. He was executed by Communist partisans in 1945.

13. For instance, Gramsci does not appear in the index to the *Politics and Letters* interviews.

References

Anderson, P. (1976). The Antinomies of Antonio Gramsci. *New Left Review*, 100, 5-78.

Avineri, S. (1968). *The Social and Political Thought of Karl Marx.* London: Cambridge University Press.

Bourdieu, P. (1971). Systems of Education and Systems of Thought. In E. Hopper (Ed.), *Readings in the Theory of Educational Systems* (pp. 159-83). London: Hutchinson University Library.

Cavalcanti, P., & Piccone, P. (Eds.). (1975). *History, Philosophy and Culture in the Young Gramsci.* St. Louis: Telos.

Davidson, A. (1977). *Antonio Gramsci: Towards an Intellectual Biography.* London: Merlin.

De Grazia, V. (1981). *The Culture of Consent: Mass Organization of Leisure in Fascist Italy.* Cambridge: Cambridge University Press.

Fieldhouse, R. (1993). Oxford and Adult Education. In W. J. Morgan & P. Preston (Eds.), *Raymond Williams: Politics, Education, Letters* (pp. 47-64). London: Macmillan.

Fiori, G. (1973). *Antonio Gramsci: Life of a Revolutionary.* New York: Schocken.

Genovese, E. (1972). *Roll Jordan Roll.* New York: Vintage.

Gramsci, A. (1985). *Selections from Cultural Writings* (D. Forgacs & G. Nowell Smith, Eds.). London: Lawrence & Wishart.

Gramsci, A. (1971). *Selections from the Prison Notebooks* (Q. Hoare & G. Nowell Smith, Eds.). London: Lawrence & Wishart.

Grunberger, R. (1979). The Workers. In A *Social History of the Third Reich* (pp. 239-60). Harmandsworth: Penguin.

Hobsbawm, E. J., & Ranger, T. (Eds.). (1983). *The Invention of Tradition.* Cambridge: Cambridge University Press.

Jarman, A. O. H. (Ed.). (1950). *The Historical Basis of Welsh Nationalism.* Cardiff: Plaid Cymru.

Kann, M. E. (1980). Antonio Gramsci and Modern Marxism. *Studies in Comparative Communism,* 13 (2-3), 250-66.

Leavis, F. R. (1972). *Nor Shall My Sword Sleep in My Hand: Discourses on Pluralism, Compassion and Social Hope.* London: Chatto & Windus.

Leavis, F. R., & Thompson, D. (1933). *Culture and Environment.* London: Chatto & Windus.

Mally, L. (1989). Intellectuals in the Proletkult: Problems of Authority and Expertise. In D. P. Koenher et al. (Eds.), *Party, State and Society in the Russian Civil War: Explorations in Social History* (pp. 296-311). Bloomington: Indiana University Press.

Marx, K., & Engels, F. (1970). *The German Ideology.* New York: International.

McGuigan, J. (1993). Reaching for Control: Raymond Williams on Mass Communication and Popular Culture. In W. J. Morgan & P. Preston (Eds.), *Raymond Williams: Politics, Education, Letters* (pp. 163-88). London: Macmillan.

McIlroy, J., & Westwood, S. (Eds.). (1993). *Border Country: Raymond Williams in Adult Education.* Leicester: National Institute of Adult Continuing Education.

Miliband, R. (1973). *The State in Capitalist Society.* New York: Basic.

Moglen, S. (1994). Contributions to the Long Revolution: Raymond Williams and the Politics of the Post-War New Left. In W. J. Morgan & P. Preston (Eds.), *Raymond Williams: Politics, Education, Letters* (pp. 65-87). London: Macmillan.

Morgan, W. J. (forthcoming). Proletarian Education and Culture in Bolshevik Russia. In D. Jones (Ed.), *Censorship: An International Encyclopaedia.* London: Fitzroy Dearborn.

Morgan, W. J. (1990). The Miners' Welfare Fund in Britain 1920-1922. *Social Policy and Administration,* 24 (3), 199-211.

Morgan, W. J. (1988). The Burning Question of Workers' Education: Ruskin College and the Plebs' League. *Education Research and Perspectives,* 15 (2), 38-48.

Morgan, W. J., & Preston, P. (Eds.). (1993). *Raymond Williams: Politics, Education, Letters.* London: Macmillan.

Mulhern, F. (1988). Living the Work. *The Guardian*, 29 (January), 49.

O'Connor, A. (Ed). (1989). *Raymond Williams on Television*. London: Routledge.

Orwell, G. (1965). *Decline of the English Murder and Other Essays*. Harmandsworth: Penguin.

Orwell, G. (1962). *Inside the Whale and Other Essays*. Harmandsworth: Penguin.

Prynn, D. (1976). The Clarion Clubs, Rambling and the Holiday Associations in Britain Since the 1890s. *Journal of Contemporary History*, 11 (2-3), 65-78.

Riordan, J. (Ed.). (1978). *Sport under Communism: The USSR, Czechoslovakia, the GDR, Cuba, China*. London: Hurst.

Roseberry, W. (1992). Marxism and Culture. In B. Williams (Ed.), *The Politics of Culture*. Washington, DC: Smithsonian Institution.

Salvemini, G. (1936). *Under the Axe of Fascism*. London: Gollancz.

Tomlinson, A. (1999). *The Game's Up: Essays in the Cultural Analysis of Sport, Leisure and Popular Recreation*. Aldershot: Arena.

Williams, R. (1993a). The Press and Popular Education. In J. McIlroy & S. Westwood (Eds.), *Border Country: Raymond Williams in Adult Education* (pp. 121-26). Leicester: National Institute of Adult Continuing Education.

Williams, R. (1993b). Our Debt to Dr. Leavis. In J. McIlroy & S. Westwood (Eds.), *Border Country: Raymond Williams in Adult Education* (pp. 103-05). Leicester: National Institute of Adult Continuing Education.

Williams, R. (1993c). A Kind of Gresham's Law. In J. McIlroy & S. Westwood (Eds.), *Border Country: Raymond Williams in Adult Education* (pp. 84-89). Leicester: National Institute of Adult Continuing Education.

Williams, R. (1989a). Adult Education and Social Change. In *What I Came to Say* (pp. 157-66). London: Hutchinson Raduss.

Williams, R. (1989b). You're a Marxist, Aren't You? In R. Gable (Ed.), *Resources of Hope* (pp. 65-76). London: Verso.

Williams, R. (1979a). *Politics and Letters: Interviews with New Left Review*. London: Verso.

Williams, R. (1979b). Television and Teaching: An Interview with Raymond Williams. *Screen Education*, 31 (Summer), 5-14.

Williams, R. (1975). Welsh Culture (BBC Radio Talk). *Culture and Politics: Plaid Cymru's Challenge to Wales* (pp. 99-104). Cardiff: Plaid Cymru.

Williams, R. (1974). *Television, Technology and Cultural Form*. London: Fontana.

Williams, R. (1965a). *The Long Revolution*. Harmandsworth: Penguin.
Williams, R. (1965b). *Culture and Society 1780-1950*. Harmandsworth: Penguin.
Williams, R. (1962). *Communications*. Harmandsworth: Penguin.

13

Metaphors for an Educative Politics: "Common Sense," "Good Sense," and Educating Adults

Diana C. Coben

Introduction

Gramsci is celebrated in many fields, including that of adult education, where he features as a "radical hero" in debates about the politics of the education of adults[1]—appropriately enough, since, for Gramsci, politics was a supremely educative process and he was himself an inveterate adult educator. Here, I want to focus on an aspect of Gramsci's work that has been somewhat neglected in the English language literature on Gramsci and education, but which I believe deserves closer examination by adult educators. This is Gramsci's conceptualization of "common sense" and "good sense" in his prison notebooks, written during his eleven-year incarceration by Mussolini's fascist government.

So what does Gramsci mean by good sense and common sense; how does he conceive of the relationship between them; and what are the implications of his concepts for adult educators today? I shall begin my exploration of these questions with a brief outline of the genealogy of the concept of common sense in what may loosely be called Western thought in order to locate Gramsci's terms in a wider philosophical context.

Common Sense before Gramsci

The concept of common sense in Western thought may be traced back at least as far as Aristotle, who attributed to a common sense (i.e., a unified faculty of perception, distinct from the physical senses) the perception of size, shape, and number, which are all perceived by motion (Irwin, 1993, p. 29). By contrast, modern concepts of common sense in the anglophone world date from the Enlightenment and are intertwined with notions of democracy, practicality, and that mythical creature, "the common man." While, for Aristotle, it is the "sense" itself that is "common," or unified, in the latter view, common sense is common by virtue of its association with those whose sense it is perceived to be.

In Britain, this view is exemplified by the Scottish School of Common Sense, founded by Thomas Reid, in contradistinction to the skepticism of David Hume. By common sense, Reid meant those beliefs: which are universally held by humankind; whose acceptance is reflected in the common structure of all languages; whose contradictory is not merely false, but absurd; that are irresistible, so that even those who question them are compelled to believe them when engaging in the practical affairs of life (Lemos, 1993, p. 72). In the New World, Thomas Paine set out his passionate argument for secession of the American colonies from the British Crown in his pamphlet, *Common Sense*. Published in January 1776, it immediately sold well over a hundred thousand copies and prepared the ground for the Declaration of Independence on July 4th of that year.

In Britain, the rather less revolutionary Reidian notion of common sense was carried forward into the twentieth century by the "commonsensism" of G. E. Moore. Advocates of commonsensism hold the view that "we know most, if not all, of those things which ordinary people think they know and that any satisfactory epistemological theory must be adequate to the fact that we do know such things" (Lemos, 1993, p. 71). Common sense is thus both a normative and a laudatory term in the anglophone philosophical tradition, a fact that can lead to confusion for those reading Gramsci's prison notes in English, since the terms "common sense" and "good sense" are nowadays almost interchangeable.

In the continental European idealist tradition exemplified by Vico and Hegel, the concept of common sense is developed in a somewhat different way. Rather than seeing it as a practical faculty which the ordinary person exercises in his or her everyday life, common sense refers to that which is expressed in the ideal being of a nation or people. Hegel's "*volksgeist*," or "spirit of the nation," exemplifies this tradition, as does Montesquieu's "general spirit" of the nation and Herder's "*volkseel*" or "collective soul of the people" (Miller *et al.*, 1991, *passim*). For the Neapolitan, Vico, political obligation depends upon what is regarded as appropriate or just, which depends in turn on the mental development or common sense of the age.

It is from this continental philosophical tradition that Gramsci springs and against which he developed his own concept of common sense. He was familiar with Vico's[2] and Hegel's thought and aware that both were important influences on Croce, the ambivalent figure who exemplifies, for Gramsci, the mystique and influence of the traditional intellectual and whose thought Gramsci critiques in many prison notes. In one, Gramsci criticizes Croce's overly-approving attitude to common sense, complaining that it "seems unclear": "In Croce, the proposition that all men are philosophers has an excessive influence on his judgment about common sense. It seems that Croce often likes to feel that certain philosophical propositions are shared by common sense. But what can this mean concretely?" (SPN, p. 422). Likewise, Gramsci criticizes the idealist-turned-fascist ideologue, Gentile, whose "flirtation with common sense" he found "quite comical" (p. 423). Gramsci ridicules the naiveté of Gentile's statement that "Philosophy could be defined as a great effort accomplished by reflective thought to gain critical certainty of the truths of common sense [. . .]." Gramsci asks, "what does a 'truth of common sense' mean?" (p. 422), arguing that to "refer to common sense as a confirmation of truth is a nonsense." He continues:

> It is possible to state correctly that a certain truth has become part of common sense in order to indicate that it has spread beyond the confines of intellectual groups, but all one is doing in that case is making a historical observation and an assertion of the rationality of history. (p. 423)

Gramsci was mining a rich seam, but his development of the concept of common sense and the distinction he made from good sense, as we shall see, are rather different from the conceptions of Gentile, Croce, Hegel, or Vico. Instead, Gramsci cites Marx to make the point that there is no necessary correlation between the strength (or "so-lidity") and the validity of popular beliefs, and to support his argu-ment for the construction of a new common sense:

> References to common sense and to the solidity of its beliefs are frequent in Marx. But Marx is referring not to the validity of those beliefs but rather to their formal solidity and to the consequent imperative character they have when they produce norms of conduct. There is, further, implicit in these references an assertion of the necessity for new popular beliefs, that is to say a new common sense and with it a new culture and a new phi-losophy which will be rooted in the popular consciousness with the same solidity and imperative quality as traditional beliefs. (pp. 423-24)

In his enormously impressive but tragically incomplete and fragmen-tary prison notebooks, Gramsci begins to make explicit the "neces-sity for new popular beliefs" that he finds implicit in Marx.

Common Sense and Good Sense in Gramsci's Writing

Gramsci's direct reference to common sense and good sense, and the distinction between them, is to Manzoni's historical novel, *The Be-trothed* (*I promessi sposi*). In the novel, a group of people is falsely blamed for causing an outbreak of the plague. Although many realize that the accusation is false, they keep silent out of fear of the ma-jority. As Manzoni puts it: "good sense was not lacking; but it was hiding for fear of common sense" (1956, p. 446). In a comment on the passage in one of the notebooks, Gramsci aligns good sense with truth: "There was, we see, a secret outlet for the truth—in domestic confidence" (FSPN, p. 557n14).

Writing under the constraints of censorship, with fascism tight-ening its grip on Italy and his health collapsing, Gramsci attempted to devise his own "secret outlet for the truth" in his prison note-books. Much has been written about the fragmentary nature of the notebooks, which Stuart Hall has memorably described as an "open text" (1987), and although references to common sense and good sense are scattered through the notebooks, usually encased in inverted commas, Gramsci did not fully elaborate his conception. Indeed, he underlined the provisional, exploratory nature of his prison notes in a sentence in parentheses at the end of a note on common sense, rendered poignant by the tragedy of his continued imprisonment and death: "(It will be necessary to establish these concepts firmly by thinking them through in depth)" (PN1, p. 173). That he was en-gaged in doing so is evidenced in a letter written in the seventh year of his imprisonment to his sister-in-law, Tania Schucht. Gramsci writes: "I would like to receive this small book: Santa Caramella, *Il senso comune: Teoria e pratica* [*Common Sense: Theory and Practice*]" (1994, p. 319).

So what does Gramsci mean by common sense and good sense? Of common sense Gramsci states:

> Its most fundamental characteristic is that it is a conception, which, even in the brain of one individual, is fragmentary, incoherent and inconsequential, in conformity with the social and cultural position of those masses whose philosophy it is. At those times when a homogeneous social group is brought into being, there comes into being also, in opposition to common sense, a homogeneous—in other words coherent and systematic—philosophy. (SPN, p. 419)

Gramsci emphasizes the chaotic and contradictory nature of common sense, describing it as "a chaotic aggregate of disparate conceptions, and one can find there anything one likes" (p. 422). It is "an ambiguous, contradictory and multiform concept." Nonetheless, although it is "crudely neophobe and conservative," it contains truths, as we have seen above in Gramsci's rejection of Gentile's "flirtation with common sense" (p. 423).

In "Some Preliminary Points of Reference" for his notes on "The Study of Philosophy," Gramsci develops his concept of common sense by comparison with philosophy, folklore, religion, and in relation to good sense (p. 323ff). In relation to philosophy, Gramsci lists common sense and good sense as constituent parts of the "'spontaneous philosophy' which is proper to everybody" (p. 323), and makes what he describes as a "practical" distinction between philosophy and common sense: "In philosophy the features of individual elaboration of thought are the most salient: in common sense on the other hand it is the diffuse, uncoordinated features of a generic form of thought common to a particular period and a particular popular environment" (p. 330n). He insists that "Philosophy is intellectual order, which neither religion nor common sense can be. It is to be observed that religion and common sense do not coincide either" (p. 325). Gramsci further maintains that this intellectual order is historically produced and actively maintained. He argues that by maintaining common sense in a

> "Ptolemaic," anthropomorphic condition and by preserving the fragmentary, incoherent, inconsequential and a-critical elements in mass spontaneous philosophy, the high philosophy assures its own intellectual superiority and dominance, and perpetuates the historical division between high and mass culture. Its historically produced "truth" is adhered to by

popular masses as a "superstition" and has the force of a social imperative. (Gramsci, quoted in Salamini, 1981, p. 90)

In another note, Gramsci again insists that common sense and good sense are historically and socially situated: "Every social stratum has its own common sense and its own good sense, which are basically the most widespread conception of life and of man" (SPN, p. 326n5). Employing an apt geological metaphor, Gramsci continues, "Every philosophical current leaves a sedimentation of common sense: this is the document of its historical effectiveness." Thus common sense is "a relatively rigid phase of popular knowledge." But in one of the seeming contradictions that can easily confuse the seeker after definitive statements in the prison notebooks, he states in another note: "Common sense is not something rigid and static; rather it changes continuously, enriched by scientific notions and philosophical opinions which have entered into common usage" (PN1, p. 173). He seems to settle on a conception of common sense as the "more or less rigidified" creator of "the folklore of the future" in the following passage:

> Common sense is the folklore of "philosophy" and stands midway between real "folklore" (that is, as it is understood) and the philosophy, the science, the economics of the scholars. Common sense creates the folklore of the future, that is a more or less rigidified phase of a certain time and place.

By folklore, Gramsci means "the entire system of beliefs, superstitions, opinions, ways of seeing things and of acting" (SPN, p. 323) of the subaltern classes, formed by the accretion of past ideas from disparate sources, including religion, modern science, and superstition. The exploration of folklore, then, is represented by Gramsci as an archaeological endeavor, a process of uncovering the remains of the common sense of past ages. As he states,

> The personality is strangely composite: it contains Stone Age elements and principles of a more advanced science, prejudices from all past phases of history at the local level and intuitions of a future philosophy which will be that of a human race united the world over. (p. 324)

Gramsci also compares common sense with religion. For example, in contending that common sense is multifaceted, he describes it as "a collective noun, like religion: there is not just one common sense" (p. 325). The comparison with religion is not fortuitous since Gramsci contends that in Italy, religion, in the form of Catholicism, provides the principal elements of common sense. Consequently the relationship between common sense and religion is much more intimate than that between common sense and the philosophical systems of those Gramsci terms "traditional intellectuals" (p. 420), i.e., those intellectuals aligned with the dominant classes.

Despite the incoherence of common sense, it is intimately connected with good sense, since common sense contains "a healthy nucleus" of good sense, which "deserves to be made more unitary and coherent" (p. 328). For Gramsci, good sense is exemplified by the "philosophy of praxis" (a term he uses throughout the notebooks for Marxism, partly to deceive the prison censor). Good sense is analogous to philosophy, in that it is inherently coherent and critical. As he says, "Philosophy is criticism and the superseding of religion and common sense. In this sense it coincides with good as opposed to common sense" (p. 326). Good sense is thus an "intellectual unity and an ethic in conformity with a conception of reality that has gone beyond common sense and become, if only within narrow limits, a critical conception" (p. 333). It is not just any "critical conception" however; for Gramsci, good sense is synonymous with the philosophy of praxis.

So what does Gramsci mean by a philosophy of praxis? In his notes on "Problems of Marxism," Gramsci states as "the fundamental concept" of the philosophy of praxis that it is

"sufficient unto itself," that it contains in itself all the fundamental elements needed to construct a total and integral conception of the world, a total philosophy and theory of natural science, and not only that but everything that is needed to give life to an integral practical organisation, that is, to become a total integral civilisation. (SPN, p. 462)

He contends that "A philosophy of praxis cannot but present itself at the outset in a polemical and critical guise, as superseding the existing mode of thinking and the existing concrete thought (the existing cultural world)" (p. 330). In developing his own critical polemical thought—his own philosophy of praxis—Gramsci is distinguishing his thought from the Marxism of his day. He deplores the positivistic, evolutionary tendencies of Second International Marxism, noting that the "deterministic, fatalistic and mechanistic element has been a direct ideological 'aroma' emanating from the philosophy of praxis, rather like religion or drugs (in their stupefying effect)" (p. 336). As Joseph Femia (1975, p. 29) puts it, in this period, Marxism was characterized by "a paralysing and debilitating optimism, which led socialists to slight the consequences of either action or inaction." Sitting back and waiting for history to take its course is not Gramsci's way, but, as always, he considers the phenomenon of "mechanical determinism" in its historical context, recognizing that: "When you don't have the initiative in the struggles and the struggle itself comes eventually to be identified with a series of defeats, mechanical determinism becomes a tremendous force of moral resistance, of cohesion and of patient and obstinate perseverance" (SPN, p. 336). But neither does he believe in spontaneity as the "be all and end all" of revolutionary politics. Rather, spontaneity must be *"educated*, directed, purged of extraneous contaminations" in order to "bring it into line with modern theory" (p. 198).

Gramsci regards the mechanicist conception that theory should be subordinate to practice as a "religion of the subaltern" (p. 337), typical of "a relatively primitive historical phase, one which is still economic-corporate" (p. 335). And theory should not be watered down in order to appeal to a popular readership, as Gramsci considers Bukharin does in his 1921 *Theory of Historical Materialism: A Popular Manual of Marxist Sociology*. Gramsci criticizes Bukharin's notion of Marxism in his "Critical Notes on an Attempt at Popular Sociology" (pp. 419-72). Deploring Bukharin's omission of any mention of the dialectic, Gramsci argues that Bukharin

> really does capitulate before common sense and vulgar thought, since he has not put the problem in exact theoretical terms and is therefore in practice disarmed and impotent. The uneducated and crude environment has dominated the educator and vulgar common sense has imposed itself on science rather than the other way round. (p. 435)

In a reference to Marx's third Thesis on Feuerbach, which states that "it is essential to educate the educator" (McLellan, 1977, p. 156), Gramsci continues: "If the environment is the educator, it too must in turn be educated" (SPN, p. 435).

Gramsci's Marxism, in contrast to Bukharin's, comprises a dialectic relationship between theory and practice, expressed in his designation of Marxism as a philosophy of praxis. As Gramsci puts it, "The identification of theory and practice is a critical act, through which practice is demonstrated rational and necessary, and theory realistic and rational" (p. 365). Good sense is, therefore, not predetermined but instead must be created, and the medium through which it is created is politics. For Gramsci, "Critical understanding of self takes place through a struggle of political 'hegemonies' [. . .] first in the ethical field and then in that of politics proper, in order to arrive at the working out at a higher level of one's own conception of reality" (p. 333). Continuing the comparison with Catholicism, Gramsci contends that it is politics that links common sense and the upper level of philosophy, just as it is politics that "assures the relationship between the Catholicism of the intellectuals and that of the simple"

(p. 331). But whereas the Catholicism of the intellectuals leaves the simple in their primitive philosophy of common sense, "The philosophy of praxis" tends instead "to lead them to a higher conception of life" (p. 332), in other words, to good sense. It affirms the need for contact between intellectuals and the simple "precisely in order to construct an intellectual-moral bloc which can make politically possible the intellectual progress of the mass and not only of small intellectual groups." Gramsci contends that a philosophy comes to be "accepted by the many, and accepted permanently [. . .] by becoming a culture, a form of good sense, a conception of the world with an ethic that conforms to its structure" (p. 346). Only Marxism can become good sense: "diffused among the many (a diffusion which precisely would be inconceivable without rationality or historicity) and diffused in such a way as to convert itself into an active norm of conduct." Gramsci argues that "every philosophy has a tendency to become the common sense of a fairly limited environment (that of all the intellectuals)." In order for common sense to be renewed, in other words, to become good sense, one must start with

> a philosophy which already enjoys, or could enjoy, a certain diffusion, because it is connected to and implicit in practical life, and elaborating it so that it becomes a renewed common sense possessing the coherence and sinew of individual philosophies. But this can only happen if the demands of cultural contact with the "simple" are continually felt. (p. 330n)

Towards Good Sense: Mapping an Educative Politics

Gramsci begins to map the route from common sense to good sense at both the individual and collective levels. At an individual level, the development of good sense entails criticizing one's own conception of the world in order to make it "a coherent unity and to raise it to the level reached by the most advanced thought in the world" (SPN, p. 324), in other words, Marxism (or good sense). It is a process of coming to "the consciousness of what one really is," not, for Gramsci, the uncovering of an essential self, but instead, the creation of a historical, political self. Gramsci stresses the necessity of "'knowing thyself' as a product of the historical process which has deposited in you an infinity of traces without leaving an inventory." Superseding the "infinity of traces" which comprises each individual's common sense does not mean "introducing from scratch a scientific form of thought into everyone's individual life," instead it entails "renovating and making 'critical' an already existing activity" (p. 331). For Gramsci, "Critical understanding of self takes place through a struggle of political 'hegemonies.'" This takes place, as we have seen, "first in the ethical field and then in that of politics proper, in order to arrive at the working out at a higher level of one's own conception of reality" (p. 333). It is politics which mediate between the individual and the group levels, and Gramsci recognizes that if it is to be politically effective, critical activity cannot remain at the individual level. As he puts it:

> Creating a new culture does not only mean one's own individual "original" discoveries. It also, and most particularly, means the diffusion in a critical form of truths already discovered, their "socialisation" as it were, and even making them the basis of virtal action, an element of co-ordination and intellectual and moral order. (p. 325)

The movement to socialized collective good sense is envisaged by Gramsci as the formation of what he calls "a collective consciousness, which is to say a living organism" which occurs "only after the unification of the multiplicity through friction on the part of the individuals" (FSPN, p. 16). This he likens to an orchestra tuning up, which, with "every instrument playing by itself, sounds a most hideous cacophony, yet these warm ups are the necessary condition for the orchestra to come to life as a single 'instrument.'" The musical metaphor is telling: Gramsci envisages the individual "musician" as the microcosm and the "orchestra"—the group—as the macrocosm. The process is the same in both cases: it is a process of bringing order (good sense) out of chaos (common sense). But the two moments are analogous rather than equivalent—the individual and the group are not of equal political weight. To become politically effective, the individual must be part of the whole (the orchestra), just as to become politically effective, good sense must be part of common sense—and *vice versa*. Gramsci insists:

> Philosophical activity is not to be conceived solely as the "individual" elaboration of systematically coherent concepts, but also and above all as a cultural battle to transform the popular "mentality" and to diffuse the philosophical innovations which will demonstrate themselves to be "historically true" to the extent that they become concretely—i.e. historically and socially—universal. (SPN, p. 348)

The orchestra must play: it comes into its own as an entity only when the musicians play their instruments. The performance brings the orchestra into being, just as political action brings the group into being as a historical and social (i.e., concrete) entity. But what of the music that the orchestra plays? To follow Gramsci's metaphor to its logical conclusion: the performance is the collective expression of a single composition; each musician must play from the same score. The achievement of such a collective expression is no easy matter. Gramsci warns that the process of elaborating a unitary consciousness "requires manifold conditions and initiatives." Among these, Gramsci identifies the following: the study of Marxism; an analysis of common sense in order to retrieve and develop the elements of good sense inherent in it, and an analysis of the ideas of traditional intellectuals. The study of Marxism is necessary because Marxism constitutes good sense, as we have seen, and, as a philosophy of praxis, it unites theory and practice; in other words, it constitutes a political method as well as a political aim of revolutionary activity. But Marxism, like everything else, must be considered critically, as Gramsci's prison notes on "Some Problems in the Study of the Philosophy of Praxis" (SPN, pp. 381-419) and his extended critique of Bukharin's *Popular Manual* (pp. 419-72), indeed his whole political biography,[3] amply demonstrate.

Gramsci argues that the incoming class must also look critically at its own culture, particularly at its own common sense. However, he recognizes that this is difficult since the history of common sense, by definition, is unwritten and "impossible to reconstruct for lack of documentary material" (p. 331). As he reflects, "how does one know which errors are deeply rooted or more widespread? Obviously, it is impossible to have 'statistics' on ways of thinking and on single individual opinions that would give an organic and systematic picture" (PN1, p. 129). In the absence of such statistics, Gramsci advocates "the review of the most widely circulated and most popular literature" to shed light on the common sense prevailing at a particular time and amongst particular groups. Gramsci maintains that in the absence of a history of common sense, the study of the history of philosophy must be the main source of reference. The aim is not to give historical information about the development of past philosophy but rather to give a cultural formation, and help the individual to elaborate his or her own thought critically so as to be able to participate in an ideological and cultural community (SPN, p. 424). This is necessary in order to develop in the individual the ability to evaluate ideas "as superseded links of an intellectual chain, and to determine what the new contemporary problems are and how the old problems should now be analyzed" (p. 331).

In the struggle for hegemony, the incoming class must conquer the "commanding heights of the adversary's culture" (FSPN, p. xxx), and Gramsci criticizes Bukharin for assuming that the ideas of traditional intellectuals are irrelevant to revolutionary workers (SPN, p.

419). Far from being dismissed as irrelevant, Gramsci argues that they should be rigorously examined and subjected to criticism in order to recover any useful elements that they might contain. The ideas of traditional intellectuals also constitute the residues of which common sense is partly comprised, Gramsci therefore advocates "the study and criticism of previous ideological currents, each of which 'may' have left a deposit in various combinations with preceding or subsequent deposits" (PN1, p. 129).

As Gramsci points out, however, it is wrong to think "that every social stratum elaborates its consciousness and its culture in the same way, with the same methods, that is, with the methods of professional intellectuals." These methods are not innate but instead acquired through specialized training:

> The ability of the professional intellectual skillfully to combine induction and deduction, to generalize, to infer, to transport from one sphere to another a criterion of discrimination, adapting it to new conditions, etc. is a "specialty," it is not endowed by common sense. (PN1, p. 128)

Accordingly, it is not enough to rely on the "simple theoretical enunciation of 'clear' methodological principles" (p. 129). Gramsci castigates as "an 'enlightenment' error" the idea "that a well propagated 'clear idea' enters diverse consciousnesses with the same 'organising' effects of widespread clarity," pointing up his argument with a brilliant metaphor:

> The same ray of light passes through different prisms and yields different refractions of light: in order to have the same refraction, one must make a whole series of adjustments to the individual prisms. Patient and systematic "repetition" is the fundamental methodological principle. But not a mechanical, material repetition: the adaptation of each basic concept to diverse peculiarities, presenting and representing it in all its positive aspects and in its traditional negations, always ordering each partial aspect in the totality. (PN1, p. 128)

Such a diversified, contingent approach is necessary because of the difficulty of "Finding the real identity underneath the apparent differentiation and contradiction and finding the substantial diversity underneath the apparent identity." Nonetheless, this is "the most essential quality of the critic of ideas and of the historian of social development" (pp. 128-29).

This is not an abstract task for the academic theorist: Gramsci envisages this "educational-formative work" as the task of "a homogeneous cultural center":

The work required is complex and must be articulated and graduated: there has to be a combination of deduction and induction, identification and distinction, positive demonstration and the destruction of the old. Not in the abstract but concretely: on the basis of the real. (PN1, p. 129)

The "concreteness" of the task is emphasized by Gramsci in his critique of the Popular Universities in Italy. He argues that the Popular Universities could only have worked properly if "the intellectuals had been organically the intellectuals of those masses, and if they had worked out and made coherent the principles and problems raised by the masses in their practical activity" (SPN, p. 330).

This process takes time. Accordingly, it is a mistake to expect sudden, "explosive" changes in popular consciousness. Gramsci argues that

changes in ways of thinking, in beliefs, in opinions do not come about through rapid and generalized "explosions," they come about, for the most part, through "successive combinations" in accordance with the most disparate "formulas." The illusion of "explosiveness" comes from the absence of a critical sense. (PN1, p. 129)

Gramsci underlines the social, historical, and geographical "situatedness" of the route from common sense to good sense with another graphic metaphor:

Just as methods of traction did not pass directly from the animal-drawn stagecoach to modern electrical express trains but went through a series of "intermediate combinations" some of which still exist (such as animal traction on tracks, etc.), and just as railway stock that has become obsolete in the United States remains in use for many years in China where it represents technical progress—so also in the cultural sphere diverse ideological strata are variously combined, and what has become "scrap iron" in the city is still an "implement" in the provinces. Indeed, in the cultural sphere, "explosions" are even less frequent and less intense than in the technical sphere. (p. 129)

Gramsci's notes on common sense and good sense thus consist of flashes of insight illuminating some general principles rather than constituting a detailed map of the route from one to the other. Before considering ways of envisaging the relationship between common sense and good sense, and their implications for adult educators, it may be helpful briefly to review some interpretations, comments, and critiques by commentators in a range of fields to see what light they may shed on Gramsci's concepts.

Some Interpretations of Gramsci's Concepts
of Common Sense and Good Sense

The literature commenting on Gramsci's development of the concepts of common sense and good sense emerges in several different fields of enquiry and has been interpreted in various ways. For example, Geoffrey Nowell Smith (1974), coeditor of Gramsci's prison notebooks (SPN), argues that, for Gramsci, common sense is a reactionary phenomenon; while the sociologist Alvin Gouldner (1980) uses Gramsci's concepts to develop a frame of reference for an analysis of the role of intellectuals in creating a progressive society.

In the field of psychology, Francesco Paolo Colucci (1991, 1994), explores the positive, transformative potentialities of Gramsci's concept of common sense, as well as its potential to shed light on the persistence of phenomena such as ethnic divisions and racial hatred. Colucci emphasizes the appeal of Gramsci's concept of common sense across fields and disciplines in support of his argument for greater openness between different areas of psychology, in particular between social cognitive psychology and activity theory, as well as between psychology and other disciplines.

In the field of cultural and media studies, Marcia Landy argues that Gramsci's writings on common sense may shed light on the contradictory cultural position of scientists, and the problematic nature of the circulation of scientific knowledge, in her book *Film, Politics and Gramsci* (Landy, 1996). In an article in *Mass Communication*, Lewis (1992) uses Gramsci's concept in developing a framework for tracking hegemony. In political theory, Jose Nun (1986) discusses Gramsci's concept in relation to theories of democracy, while Sue Golding, in her discussion of *Gramsci's Democratic Theory*, emphasizes Gramsci's concept of the will rather than his concepts of common sense and good sense, which she finds "vague and contradictory," concluding that "their value seems to lie more in their polemic and even strategic sense than in theoretical usages, strictly speaking" (Golding, 1992, p. 179n78).

Leonardo Salamini (1981, *passim*) contrasts Gramsci's concept of common sense with that of eighteenth-century philosophers such as Thomas Reid and the Scottish School, and in the nineteenth and twentieth centuries with that of the unclassifiable George Santayana and the utilitarian Henry Sidgwick, as well as with that of phenomenologists such as Alfred Schutz, Peter Berger, and Thomas Luckmann. Salamini states:

Common sense knowledge has been regarded as either theoretically more sound than philosophy (Santayana), or in opposition to the "critical nature" of philosophy and scientific methodology but ultimately reconcilable with them (Henry Sidgwick), or unmistakably superior to all types of knowledge because of its taken-for-granted, massive and universal character (Berger and Luckmann). (Salamini, 1981, p. 83)

Salamini highlights the common factor in each of these approaches to common sense as "the reduction of its content to an expression of a natural attitude, a conception-of-the-world not rational or scientific, but practical and universal." As he rightly observes, "Gramsci rejects such approaches by insisting on the historical, ideological and political characteristics of common sense."

Gramsci's concepts emerge from this brief review as contested both across and between disciplines, and, as we have seen, they remain elusive in Gramsci's own writings. As a result, it is not possible simply to apply Gramsci's concepts of common sense and good sense in relation to the education of adults as one might translate a set of instructions into another language or adapt a recipe, nor would it be in keeping with Gramsci's own way of working to seek to do so. Instead, it seems appropriate to explore the significance of Gramsci's concepts through metaphor (a technique which Gramsci himself often uses). Such an approach may provide a way of representing Gramsci's concepts of good sense and common sense which engages with key aspects of his problematic and illuminates considerations relevant to the education of adults.

Common Sense, Good Sense, and Educating Adults: Some Spatial Metaphors

Spatial metaphors may be particularly appropriate since Gramsci uses spatial metaphors throughout his writing, for example, in his designation of "terrains of struggle," "war of maneuver" and "war of position"—terms which have become hallmarks of Gramscian discourse. Spatial metaphors have also recently emerged in educational thinking and practice in order to articulate forms of critical-emancipatory pedagogy, with much reference to "border crossing," "boundaries," and so on, as Edwards and Usher (1998) point out. So, what spatial metaphors can be used to delineate common sense and good sense and the relationship between them?

An obvious metaphor to start with is a hierarchy (Figure 1). It is clear that Gramsci regards good sense as superior to common sense. Good sense is intrinsically "systematic," "coherent," "critical"—all

Figure 1

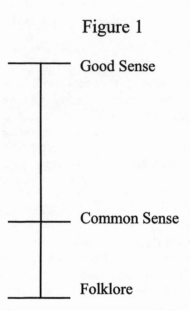

—⊤— Good Sense

—⊢— Common Sense

—⊥— Folklore

Figure 2

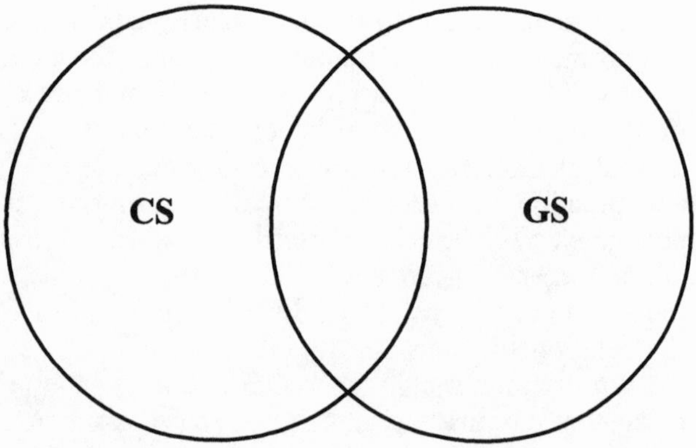

CS   GS

CS = Common Sense, GS = Good Sense

Figure 3

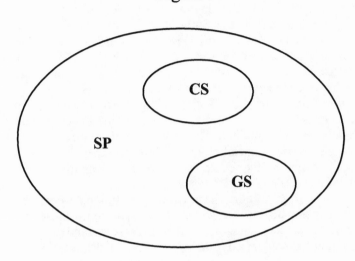

Figure 4

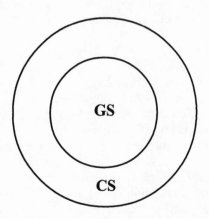

S = Common Sense, GS = Good Sense, SP = Spontaneous Philosophy

positive terms for Gramsci—whereas common sense is the obverse: "chaotic," "incoherent," "ambiguous." Extrinsically, also, good sense is superior to common sense because it has the capacity to become politically effective, to become "diffused" into a new "collective consciousness" expressed in organized political action. He explicitly states that good sense is at a "higher level" (SPN, p. 333). As we have seen, Gramsci also uses archaeological and geological metaphors (common sense as a remnant of the Stone Age personality, common sense as sediment). The relationship between common sense and good sense thus appears as hierarchical, with good sense at the apex and common sense at the base of the hierarchy. Or rather, not quite at the base: folklore occupies a lower position still, as Salamini observes. He notes that Gramsci distinguishes "various levels in hegemonic ideologies [. . .] philosophy, religion, common sense and folklore, each representing qualitatively different conceptions of the world adhered to by various social strata," while acknowledging that each contains elements of the other, so that "No clear distinction between them exists" (Salamini, 1981, p. 89).

Salamini is surely right to emphasize Gramsci's ranking system in this way, but he is right, also, to insist that there can be no clear distinction between the ranked categories. This may be paradoxical—it certainly undermines the hierarchy metaphor—but I do not believe that it is accidental. Gramsci is arguing that common sense is part of good sense, not that the two are entirely antithetical. Common sense is integral to, and supports, good sense, just as the base of the hierarchy is integral to, and supports, the apex. In any case, Gramsci is interested in the hierarchy as a whole, not just the apex—and he is in no doubt as to which way is up. Nevertheless, the hierarchy metaphor is not entirely satisfactory as a representation of Gramsci's conceptual schema because it implies a rigid separation between the elements which is not borne out in Gramsci's references to common sense and good sense.

Another spatial metaphor, the Venn diagram, borrowed from mathematics (where it denotes the set of all points within a closed figure), offers another way of representing the relationship between common sense and good sense—or rather, several ways of representing the relationship. Common sense and good sense may be seen as overlapping categories (Figure 2). There is some support for this in Gramsci's notes, but it is confusing. As we have seen, he also describes common sense and good sense as constituent parts of the "'spontaneous philosophy' which is proper to everybody" (SPN, p. 323). In this formulation, common sense and good sense are both contained within a larger entity: the individual's "spontaneous philosophy" (Figure 3). Gramsci also uses the biological metaphor of a cell, noting that common sense contains "a healthy nucleus" of good sense, which "deserves to be made more unitary and coherent" (p. 328). Here good sense is contained within common sense (Figure 4).

To sum up then: the Venn diagrams reveal the multiple ambiguities, the paradoxical nature of Gramsci's concepts, but they do not provide us with a single definitive visual representation. Part of the problem perhaps is that a Venn diagram is a static representation, whereas, as I have argued elsewhere, Gramsci sees both common sense and good sense as dynamic concepts, in keeping with his dynamic theory of hegemony:

> Hegemony is characterized by a blend of force and consent; power is articulated through a complex of historically-specific forces and counter-forces; any settlement is inevitably provisional. Accordingly, any victory of good sense over common sense is temporary, holding only for as long as good sense is able to renew itself, partly through its relationship with common sense. Good sense is constantly being developed or deteriorating, as is common sense, and the relationship between the two is constantly developing or deteriorating also. (Coben, 1997a, p. 44)

Accordingly, history, for Gramsci, as for Marx in the *Grundrisse*, is created by human agency; it does not just roll on in a preordained sequence. Progress is not the "simple unilinear evolution," the "chronological succession of epochs" that "became canonical" in Marxism (Bottomore, 1983, p. 20). A correspondingly nonunilinear idea of technological progress is proposed by Gramsci in the metaphor discussed above, where he states that "what has become 'scrap iron' in the city is still an 'implement' in the provinces" (PN1, p. 129).

Another spatial metaphor from the world of fractal mathematics,[4] may have greater explanatory power than either the Venn diagram or the simple hierarchy, because it engages with the dynamic nature of Gramsci's concepts of common sense and good sense. In mathematics, a dynamic system is "any natural process [. . .] or any mathematical model in which each successive state is a function of the preceding state"—a statement which stands, also, for Gramsci's historically contingent notion of common sense and good sense. The parallels with Gramsci's educative politics become more striking as the definition proceeds:

> The *orbit* of the system is the sequence of the repeated compositions of this function, starting from an initial state or *seed*. If the system reaches an equilibrium or cycles between a number of states, the equilibrium points [. . .] are called the *attractors* of the system. If the initial seed determines the equilibrium state, a system with two or more attractors di-

vides the complex plane into equivalence classes, and the boundary between such states is typically a fractal curve. (Borowski & Borwein, 1989,
p. 180)

To translate into politicoeducational terms after the initial "seed"—
the event which triggers the start of the educative process—the "or-
bit" of activities is established and reaches an equilibrium, denoted by
the "attractors of the system." Common sense and good sense may
thus both be considered as "classes of equivalence" in a dynamic system and the boundary between them may be considered a fractal
curve rather than a one-dimensional line.

The mathematical definition of dynamic (or dynamical) systems
continues, describing the element of chaos theory which has caught
the public imagination—the butterfly flapping its wings in Japan
which effects the weather on the other side of the world:

> In many natural processes [. . .], apparently random ("*chaotic*") behaviour
> is nonetheless deterministic and may be modelled by a dynamical system
> in which the nature of the attractor depends upon minute variations of
> some seemingly irrelevant parameter of the system; a point at which the
> attractor changes is called *bifurcation*. In a chaotic system, bifurcation
> may be observed to recur at all levels of analysis or magnification, show-
> ing the self-symmetry typical of fractals; in fact such a system has an at-
> tractor that bifurcates infinitely often and is a fractal set (a *strange attrac-
> tor*). (Borowski & Borwein, 1989, p. 180)

Just so does the form of common sense change in response to seemingly irrelevant factors. Bifurcation, the point at which the attractor
changes, may be seen as the beginning of the revolutionary process—the shift towards the establishment of a new hegemony. Bifurcation occurs "at all levels of analysis or magnification, showing the
self-symmetry typical of fractals"; this too is symptomatic of common sense and good sense in Gramsci's schema.

The same argument may be traced in terms of the relationship
between the educator and the student. Gramsci, as we have seen, does
not see good sense as exclusively embodied in the educator; the educator embodies both common sense and good sense and works to develop the latter—in both the learner and the educator—on the basis
of the former. The educational encounter is conceived as an active,
dynamic one. Common sense and good sense are not static qualities
vested in one or the other party; it is not a case of the all-knowing
educator endowing the ignorant learner with knowledge. In any case,
knowledge alone is not enough for Gramsci, as his predilection for
the eleventh of Marx's Theses on Feuerbach reveals: "The philosophers have only interpreted the world, in various ways, the point is

to change it" (McLellan, 1977, p. 158). Similarly, it is not the case that good sense is equated with truth and common sense with falsehood, or that the educator already knows the truth and the student is trapped in false apprehensions: common sense is not a Gramscian version of "false consciousness."[5] Gramsci rejects the dichotomized notion of consciousness as either true or false in favor of what Femia (1975, p. 29) calls his "expansive vision of the role of consciousness within the framework of historical materialism."

Undeniably, however, Gramsci is writing from the perspective of the educator; he sees the educator, in principle, as both knowing more and knowing better than the student and having the organizing capacity to diffuse that knowledge. In his educative politics, organization, coherence, and homogeneity are valued highly; these are all qualities of good sense rather than common sense, and the task of organization is that of the "educator," whether he, she, or it is the organic intellectual of the working class, the revolutionary political party, the state, or any other formation. Here again, the analogy with fractal mathematics is telling, since at each point on the scale the educative process is self-similar in the way of fractals. Furthermore, as Tim Robinson (1998) has pointed out:

> With attractors, the universe of discourse is phase-space; i.e. each point represents a possible state of the system under consideration. So, metaphorically [. . .] it represents where an individual stands, in terms of some parameters of ability, knowledge, educational attainment etc. Someone starting from or passing through certain points will pursue an educational orbit leading to good sense; others, starting elsewhere, won't.

Whoever (or whatever) the educator is, the starting point must be the student's common sense, as Gramsci insists in this sketch of the educational process:

> it is necessary to take as one's starting point what the student already knows and his philosophical experience (having first demonstrated to him precisely that he has such an experience, that he is a "philosopher" without knowing it). And since one presupposes a certain average cultural and intellectual level among the students, who in all probability have hitherto only acquired scattered and fragmentary bits of information and have no methodological and critical preparation, one cannot but start in the first place from common sense, then secondly from religion, and only at a third stage move on to the philosophical systems elaborated by traditional intellectual groups. (SPN, pp. 424-25)

Gramsci's aim is that every citizen should be educated so that he or she is formed "as a person capable of thinking, studying and ruling—or controlling those who rule" (SPN, p. 40). In other words, he conceives of the educator and the student as "classes of equivalence" in the educational process. The boundary between the student and the educator is therefore also fractal, endlessly iterating and recurring at all scales.

Gramsci, however, was writing before Benoit Mandelbrot (in the 1960s) brought together the concept of the virtually infinite length of coastlines and the concept of nonintegral dimensionality, and, in 1975, coined the term "fractal," thereby opening up practical and theoretical possibilities in fields ostensibly far removed from pure mathematics (Paulos, 1992, pp. 82-86; Robinson, 1996, p. 86). Both concepts had been suggested separately by earlier mathematicians, a fact that raises the intriguing possibility that Gramsci (who had an extraordinarily wide range of interests) might have had some knowledge of, for example, the work of the Italian mathematician, who discovered—or created, depending on one's point of view—the Peano curve, at the turn of the century.[6] Does Gramsci intuitively anticipate chaos and complexity theory in his formulation of common sense, and the relationship between common sense and good sense? Was his formulation of common sense and good sense hampered, not only by his own poor health and the conditions of his imprisonment, but also by the fact that the mathematics which might have expressed something of the nature of common sense, and the elusive relationship between common sense and good sense, was simply unavailable to him in the 1930s?

A Tentative Conclusion

So where does this leave us? Is Gramsci's distinction between good sense and common sense relevant to adult educators post-1990? I believe it is. As I argue in my book (Coben, 1998), Gramsci's concept of common sense as something to be transcended rather than rejected implies an educative process rooted in, and respectful of, people's lived experience. By problematizing common sense rather than simply opposing it to good sense, Gramsci's distinction offers a way of thinking about common sense as a basis for further development, rather than as something to be excised before "proper" learning can take place. Accordingly, Gramsci's distinction between good sense and common sense may be seen as

> conceptual rather than empirical, since the categories are not mutually exclusive. It is also both epistemological and sociological: both a distinction between different forms of knowledge and a distinction between the "knowledges" characteristic of different social groups. But again, the dis-

tinctions are not mutually exclusive in either case. In epistemological terms, common sense includes elements of good sense. In sociological terms, good sense is not the preserve of an elite, and common sense is common to us all. (Coben, 1998, pp. 213-14)

It seems that aspects of these apparent paradoxes may be expressed in terms of an endlessly iterating fractal curve forming the boundary between classes of equivalence in a dynamic system with strange attractors. But this is to propose a way of envisaging the relationship between common sense and good sense, which seems more in keeping with Gramsci's political project, it is not to propose a theory. A great deal of further work must be done before anything approaching a Gramscian theory of adult education might be developed drawing on Gramsci's brilliant, elusive concepts of good sense and common sense. As Gramsci himself says, "It will be necessary to establish these concepts firmly by thinking them through in depth" (PN1, p. 173).

Gramsci's distinction between good sense and common sense has been revealed as multifaceted and complex, its complexity compounded by the fact that his prison notes are fragmentary and incomplete. Any attempt to draw out the implications for adult educators must, therefore, be somewhat tentative and have regard to Gramsci's own exploratory method of working in the prison notebooks. It also necessarily involves translation from political philosophy to educational theory in a field (the education of adults) that is acknowledged to be undertheorized (Field et. al., 1991), and whose practitioners do not necessarily share Gramsci's political aims.

Gramsci writes: "It is necessary to create sober, patient people who do not despair in the face of the worst horrors and who do not become exuberant with every silliness" (PN1, p. 172). How are such "sober, patient people" to be created? Gramsci envisages this task in terms of an educative revolutionary politics encompassing "education" in the conventional sense of the word, as well as a myriad of other forms of educative activity, much of it organized through the revolutionary political party. It is a task that extends far beyond the academy and requires politically committed "organic intellectuals"—revolutionaries who conceive their task somewhat differently from even the most progressive of liberal adult educators.

Meanwhile, the question of what constitutes good sense, the question that Gramsci spent his life trying to answer, has been thrown into sharp relief by the collapse of the Soviet version of Marxism-Leninism in 1989-90, especially since Gramsci was honored in the Soviet Union. In the years since his death, Gramsci has been claimed as a Leninist, a Eurocommunist, an idealist Crocean, and even a crypto-feminist (see my discussion of "Gramscism after Gramsci," 1998, pp. 41-49). There is even a "right-wing Gramscianism," a perversion of Gramsci's ideas perpetrated by the French *Nouvelle Droite* and the Flemish *het Vlaams Blok* (van Kranenburg, 1999). Gramsci himself would surely disown some of the causes to which his name has been attached—especially the last two, but the very diversity of these "Gramscisms" is an indication of the contested nature of Gramsci's legacy.

In his prison notebooks, Gramsci is writing from a position of crushing defeat; his call for "pessimism of the intelligence, optimism of the will" (PN1, p. 172) has especial resonance, emerging as it does from a prison cell. That he continued to assert the necessity for "a new common sense and with it a new culture and a new philosophy which will be rooted in the popular consciousness with the same solidity and imperative quality as traditional beliefs" (SPN, pp. 423-24) under such circumstances, is inspiring. It should inspire us to consider again the good sense and common sense of our own troubled times.

Postscript

A reminiscence of Gramsci by Felice Platone, who worked with him on the editorial board of the political newspaper, *L'Ordine Nuovo*, is recorded in the Introduction to an early collection of Gramsci's writings in English translation. It gives us a glimpse of what the concepts of good sense and common sense meant to Gramsci in practice. Platone describes an occasion when Gramsci was visited in his office by a young, opinionated, and supercilious university lecturer:

> The young professor said that he intended to "help" the workers, "instruct them," "educate them," and all this disinterestedly. The workers would find him a loyal and capable "teacher." From the beginning Gramsci fumed in silence; he kept taking off and putting on his spectacles. I saw that he was about to lose his patience. Then he calmed down and listened to the end, without raising his eyes, entirely absorbed in folding and refolding, with great care, a sheet of paper. When the professor had finished, Gramsci, as if he had heard nothing and had been thinking about something completely different, asked him:
>
> "What in your opinion was the most fruitful and important step forward made by man after he had learned to use fire?"
>
> When he saw that the other man gaped astonishedly, he continued:
>
> "Excuse me, this really is not good enough. But tell me, how many years have you been at school with the workers?"
>
> "Really, I never intended to become a worker . . ."
>
> "That is not what I meant. Who do you think is more qualified to be classed as an intellectual: a lecturer, or even a professor, who has stored up

a certain number of more or less disconnected notions and ideas, who knows nothing except his own job; or a worker, even a not very cultured worker, but one who coherently organises and co-ordinates those modest and elementary notions he has been able to acquire around this idea?" "But I know Marxism very well; moreover, I have given it an idealistic basis."

That was enough for Gramsci. After a few minutes the professor, as if by magic, had lost his affectation and went away saying, in the tone of one who does not want to show his wounded pride: "I shall think about his advice to learn from the workers." (Gramsci, 1957, p. 15)

Notes

1. I discuss the relationship between common sense and good sense in Gramsci's writings in my book, *Radical Heroes: Gramsci, Freire and the Politics of Adult Education* (Coben, 1998); that discussion is extended and continued here. I have also explored the relationship between common sense and adults' mathematical knowledge and understanding in a series of papers based on my research with Gillian Thumpston on adults' mathematics life histories (Coben, 1997a, 1997b; Coben & Thumpston, 1996).

2. The philosophical route "From Vico's Common Sense to Gramsci's Hegemony" is explored by Jacobitti (1983).

3. Readers in search of biographical information are referred to Davidson (1977), Fiori (1970), and Frank Rosengarten's Introduction to his edition of Gramsci's prison letters (Gramsci, 1994).

4. For an accessible introduction to fractals for the non-mathematician, see Paulos (1992, pp. 82-86); for more detail, see Mandelbrot (1982).

5. David McLellan points out that although the notion of false consciousness is generally regarded as Marxist, it does not in fact come from Marx. It is too clear-cut, in that Marx does not operate with a true/false dichotomy, and too general to encompass Marx's meaning because it is essential to know what kind of falsity is involved, "indeed, Marx's point is often that ideology is not a question of logical or empirical falsity but of the superficial or misleading way in which truth is asserted" (McLellan, 1986, p. 18).

6. I am grateful to Tim Robinson for this point and for his other insightful comments on an earlier draft of this paper (private communication). Elsewhere, in a wonderful essay about the mathematics of mapmaking, "A Connemara Fractal" (1996, p. 87), Robinson describes his encounters with fractal geometry and with the Peano Curve: "discovered—or created, according to one's view of the na-

ture of mathematical objects—by the Italian mathematician Peano around the turn of the century." Gramsci refers to Giuseppe Peano in PN1 (p. 233), though on an educational rather than a mathematical point. An editorial note on the passage indicates that "Giuseppe Peano taught at the University of Turin when Gramsci was a student there" (PN1, p. 520n5). It was Tim Robinson's essay which set me off on the intellectual journey described in this paper, however, the route I have chosen is my own, as is the responsibility for any wrong turnings along the way.

References

Borowski, E. J., & Borwein, J. M. (1989). *Collins Dictionary of Mathematics*. London: Harper Collins.

Bottomore, T., Harris, L., Kiernan, L., & Miliband, R. (Eds.). (1983). *A Dictionary of Marxist Thought*. Oxford: Basil Blackwell.

Coben, D. (1998). *Radical Heroes: Gramsci, Freire and the Politics of Adult Education*. New York: Garland.

Coben, D. (1997a). Mathematics or Common Sense? Some Reflections on Research into Adults' Mathematics Life Histories. In G. E. FitzSimons (Ed.), *Adults Returning to Study Mathematics: Papers from Working Group 18, 8th International Congress on Mathematical Education, ICME-8* (pp. 37-48). Adelaide, SA: Australian Association of Mathematics Teachers.

Coben, D. (1997b). Mathematics Life Histories and Common Sense. In *Adults Learning Mathematics-3. Proceedings of ALM-3, 3rd International Conference of Adults Learning Maths—A Research Forum (ALM)* (pp. 56-60). London: Goldsmiths College, University of London.

Coben, D., & Thumpston, G. (1996). Common Sense, Good Sense and Invisible Mathematics. In T. Kjaeregaard, A. Kvamme, & N. Linden (Eds.), *Numeracy, Race, Gender and Class: Proceedings of the Third International Conference of Political Dimensions of Mathematics Education (PDME) III, Bergen, Norway* (pp. 284-98). Landaas, Norway: Caspar.

Colucci, F. P. (1994). Common Sense, Transformation, and Elites. In *Multidisciplinary Newsletter for Activity Theory*, 15-16, 45-52.

Colucci, F. P. (1991). Praxis as Tatigkeit: Antonio Gramsci's Ideas on the Subject of Common Sense and their Relevance to Psychology. *Multidisciplinary Newsletter for Activity Theory*, 9-10, 41-49.

Davidson, A. (1977). *Antonio Gramsci: Towards an Intellectual Biography*. London: Merlin.

Edwards, R., & Usher, R. (1998). Globalisation, Diaspora Space and Pedagogy. Paper presented at the American Educational Research Association Annual Meeting, San Diego.

Femia, J. V. (1975). Hegemony and Consciousness in the Thought of Antonio Gramsci. In *Political Studies*, 23 (1), 29-48.

Field, J., Lovett, T., & Weller, P. (1991). *Research Quality in Continuing Education: A Study of Citations Patterns*. Research paper, University of Warwick, Coventry.

Fiori, G. (1970). *Antonio Gramsci: Life of a Revolutionary* (T. Nairn, Trans.). London: NLB.

Golding, S. (1992). *Gramsci's Democratic Theory: Contributions to a Post-Liberal Democracy*. Toronto: University of Toronto Press.

Gouldner, A. (1980). *The Future of Intellectuals and the Rise of the New Class: A Frame of Reference*. New York: Continuum.

Gramsci, A. (1994). *Letters from Prison* (F. Rosengarten, Ed. and R. Rosenthal, Trans.). 2 vol. New York: Columbia University Press.

Gramsci, A. (1957). *The Modern Prince and Other Writings* (L. Marks, Trans. and Intro.). New York: International.

Hall, S. (1987). *Speaking at Gramsci '87 Conference*. London: Marxism Today.

Irwin, T. (1993). Aristotle. In J. Dancy & E. Sosa (Eds.), *A Companion to Epistemology* (pp. 27-31). Oxford: Basil Blackwell.

Jacobitti, E. E. (1983). From Vico's Common Sense to Gramsci's Hegemony. In G. Tagliacozzo (Ed.), *Vico and Marx: Affinities and Contrasts* (pp. 367-87). London: Humanities.

van Kranenburg, R. (1999). Whose Gramsci? Right-wing Gramscianism. In *International Gramsci Society Newsletter*, 9, 14-18.

Landy, M. (1996). *Film, Politics and Gramsci*. Minneapolis: University of Minnesota Press.

Lemos, N. H. (1993). Commonsensism and Critical Cognitivism. In J. Dancy & E. Sosa (Eds.), *A Companion to Epistemology* (pp. 71-74). Oxford: Basil Blackwell.

Lewis, C. (1992). Making Sense of Common-Sense: A Framework for Tracking Hegemony. *Critical Studies in Mass Communication*, 9 (3), 277-92.

Mandelbrot, B. (1982). *The Fractal Geometry of Nature*. San Francisco: W. H. Freeman.

Manzoni, A. (1956). *The Betrothed* (A. Colquhoun, Trans.). London: Dent.

McLellan, D. (1986). *Ideology*. Minneapolis: University of Minnesota Press.

290 Diana C. Coben

McLellan, D. (Ed.). (1977). *Karl Marx: Selected Writings*. Oxford: Oxford University Press.
Miller, D., Coleman, J., Connolly, W., & Ryan, A. (Eds.). (1991). *The Blackwell Encyclopedia of Political Thought*. Oxford: Basil Blackwell.
Nowell Smith, G. (1974). Common Sense. *Radical Philosophy*, 7, 15-16.
Nun, J. (1986). Elements for a Theory of Democracy: Gramsci and Common Sense. *Boundary 2*, 3, 197-225.
Paulos, J. A. (1992). *Beyond Numeracy: An Uncommon Dictionary of Mathematics*. London: Penguin.
Robinson, T. (1998). Personal communication.
Robinson, T. (1996). A Connemara Fractal. In *Setting Foot on the Shore of Connemara and Other Writings* (pp. 78-102). Dublin: Lilliput.
Salamini, L. (1981). *The Sociology of Political Praxis: An Introduction to Gramsci's Theory*. London: Routledge.

Abbreviated Titles

FSPN: *Further Selections from the Prison Notebooks of Antonio Gramsci* (D. Boothman, Ed. and Trans.). Minneapolis: University of Minnesota Press (1995).
PN1: *Antonio Gramsci: Prison Notebooks Vol. I* (J. A. Buttigieg, Ed. and Intro., and J. A. Buttigieg & A. Callari, Trans.). New York: Columbia University Press (1992).
SPN: *Selections from the Prison Notebooks of Antonio Gramsci* (Q. Hoare & G. Nowell Smith, Eds. and Trans.). London: Lawrence & Wishart (1971).

14

Gramsci and the Current Debate on Multicultural Education

Ursula Apitzsch

The concept and the politics of "multicultural society" contain a strange mixture of tendencies that are both amicable and hostile towards foreigners. The concept of multicultural society involves the basic acceptance of the "inside views" of the respective ethnic groups, while at the same time it affords society a variety of cultures "free of charge"—without having to concern itself with the problems that give rise to migration. The symbolic representation of traditional cultures of origin within the diversity of immigrant cultures made it seem feasible to conceive of these "ancestral" cultures as the real territory to which migrants could withdraw in both the economic and the psychological sense.

Awareness that such a multicultural model for society is essentially ambivalent did not develop in Germany until attention was drawn to the "New Racism" debate in France (Balibar, Finkielkraut, and so forth). The contribution of social science to the creation of the model was seen in "intellectual articulations of the segregation deception" (Balibar, 1989, p. 369). In his very polemic critique of "the pedagogics of relativism" in multicultural society, Alain Finkielkraut has attempted to unmask the implications and consequences that are implied by the excessive "respect" for all that is alien.[1] These are manifested both in the "Third World" argument (Tiersmondisme)—the plea for each people to be conceded its own cultural peculiarities, and each culture its own system of moral values and political traditions—as well as in the manner in which the "New Right" in France exploits the notion of "cultural differences" in pursuing its political objectives: "To speak of culture in the plural is to deny people from different epochs or distant civilisations the opportunity to establish contact with each other through conceivable meanings or values that extend beyond the original source from which the latter may have arisen" (Finkielkraut, 1989, p. 97ff).

The definitive features of multicultural society—the acceptance of mere physical proximity and the emphasis on cultural differences—are quite obviously nonidentical with the principle of universalist morality as it has developed within the Enlightenment tradition in Europe. "Right" (Recht) is either founded on universalist principles or culture has the last word, and—as Marx says—the feudal serf who suffers under the knout must suppress a cry of rebellion "once the knout is time-honored, ancestral, and historical" (Marx, 1977, p. 132).

Finkielkraut's critique points the way back to the "constitutional patriotism" of the democratic social and legal order in the tradition of the French Revolution as the sole foundation for a multicultural society capable of intercultural discourse. But can such a synthesis of the general and the particular actually succeed without more precise knowledge of the relations between cultures in an immigration society? Does the French example, or the example of Great Britain, not show instead that granting civil rights to immigrants from former colonies is no protection against social exclusion and marginalization? As soon as nationality no longer functions as the criterion for exclusion, the ethnic and the cultural dimension is constructed as the main determinant. Academic disciplines with a humanist ethos, such as pedagogy, have aided this process in that for years they have offered their services as mediators between the supposedly "indigenous" and "foreign." The problematic nature of multicultural thinking thus seems to consist not only in defining the main differences in society in cultural terms, but also in the fact that it is liable to underestimate those social forces that distinguish not only between different cultures but also between the "indigenous" and the "foreign." Such distinctions and demarcations also involve elements of domination, coercion, and subordination, disguised behind the label of culture or "ethnicity." A study entitled *The Empire Strikes Back*, which was published by the Centre of Contemporary Cultural Studies (CCCS) in 1982, argued that colored immigrants in particular were only able to form a so-called "cultural identity" in a position of marginality, in other words, in those sections of society that are excluded from positions of social power.

In order to recognize the subtle traps into which a well-intended concept of multiculturalism can fall, some thoughts and categories developed by Antonio Gramsci from the "Ordine Nuovo" period to the *Prison Notebooks* would seem appropriate. Gramsci's ideas on culture and multiculturalism seem particularly relevant in that: (a) he views emigration and immigration processes as social phenomena of one and the same Italian society; (b) he thinks from the perspective of those countries from which there is high migration, bearing in mind the spread of Italian labor over the whole world; (c) he wants to see the culturally particular, in its marginalized and folklorized form, defended as "collective memory" and integrated into a new, modern form of civil society. In the following, I would like to pursue these aspects of Gramci's thought in greater detail.

Migration and Culture: The Familiar from Afar and the Alien in Ourselves

The theme of "emigration" is one of the "*argomenti principali*" (i.e., main themes) listed by Antonio Gramsci on 8 February 1929 on the opening page of his first prison notebook. His concern is very clearly to criticize culturalist analyses of emigration from the Italian South, and to counter these with a more rationalist approach. Gramsci makes particular reference to the fact that a society that loses emigrants is very reluctant to reflect on the phenomenon of migration. Nor does migration comply with the notion of human worth inherent in popular consciousness in the North. It provokes images of the terrible and reluctantly discussed side of the Italian Risorgimento—the unresolved issue of the economic and social backwardness of the South. In response to an article printed in the periodical, *Pègaso*, in September 1930 (which discussed the curious phenomenon that while Italian labor is globally distributed, hardly any literature deals with the subject), Gramsci writes: "That writers concern themselves little with the emigrant abroad is less surprising than the fact that they do not deal with the life he leads before he emigrates, with the conditions that compel him to emigrate" (QC, p. 2254).

One of the few literary works about migration from Italy known in Gramsci's time (besides those portraying the "American Myth," such as De Amici's work) was Francesco Perri's novel, *The Emigrants*. This story deals with the historical conflict that gave rise to emigration from Calabria; but, in Gramsci's view, it obscures and mystifies more than it reveals:

> It is apparent that Perri is not directly familiar with the simple life of the Calabrians through his own emotional and psychological experience, but that he makes use of the old regionalist clichés. [. . .] The absence of any historical sense is intentional, since this enables him to treat all folkloric themes as a homogenous mass, whereas in reality they differ greatly in space and time. (QC, p. 2201-02)

Gramsci is referring here to a procedure within culturalism that ascribes and typifies particular characteristics, something that can frequently be observed in present-day studies on migration. Gramsci returns to the real historical background of migration processes by discussing Fiat's policies for the recruitment of migrant laborers. He refers to Agnelli's policy in 1925-26, when 25,000 Sicilians were recruited as labor migrants for the factories in Turin. The attempt failed miserably. The Sicilians, who were expected to live in barracks-like accommodations with strict internal discipline, fled in droves from the factory to nearby farms in search of work. The criminal records of those years further reinforced the Sicilians' bad reputation as brigands.

What is interesting here is that Gramsci's treatment of the event does not include any reference to general cultural peculiarities of the Sicilians. Instead, he sees it as a continuation of the old struggle between the Piedmontese and the Sicilians, between the industrial North and the peasant South. The migrants, who originally came on a "voluntary" basis, recognized immediately on entering the barracks that there was a connection between migration and the history of their colonization. For Gramsci, the Sardinian chronicler who can draw parallels very quickly with the state of virtual war between the Piedmontese and the Sardinians, these Sicilians and their ways of behaving are in no sense "alien."

With a methodological approach familiar to us from ethnomethodology and psychoanalysis, Gramsci reverses the angle of vision to that of "the alien" himself.[2] It is not the emigrants that are alien, since the causes for their collective behavior are easily identified; instead, it is those groups and social formations that come into being in the large factories (as a consequence of capitalist factory owners' behavior) that are the alien subjects in the eyes of politicians and political scientists. This is an aspect that Gramsci discussed even before the *Ordine Nuovo* period, shortly after the end of the First World War, and to which he often returned in the *Prison Notebooks*. Unlike other Marxist theorists, Gramsci finds the idea of uniting all proletarians both abstract and insufficient—what interests him, instead, is the specifically new that comes into being in the melting pot of the large factory. For Gramsci, it is important that the new can only be created when what happens to the subjects in this process is grasped as something essentially new. In one of his first articles about "Socialism and Culture," written in 1916 (SG, pp. 22f), Gramsci quotes Novalis to show that the prerequisite for understanding the alien is understanding oneself. In 1916, Gramsci termed this a "transcendental" aspect. By linking the "transcendental" component of early Romanticism with Vico's "Corollaries concerning Speech by Poetic Characters among the First Nations," Gramsci goes a step further in his analysis of the "alien." The members of the dominant minority do not have to "understand" the majority; instead, it is the subordinated groups who should discover themselves and thereby develop their universal claim to equal civil rights:

> Vico [in the First Corollary concerning Speech by Poetic Characters among the First Nations in *Scienza Nuova*] gives a political interpretation of the famous dictum of Solon which Socrates subsequently made his own in relation to philosophy: "Know thyself." Vico claims that in this dictum Solon wished to admonish the plebeians, who believed themselves to be of bestial origin and the nobility to be of divine origin, to reflect on themselves and see that they had the same human nature as the nobles and hence should claim to be their equals in civil law. Vico then points to this consciousness of human equality between plebeians and nobles as the basis and historical reason for the rise of the democratic republics of Antiquity. We have not chosen these two fragments entirely at random. In them we believe the writers touch upon, though admittedly in a vaguely expressed and defined manner, the limits and principles governing the correct comprehension of the concept of culture even in relation to socialism. (GR, p. 56)

Critique of "Understanding the Alien" as "Intracultural Reductionism"

What makes Gramsci's writings such a rich source of material today for solving the problems of multinational and multicultural coexistence is the fact that he does not reduce the social problems associated with differing degrees of modernity to the relationship between native people and foreigners, but defines these differences as a problem of modern consciousness generally. Modern consciousness is characterized for him by the fact that only through "folkloristic" distortions is it able to retain certain moments of its rural prehistory and the counterknowledge rooted in and dominated by the process of modernization. The relationship of such sedimented collective experience to industrial society is by no means identical to the relationship between traditional and modern societies; this difference in degree of modernity is a crucial defining aspect of modern society itself. Gramsci developed this aspect with extraordinary clarity in his twenty-seventh prison notebook. According to his analysis, so-called "folklore" research cannot be conducted in isolation from "official" worldviews in the dominant society:

> Folklore should instead be studied as a "conception of the world and life" implicit to a large extent in determinate (in time and space) strata of society and in opposition (also for the most part implicit, mechanical and objective) to "official" conceptions of the world (or in a broader sense, the conceptions of the cultured parts of historically determinate societies) that have succeeded one another in the historical process. (Hence the strict relationship between folklore and "common sense," which is philosophical folklore.) This conception of the world is not elaborated and systematic because, by definition, the people (the sum total of the instrumental and subaltern classes of every form of society that has so far existed) cannot possess conceptions which are elaborated, systematic and politically organised and centralised in their albeit contradictory development. It is, rather, many-sided—not only because it includes different and juxtaposed elements, but also because it is stratified, from the more crude to the less crude—if, indeed, one should not speak of a confused agglomerate of fragments of all the conceptions of the world and of life that have succeeded one another in history. In fact, it is only in folklore that one finds surviving evidence, adulterated and mutilated, of the majority of these conceptions. Philosophy and modern science are also constantly contributing new elements to "modern folklore" in that certain opinions and scientific notions, removed from their context and more or less distorted, constantly fall within the popular domain and are "inserted" into the mosaic of tradition. (GR, pp. 360-61)

Gramsci's reflections on folklore are provoked by a question that could be posed today, in a somewhat adapted form, without losing any of its relevance. Gramsci states his position on the question as to whether or not folklore should be taught at teachers' training institutions: "To deepen the impartial culture of the teachers? To show them the object that they should not destroy?" (QC, p. 2313). Gramsci poses this question in precisely the same sense in which one could ask today whether it is necessary to include an introduction to folk cultures in teachers' training courses. The answer, for Gramsci, depends significantly on whether the introduction of such new syllabus content is nothing more than "firing broadsides at folklore"—in other words, convincing the younger generations that they are caught up in a culture that must be overcome, or that is seen "as an eccentricity, an oddity or a picturesque element"—or whether such activity should be seen as a very important matter that should be taken seriously: "It is clear that, in order to achieve the desired end, the spirit of folklore studies should be changed, as well as deepened and extended. Folklore must not be considered an eccentricity, an oddity or a picturesque element, but as something which is very serious and is to be taken seriously" (GR, p. 362). In Gramsci's view, the issue is not about choosing between the illusory alternatives of pluralism and universalism—in other words, the point is not whether one accepts the Ptolemaic system as an element of folklore or whether it is combatted as archaic and a barrier to progress. Both approaches would be an expression of thought that is confined by categories of cultural difference, one in which the culture of the oppressed masses is disqualified out of hand as something backward and as something that has therefore been removed from the dominant culture.

Gramsci, therefore, sees the debate between universalists and relativists as a "mock battle." The real issue for him is to identify within historically real "common sense," in all its specific variations, that reformative element which Solon and Vico had already mentioned, namely the consciousness of fundamental human rights and of the dignity and worth of each individual human being. If, by contrast, popular consciousness as "pre-history in the present" obstructs such reformative strivings, it can easily prove to be an element hostile to the simple individual and something he must rid himself of, since "folklore has always been linked to the culture of the dominant classes, and has extracted elements that have become joined with existing traditions" (QC, p. 1105).

The principal concern should be (and here Gramsci refers to the Catholic population in Italy, as befits his specific historical situation) to assess the extent to which a new "reformed" *civiltà* could arise from the complex of popular culture:

> Only in this way will the teaching of folklore be more efficient and really bring about the birth of a new culture among the broad popular masses, so that the separation between modern culture and popular culture of folklore will disappear. An activity of this kind, thoroughly carried out, would correspond on the intellectual plane to what the Reformation was in Protestant countries. (GR, p. 362)

Cultures as Elements in the Development of "*Civiltà*"

The return to the pluralist understanding of the "many cultures" in society which developed out of the protest against the ethnocentricity of western-universalist cultural constructs has led insidiously, in the concept of the "multicultural society," to a new form of thought in which differences between cultures are brought forward. Individual developments and crises of migrants not only of the first, but also of the second generation, were purposively explained in terms of the closed cultural context of the society of origin in order to arrive at a "better understanding." Especially in studies conducted in the fields of education, sociology, and cultural anthropology, the society of origin was interpreted unquestioningly in the name of cultural identity as something "immutable." A contrast is thus constructed, creating two clinically separated worlds in which there is an opposition between each of their respective central components. Once this polarity has been established, it will control subsequent perceptions, thus reinforcing the prejudice and vice versa. The migrant is locked within the ideological structure of his or her society of origin, while at the same time western values are assumed to be the superior ones.

Existing approaches to multicultural policymaking, as could be observed in some German cities in recent years, seek to promote legal equality and rational discourse. But this does not do away with the problem that the debate on the multicultural society is barely able to include the question of societal sub- and superordination. As long as the population of rich industrial countries continues to be underclassed by immigrants, the stress on cultural identity can have a certain functional utility in the sense of subordination under the dominant culture.[3] The question of cultural relations cannot be discussed without referring it back to the question of hegemonic structures.

Gramsci's thoughts regarding the so-called "subaltern social strata" (in Notebook 25, as well as in many other writings on cultural hegemony) appear to supply a wealth of ideas relating to precisely this problem. Gramsci's concept permits us to base our analysis not only on one but on many cultures within a given national society. Important elements of the "pre-history of the present" are not eliminated within the dominant culture, according to Gramsci. His approach thus lends itself very well to the critique of ethnocentric pseudouniversalism. His concepts are used by migration researchers who criticize, from the perspective of migrants, the logic in western recipient countries, according to which the economic value of migrants is the only factor that counts: "Different cultures live side by side within the same society, and the locations of identity are the locations where there is mutual recognition of the social groups" (Di Carlo, 1986, p. 28f). At the same time, however, it is clear that the "many cultures" cannot be separated from the context that binds them to the structures of domination in both the country of origin and the country of emigration. The concept of "national culture" takes effect for Gramsci at this point as a hegemonic framework in which dominant and subordinate cultures encounter each other. This means that "popular" or "folk" culture cannot be reduced to national culture, or vice versa (QC, p. 1660f). Because dominant and subordinate cultures are described in terms of their opposition and their mutual interdependency, it is necessary to reflect further on the process by which the entire complex develops and the direction which that development takes. As the historical example of the Reformation shows, Gramsci is not thinking here of educational processes with schools as the medium, but of a fundamental change in consciousness throughout society, of a new *civiltà*.[4] Without such a reform of consciousness, political changes are unthinkable. For Gramsci, the formation of national consciousness between the seventeenth and nineteenth centuries in Europe ran parallel to a mental reformation that involved overcoming particularist as well as dogmatic universalist tendencies. Gramsci sees the history of the Jews in Italy as the clearest example of this: "In Italy there did not exist [. . .] any anti-Semitism precisely because national consciousness was formed and indeed had to be formed through the conquest over two forms of culture: town hall particularism on the one hand, and Catholic cosmopolitanism on the other" (QC, p. 1801).[5]

The lack of anti-Semitism in Italy appears as part of that new *civiltà* that can only be developed beyond the abstract opposition of universal and particular cultures. Italian cosmopolitanism, which Gramsci criticizes so vehemently in Croce (who is seen as a prime example of the great intellectual from southern Italy on account of his functional support for the regional and social divisions in Italy), can turn into a desirable and interested cosmopolitanism to the extent that it relates to the phenomenon of migration as the specific relation to the world for the peasant masses in Italy:

> Traditional Italian cosmopolitanism would have to become cosmopolitanism of the modern type, i.e., it would have to ensure the best conditions for the development of the Italian "uomo-lavoro" [man-labor] wherever in the world he might happen to be—not as a citizen of the world, to the extent that he is a *civis romanus* or a Catholic, but to the extent that he is a producer of *"civiltà."* (QC, p. 1988)

This quote is expressive of Gramsci's very own personal aim—to apply a universalist spirit to the critique of particularist and folklorist elements in the "plurality of cultures"; to recognize the gesture of submission that these elements entail, but also to identify the universal or the global in the particular, the subaltern, and the "foreign." This is the struggle against any sociological analysis of everyday culture which is "permanently afraid that modernity is going to destroy the object of [its] study" (QC, p. 1506).

Multicultural Society and Adult Education

From the perspective of Gramsci's argumentation we have to ask: Is it really true that we can learn from alien cultures? More precisely, is it possible to learn from foreign cultures in adult education?

The most common opinion or concept regarding the diversity of cultures in adult education in modern democratic societies is based on pluralism: we owe equal respect to all cultures because we know (for example, from anthropologists like Lévi-Strauss) that all human cultures have something important to say to all human beings. But this immediately raises the questions: "Aren't there some cultures that have done much more for universal humankind than others? And aren't there cultures undergoing phases of crisis and collapse?" What about the difference between the contribution of Zulu culture as compared with the contribution of classical Greek culture or nineteenth-century Russian literature? We all remember the famous sentence attributed to Saul Bellow: "When the Zulus produce a Tolstoi, we will read him."

This sentence was considered by the famous Canadian philosopher Charles Taylor—defender of the "Politics of Recognition"—to be "a quintessential statement of European arrogance," regardless of whether it was Saul Bellow who actually made the statement or not. The error here would not have been an error in evaluation, but in the denial of a fundamental human principle, namely "the acknowledgement of the equal value of all humans potentially" (Taylor, 1992, p. 42). For Taylor, the above is a fine example of what many critics of the universal idea of formal equal dignity call Western ethnocentrism:

The claim is that the supposedly neutral set of difference-blind principles of equal dignity is in fact a reflection on the one hegemonic culture. As it turns out, then, only the minority or suppressed cultures are being forced to take alien form. Consequently, the supposedly fair and difference-blind society is not only inhuman (because suppressing identities) but also, in a subtle and unconscious way, itself highly discriminatory. (Taylor, 1992, p. 43)

In her interview with the German weekly, *Die Zeit*, the Nobel prizewinner Rigoberta Menchù from Guatemala answered, when asked what the United Nations could do for the so-called "indigenous communities" like the Quiché-Maya Indians (Menchu's own people):

> In any case, we don't want to be treated like a caterpillar in a glass of formaldehyde. The indigenous people are living people with their own wishes, hopes and with the need for participation in the development of mankind. We do not want to be treated as a piece of nature, like a rare animal that has to be saved at any costs. This sort of romanticizing is deeply racist. We are human beings like everybody else. What we need from the United Nations? Concrete help that gives us the chance to participate in our own development. (1995, p. 10)

This sentence recalls the critical conception of folklore studies that Gramsci elaborated in his *Prison Notebooks*. According to his analysis, so-called "folklore research" cannot be conducted in isolation from "official" worldviews in the dominant society. This concept leads to an understanding of culture that is socially and interactively constituted—far removed from any totalitarian tendencies, or any "atomistic" view of individuals. It seems appropriate to link it with the tradition of George Herbert Mead's symbolic interactionism, or John Dewey's critical pragmatism. Amy Gutmann interprets the essential cultural message of this tradition as follows:

> Part of the uniqueness of individuals results from the ways in which they integrate, reflect upon and modify their own cultural heritage and that of other people with whom they come into contact [. . .]. If human identity is dialogically created and constituted, then public recognition of our identity requires a politics that leaves room for us to deliberate publicly about those aspects of our identities that we share, or potentially share, with other citizens. (1992, p. 7)

What does this mean for the educational process in general, and adult education in particular? The motivation behind the European Enlightenment notion of learning from foreign cultures was the idea of reflecting upon and morally improving one's own culture. Leibniz, for example, "regarded his own culture as corrupt; so he came to the conclusion that we should not be sending missionaries to China, but rather the Chinese should send missionaries to us" (Bredella, 1992, p. 560). What Leibniz expected from the study of Chinese culture was something that applied, in the opinion of Rüdiger Bubner, to the Enlightenment in general: "When we hear about other peoples, we learn

to know ourselves better as human beings, discover more about a correct way of life, break away from the ethnocentric haughtiness of
Europeans and begin to comprehend the moral decay of the present"
(1983, p. 186).

The idea that we can learn from foreign cultures is based here on
the conviction that the foreign culture will change our own cultural
identity. The Enlightenment idea of tolerance does not move from
the assumption that cultures are self-enclosed units that need only
respect one another, but implies that recognition of the other must
lead to the transformation of ourselves. However, during the development of modern societies and the rise of nation-states, this nonplu-
ralistic idea of tolerance has led to a strange dialectics—i.e., to the
present-day defense of exclusion procedures within the universalist
liberal tradition itself. The logic of this exclusion is quite clear: if foreign cultures are able to change our cultural identity, then they will
also be able to invade and destroy us. This fear becomes a threat when
linked to the immigration processes currently occurring in Western
Europe, and also affects the discussion on intercultural adult education. To illustrate this, I quote Horst Siebert, a well-known German
author in the field of adult education. In an article entitled "Political
Aspects of Intercultural Learning," Siebert writes:

> Doesn't intercultural learning lead to permanent irritation and disorienta-
> tion if we ourselves are not in possession of a stable cultural identity?
> Doesn't there exist the danger of over-identification with everything that is
> foreign and extra-European? The mentalities, needs and obstacles of learners
> have in fact been neglected in all literature on intercultural learning. The
> proclamation of ambitious aims is dominating the discussion and suppress-
> ing the question whether these aims are acceptable for the subjects and cli-
> ents of adult education. (1989, p. 29f)

This fear about the consequences of transformation processes is
not the only type of response to the Enlightenment conception of
learning from foreign cultures. The opposite viewpoint can be found
in postmodern discourse. Jean Francois Lyotard, for example, calls
understanding "a form of terror"—not because it invades us, but because it invades and converts the other. We cannot mediate between
cultures because "a universal rule of judgment between heterogeneous
genres is lacking in general" (Lyotard, 1988, p. xi). Therefore, the
only legitimate activity that remains—according to Lyotard—is to
deconstruct understanding (as a form of violence) and protect the
heterogeneous from being understood. Both positions—the closure of
liberality and the postmodern argument, the fear of being converted
and the fear of converting the other—share the assumption that cul-

ture in itself is something like an authentic historical heritage where the activity of the subject should be excluded.

I would like to criticize this aesthetic understanding of authentic culture. Authenticity in the context of social life can never consist in a collective ascription (such as Herder's concept of authentic folk culture, which ascribes collective authenticity). On the contrary, authentic culture can be nothing else than a transformative act by a concrete person or network of persons (Habermas, 1993). Culture as a collective heritage of a special group or class may exist as a "habitus" (in Bourdieu's terms), but this habitus is nothing other than a condition for and competence of individuals to "gain possession" of their own particular culture. What Bourdieu fails to see is that the scheme of a collective habitus can never be identified with the reflexive form of individual consciousness of culture. Bourdieu, thus, criticizes social interactionism for overemphasizing the meaning of individual culture (1979, p. 181f). Indeed, symbolic interactionism as well as Antonio Gramsci's cultural criticism insist on the hypothesis that everyone's authentic understanding of his or her own culture should be interpreted as the potential critique of, and also the possibility of forever leaving, a traditional culture.

According to this interpretation, intercultural adult education must not involve studying a strange habitus and should not lead in any sense to an aesthetic view of alien cultures as self-enclosed hermetic units. On the contrary, it must mean learning how people in a certain determined social and historical context develop their culture in a double dialogue with "the other" and with their own tradition, and in this way construct their culture for themselves, involving "the other" in this process at the same time. Only in this way—reconstructing the self-reflexivity of any culture in modern societies—does one get to learn what it means to transform, reform, and thus develop one's own culture. On the basis of this sociological concept, I think it is also possible to give a very clear answer about the role of intercultural adult education as an intrinsic part of the intercultural creation of culture.

Notes

1. Finkielkraut's critique of cultural relativism is convincing, of course, in that the latter implies a renunciation of the very universalism which enables epochs to be jumped, frontiers to be crossed, and a world which transcends the differences between nations to be entered

(an idea that Finkielkraut illustrates with Goethe's concept of "world literature"); but his restriction of the concept of the universal to a canon of classical aesthetic works from western Europe mars this critique.

2. A similar methodological reversal of "familiar" and "alien" could possibly be found in Walter Benjamin's writings.

3. A number of studies on this have been produced since the 1970s—the CCCS study in Great Britain mentioned above, as well as a series of American studies. Poor achievement in school, for example, can be due to other factors than those typically cited by way of explanation (loss of one's own culture, cultural differences, lack of resources in schools). In the United States, children from social minorities which had not been able to establish any links to structures of social power through the development of social networks, developed low school achievement as a strategy of adaptation to the prevalence of discrimination and the barriers to success in working life and society generally in later adult life (Ogbu, 1974).

4. In the debate he conducted with Henri De Man, Gramsci demands a "catarsi di civiltà moderna" (QC, p. 1506) to replace De Man's psychology of depraved worker consciousness, which found considerable acceptance during Italian fascism. Gramsci accuses De Man of being a "scholarly student of folklore who is permanently afraid that modernity is going to destroy the object of his study."

5. Years before the holocaust, Gramsci provides a very detailed explanation for a phenomenon which Hannah Arendt was later to mention in her analysis of the Eichmann trial.

References

Apitzsch, U. (1995). Lavoro, cultura ed educazione tra fordismo e fascismo. In G. Baratta & A. Catone (Eds.), Antonio Gramsci e "il progresso intellettuale di massa" (pp. 115-32). Milano: Edizioni Unicopli.

Arendt, H. (1990). Eichmann in Jerusalem. Leipzig: Reclam.

Balibar, E. (1989). Gibt es einen "Neo-Rassismus"? In Das Argument, 175, 369-80.

Bourdieu, P. (1979). Entwurf einer Theorie der Praxis. Frankfurt: Suhrkamp.

Bredella, L. (1994). Intercultural Understanding between Relativism, Ethnocentrism and Universalism: Preliminary Considerations for a Theory of Intercultural Understanding. In G. Blaicher & B.

Glaser (Eds.), *Anglistentag 1993* (pp. 287-306). Tübingen: Niemeyer.

Bredella, L. (1992). Towards a Pedagogy of Intercultural Understanding. In *American Studies, 37* (4), 559-94.

Bubner, R. (1983). Ethnologie und Hermeneutik. In G. Baer & P. Centlivres (Eds.), *Ethnologie im Dialog (L'ethnologie dans le dialogue interculturel)* (pp.183-90). Fribourg: Editions Universitaires.

CCCS. (Eds.). (1982). *The Empire Strikes Back.* London: Hutchinson.

Di Carlo, A., & S. (1986). *I luoghi dell'identità.* Milano: Franco Angeli.

Di Carlo, S. (1987). Die Kultur der Emigration in Europa. In U. Apitzsch et al. (Eds.), *Emigration und kulturelle Identität.* Frankfurt: CGIL.

Finkielkraut, A. (1989). *Die Niederlage des Denkens.* Reinbek: Rowohlt.

Gutmann, A. (Ed.). (1992). Introduction. In *Multiculturalism and the Politics of Recognition* (pp. ix-xv). Princeton: Princeton University Press.

Habermas, J. (1993). Anerkennungskämpfe im demokratischen Rechtsstaat. In A. Gutmann & S. Fischer (Eds.), *Multikulturalismus und die Politik der Anerkennung.* Frankfurt: S. Fischer.

Hamburger, F. (1994). *Pädagogik der Einwanderungsgesellschaft.* Frankfurt: Cooperative Verlag.

Kristeva, J. (1990). *Fremde sind wir uns selbst.* Frankfurt: Suhrkamp.

Leggewie, C. (1990). *Multi Kulti.* Berlin: Rotbuch.

Lyotard, J. F. (1988). *The Differend: Phrases in Dispute* (G. Van Den Abbeele, Trans.). Minneapolis: University of Minnesota Press.

Marx, K. (1977). Introduction. In *Critique of Hegel's "Philosophy of Right."* Cambridge: Cambridge University Press.

Menchù, R. (1995, March 10). [Interview.]. *Die Zeit,* p. 10.

Ogbu, J. U. (1974). *The Next Generation: An Ethnography of Education in an Urban Neighbourhood.* New York: Academic.

Siebert, H. (1989). Zur Theorie des interkulturellen Lernens. Politische Aspekte des interkulturellen Lernens. In *Literatur—und Forschungsreport Weiterbildung, 23,* 20-36.

Taylor, C. (1992). The Politics of Recognition. In A. Gutmann (Ed.), *Multiculturalism and the Politics of Recognition* (pp. 25-73). Princeton: Princeton University Press.

Walzer, M. (1992). Comment. In A. Gutmann (Ed.), *Multiculturalism and the Politics of Recognition* (pp. 99-103). Princeton: Princeton University Press.

Abbreviated Titles

GR: *A Gramsci Reader* (D. Forgacs, Ed.). London: Lawrence & Wishart (1988).

QC: *Quaderni del carcere* (V. Gerratana, Ed.). Edizione critica dell' Istituto Gramsci. 4 vol. Torino: Einaudi (1977).

R: Il Risorgimento. In V. Gerratana (Ed.), *Il pensiero di Gramsci.* Nuova ed. riveduta e integrata sulla base dell'edizione critica dell'Istituto Gramsci. Roma: Editori Riuniti (1987).

SF: Socialismo e Fascismo: L'Ordine Nuovo 1921-1922. In *Opere de Antonio Gramsci 1914-1918.* Torino: Einaudi (1975).

SG: *Scritti Giovanili 1914-1918.* Torino: Einaudi (1975).

15

The Postmodern Prince: Gramsci and Anonymous Intellectual Practice

Jerrold L. Kachur

> You should understand, therefore, that there are two ways of fighting: by law or by force. (Machiavelli, *The Prince*)
>
> The modern Prince must be and cannot but be the proclaimer and organizer of an intellectual and moral reform, which also means creating the terrain for a subsequent development of the national-popular collective will towards the realization of a superior, total form of modern civilization. (Gramsci, *Prison Notebooks*)

Introduction

Three ingredients are required to restructure social reality: an understanding of actually existing society, a vision of the future, and a strategy linking "what is" to "what ought to be" (Livingstone, 1983). New Right school reformers articulate these ingredients into the formation of a collective will by providing populist movements with a

vision that intends to resolve the crisis of postmodernization and ex-
acerbate the existing social relations of subordination and profit-
taking. This conservative visioning process emphasizes individualism,
globalism, managerialism, consumerism, market-speak, and contempt
for the accomplishments of the modern social welfare State in advanced capitalist countries. Education forecasters now focus on technological rationalization and adapting education to the age of the
semiconductor and microprocessor, promoting more efficient and effective techniques to reduce expenditures in the face of an increasing
diversity of needs.

Along with the educator's compliance to the above economic imperative, the "natural" forms of collective organization, such as public schooling, are losing legitimacy. Social relations are fragmenting
into their constituent parts based on the practical experiences of people and have increased the demand for States to encourage different
kinds of schools for different kinds of people according to a cultural
logic labeled "postmodernism" (e.g., Jameson, 1991). Objective class
characteristics underlying these competing and disaggregated morali-
ties are fluid, layered with cultural divisions based on socioeconomic
status, race, sex, language, region, and so on. Social reintegration—or
steering through the crisis of accumulation and legitimation—also requires the differential mobilization of the media of language, force,
and money and the reconstitution of subjectivities and reestablish-
ment of dominant norms. Within this flux, changes to the nature of
intellectual practice have occurred, introducing new mechanisms of
social control informed by two systemic movements: (1) the increasing division and anonymous regulation of intellectual labor; and (2)
the increasing importance of scientific management in the mobilization of public desires.

How might researchers theorize the changed nature of intellectual
practice today?[1] Of central importance is the way Gramsci articulates
a definition of intellectuals as agents of cultural power and party formation. Given the New Right's attempt to rescript subjectivities and
to maintain relations of subordination via new mechanisms of social
control, this chapter argues that Gramsci's conception of the "Modern Prince" provides a theoretical and methodological basis for rein-
terpreting the functioning of the contemporary State and public
sphere, the mobilization of consent in a representative democracy,
the intellectual production and politics of culture, and the reformation
of social and education systems by contemporary political parties. I
describe how Gramsci defines intellectuals according to their practices
and I identify the variety of Gramsci's useful conceptions for educational research. I also show how Gramsci thinks about the relationship

between the State and the people as one of practical consent and I outline his arguments for how and why a political party necessarily plays an important mediating role in the formation of a hegemonic counterculture. I conclude with a specification of Gramscian ideas for rethinking intellectual practice in the contemporary period and for analyzing the special source of power that can be attributed to what I call the "anonymous intellectual." These collective expressions by the intelligentsia monopolize cultural production, coordination, and regulation. When anonymous intellectuals are politicized as agents of capital, State, or parties, they become "postmodern princes" who take the place of a divinity in refashioning all aspects of life and customary relationships.

Gramsci Defines Intellectuals and their Varied Practices

Gramsci provides a definition of and a mode for defining "intellectuals." He starts with concrete social practice and uses a reconstructive synthesis of historical and structuralist theories and methods. He also specifies a variety of intellectual practices that inform the Italian social formation: traditional, community, universal, and organic. Not only does this strategy distinguish his approach from historicist and functionalist analytical strategies, it provides a way to situate the practices of intellectuals as important agents of hegemonic activity and party organization.

Gramsci (1971) writes in an oft quoted phrase: "All men[2] are intellectuals [. . .] not all men have in society the function of intellectuals" (p. 9). This functional stipulation situates intellectuals in an intersecting space or "intellectual sphere," a point of mediation between "political society [and] the State" and "civil society [and] the private" (p. 12). Intellectuals are further distinguished as historical actors but are unlike those with direct productive relationships: "the fundamental social groups" (e.g., capitalists and their workers). According to Eyerman (1994), "*Intellectual* is thus understood as a situated social practice, not a fixed quality, and *intellectuals* by the specific social relations which constitute that practice" (p. 6).

According to Gramsci, the relationship of intellectuals to the world of production is mediated by the "whole fabric of society and by the complex of superstructures," and the work of intellectuals can be mobilized for "hegemony" in society or as "direct domination" through the State and juridical government. By defining intellectuals according to a particular set of social relationships and practices,

Gramsci's approach is sensitive to the enablements and constraints of causal structures, the personal characteristics of individual actors, the cultural context of meaning systems, and the transformative effect of political movements. It accommodates the assumptions of self-understanding, individual agency and social organization. Defining both the characteristics and functions of intellectuals points to the importance of Gramsci's method in keeping with the new debates about agency and how intellectual activity is historical practice (Aronowitz, 1992, p. 26).

Finally, Gramsci understands the capitalist class as being at the center of a historically constituted ruling bloc and that it could pass away. What this "ruling class" *is*, whether it is in control, how it is in control, and how intellectual practice participates in this struggle are key empirical questions that cannot be presumed to be answered before investigation starts (Gramsci, 1971, p. 408). By implication, however, the definition of intellectual practice is not a fixed idea. Intellectual activity constantly changes and is open to redefinition. "The idea" of what an intellectual "is" also has a history that must be situated in the context of its enunciation. So, according to Gramsci, "the elaboration of intellectual strata in concrete reality does not take place on the terrain of abstract democracy but in accordance with very concrete traditional historical processes" (p. 11).

In Italy during the 1920s and 1930s, Gramsci analyzed four intellectual models: traditional, community, universal, and organic. These models are significant because they clarify the complex relationships among intellectuals and the producing classes. The "traditional" model comprehends intellectuals as autonomous philosophers, artists, or poets and conforms to particular public figures such as academics, artists, and publishers who represent moral and ideological positions in the public sphere. These are the organizers of culture (e.g., creative artists, scholars) and the vestiges of organic intellectuals from previous social formations (e.g., ecclesiastics), who fuse in a common illusion that they are autonomous from class interest. While traditional intellectuals do not necessarily share the worldview of the ruling class, they eventually effect a compromise with it, partially because of institutional pressures and financial inducements. They incorporate instances of power whereby their social function is fulfilled as the "non-neutral" producers and transmitters of knowledge. Nevertheless, their common consciousness is conservative, and they act in the name of the social order. In most cases, the purpose of a conservative culture is to provide an integrating function to compensate for capitalist revolution.

The "community culture" model comprises the "structure of feeling" and "intellectual community" as a supraindividual subject. This model identifies the material conditions of possibility for mobilizing traditional intellectual practices for a democratic cause and the potentialities for mobilizing social change by "universal intellectuals" in their relationship with subaltern groups. It focuses on the activities that are carried out in churches, educational institutions, and cultural spheres by doctors, pharmacists, teachers, priests, and other professionals and semi-professionals in the dissemination of knowledge, which either challenges or produces hegemony via the spontaneous consent of the people in their everyday lives. This professional stratum may not share a common language with the subaltern people but it does share a "structure of feeling," whereby the professional is accorded privilege and prestige in the community. Without the mediation of this stratum, the hegemonic relationship between the masses and the predominant class cannot be maintained. Furthermore, the role of mediation and its privileges does not have to be limited to professional or institutional power but can be gained by any person who is capable of reasoning and promoting an analysis about the practices of everyday life within the cultural sphere. This universal condition for the exchange of ideas identifies the practical foundation for the emergence of the "universal intellectual," a world-historical individual with insights into the requirements of the times such as Lincoln, Napoleon, and Lenin.

The fourth model is the "organic intellectual," the most well-known and the most simplistically—if not inaccurately—characterized. Organic intellectuals emerge directly out of the class whose consciousness they help articulate. As an organic functionary, the new hegemonic intellectual has a distinctive practical orientation.

> The mode of being of the new intellectual can no longer consist in eloquence, which is an exterior and momentary mover of feelings and passions, but in active participation in practical life, as constructor, organiser, "permanent persuader" and not just a simple orator (but superior at the same time to the abstract mathematical spirit); from technique-as-work one proceeds to technique-as-science and to the humanist conception of history, without which one remains "specialised" and does not become "directive" (specialized and political). (Gramsci, 1971, p. 10)

Within the hegemonic organic formation two types of intellectuals are distinguished as "accommodating" or "hegemonic" by their distinctive self-conceptions and practical interests and by their relationship to the texts, each other, and the fundamental ruling group. In times of revolutionary transformation some traditional intellectuals, such as Marx and Engels, form a common cause with organic intellectuals and the working class, and may herald a new hegemony as universal intellectuals (Jay, 1984).

Gramsci differentiates at least three different forms of organic intellectuality: "orthodox organic," "new intellectual," and "critical specialist" (Holub, 1992). The orthodox organic intellectual is the product of each organization and differentiated according to complex class and cultural interests. Because every social and economic formation develops unequally, it also produces a variety of these organic intellectuals—a result of the functioning of regional, patriarchal, capitalist, and socialist organizations. The new intellectual is a technocrat who must know how his or her role is related to the roles of others in the functioning of complex capitalist relations. The critical specialist understands his or her own activity as a partial activity, yet also understands that because this activity is partial, it is also related to other activities in a system of social, political, and economic relations.

Hegemony as Practical Consent

The transition to a new hegemony was based on Gramsci's optimism about the working class generating its own organic intellectuals, but except for exceptional cases, most radical intellectuals have been renegades from the middle class. Although Hegel and Marx were the first to consider the mediating role of "world historical" or "universal" intellectuals in conferring intelligibility on practical activity, Gramsci's significance lies in his identification of how world visions are transmitted throughout society by lesser intellectuals such as teachers, activists, journalists, and priests and how this vision is to become eventually embodied as new "common sense."

Gramsci's models of intellectual practice allow researchers to link traditional historical and sociological analysis of intellectuals to a more comprehensive and unique understanding of intellectual practice, the role of cultural struggle, and the potential formation of a new political authority. To accomplish this task, Gramsci builds on and revamps Lenin's concept of "hegemony" as political leadership in the democratic revolution, based on a working class alliance with sections of the peasantry. By viewing leadership as practical consent, Gramsci argues that a class maintains its dominance not simply through the special organization of force but through the extension of its corporative interest to exert moral and intellectual leadership. Through alliance building and limited compromises, a social bloc is unified to represent the basis of consent for a social order. This hegemony of a dominant class is constituted and reconstituted in a network of institutions, social relations, and ideas woven by intellectuals in their organizational role. Gramsci realizes that while coercion might work with enemies, favorable alliances with other social classes, such as the peasantry, require consent and compromise to achieve legitimate and effective action.

Gramsci's critique of Italian national culture, the two worlds of a liberal north and conservative south, and the rise of Mussolini demonstrated the total inability of workerist purism and proletarian sectarianism to build radical socialist alliances. Gramsci calls for the development of a "historic bloc" of tactical alliances united "from below." This idea is quite different from those alliances promulgated as Popular Front strategies in the 1930s which were more concerned with preserving bourgeois institutions and defending an alliance with the Soviet Union than they were concerned with furthering a socialist revolution in the capitalist West. The failure of socialist revolution in the West required revolutionaries to rethink Marx's intellectual legacy and his theory of motivation. Central to Marx's theory were two components: the external pressures of force, fraud, and compulsion on individuals and the internal contradictions of class interest and the formation of ideology. Gramsci's work revisits the relationship between coercion and consensus, and focuses primarily on how individuals agree on basic values and how they voluntarily support a social system and eagerly perform their roles.

For Gramsci, conforming consent arises from some degree of conscious attachment to or agreement with certain core elements of the society. Although bound up with the concept of "legitimacy," the concept of hegemony embodies a hypothesis that "within a stable social order, there must be a substratum of agreement so powerful that it can counteract the division and disruption arising from conflicting interests. And this agreement must be in relation to specific *objects*—persons, beliefs, values, institutions or whatever" (Femia, 1981, p. 39).

Further, empirical evidence of consent cannot be limited to verbal affirmations readily catalogued (e.g., survey research), but rather is to be extended to include the historical analysis of political performance. Prudent consent based on the empirical evidence of social harmony and a balance of interests fails to identify why certain people define their interests as they do (e.g., why consumer hedonism should be treated as a natural and transhistorical human need). The degree of contradiction between verbal affirmation and social performance marks both the empirical degree that ideology as false consciousness is evident in the practical activity of a society and the way intellectuals provide moral-political leadership.

Gramsci deploys the concept of hegemony to suggest that narrow economic notions of politics or ideology are not capable of assessing accurately the political situation, the balance of forces, and the adequacy of dominant class power vis-à-vis the State. By contrasting "hegemony" (as moral-political leadership) and "domination" (as the direct coercive force of the State), Gramsci shows how the maintenance of the capitalist State continues to control society through a political strategy of alternating uses of consensual and coercive power. By maintaining this dual perspective on superstructural politics, he is able to argue for the creation of working-class hegemony as a prefigurative counter-hegemony and challenge the power of capitalist ideology through education. Gramsci (1971) thus conceives of the State as necessarily an "educator,"

> in as much as it tends precisely to create a new type or level of civilization. Because one is acting essentially on economic forces, reorganizing and developing the apparatus of economic production, creating new structures, the conclusion must not be drawn that superstructural factors should be left to themselves, to develop spontaneously, to a haphazard and sporadic germination. The State, in this field, too, is an instrument of "rationalization," of acceleration and of Taylorization. (p. 247)

Gramsci's identification of the State as educator points to the importance of analyzing the relationships between the State, individual intellectuals, and the collective organization of intellectual activists and the masses. In the latter form, intellectual and moral practice has to find a place in a political party.

The Modern Prince

The Modern Prince, or political party, is the initiator of political change organically linked to the working class, a complex element in society, and "the first cell in which there come together germs of a collective will tending to become universal and total" (Gramsci, 1971, p. 129). Crucial for Gramsci is how a strategic and legitimate political movement can be collectively coordinated via an organic party. The intellectual terrain, he argues, is the field of culture (although not entirely), and the vehicle is a strategically organized political movement, a party. While Lenin theorized the "vanguard party" and assumed an essential organic link between the radicalized intellectuals and the working class, Gramsci's interest lies more in understanding the mediation between the party, intellectuals, and the working class.

The party, he says, provides the institutional context for elaborating and disseminating a new counter-hegemonic culture. Gramsci's considerations of the political party are much broader than is usually thought in political discourse. Furthermore, his emphasis on universality and totality should not be misconstrued in light of the Soviet experience and State Socialism. Gramsci clearly focuses on the key problematic for any political movement intent on State power: how to maintain solidarity and diversity while accounting for the logics of democracy and bureaucracy.

"Parties," he writes, "may present themselves under the most diverse names, even calling themselves the anti-party or the 'negation of the parties'" (1971, p. 146). The political party might be more accurately described as a political movement with strategic and moral intent. The effective party is composed of three elements: a "mass element" that is the spontaneous force of ordinary people which alone cannot form a party; a "cohesive element" that leads, innovates, and disciplines, but alone is ineffective as a party; and an "intermediate element," that articulates the first two elements and provides moral and intellectual authority. In other words, the revolutionary party—as political movement—is not only a strategic organization, it is an organization with an empirical analysis of reality and a moral-ethical goal. It presupposes a new hegemony: a postrevolutionary State, which accommodates sociocultural difference and moral-political direction.

Gramsci's chief concern is to develop a new hegemony that can account for the tenuous relationship between bureaucracy and democracy in political movements and the tendency of political parties to regress into "bureaucratic centralism" (1971, p. 155). Marx considered the party as the political form of the proletarian movement but rejected any notion of a political arm distinct from the proletariat's existence. Lenin (1975) retained Marx's notion of an organic movement but undertheorized the nature of the organicity. However, Lenin's theory of the vanguard party tended to fuse intellectuals, party functionaries, and workers, and to bring socialist theory from the "outside" to the workers. Gramsci agrees with Lenin that the working class could not spontaneously develop its own intellectual leadership in the production process or from class struggle and the party was a necessary mediating force to transcend working-class mystification. To accomplish this task, Gramsci develops the idea of a "third element." Gramsci's concern for the "simple folk" and their involvement in the formulation of party policy meant reassessing the instrumental leadership of the party as the crucial factor in building socialism. Gramsci argues that intellectuals should mediate the "ethical State" of the people and forge a national culture based on practical consent. According to Gramsci, the function of the socialist intellectual is to build the party as a linguistic community and a basis for socialism. Gramsci's concern? Without the activating effects of intellectual and moral activity, the party would regress into "bureaucratic centralism" as "a simple, unthinking executor" (1971, p. 155). This central importance given to intellectual practice and the mediation of history contrasts with anarchist hostility to intellectuals and naive "workerist" celebration, which infused most party colleagues. Gramsci's thesis, thus, confronts in a subtle and complex way the dilemma of integrating party organization, intellectual culture, and mass culture without the party succumbing to bureaucratization or the masses to marginalization, and without reintroducing a new aristocratic caste or priesthood. The party, however, must remain organic through its articulation of the fundamental values and concerns that unite the leadership with the rank and file (Femia, 1981, pp. 147-57, 190; Fontana, 1993; Kolakowski, 1978, p. 250).

A second distinction from Lenin's conception of the revolutionary party is that Gramsci accepts the traditional social democratic notion that the party is a State in miniature, and that the party in its being anticipates the character of the collective future. For Gramsci, all true organic parties are not merely instruments but are a complex of cultural, social, and political institutions that serve a class and a worldview. His remarks about the Communist Party are to be considered in light of what he wrote about "organic" parties in general (*The Modern Prince*) and their potential application to the analysis of forces constituting the Right. Nevertheless, Gramsci does agree with Lenin that without revolutionary intellectual agitation, the dominance of bourgeois ideology would impose itself on the working class. Gramsci's focus, though, is more general than Lenin's in articulating the need for an ideological solution grounded in cultural and ethical terms rather than propaganda and political agitation. For Gramsci, the "new man" will precede the revolution, not follow it. However, Kolakowski (1978, p. 244) emphasizes that Gramsci's notes lack order and consistency on this point, and the creation of "new values" is relegated to an uncertain future following a postrevolutionary and economic-corporative phase.

Finally, Gramsci distances himself from Lenin's naive psychology, which assumed that capitalist social relations automatically generated great class hostility. Gramsci wishes to extend the sort of relationships Lenin envisaged for a small movement based on comradeship to the movement as a whole and to block the development of the party into an "autonomous divinity" or degenerating into "bureaucratic centralism." Although other Marxist thinkers, such as Luxemburg and Trotsky, had articulated a fear of bureaucracy, Gramsci was the first to treat it as a universal problem. For the most part, the struggle for unity could not block free and open discussion, critical research, and understanding of political complexity. Intellectual thought had to be liberated from mechanical and schematic application of abstract formulae. Gramsci challenges Kautsky's, Lukacs', and Lenin's versions of a revolutionary consciousness produced exclusively at the intellectual level. Where the actual consciousness of the empirical proletariat appeared as an impediment to the Marxist vanguard, Gramsci sees it as a source of theoretical reflection in keeping with Marx's revolutionary science. The truth that the party represents and elaborates has to be developed in a dialectical relationship with the life of the class and permanently subject to change and reformulation. Class practice is understood as influencing theory, posing new problems, and challenging theoretical propositions. The desired relationship is reciprocal, where "every teacher is always a pupil and every pupil a teacher" (Gramsci, cited in Femia, 1981, p. 161).[3]

From the Modern to Postmodern Prince

Gramsci's conceptions of intellectual practice, hegemony, and the Modern Prince have value in light of recent changes in the North American "information" economy; the rising power of "knowledge-based" classes and the New Right; and the declining influence of socialist movements and political parties. Although Gramsci's preliminary musings about intellectual practice in North America are sparse, he nevertheless shares some insights related to American research on the topic.[4] Richard Hofstadter (1962) was one of the first American historians to identify the rising power of technocratic experts in the United States. He also showed how antiintellectualism defined the American intellectual tradition. In response to McCarthyism in the 1950s, Hofstadter argues that the rise of technocratic thought and political integration meant a further degeneration of intellectual activity. The rising power of the expert in the twentieth century and the purifying power of an expanding administrative State subjected the American population to increasing measures of control. Professional educators, without being subjected to intellectual discipline, were left to develop their ideas in isolation from academics. Mass schooling and the extension of professional managerialism became key vehicles for social engineering. The rise of this technocratic-professional "class" in the postwar period appears to have been most prevalent in the United States and its economic and cultural colony, Canada.

The identification of the "technocratic class" in North America is also evident to Gramsci. Gramsci (1971, p. 18) understands English organic intellectuals at the beginning of the twentieth century as closely allied with economic-corporate development and marginalized in the intellectual-political sphere which was dominated by traditional intellectuals from the declining landowning aristocracy. In the United States, without a landed aristocracy, Gramsci identifies a considerable absence of traditional intellectuals and a different equilibrium among intellectuals in general. Rather than a split between traditional and hyperorganic intellectuals, which required integration, American society needed the formation of a unitary culture based on cultural diversity. It also needed to deal with the vast sedimentation of traditional intellectuals which produced two major political parties (reduced in fact to one party) and an enormous proliferation of religious sects. However, he identified the formation of a unitary culture as extremely difficult in light of the subjugation of "American Negroes" and a negative national and racial spirit. So even for Gramsci, the Anglo-American countries exhibited intriguing phenomena reflecting many of today's issues: the tendency to deintellectualize organic intellectual practice in the name of technocratic efficiency and the concentrated focus on creating a national-popular identity in the face of fragmented and centrifugal forces (pp. 20-21).

The increasing division of intellectual labor and the displacement of agricultural workers by service workers mark the emergence of a new kind of economy today. Whether this new economy is postindustrial, postcapitalist, post-Fordist, or at the end of history is the subject of important debates is the changing function of intellectuals. Nevertheless, one of the most dramatic developments for Western industrial societies has been the rapid growth and commodification of cultural production.[5] How might Gramsci formulate a new way to conceptualize intellectual practice within the contemporary context of economic production and social reproduction?

Many of the traditional approaches to intellectual practice fail to recognize the importance of new communication technologies, the politics of strategic management in the postmodernization process, and the role of corporatism in contemporary liberal reform. Increasingly, the lines between knowledge, class, and power are blurred, suggesting that researchers revisit history with new methods and concepts in mind. Furthermore, the canonical interpretations of intellectual practice focus on the heroic practices of public intellectuals or expert opinionmakers. The primary limitation of these theories is an emphasis on intellectuals as individuals (or aggregates of individuals) rather than as collectively structured practices of symbolic mediation and production. Missed are the emergent powers of "collective" agency and the increasingly "anonymous" nature of intellectual practice.

In his reflections about the separation of intellectual elites from the masses, Gramsci is critical of two kinds of volunteerism (still prevalent in the U.S. today): individual superhuman activists or vanguards without armies to back them up. He calls for a struggle against "false heroisms and pseudo-aristocracies," and for the stimulation of "the formation of homogeneous, compact social blocs, which will give birth to their own intellectuals, their own commandos, their own vanguard—who in turn will react upon those blocs in order to develop them, and not merely so as to perpetuate their gypsy domination" (1971, p. 205). Gramsci's "Modern Prince" might best describe the collective organization of intellectual activists. He conceives of the "organic party" in the broadest political sense: a State in waiting. He often refers to the New Party as a "collective intellectual" and, after the fashion of Machiavelli's Prince, the ruler who justifies domination. Justifying domination also means mystifying domination through mythmaking (see Lefort, 1964, pp. 246-50), a practice New Right intellectuals seem gifted at.

Just as Machiavelli's Prince tried to free politics from the limitations of religion and morality and speak to the historical task of the bourgeoisie blinded by tradition, Gramsci's "Modern Prince" intends to free Marxism from economic reductionism and to force socialist intellectuals to elaborate strategies for the working class to obtain and maintain an authoritative leadership. To accomplish this task, Gramsci emphasizes the populist and consensual side of Machiavelli's thought and reinterprets the Jacobin tradition as strong leadership tied to a democratic mission. But he also identifies the importance of myth (in the Sorelian sense) as the prefigurative form of Machiavelli's *Prince*. For Gramsci, political ideology is a concrete fantasy, which organizes and arouses the collective will. He argues that in an era of bourgeois hegemony a "Modern Prince" is required:

> a myth-prince, [who] cannot be a real person, a concrete individual. It can only be an organism, a complex element of society in which a collective will, which has already been recognized and has to some extent asserted itself in action, begins to take concrete form. History has already provided this organism, and it is the political party—the first cell in which there

come together the germs of a collective will tending to become universal
and total. (1971, p. 129)

In so doing, the Prince as proclaimer and organizer of intellectual reform becomes the basis for a modern divinity and replaces the old divinity in the people's consciousness (p. 133).

It is beyond the scope of this chapter to deal with the many limitations of Gramsci's thought, but suffice it to state here that his conception of the "Modern Prince" as an organic organization points
toward a kind of analysis that does not focus solely on the issue of
organicity or instrumentality but also on the division and coordination of collective intellectual practice and new organizational forms
of cultural production, political legitimacy, and the functioning of
"myth-Princes."

Gramsci confronts the problematic of organicity by identifying
the principle of revolutionary action for the intellectual as the complete articulation of a worldview, uniting theory, practice, and myth.
Human liberation does not merely consist of formulating a unique vision of social and economic structures but requires the creation of an
all-embracing and distinctive *Weltanschauung*. This new worldview is
the precondition for political revolution, and Gramsci suggests that
researchers study the organicity established by the Roman Catholic
Church and the ideology of Catholicism in maintaining the organizational and ideological relations between the religion of the learned and
the simple folk (Gramsci, 1971, pp. 328, 409). Researchers might do
well to follow Gramsci's analysis of the "party" as constituted in New
Right coalitions and to rethink the functioning of a counterhegemonic party in contemporary society.

From the Individual as Intellectual to the
"Anonymous Intellectual"

While Gramsci's work provides a theory and method to approach
contemporary intellectual practice, the objects of debate about mod-
ernity/postmodernity need to be explored anew. From Sartre's "universal intellectual" to Foucault's "specific intellectual," discussion
about intellectual practice is usually framed according to the exemplary practice of particular kinds of "individuals" who might be
grouped together according to similar characteristics or roles. The
transformative potentials of these agents and the changing densities
of education, research, and communication mean that contemporary
research may not be fully acknowledging the present discontinuous

aspects of technocapitalism and postmodernity with past relations of capitalist power (e.g., Harvey, 1989; Jameson, 1991; Kellner, 1989; Poster, 1989, 1990). The era of information technology may mark not only the end of Sartre's public space but also Foucault's biopower. Normalizing power is increasingly being replaced by forms of power that rely on connections, and networking and docile bodies are being supplanted by body/machine hybrids. These "anonymous" dispersions of intellectual power will require new ways for analysts to conceive rationality, cognitive practices, and subjects of knowledge.

While Habermas (1987) and Lyotard (1984) point beyond Gramsci in different ways, they nevertheless owe much of their genealogy to the Italian theorist. With an eye to the "postmodern," they identify the challenges of an organizational logic called "performativity": a generalized spirit which reduces value to increasing the efficiency of inputs and outputs between truth, science, technology, profits, and power. In a regime of "performativity," public discourse is subordinated to corporate management interest. The organized stock of established knowledge and the means to transmit it are reevaluated according to a logic which answers the question "What use is it?" rather than "Is it true?" In the contemporary context of economic commercialization and State expansion this utilitarian quest finds its true equivalencies for intellectual practice in "Is it saleable?" and "Is it efficient?" (Lyotard, 1984, p. 51). The transformation of a liberal technocratic logic to a corporatist postmodernization logic marks a change in the way hegemony is exercised, introducing new means of social control via futurology and strategic management. The new combination of ideology and administration establishes a political agenda for social reform and marks a transformation in intellectual practice.

The first element in the transformation is the increasing division of labor once applicable to the factory mode of manual production that is now colonizing the office mode of intellectual production. Cybernetic feedback systems of information processing have been incorporated as regimes of scientific management, rendering obsolete traditional approaches to the analysis of the formation of "political consensus" in a modern public sphere.

The second element is the changing nature of cultural regulation brought about by the revolution in new communication technology and the applications of the science of consumer management. Not only has cultural regulation become more anonymous, it is increasingly used to mobilize people's desires rather than develop their intelligence. Through this "science of desire," managerial elites secure their political and economic agenda—as, for example, in the advertising and polling industries, and in fomenting consumerism as the basis for social service provision.

The third element is a cluster of linkages among populism, the public sphere, the State, and the rise of liberal corporatism. The process of "massification" and the use of "emotion" for political purposes have long been under careful scrutiny in the study of authoritarian and democratic populism, but the fundamental premise of any analysis of "populism" presupposes what corporatism denies, a politicized public sphere, albeit deintellectualized and divided by religious affections.

In reconsidering a theory of intellectual practice based on both cybernetic systems regulating the division of intellectual labor and the mobilization of an economy of desire through the science of management, it seems that the concept of "populism" is problematic and increasingly irrelevant in light of the growing importance of "anonymous intellectual" practice. In a "postmodern" age, the conception of the "anonymous intellectual" captures the sensibility evident in Gramsci's "Modern Prince" as a collective mythmaking enterprise that might be applied to the contemporary period. In a world without individual prophets and public space, then, how is the population mobilized?

Gramsci emphasizes many points about the functioning of an "organic party" and describes activities similar to many contemporary political parties and governments. As Laclau and Mouffe (1985, p. 176) point out, the conservative reaction has a clearly hegemonic character in that it seeks to transform the terms of political discourse and create a new definition of reality. For Gramsci, the exercise of hegemony is mainly a process that defines the creation of a ruling bloc. In the context of contemporary consensus-building forums, the political elite is united as "stakeholders." They determine and implement policy and, in the process, instill or maintain conformity for the mass of the population.

Furthermore, Gramsci identifies the conjunction of futurism and corporatism. The rise of corporatist institutions has shifted decision-making power away from elected legislatures to appointed stakeholder councils reminiscent of Italian politics in the 1920s and 1930s. In contemporary liberal societies, visioning and corporatist practices are evident in four ways: (1) the presence of a core intellectual elite articulating the needs of the ruling elites while still incorporating the language of a broader stratum of "party" activists; (2) the intermediate role played by conference and consultation strategists and the private media, espousing objectivity and neutrality in the identification of problems and solutions; (3) the instrumental relationship established with "non-stakeholders" in interest-group relations; and (4) the replacement of future rewards or present punishments for authentic democratic participation.

The rise of corporatism is also concurrent with delegational democracy, where elections are treated as plebiscites. Contemporary politics in advanced capitalist countries, such as Canada and the United States, are defined by the presence of a weak oppositional party structure and ongoing "public consultations" and polling geared to strategic manipulation of the population. Rather than look to communicative action as the basis for authority, strategic managers manipulate popular consent and lack democratic legitimacy according to Gramsci's conception of practical consent.

As the cultural core of a hegemonic bloc, accommodating and hegemonic intellectuals rescript valuable texts which symbolically represent the "economy" and "the class struggle" (or lack of it). These texts also provide the crucial mediating artifacts by which a highly fragmented set of subject positions resulting from specialization can be articulated into self-conscious social interests. In the transformation of the social order, the ruling group not only transforms others it also transforms itself. If the "anonymous intellectual" is considered the voice that "speaks" anonymously as a "divinity" through the production of "unauthored" texts, then the Postmodern Prince is the collectivity that acts as an extended political mobilization with economic, political, intellectual, and managerial functions coordinated as if a State in waiting.

Thus, drawing on Gramscian assumptions, five potential ways are open to analyze the political mediations of intellectuals, the intelligentsia, and knowledge workers in society.[6] The Anonymous Intellectual could signify a residual social artifact of a communicative occurrence. In this case, the Anonymous Intellectual refers to the passive element, the physical text, a sign that "God" has been present, as in the case of the "Bible" as the Word of God. Second, the Anonymous Intellectual, when politicized, may be treated as equivalent to Gramsci's "Modern Prince," that is, to the objective basis for the proliferation of politicized supraindividual subjects or anonymous intellectual communities. In this case, the collectivity may be referred to as either class or stratum but with the specific intent to include the material conditions of possibility for mobilizing the institutional resources for intellectual practice. Third, and closely related to Gramsci's concept of the Modern Prince, the Anonymous Intellectual can mean the charismatic authority of the intelligentsia indicated by their privilege and prestige to profess on issues of fact, value, and taste. In this case, I refer to the "structure of feeling" or emotive relationship of trust established by the "petty prophets" within the general population.

Fourth, the specific postmodern form of collective intellectual practices is an extension of the second and third cases. At the material level, this practice is marked by the increasing division and anonymous regulation of intellectual labor and its emergent powers. At the aesthetic-erotic level, it is marked by the increasing importance of scientific management in the mobilization of desire. Here, the intelligentsia and knowledge workers are collectively organized as "an intellectual." Authorship, in this case, is not attributable to any one individual, but rather to a corporate entity and postmodern princes, e.g., the Government of Canada, the Hudson Institute, or The Business Roundtable on Education. Finally, the Anonymous Intellectual could mean Gramsci's "divinity" as Nation, God, Nature, Market, or Man. Here Gramsci's "Sorelian Myth" shares much with Anderson (1983) and Wilden's (1980) conception of the "Social Imaginary" (whether Althusserian or Lacanian) in filling the gap of desire between culture and politics as an image of possibility: the Anonymous Intellectual as the Postmodern Prince.

How, then, can imaginary evaluations of future orientations be situated in their sociohistorical presence, that is, in their capacity for circulation, exchange, consumption, and transformation as an asset in the administration of scarce resources, that is, as an economy of action? Much of prophecy can now be found routinized in strategic planning, that is, the conjunction of scientific prediction and political plan whereby the imagination of social scientists, leading politicians, and dominant entrepreneurs can be realized as public policy. In order to engineer history for their own interest, the language of action, scientific cause, and a new normality must be revisioned in such a way as to mobilize public opinion and to guarantee moral and political leadership to the dominant groups.

At the dawn of the postmodern, prophetic practices are still recognizable as a form of situated social practice, whereby "intellectuals" in their various guises (as heroic or anonymous, universal or specific) signify the actions and experiences of everyday life. Hegemonic intellectuals rework a metalanguage which can suture the language of the dominant players working in science, politics, and business to that of the general population (Laclau & Mouffe, 1985). Thus, intellectuals, ideal-typically, may be defined as the metatheorists of post/modernity. Furthermore, the postmodern emergence of scientific regulation and commercialization of communication creates a revolution in politically efficient justification. Forms of anonymous or "arms-length" communication are regulated by the intelligentsia and embody an intellectual formation, which increasingly functions as a cyborg-like

Anonymous Intellectual, rather than an aggregation led by heroic individuals.

Gramsci's "Modern Prince" provides the basis for comprehending anonymous intellectual practice. The conception of the Postmodern Prince is crucial for understanding postmodern and political aspects of intellectual practice related to the increasing division—and anonymous—regulation of intellectual labor and the increasing importance of the scientific management of public desires and the mobilization of an aesthetic politics. Hegemonic intellectual practice today lends itself to an analysis of how an everyday normality can survive without prophets and how new intellectual practices might mediate social movements in the mobilization of consent, conformity, liberation, or domination. The analysis of the regulation of discourse and the routines of the intelligentsia is crucial for understanding how the real, symbolic, and imaginary orders mediate expert and popular culture, how language and image have been mobilized in the implementation of conservative postmodernization from above, and whether Gramsci's realism might still meaningfully contribute to socially transformative politics.

Notes

1. Some of the literature: Bauman (1987, 1992), Boggs (1993), Brooks and Gagnon (1988, 1990, 1994), Brym (1980, 1987), Coser (1965), Eyerman (1994), Eyerman, Svensson, and Soderqvist (1987), Gouldner (1979), Jacoby (1987, 1994), Jennings and Kemp-Welch (1997), Larson (1977), Lemert (1991), Robbins (1990, 1993), Shils (1982).

2. The term "man" is used if keeping with Gramsci's words.

3. See Gramsci (1949, p. 26).

4. For various critical perspectives on the "new class" see J. and B. Ehrenreich (1979, 1990), Gouldner (1979, 1985), Szelenyi and Konrad (1979), Szelenyi and Martin (1987, 1991), Collins (1979), Murphy (1988), Bourdieu (1984, 1988, 1993), Chomsky (1967, 1978, 1989), E. O. Wright (1978, 1985), Bowles and Gintis (1976, 1987, 1988). The managerial thesis was first presented by Berle and Means (1932), who approved of the advancing managerial power in the United States. They argued that capitalism was undergoing a transformation, private property was disappearing, and private owners were being displaced by managers in a position of economic power. Various defenses of this technocratic position are made: Galbraith

(1972), Drucker (1993), and Bell (1973, 1976, 1980). Also, see Burnham (1962) for his conception of the "managerial revolution" as technocratic domination which also imputed a special and independent role for intellectuals concerned with planning and managing the new bureaucratic societies. Burnham influenced George Orwell and Alvin Toffler. Milovan Djilas's (1957) analysis of the rise of the Soviet *nomenclatura* provided the basis for an anti-Communist and anti-statist critique, which could be appropriated by American theorists for a critique of university dons and state mandarins. This New Class thesis also found sympathy with neoconservatives such as Daniel Bell, Seymour Lipset, Irving Kristol, Norman Podhoretz, and others, who pushed the analysis of benign technocrats and political elites into a liberal critique of a new "class" (Lipset, 1988; Bruce-Briggs, 1981; Kristol, 1978).

5. See, for example, Aronowitz and DiFazio (1994), Bauman (1992), Derber et al. (1990), Harvey (1989), Jameson (1991), Kellner (1989), Lash (1990), Rifkin (1995), Sayer and Walker (1992), Teeple (1995), Tomlinson (1991).

6. I use the term "knowledge workers" to identify a category of labor more akin to manual or skilled laborers who, unlike the intelligentsia, do not require "expertise" to do their jobs although they do require knowledge and work in the knowledge-based industries.

References

Anderson, B. (1983). *Imagined Communities*. London: Verso.

Aronowitz, S. (1992). On Intellectuals. In B. Robbins (Ed.), *Intellectuals* (pp. 3-56). Minneapolis: University of Minnesota Press.

Aronowitz, S., & DiFazio, W. (1994). *The Jobless Future*. Minneapolis: University of Minnesota Press.

Bauman, Z. (1992). *Intimations of Postmodernity*. London: Routledge.

Bauman, Z. (1987). *Legislators and Interpreters*. Cambridge: Polity.

Bell, D. (1980). *The Winding Passage*. Cambridge, MA: Abt.

Bell, D. (1976). *The Cultural Contradictions of Capitalism*. New York: Basic.

Bell, D. (1973). *The Coming of Post-Industrial Society*. New York: Basic.

Benda, J. (1955). *The Betrayal of the Intellectuals*. Boston: Beacon.

Berle, A. A., & Means, G. C. (1932). *The Modern Corporation and Private Property*. New York: Macmillan.

Boggs, C. (1993). *Intellectuals and the Crisis of Modernity*. Albany, NY: State University of New York Press.

Bourdieu, P. (1993). *The Field of Cultural Production*. New York: Columbia University Press.

Bourdieu, P. (1988). *Homo Academicus*. Cambridge: Polity.

Bourdieu, P. (1984). *Distinction*. London: Routledge.

Bowles, S., & Gintis, H. (1988). Schooling in Capitalist America: Reply to Our Critics. In M. Cole (Ed.), *Bowles and Gintis Revisited*. London: Falmer.

Bowles, S., & Gintis, H. (1987). *Democracy and Capitalism*. New York: Basic.

Bowles, S., & Gintis, H. (1976). *Schooling in Capitalist America*. New York: Basic.

Burnham, J. W. (1962). *The Managerial Revolution*. Bloomington: Indiana University Press.

Brooks, S., & Gagnon, A. (Eds.) (1994). *The Political Influence of Ideas*. Westport, CT: Praeger.

Brooks, S., & Gagnon, A. (Eds.) (1990). *Social Scientists, Policy and the State*. New York: Praeger.

Brooks, S. & Gagnon, A. (Eds.) (1988). *Social Scientists and Politics in Canada*. Kingston: McGill-Queen's University Press.

Bruce-Biggs, B. (1981). *The New Class?* New York: McGraw-Hill.

Brooks, S., & Gagnon, A. (Eds.) (1988). *Social Scientists and Politics in Canada*. Kingston: McGill-Queen's University Press.

Brym, R. J. (1987). The Political Sociology of Intellectuals. In A. Gagnon (Ed.), *Intellectuals in Liberal Democracies: Political Influence and Involvement* (pp. 210-19). New York: Praeger.

Brooks, S., & Gagnon, A. (Eds.) (1988). *Social Scientists and Politics in Canada*. Kingston: McGill-Queen's University Press.

Chomsky, N. (1989). *Necessary Illusion*. Boston: Southend.

Chomsky, N. (1978). *Intellectuals and the State*. Amsterdam: Het Wereldvenster Baarn.

Chomsky, N. (1967). *American Power and the New Mandarins*. New York: Pantheon.

Collins, R. (1979). *The Credential Society*. New York: Academic.

Coser, L. (1965). *Men of Ideas*. New York: Free.

Derber, C., Schwartz, W. A., & Magrass, Y. (1990). *Power in the Highest Degree*. Oxford: Oxford University Press.

Djilas, M. (1957). *The New Class: An Analysis of the Communist System*. New York: Praeger.

Drucker, P. (1993). *Post-Capitalist Society*. New York: Harper Business.

Ehrenreich, B. (1990). The Professional-Managerial Class Revisited. In B. Robbins (Ed.), *Intellectuals* (pp. 173-85). Minneapolis: University of Minnesota Press.

Ehrenreich, J., & Ehrenreich, B. (1979). The Professional-Managerial Class. In P. Walker (Ed.), *Between Labor and Capital*. Boston: South End.

Eyerman, R. (1994). *Between Culture and Politics*. Cambridge: Polity.

Eyerman, R., Svensson, L., & Soderqvist, T. (1987). *Intellectuals, Universities, State in Western Modern Societies*. Berkeley: University of California Press.

Femia, J. V. (1981). *Gramsci's Political Thought*. Oxford: Clarendon.

Fontana, B. (1991). *Hegemony and Power: On the Relationship Between Gramsci and Machiavelli*. Minneapolis: University of Minnesota Press.

Galbraith, J. K. (1972). *The New Industrial State*. Boston: Houghten Mifflen.

Gouldner, A. (1985). *Against Fragmentation*. New York: Oxford University Press.

Gouldner, A. (1979). *The Future of Intellectuals and the Rise of the New Class*. New York: Seabury.

Gouldner, A. (1976). *The Dialectic of Ideology and Technology*. New York: Seabury.

Gramsci, A. (1971). *Selections from the Prison Notebooks*. New York: International.

Gramsci, A. (1948). *Il materialismo storico e la filosofia di Benedetto Croce*. Torino: Einaudi.

Habermas, J. (1987). *The Theory of Communicative Action: Volume II*. Boston: Beacon.

Harvey, D. (1989). *The Condition of Postmodernity*. Cambridge: Blackwell.

Hofstadter, R. (1962). *Anti-intellectualism in American Life*. New York: Vintage.

Holub, R. (1992). *Antonio Gramsci: Beyond Marxism and Postmodernism*. London: Routledge.

Jacoby, R. (1994). *Dogmatic Wisdom*. New York: Anchor.

Jacoby, R. (1987). *The Last Intellectuals*. New York: Noonday.

Jameson, F. (1991). *Postmodernism*. Durham, NC: Duke University Press.

Jay, M. (1984). The Two Holisms of Gramsci. *Marxism and Totality* (pp. 150-73). Berkeley: University of California Press.

Jennings, J., & Kemp-Welch, A. (1997). *Intellectuals in Politics*. London: Routledge.

Kachur, J. L. (1995). *Hegemony and Anonymous Intellectual Practice.* Unpublished doctoral dissertation, University of Alberta, Edmonton, Canada.

Kellner, D. (1989). *Critical Theory, Marxism and Modernity.* Baltimore: Johns Hopkins University Press.

Kolakowski, L. (1978). Antonio Gramsci: Communist Revisionism. *Main Currents of Marxism: 3—The Breakdown* (pp. 220-52). Oxford: Oxford University Press.

Kristol, I. (1978). *Two Cheers for Capitalism.* New York: Basic.

Laclau, E., & Mouffe, C. (1985). *Hegemony & Socialist Strategy.* London: Verso.

Larson, M. S. (1977). *The Rise of Professionalism.* Berkeley: University of California Press.

Lash, S. (1990). *The Sociology of Postmodernism.* London: Routledge.

Lefort, C. (1964). Bureaucratic Society and Traditional Rationality. In D. Howard (Ed.), *The Marxian Legacy.* New York: Urizen.

Lemert, C. C. (Ed.). (1991). *Intellectuals and Politics.* Newbury Park, CA: Sage

Lenin, V. I. (1975). *What is to be Done?* Peking: Foreign Languages.

Lipset, S. M. (1988). Neoconservatism: Myth and Reality. *Society, 25* (5).

Livingstone, D. W. (1983). *Class Ideologies and Educational Futures.* Sussex: Falmer.

Lyotard, J-P. (1984). *The Postmodern Condition.* Minneapolis: University of Minnesota Press.

Murphy, R. (1988). *Social Closure.* Oxford: Clarendon.

Poster, M. (1990). *The Mode of Information.* Chicago: University of Chicago Press.

Poster, M. (1989). *Critical Theory and Poststructuralism.* Ithaca, NY: Cornell University Press.

Radhakrishnan, R. (1990). Toward an Effective Intellectual: Foucault or Gramsci? In B. Robbins (Ed.), *Intellectuals* (pp. 57-99). Minneapolis: University of Minnesota Press.

Rifkin, J. (1995). *The End of Work.* New York: J. P. Putnam's Sons.

Robbins, B. (1993). *Secular Vocations.* London: Verso.

Robbins, B. (Ed.) (1990). *Intellectuals.* Minneapolis: University of Minnesota Press.

Ross, A. (1996). *Science Wars.* Durham, NC: Duke University Press.

Sayer, A., & Walker, R. (1992). *The New Social Economy.* Cambridge, MA: Blackwell.

Shils, E. (1982) [1971]. Intellectuals and the Center of Society. *The Constitution of Society.* Chicago: University of Chicago Press.

Szelenyi, I., (1991). The Intellectuals in Power. *After the Fall: The Failure of Communism and the Future of Socialism*. London: Verso

Szelenyi, I., & Konrad, G. (1979). *Intellectuals on the Road to Class Power*. New York: HBJ.

Szelenyi, I., & Martin, B. (1991). The Three Waves of New Class Theories and a Postscript. In C. C. Lemert (Ed.), *Intellectuals and Politics*. Newbury Park, CA: Sage.

Szelenyi, I. & Martin, B. (1987). Beyond Cultural Capital. In R. Eyerman et al. (Eds.), *Intellectuals Universities State in Western Modern Societies*. Berkeley: University of California Press.

Teeple, G. (1995). *Globalization and the Decline of Social Reform*. Toronto: Garamond.

Tomlinson, J. (1991). *Cultural Imperialism*. Baltimore: Johns Hopkins University Press.

Wilden, A. (1980). *The Imaginary Canadian*. Vancouver: Pulp.

Wright, E. O. (1985). *Classes*. London: Verso.

Wright, E. O. (1978). *Class, Crisis and the State*. London: New Left.

About the Contributors

PAULA ALLMAN is the author of *Revolutionary Social Transformation: Democratic Hopes, Political Possibilities, and Critical Education* (Bergin & Garvey, 1999) and the forthcoming *Critical Education Against Global Capital: Karl Marx and Revolutionary Critical Education* (also Bergin & Garvey). She has also written a number of articles and/or book chapters on Paulo Freire and Antonio Gramsci that emphasize their contributions to radical education as well as Marx's influence on their thinking. At present, she is an Honorary Research Fellow with the School of Continuing Education at the University of Nottingham.

ESTANISLAO ANTELO is assistant professor at the National University of Rosario (Santa Fe, Argentina). He is one of the co-editors of *Cuadernos de Pedagogia-Rosario* a biannual peer-reviewed journal, and the author of *Instruciones para ser profesor* (Santillana, Buenos Aires, 2000) and several articles on critical pedagogy and teacher education.

URSULA APITZSCH is Professor of Sociology and Political Science at the J. W. Goethe-University Frankfurt/Main. She is a member of the Board of Directors of the German edition of Gramsci's "Letters from Prison" which for the first time will be published in their entirety together with the letters of his correspondents. The first of the four projected volumes (Gramsci's correspondence with his wife Giulia Schucht) appeared in 1995. Ursula Apitzsch is also the author of numerous articles on Gramsci in Italian, English, and German on the issues of culture, education, and political theory. Her book, *Neurath-Gramsci-Williams. Theorien der Arbeiterkultur und ihre Wirkung*, was published in 1993 by Argument-Verlag (Hamburg).

STANLEY ARONOWITZ is Distinguished Professor of Sociology and Cultural Studies at the Graduate Center, City University of New York, and Director of its Center for the Study of Culture, Technology, and Work. He is a member of the executive council of the Professional Staff Congress, the CUNY faculty and staff union. He is author of eighteen books including *The Knowledge Factory*, *Dismantling the Corporate University*, and *Creating True Higher Learning*.

JOHN BALDACCHINO is currently Lecturer of Critical and Contextual Studies at Grays School of Art, The Robert Gordon University in Aberdeen, Scotland. From 1993 until 2000 he was lecturer of visual arts and cultural theory at the University of Warwick, England. He has published on the visual arts, music, aesthetics, cultural theory, and education, and is the author of two books: *Post-Marxist Marxism: Questioning the Answer* (Avebury, 1996) and *Easels of Utopia: Art's Fact Returned* (Ashgate, 1998). He is currently working on a new book on Mediterranean aesthetics and a volume of philosophical essays on art, culture, and learning.

CARMEL BORG is Senior Lecturer and Head of the Department of Primary Education, University of Malta. He coordinates the Teaching for Diversity Programme at the same University. He lectures and researches in the areas of Curriculum Studies, Critical Pedagogy, and Parental Involvement in Education. He was heavily involved in the process of curriculum reform in Malta. His papers have appeared as chapters in books or as articles in a number of international refereed journals. His books include *Children and Youth at Risk* (coedited with C. Calleja; Agenda, forthcoming). Borg is also the cofounding editor of the *Journal of Postcolonial Education* (James Nicholas Publishers).

JOSEPH A. BUTTIGIEG is the William R. Kenan, Jr. Professor of Literature and a Fellow of the Nanovic Institute for European Studies at the University of Notre Dame. His complete critical edition in English of Antonio Gramsci's *Prison Notebooks* (of which the first two volumes are already in print) is being published by Columbia University Press. He is a founding member and secretary of the International Gramsci Society.

DIANA COBEN is a Senior Lecturer in Continuing Education in the School of Continuing Education, University of Nottingham. She specializes in the politics of adult education and adult mathematics/numeracy education. She is the author of *Radical Heroes: Gramsci, Freire and the Politics of Adult Education* (Garland, 1998; also to be published shortly in Spanish translation) and "Revisiting Gramsci" in *Studies in the Education of Adults* (April 1995). Dr Coben has long been fascinated by Gramsci's concepts of "good sense" and "common sense" and has explored their significance in relation to adults learning mathematics in various writings, including a chapter *in Perspectives on Adults Learning Mathematics: Research and Practice* (Kluwer Academic Publishing, 2000), which she also coedited.

GUSTAVO FISCHMAN is an Assistant Professor in the division of Curriculum and Instruction, at Arizona State University. His research interests are in the areas of comparative and international education, cultural studies, and popular education. Dr Fischman is the author of several articles on Latin American education, teacher education, cultural studies and education, and gender issues in education. His books include *Imagining Teachers: Rethinking Teacher Education and Gender* (Rowman & Littlefield, 2000) and (with I. Hernandez), *La Ley y La Tierra: Historia De Un Despojo En La Tribu Mapuch De Los Toldos* (Centro Editor para América Latina/Centro de Estudios Avanzados-UBA, Buenos Aires, Argentina, 1991).

BENEDETTO FONTANA is Assistant Professor of political theory at Baruch College and the Graduate Center of the City University of New York. The author of *Hegemony and Power: On the Relation between Gramsci and Machiavelli,* he has written numerous articles in such journals as the *History of Political Thought,* the *Journal of the History of Ideas, The Philosophical Forum,* and the *Cardozo Law Review.* Currently, he is working on the relation between democratic politics and rhetoric; he is also completing a book on *Gramsci and the State.*

HENRY A. GIROUX is the Waterbury Chair Professor in Education and Cultural Studies at Penn State University. His most recent books are *Stealing Innocence: Youth, Corporate Power and the Politics of Culture* (St. Martin's Press) and *Impure Acts: The Practical Politics of Cultural Studies* (Routledge). He has a forthcoming coedited book, *Beyond the Corporate University* (with Kostas Myrsiadis) and a collection of essays on film and cultural studies with Basil Blackwell tentatively titled, *Framing the Present.*

JERROLD L. KACHUR is an Associate Professor in the Department of Educational Policy Studies at the University of Alberta and specializes in the international sociology of education. He is co-editor, with Trevor Harrison, of *Contested Classrooms: Education, Globalization and Democracy in Alberta* (Edmonton: University of Alberta Press/Parkland Institute, 1999). He is currently coauthoring, with Carlos Torres et al., a book on *Globalization, Teachers' Unions and the State: Comparative Perspectives.* His other interests include Canadian welfare-to-work programs and their effect on children's well-being, and the influence of multinational corporations on university restructuring in Africa, Asia, and Latin America.

D. W. LIVINGSTONE is head of the Centre for the Study of Education and Work at OISE/University of Toronto and leader of the Working Class Learning Strategies Project. His recent publications include *The Education-Jobs Gap*; *Down-to-Earth People*; *Working and Learning in the Information Age*; and *Hidden Dimensions of Working Class Learning* (forthcoming), which extends the activity theory of learning based on case studies with members of several labor unions and their families.

PETER MCLAREN is a Professor in the Urban Schooling Division, The Graduate School of Education and Information Studies, University of California, Los Angeles. He is the author and editor of over thirty books on topics that include critical social theory, the sociology and anthropology of education, and critical pedagogy. His most recent books include *Revolutionary Multiculturalism* (Westview Press), *Critical Pedagogy and Predatory Culture* (Routledge), and *Che Guevara, Paulo Freire and the Pedagogy of Revolution* (Rowman & Littlefield). His forthcoming book is entitled *The Critical Pedagogy Manifesto: A Revolutionary Politics for Everyday Struggle* (Rowman & Littlefield). Professor McLaren lectures worldwide and his works have been translated into thirteen languages.

PETER MAYO is Lecturer in Sociology of Education and Adult Education at the University of Malta. His books include *The National Museum of Fine Arts* (Midsea, 1997), *Beyond Schooling. Adult Education in Malta* (coedited with G. Baldacchino, Mireva, 1997), and *Gramsci, Freire and Adult Education. Possibilities for Transformative Action* (Zed Books, 1999; also forthcoming in German by Argument Verlag). He is Reviews Editor of the *Mediterranean Journal of Educational Studies* and founding Editor of the *Journal of Postcolonial Education*.

ATTILIO MONASTA is Professor of Educational Research at the University of Florence (Italy). Since 1982, he has been actively involved in European projects for teacher education, and he is now leading national initiatives for school reform in Italy. In addition to many essays on education and the function of intellectuals, he has proposed a complete reassessment of the two editions of Gramsci's notebooks where differences and original findings were discovered and outlined (see A. Monasta, *L'educazione tradita. Criteri per una* *diversa valutazione complessiva dei Quaderni del carcere di A. Gramsci*, Giardini, Pisa, 1985; reprint, McColl Publisher, Florence, 1993).

W. J. MORGAN is Professor of Comparative and International Education and Director of the Centre for Comparative Education Research and Commonwealth Education Documentation, the University of Nottingham. He was formerly Director of the Centre for Research into the Education of Adults at the same University. In 1993, he edited, with Peter Preston, *Raymond Williams: Politics, Education, Letters* (Macmillan and St. Martin's Press, London and New York), a collection of critical essays. He has been commissioned by the Welsh Academic Press to prepare a political biography of Raymond Williams.

RAYMOND A. MORROW is Professor of Sociology and Adjunct Professor of Educational Policy Studies at the University of Alberta, Edmonton, Canada. His publications include *Critical Theory and Methodology* (Sage, 1995), and with Carlos A. Torres, *Social Theory and Education* (SUNY Press, 1995), and *Critical Social Theory and Education: Freire, Habermas and the Dialogical Subject* (in press, Teacher's College Press, Columbia University).

SILVIA SERRA is the Director of the Center of Studies on Critical Pedagogy and Assistant Professor of Pedagogy at the National University of Rosario (Santa Fe, Argentina). She is one of the editors of *Cuadernos de Pedagogia-Rosario*, a biannual peer-reviewed journal, and the author of several articles on critical pedagogy and the politics of education.

CARLOS ALBERTO TORRES is a political sociologist of education, Professor of Social Sciences and Comparative Education, University of California, Los Angeles, Director of the Latin American Center at UCLA, and Director of the Paulo Freire Institute, São Paulo, Brazil. His books include *Social Theory and Education* (with R. A. Morrow, SUNY Press, 1995), *Education, Power and Personal Biography* (Routledge, 1998), *Democracy, Education and Multiculturalism* (Rowman & Littlefield, 1998), and *Sociology of Education: Emerging Perspectives* (with T. Mitchell, SUNY Press, 1998).